MEDIEVAL
AND
RENAISSANCE
DRAMA
IN ENGLAND

Editorial Board

Leeds Barroll
University of Maryland (Baltimore)

Catherine Belsey
University of Wales
College of Cardiff

David M. Bevington
University of Chicago

Barry Gaines
University of New Mexico

Jean E. Howard
Columbia University

Arthur F. Kinney
University of Massachusetts

Anne C. Lancashire
University of Toronto

William B. Long
Independent Scholar

Barbara Mowat
Folger Shakespeare Library

Lee Patterson
Yale University

John Pitcher
St. John's College, Oxford

E. Paul Werstine
University of Western
Ontario

MEDIEVAL AND RENAISSANCE DRAMA IN ENGLAND

Volume 22

Edited by
S. P. Cerasano

Book Review Editor
Heather Anne Hirschfeld

Madison • Teaneck
Fairleigh Dickinson University Press

© 2009 by Rosemont Publishing & Printing Corp.

All rights reserved. Authorization to photocopy items for internal or personal use, or the internal or personal use of specific clients, is granted by the copyright owner, provided that a base fee of $10.00, plus eight cents per page, per copy is paid directly to the Copyright Clearance Center, 222 Rosewood Drive, Danvers, Massachusetts 01923. [978-0-8386-4252-8/09 $10.00 + 8¢ pp, pc.]

Associated University Presses
2010 Eastpark Boulevard
Cranbury, NJ 08512

The paper used in this publication meets the requirements of the American National Standard for Permanence of Paper for Printed Library Materials Z39.48-1984.

International Standard Book Number 978-0-8386-4252-8 (vol. 22)
International Standard Serial Number 0731-3403

All editorial correspondence concerning *Medieval and Renaissance Drama in England* should be addressed to Prof. S. P. Cerasano, Department of English, Colgate University, Hamilton, N.Y., 13346. Orders and subscriptions should be directed to Associated University Presses, 2010 Eastpark Boulevard, Cranbury, New Jersey 08512.

Medieval and Renaissance Drama in England disclaims responsibility for statements, either of fact or opinion, made by contributors.

PRINTED IN THE UNITED STATES OF AMERICA

Contents

Foreword	9
Contributors	11

Symposium: Women and Theater

Introduction: Orange-Women, Female Spectators, and Roaring Girls: Women and Theater in Early Modern England MARION WYNNE-DAVIES	19
The Merry Tanner, the Mayor's Feast, and the King's Mistress: Thomas Heywood's *1 Edward IV* and the Ballad Tradition NORA L. CORRIGAN	27
"That which Marreth All": Constancy and Gender in *The Virtuous Octavia* YVONNE BRUCE	42
"A Fine and Private Place": Chapman's Theatrical *Widow* ELIZABETH HODGSON	60

Articles

Playing in the Provinces: Front or Back Door? BARBARA D. PALMER	81
Dux Moraud: Criminality and Salvation in an East Anglian Play CLIFFORD DAVIDSON	128
Alice Layton and the Cross Keys DAVID KATHMAN	144
Puritanism and the Closing of the Theaters in 1642 N. W. BAWCUTT	179
My Magic Can Lick Your Magic RICHARD LEVIN	201

New Books on Theater History

Farah Karim-Cooper, *Cosmetics in Shakespearean and Renaissance Drama* FRANCES TEAGUE	231

CONTENTS

Gina Bloom, *Voice in Motion: Staging Gender, Shaping Sound in Early Modern England*   234
GENEVIEVE LOVE

Karen Britland, *Drama at the Courts of Queen Henrietta Maria*   237
SUZANNE GOSSETT

Sophie Tomlinson, *Women on Stage in Stuart Drama*   239
KAREN RABER

Lucy Munro, *Children of the Queen's Revels: A Jacobean Theatre Repertory*   242
MARY BLY

Barbara Ravelhofer, *The Early Stuart Masque: Dance, Costume, and Music*   248
TIMOTHY RAYLOR

Simon Palfrey and Tiffany Stern, *Shakespeare in Parts*   251
MELISSA AARON

Elza C. Tiner, *Teaching with the Records of Early English Drama*   253
ROSLYN L. KNUTSON

Reviews

Michelle Ephraim, *Reading the Jewish Woman on the Elizabethan Stage*   261
MATTHEW BIBERMAN

David M. Bergeron, *Textual Patronage in English Drama, 1570–1640*   263
ALISON V. SCOT

Lynette R. Muir, *Love and Conflict in Medieval Drama: The Plays and their Legacy*   266
CHET SCOVILLE

Heather Hill-Vasquez, *Sacred Players: The Politics of Response in the Middle English Religious Drama*   267
ANDREA R. HARBIN

Oliver Arnold, *The Third Citizen: Shakespeare's Theater and the Early Modern House of Commons*   270
CHRIS FITTER

Rebecca Lemon, *Treason by Words: Literature, Law, and Rebellion in Shakespeare's England*   273
DENNIS KEZAR

Lorna Hutson, *The Invention of Suspicion: Law and Mimesis in Shakespeare and Renaissance Drama*   275
DEBORA K. SHUGER

CONTENTS

Timothy Rist, *Revenge Tragedy and the Drama of Commemoration in Reforming England* 279
THOMAS P. ANDERSON

Lena Orlin, *Locating Privacy in Tudor London* 282
AMY SMITH

Lukas Erne, *Shakespeare's Modern Collaborators* 284
ROBERT E. STILLMAN

Index 288

Foreword

Medieval and Renaissance Drama in England, now over twenty years in publication, is an international journal committed to the publication of essays and reviews relevant to drama and theater history to 1642. In keeping with the precedent set by previous volumes, *MaRDiE* 22 features a symposium on women and the theater, introduced by Marion Wynne-Davies. Contributors include Yvonne Bruce on constancy and gender in *The Virtuous Octavia,* Nora L. Corrigan on Heywood's *1 Edward IV* and the ballad tradition, and Elizabeth Hodgson on Chapman's *The Widow's Tears.* Volume 23—to be published in 2010—will offer a collection of essays concentrating on the plays of Thomas Middleton, and is to be edited by Mary Bly (Fordham University), the new Associate Editor of *MaRDiE,* who is a welcomed addition to our crew.

Additionally, volume 22 of *Medieval and Renaissance Drama in England* includes essays by Barbara D. Palmer on playing in the provinces, by David Kathman on a seldom discussed playing space—the Cross Keys Inn—and by Richard Levin on magic contests in plays of the period. Nigel Bawcutt reconsiders the closing of the theaters in 1642. Finally, a special review section highlights new books in theater history, while nine further reviews address recently published books on topics ranging from the Jewish woman on the Renaissance stage to the House of Commons and legal issues, to revenge tragedy and Shakespeare's modern collaborators.

As ever, the publication of *MaRDiE* would not be possible without its many contributors and supporters. On this occasion special thanks go to Marion Wynne-Davies whose long acquaintance with women's drama in early modern England made her the perfect person to write the introduction to "Women and Theater."

S. P. CERASANO
Editor

Contributors

MELISSA AARON is Professor of English and Foreign Languages at California Polytechnic State University at Pomona. She is the author of *Global Economics: A History of the Theater Business, the Chamberlain's/King's Men, and their Texts, 1599–1642* (University of Delaware Press, 2005) and, more recently, of "'A Queen in a Beard': A Study of All-Female Shakespeare Companies," in *Shakespeare Re-Dressed: Cross-Gender Casting in Contemporary Performance,* ed. James C. Bulman (FDVP, 2008).

THOMAS P. ANDERSON is Assistant Professor of English at Mississippi State University. He is the author of *Performing Early Modern Trauma from Shakespeare to Milton* (2006), as well as articles on Marvell, Shakespeare, Milton, and Webster. He is currently coediting a volume of scholarly essays on John Foxe's *Actes and Monuments* (UVP, forthcoming).

N. W. BAWCUTT, now Senior Research Fellow, was formerly Reader in English at the University of Liverpool. His recent publications include "The 'Myth of Gentillet' Reconsidered: An Aspect of Elizabethan Machiavellianism," *Modern Language Review* 99 (2004): 863–74, and "The Assassination of Alessandro de'Medici in Early Seventeenth-Century English Drama," *English Studies,* n.s. 56 (2005): 412–23.

MATTHEW BIBERMAN, Associate Professor of English at the University of Louisville, is the author of *Anti-Semitism, Masculinity and Early Modern English Literature* (2004). He has published scholarly essays in various forums including *SEL, Milton Quarterly, Religion and Literature,* and most recently in the collection *Milton and the Jews* (2008).

MARY BLY is Associate Professor of English Literature at Fordham University. She is currently working on *The Geography of Puns,* a project addressing the geographical and linguistic economies of early modern London with particular attention to the liberties. An article from this book was published in the *PMLA* (January 2007).

YVONNE BRUCE is an Instructor of English at the University of Akron and John Carroll University in Ohio. Her recent publications include the edited

12 CONTRIBUTORS

collection *Images of Matter: Essays on British Literature of the Middle Ages and Renaissance* (2005).

NORA CORRIGAN is Assistant Professor at Mississippi University for Women. Her article is part of a longer project about English commoners and communities in Renaissance drama.

CLIFFORD DAVIDSON is Professor of English and Medieval Studies Emeritus at Western Michigan University, where he was a coeditor of *Comparative Drama* and director of the Early Drama, Art, and Music project in the Medieval Institute. He has published extensively on early English drama, iconography, and other topics, and is the author of numerous books, including *History, Religion, and Violence: Cultural Contexts for Medieval and Renaissance Drama* (2002) and *Deliver Us from Evil: Essays on Symbolic Engagement in Early Drama* (2004). He is the coeditor of *The Coventry Corpus Christi Plays* (2000) and of *Everyman* (forthcoming).

SUZANNE GOSSETT is Professor of English at Loyola University Chicago. She is the editor of the Arden 3 *Pericles* (2004) and a General Editor of Arden Early Modern Drama. She writes on issues of editing, feminism, and collaboration, and is the editor of many early modern plays, including Middleton and Rowley's *A Fair Quarrel* (2007), Chapman, Jonson, and Marston's *Eastward Ho!* for the *Cambridge Works of Ben Jonson,* and Beaumont and Fletcher's *Philaster* (forthcoming).

ANDREA R. HARBIN is currently Assistant Professor of English at the State University of New York, College of Cortland. She is the author of "The Citizens of York and the Archetypal Christian Journey: Pilgrimage and Ritual in the York Cycle," *Medieval Perspectives XIV* (1999); 84–98.

ELIZABETH HODGSON is Associate Professor of English at the University of British Columbia. She has published *Gender and the Sacred Self in John Donne* (UDP, 1999) as well as articles in *Milton Studies, SEL, Early Modern Literary Studies, Prose Studies,* and *Women's Writing.*

DAVID KATHMAN is an independent scholar in Chicago, Illinois. His recent research has focused on theatrical apprentices and on sixteenth-century playing venues other than custom-built playhouses, including inns, taverns, and halls. His work has recently appeared in *Shakespeare Quarterly, Shakespeare Survey, Early Theatre,* and *Notes and Queries,* and he has contributed to the *Oxford Dictionary of National Biography,* the *Shakespeare Encyclopedia,* and the *Oxford Handbook on Theatre History.*

CONTRIBUTORS

DENNIS KEZAR is Associate Professor of English at the University of Utah. He is the author of *Guilty Creatures: Renaissance Literature and the Ethics of Authorship* (2001); editor of *Solon and Thespis: Law and Theater in the English Renaissance* (2006) and of numerous essays on Shakespeare, Jonson, Milton, and other Renaissance authors appearing in journals such as *ELR, ELH,* and *Critical Inquiry.*

ROSLYN L. KNUTSON, Professor of English at the University of Arkansas at Little Rock, has published widely in theater history, including two books and articles in various journals and annuals. She is currently the president of the Marlowe Society of America, and is researching the reportorial context of Christopher Marlowe's plays and the narratives behind the lost plays in Philip Henslowe's diary.

RICHARD LEVIN is Professor Emeritus of English at Stony Brook University. His most recent book is *Looking for an Argument: Critical Encounters with the New Approaches to the Criticism and His Contemporaries* (FDUP, 2003).

GENEVIEVE LOVE is Associate Professor of English at Colorado College. She has published essays on Shakespeare and his contemporaries in performance in *Renaissance Drama, Shakespeare Bulletin,* and *Borrowers and Lenders,* and serves as book review editor for *Shakespeare Bulletin.*

BARBARA D. PALMER is Professor of English Emerita at the University of Mary Washington and an adjunct professor in Mary Baldwin College's M.Litt./ MFA Shakespeare and Renaissance Literature in Performance program. Author of *The Early Art of the West Riding of Yorkshire* and numerous articles on early modern drama, she is currently editing the West Riding (Yorkshire) and Derbyshire collections for REED. She is secretary of the REED Executive Board and president of REED-USA, Inc.

KAREN RABER is author of *Dramatic Difference: Gender, Class and Genre in the Early Modern Closet Drama* (UDP, 2001); coeditor, (with Treva Tucker) *The Culture of the Horse: Status, Discipline and Identity in the Early Modern World* (2005); coeditor (with Ivo Kamps), *William Shakespeare,* Measure for Measure*: Texts and Contexts* (2004); and author of numerous articles on women writers, animals, and ecocriticism.

TIMOTHY RAYLOR is Professor of English at Carleton College, Minnesota. He has written on the masques sponsored by Viscount Doncaster, on the circle of intellectuals and writers patronized by William Cavendish, Earl of Newcastle, and is currently engaged (with Michael P. Parker) upon an edition of the poems of Edmund Waller.

ALISON V. SCOTT is lecturer in Renaissance literature at the University of Queensland, Australia. She is the author of *Selfish Gifts: The Politics of Exchange and English Courtly Literature* (FDUP, 2006) and coeditor of *Ben Jonson and the Politics of Genre* (forthcoming). She is currently completing a book on languages of luxury in early modern England.

CHESTER N. SCOVILLE teaches in the Department of English and Drama at the University of Toronto Mississauga. His first book, *Saints and the Audience in Middle English Biblical Drama,* was published in 2004. He is currently at work on a second book.

DEBORA SHUGER is Professor of English at UCLA. She is the author of many books and articles and, most recently, of *Censorship and Cultural Sensibility: The Regulation of Language in Tudor-Stuart England* (2006), and *Political Theologies: The Sacred and the State in "Measure for Measure"* (2001).

AMY L. SMITH is Associate Professor of English at Kalamazoo College. She has published articles on performing marriage on and off the stage in early modern England in journals such as *SEL* and *Comparative Drama.*

ROBERT E. STILLMAN is Professor of English at the University of Tennessee, Knoxville. His most recent book is *Philip Sidney and the Poetics of Renaissance Cosmopolitanism.* (2007). He is currently at work on a project about Shakespeare and the concept of popular culture.

FRANCES TEAGUE is the Josiah Meigs Professor of English at the University of Georgia. Her most recent book is *Shakespeare and the American Popular Stage* (2007).

MARION WYNNE-DAVIES holds the Chair of English Literature in the Department of English at the University of Surrey. Her main areas of interest are early modern literature and women's writing. She has published two editions of primary material, *Renaissance Drama by Women: Texts and Documents* (with S. P. Cerasano, 1996) and *Women Poets of the Renaissance* (1998), as well as several collections of essays in the same field. She has written four monographs, *Women and Arthurian Literature* (1996), *Sidney to Milton* (2002), *Margaret Atwood* (2003), and *Women Writers of the English Renaissance: Familial Discourse* (2007).

MEDIEVAL
AND
RENAISSANCE
DRAMA
IN ENGLAND

Symposium: Women and Theater

Orange-Women, Female Spectators, and Roaring Girls: Women and Theater in Early Modern England

Marion Wynne-Davies

At the beginning of Ben Jonson's *Epicene* (1609) Morose's friends discuss how sensitive he is to noise, in particular, the cries of "fishwives and orange-women."[1] In a play that satirizes women, and particularly vocal ones, the inclusion of these street criers as abhorrent to Morose hardly comes as a surprise. However, they are also significant in that they problematize the way in which we interpret how women engaged with early modern theater. In this introduction to the forum on women and theater, I would like to begin by exploring how and why women went to the theater, what they expected of it, who they were, and how they were represented. Since the 1980s considerable scholarship has been undertaken to uncover plays written by women and to analyze from various feminist perspectives the way women were represented on stage by male authors and by boy actors. This was pathbreaking and essential work, but we also need to consider how plays in performance might not always align neatly with critical readings of dramatic texts, and that the performances themselves were very different in the early modern period than in our own respectful auditoria. Moreover, while theater history often offers tantalizing snapshots of female participation in court masques and drama, as well as accounts of attendance at publically performed plays, little is known of women's vocal and physical activity during performances. The presence in the theater of orange-women primarily interested in selling their wares, of female playgoers intent upon a variety of entertainments, and of idiosyncratic characters like Mary Frith, the Roaring Girl, suggest that a more complex analysis of the way in which women negotiated their roles as mute viewers within a space dominated by men is necessary.

The attendance of orange-women at plays in London theaters is most commonly known from the story of Nell Gwynn, who became the mistress of Charles II, but her career was not commonly replicated by other working women in the theater, particularly before the Restoration. In her essay "Gender at Work in the Cries of London," Natasha Korda excavates the ways in which these lower-class women are portrayed in ballads, printed texts, and plays. Alongside the orange-women, she identifies women selling "tobacco, gingerbread, pippins, nuts and even cheap print," pointing out that, "The visibility and vocality of working women within the walls of the theaters would thus seem to have represented a significant performative aspect of the playgoer's theatrical experience, an aspect that has hitherto been overlooked by theater historians . . . what were the attitudes of the all-male playing companies towards this largely female, boisterous 'side-show'?"[2] Korda argues that the denigration of the street criers in early modern drama, such as Jonson's satirical attack, served to legitimize the professional players as they defined themselves against itinerant forms of entertainment, from which they themselves had recently evolved. But, as Korda astutely notes, by inscribing the female vendors as a marginalized and illegitimate presence within the theater, the male professionals simultaneously foregrounded their own commercial and transient origins. The construction of a gendered dialectic in which men are legitimate performers within an authorized commercial space and in which women provide an informal "sideshow" in an unlawful market cannot be sustained precisely because they occupy the same theatrical site. As the orange-women demonstrate, early modern theaters provided public exchange as well as performance. The working women's presence complicates the representation of women on stage through their vocalization of economic independence, which was linked in popular perception with sexual availability. Jonson's city comedy indicates this destabilization of patriarchal discourse by mocking Morose's complaints about the noise made by orange-women, while simultaneously satirizing women through the supposedly ideal silence of Epicene.

In a misogynistic diatribe, heavily indebted to Juvenal's Satire VI, Jonson presents a comprehensive catalogue of women's faults, from the licentious behavior of "fair" and "foul," to the excessive demands of those who are "rich . . . fruitful . . . [and] learned." Intriguingly, Truewit begins this traditional querrelle des femmes attack by linking women's sexual behavior with the theater: "Alas, sir [Morose], do you ever think to find a chaste wife in these times? Now? When there are so many masques, plays, Puritan preachings, mad folks, and other strange sights to be seen daily, private and public."[3] Subsequently, women's craving for public entertainment is underscored by the play's Collegiate Ladies, who demand that Morose puts on a masque, confirm that attendance at plays is associated with amorous dalliance, "kiss our hands all the playtime," and freely visit "Bedlam . . . china houses" and the "church" for their amusement.[4] Jonson's representation of how women participated in London's varied spectacles suggests a vocal, independent, and adventurous presence. Moreover, although the play's final address to the audience indicates that the women watching the performance have been made "mute" by the discovery that Epicene is a boy, Truewit

INTRODUCTION: ORANGE-WOMEN, FEMALE SPECTATORS, ROARING GIRLS   21

concludes by asking all the "spectators" (men and women alike) to stand, applaud, and make a "noise." [5] Thus, in a particularly Jonsonian volte farce, Truewit shifts from a satire against women, to the unleashing of gender misrule through a powerful avocation of pleasure that may, only tenuously, be linked to virtue.

The Collegiate Ladies describe how women actively seek pleasure at theatrical performances, but, although the play's satire demands that their desires are interpreted as grotesque exaggerations, there is evidence that this behavior might be an authentic account. There are a number of satirical texts that refer to women attending the theater for illicit sexual encounters, including: the "Cheapside dame [who will] . . . invite us [gallants] home, We'll thrust hard for it, but we'll find her room"; Amanda, the reformed whore who goes "to some playhouse in the afternoon. And for no other meaning or intent, But to get company to sup with soon"; and the "unwholesome enticing harlots, that sit there merely to be taken up by prentices or lawyers clerks."[6] Perhaps the most comic of these accounts occurs in Henry Peacham's *The Art of Living in London* (1642) where he tells the tale of a tradesman's wife whose purse was stolen when she went to the theater and her subsequent explanation: "Quoth her husband, 'Where did you put it?' 'Under my petticoat, between that and my smock.' 'What,' qouoth he, 'did you feel nobody's hand there?' 'Yes,' quoth she, 'I felt one's hand there; but I did not think he had come for that.'"[7]

While these offer a comic portrayal, the commonality of such representations confers an authenticity upon the way in which early modern women went to the theater for a variety of reasons, only one of which seems to have been to watch the play. Andrew Gurr, in his invaluable analysis, *Playgoing in Shakespeare's London* (1987), provides information about female spectators, including their station, from ladies to prostitutes, and makes the important point that we need to be aware of the variable represented by different theaters, periods, and dramatists, while succeeding scholarship has tended to concentrate exclusively upon female spectators and how they are addressed in prologues and epilogues.[8] The amorous encounters that occurred alongside the orange-women and other female vendors selling their wares were, however, not nearly as infamous as the presence of Mary Frith.

An entry in *The Consistory of London Correction Book* (1612) recounts how Frith dressed and acted like a man, visiting, "alehowses Tavernes Tobacco shops & also to play howses . . . [where] she there vppon the stage in the publique viewe of all the people there presente in mans apparel & playd vppon her lute and sange a songe."[9] Frith's presence in the theater is attested to by her inclusion in Thomas Middleton's and Thomas Dekker's play *The Roaring Girl* (1611) which claims to represent her life and at its close promises,

22   MARION WYNNE-DAVIES

> The Roaring Girl herself, some few days hence,
> Shall on this stage give larger recompense.
> Which mirth that you may share in, herself does woo you,
> And craves this sign, your hands to beckon her to you.[10]

The epilogue assures the audience that Firth will present herself on stage, and elides the distinction between women and character through the processes of "mirth" and the pleasure recorded by the audience as they applaud the performance. There is no castigation of Frith's promised presence and, unlike Jonson's satirical attack on the orange-women and the Collegiate Ladies, the play welcomes Frith's interaction with the audience. Indeed, Middleton and Dekker imply that real Roaring Girl's appearance acts as an inducement to theatergoers, an argument that is underscored by a parallel usage of her character in Nathan Field's *Amends For Ladies* (1618). As Janet Todd and Elizabeth Spearing comment in their edition of Mary Frith's life, "it must have seemed that her notoriety would be good box office or good for the publisher's receipts."[11] Frith's vocal presence on stage is further affirmed by the *London Correction Book,* which records her addressing the audience with "immodest & lascivious speaches," informing them that, although she looked like a man, she would prove she was a woman.[12] Mary Frith was an unusual and idiosyncratic character and it would be wrong to assume that her presence on stage, together with playing the lute, singing, and making "lascivious" speeches, was emulated, or even admired, by other women. Nevertheless, there are elements common to the orange-women, the amorous female spectators, and Frith that suggest a distinct gender-specific discourse, which might have been illicit, but which ran parallel with the authorized entertainment being acted out on stage.

The first point of convergence is class; none of the women depicted is noble, some are middle class, most are poor. The itinerant sellers of oranges, apples, and tobacco were forced into such labor because of the strict rules applied to retailers in early modern England. Although trading in London was not policed as stringently as in the provinces, regrating (purchasing food items in bulk and selling them on in smaller quantities) was perceived as threatening the profits of shop holders. A sign on London Bridge warned women, "Let no Regrateress pass *London Bridge* towards *Suthwerk* . . . to buy Bread, to carry it into the City of *London* to sell."[13] The use of the feminine, "Regrateress," indicates that this occupation was considered to be one taken up mainly by women and it was one of the few ways that a poor woman could earn a living. The female spectators described are not always poor—the Collegiate Ladies and the tradesman's wife, for example, belong to the bourgeoisie—but these women are often depicted as selling their company and/or sexual favors. Finally, Mary Frith was not only a cross-dresser but also a thief, as a further name applied to her—Moll Cutpurse—attests. In this analy-

INTRODUCTION: ORANGE-WOMEN, FEMALE SPECTATORS, ROARING GIRLS   23

sis of class a further commonality becomes apparent; the poor, the prostitutes, and the thieves are all on the margins of legitimate society and all are perceived as transgressing the law. Another element emerges through the concept of misdemeanor, in that all groups of women are alleged to be sexually transgressive: the orange-women were depicted as selling sexual favors as well as fruit; the female spectators, even if not selling their bodies, were clearly at the theater with amorous intent; and Mary Frith through her dress, habits, and "lascivious speech" challenged moral codes. Finally, the most powerful link between these women is that they did not sit silently watching the play. It is important to recognize that early modern theaters would have been alive with women's actions and voices—the cries of orange-women, the dalliances of female spectators, and the songs of Mary Frith. Together these provided, as Natasha Korda indicates, a "female, boisterous 'side-show.'" Moreover, while these women might be perceived as challenging the legitimate all-male theatrical activities, dramatists like Jonson, Middleton, Dekker, and Fielding clearly recognized the compelling power of their voices and, tellingly, linked them to applause, "box office," and other female members of the audience.

There is still work to be undertaken on how Renaissance plays negotiated the fact that the women present during performances engaged with the experience of early modern theater in a variety of ways—ways that, in turn, complicate how criticism interprets the roles of female characters on stage. The essays collected here, however, begin to shed new light on the elements that have been identified as linking the orange-women, female spectators, and the Roaring Girl.

Nora Corrigan's essay, 'The Merry Tanner, the Mayor's Feast, and the King's Mistress: Thomas Heywood's *1 Edward IV* and the Ballad Tradition," describes, in the main plot, the tale of a tanner, Hobs, and his meeting with the king, and, in the subplot, the story of Jane Shore who is taken by the King to be his mistress. The account of Hobs was originally circulated in ballad form before being reworked by Heywood, but the Jane narrative was taken from the popular retelling in poetry and drama of her story in the late sixteenth century. Corrigan points out that a "citizen's wife turned royal paramour was an unlikely heroine in a culture that valued female chastity," and goes on to stress that Heywood differs from the earlier material by making Jane a chaste and loyal wife before the king seduces her. Indeed, within the play Jane is aware of her own "powerlessness and the dangers of disobeying the monarch," and rather than being vilified she is supported by her community and presented as a sympathetic character to the audience. As Corrigan concludes,

In Heywood's plays, the commoners' primary relationships are with other commoners, and these social networks are permanently disrupted by the king's actions.

24   MARION WYNNE-DAVIES

> By placing . . . Jane at the heart of a vital and supportive community, Heywood
> makes us acutely aware of what these characters—with whom Heywood's original
> audience would have had much in common—stand to lose through their familiarity
> with the king.[14]

The two key themes of class and sexual exploitation are centered upon the character of Jane in Heywood's play and Corrigan's telling analysis of the role of the "original audience" in her construction and reception allies Shore with the female vendors and spectators who were certainly present during the play's staging in the late sixteenth century.

The emphasis upon marginalized characters and sexual availability is echoed in Elizabeth Hodgson's essay, "A Fine and Private Place: Chapman's Theatrical *Widow,*" in which she reads George Chapman's play *The Widow's Tears* (ca.1605) through the perspective of conduct books for widows and popular widow-narratives. The play's first plot focuses on Lysander, who pretends to be dead in order to test his wife's faithfulness, while in the second plot the widowed countess, Eudora, is successfully wooed because her suitor realizes that "her desires are far stronger than her grief."[15] Lysander woos his "wife" in the disguise of the soldier who has killed her husband and, predictably, the "widow" succumbs to his advances. Hodgson argues that this play offers a "persistent analogy between theatrical performativity and widows' performatively private grief," concluding that the unknowability of the widows' inner feelings acts as a metaphor for the play's own "inscrutable" meaning.[16] This reading challenges traditional criticism of the play, which tends to read Chapman's representation of lusty widows as misogynistic and reductive, but by drawing on the earlier ballad and conduct book traditions Hodgson is able to complicate interpretation through awareness of contemporary discourse. Like the early modern theater, widows occupied a marginal position in which unknowability served both to protect and entertain.

Yvonne Bruce's essay, "'That Which Marreth All': Constancy and Gender in *The Virtuous Octavia,*" deals with a very different form of theater, choosing to focus on Samuel Brandon's 1598 closet drama. Bruce investigates the character of Octavia, Anthony's "long-suffering and long-virtuous wife," in relation to Christian Stoicism, pointing out that its tenets provided inadequate moral guidance for early modern women who were faced with "the messy fragilities of human nature."[17] In addition to her careful analysis of the play's "ironic reminder that the gulf between human passion and the ideals of divine reason remains unbridgeable," Bruce compares Octavia to the licentious Sylvia who "claim[s] the sexual freedom of a man" and she quotes Sylvia's speech, "I hate subjection and will nere be brought."[18] The strident independence of Brandon's character parallels that of Salome in Elizabeth Cary's *The Tragedy of Mariam* (ca. 1603), in which the character claims "to show my sex the way to freedom's door."[19] While both Sylvia and Salome

INTRODUCTION: ORANGE-WOMEN, FEMALE SPECTATORS, ROARING GIRLS   25

serve as dark contrasts to the heroines' ideal virtue—both Octavia and Mariam are unquestionably virtuous—their vocal claim for independent subjectivity, particularly in a sexual context, demonstrates that such disputes could, and were, aired in security of the closet dramas. Unlike the public theater, the restricted nature of any "audience" allowed Cary, as a female dramatist, to deal with a range of sexual roles for women in her text. Women's contribution to and involvement with closet drama has attracted considerable critical attention and Bruce's essay is a valuable correlative to inquiries based on women writers.

What each essay demonstrates is that, in order to excavate the way in which women negotiated the theater in early modern England, it is essential to appreciate the context of the "original audience," their cultural contexts, their understanding of the narratives' traditions, and their social codes. The invaluable work undertaken by theater historians on the material circumstances of production needs to be set against critical analyses of texts in order to uncover the complex negotiation between how women were represented on stage and how they presented themselves as playgoers. For us to appreciate fully the nuances of characters, from Jane Shore, the royal mistress, to Eudora, the widowed countess, it is important to remember that, while they were being acted on stage by boy-actors, the theater itself was full of vocal and active women, such as the orange-women, the amorous female spectators and, maybe, even a roaring girl.

Marion Wynne-Davies
University of Surrey

Notes

1. Ben Jonson, *Epicene,* ed. Gordon Campbell (Oxford: Oxford University Press, 1995), 127; I.i.137.
2. Natasha Korda, "Gender at Work in the Cries of London," in *Oral Traditions and gender in Early Modern Literary Texts* ed. Mary Ellen Lamb and Karen Bamford (Aldershot: Ashgate, 2008), 117–35; pp.131–32.
3. Jonson, *Epicene,* pp. 136; 135–36. II. Ii. 57, 59, 60, 62, 65.
4. Ibid., p.164, III.vi.81; p. 175, IV.iii.43; p.174, IV.iii.22; p.178, IV.iv.108.
5. Ibid., p. 208, V.iv.219, 226–27.
6. These three references are taken from, in sequence: Henry Fitgerald's *Satyres and Satirical Epigrams, with Certyain Observations at Blackfriars* (1617); Thomas Cranley, *Amanda, or the Reformed Whore* (1635); and Anon., *The Actor's Remonstrance* (1643). All quoted from: S. P. Cerasano and M. Wynne-Davies, eds., *Renaissance Drama by Women: texts and Documents* (London: Routledge, 1996), 165–66.
7. Ibid., 166.
8. Andrew Gurr, *Playgoing in Shakespeare's London* (Cambridge: Cambridge

University Press, 1987), 55–63. See also Richard Levin, "Women in the Renaissance Theatre Audience," *Shakespeare Quarterly* 40 (1989): 165–74.

9. Quoted in *Counterfeit Ladies. The Life and Death of Mal Cutpurse. The Case of Mary Carleton,* ed. Janet Todd and Elizabeth Spearing (London: William Pickering, 1994), xvi–xv.

10. Thomas Middleton and Thomas Dekker, *The Roaring Girl* in *The Routledge Anthology of Renaissance Drama,* ed. Simon Barker and Hilary Hinds (London: Routledge, 2003), 326–77; p.377.

11. Todd and Spearing, *Counterfeit Ladies,* xv–xvi.

12. Ibid., xiv.

13. Alice Clark, *Working Life of Women in the Seventeenth Century* (London: Routledge, 1992), 208. First edition 1919.

14. See below, p. 40.

15. See below, p. 66.

16. Ibid., p. 65.

17. Ibid., p. 42.

18. Ibid., p. 53.

19. Cerasano and Wynne-Davies, *Renaissance Drama,* 53.

The Merry Tanner, the Mayor's Feast, and the King's Mistress: Thomas Heywood's *1 Edward IV* and the Ballad Tradition

Nora L. Corrigan

ALTHOUGH Thomas Heywood's *The First and Second Parts of King Edward the Fourth* (1599) are nominally chronicle history plays, Heywood often seems to stretch the definition of history to the breaking point. The play's title page, which promises to present the king's "merrie pastime with the Tanner of Tamworth, as also his love to faire Mistresse Shore, her great promotion, fall, and miserie, and lastly the lamentable death of both her and her husband," gives a fair indication of Heywood's priorities. The real heroine of the piece is Jane Shore, the king's mistress, and Edward's friendship with a tanner named Hobs is given equal weight with his wars in France. The blurring of the line between the personal and political in this text has confounded modern critics; Peter Holbrook argues that these plays do not "qualify as . . . history by Wilson's definition (that its 'chief interest' be 'political')" (155, n.18). Esther Yael Beith-Halahmi, similarly, argues that Heywood "is not concerned with the more abstract problems of government" (311). Comparing Heywood's treatment of this material with his popular ballad sources, however, throws his political agenda into sharp relief. In Heywood's world, politics are not confined to the court and battlefield; rather, they play out in the greenwood, the private home, and the artisan's shop.

The Elizabethan history play owes an immense debt to another form of popular historical narrative, the ballad—a genre which D. R. Woolf describes as "masterless history," uncensored and irreverent (37). Richard Helgerson, quoting William Chappell's notes to the Roxburghe ballad collection, suggests that the ballad tradition constitutes a "'people's history of England' in two senses: they were the history commoners heard and knew, and they were history from a commoners' point of view" (*Forms* 237). Gerald Porter describes the "dense relation between working life, popular song, and the theatre," citing a number of elements in Shakespeare that seem to have been drawn from ballads or other aspects of the popular oral tradition (168). In the history plays, these range from the wooing scene in *Henry V* to the snatches of popular ballads that Falstaff quotes incessantly. Porter argues that "within the world of the plays, ballads function as part of the cultural resources of those who are disempowered"; Shakespeare associates the genre with working people, with frequent references to songs being sung by weavers, shoemakers, and other laborers (175). Heywood's tanner, likewise, quotes snatches of ballads incessantly in *1 Edward IV.*

Ballads about historical topics performed similar cultural work to drama: they provided a narrative about England's past that was both entertaining and accessible to people who were illiterate or unable to afford books. This narrative was at once bound by a particular historical context and timeless in its use of folk motifs; it sought to humanize kings and emphasize the personal interaction between king and commoner. As Francis James Child explains in his exhaustive collection of English popular ballads, "Next to the adventures of Robin Hood and his men, the most favorite topic in English popular poetry is the chance-encounter with a king, unrecognized as such, with one of his humbler subjects" (69). Child surveys a dozen examples of such texts in his introduction to the ballad of "King Edward the Fourth and a Tanner of Tamworth," one of Heywood's sources for *1 Edward IV.* These ballads feature kings ranging from Alfred the Great to William III, although the monarchs are usually generic figures undistinguished from each other by any topical references or explicit political commentary. Several common threads recur in these narratives: the king receives an invitation to dine and drink in a humble household, sometimes featuring venison poached from the royal preserve or some similarly incriminating item. Further dramatic irony results from the subject being overly free with his speech in front of his disguised guest, although he never says anything truly seditious or critical of the king. The meal is always a harmonious occasion, with much wine drunk by all. During the course of the feast, the host often teaches the king a particular drinking ritual that serves as a symbolic way of initiating the king into the community.[1] The words of this ritual may later identify subject and king to one another, or they may agree on some other sign or token by which they will know each other when they meet again. When recognized, the subject is invariably terrified that he is going to be hanged for poaching or general disrespect; instead, the king pardons him and offers largesse (Child 67–87).

The "king disguised" narrative was a favorite on stage as well; Shakespeare, for example, employs it on multiple occasions in the second tetralogy. The episode that most overtly evokes the ballad tradition is the scene before the battle of Agincourt in *Henry V,* in which Henry wanders his army's camp in disguise and encounters one unwitting subject after another. The first man he meets is Pistol, the last survivor of the Boar's Head crowd, who praises the king in crude but hearty terms that resemble those of the ballad commoners. After a brief interlude with Captains Fluellen and Gower, Henry meets three common soldiers and converses with them at length. The most outspo-

THE MERRY TANNER, THE MAYOR'S FEAST, AND THE KING'S MISTRESS   29

ken of the three, Michael Williams, unaware that he is face to face with the king, vents his displeasure freely. Henry and Williams exchange tokens by which they agree to recognize each other. When they meet again, Williams is accused of treason for offering to strike the king, but Henry pardons him and gives him a glove full of crowns.

The outward trappings of this scene are thus virtually identical to those of the disguised-king ballads, but Anne Barton argues that Shakespeare draws on popular ballad motifs in this episode "in order to question, not to celebrate, a folk convention" (99). Unlike the ballad kings who discover concord and mutual respect with their subjects wherever they go, Henry quarrels with his soldiers, fails to provide adequate answers to their questions about the justice of his cause, and finally retreats into a resentful soliloquy. His apparent reconciliation with Michael Williams, though accompanied by a lavish gift,

> provides not a ghost of an answer to the questions raised during this particular encounter between common man and king disguised. Is the king's cause just? If not, what measure of guilt does he incur for requiring men to die for anything but the strict necessity of their country? Can the opinions and judgments of private men influence a sovereign on his throne? Henry is generous to Williams, but it is a dismissive generosity which places the subject firmly in an inferior position and silences his voice. The two men do not sit down at table together to any common feast, in the manner of Dekker's Henry V or Heywood's Edward IV.
>
> ("The King Disguised" 101)

Here and elsewhere in her article, Barton uses the Hobs scenes from *1 Edward IV* as a paradigm of a more "conventional" disguised-king episode, one that "generate[s] harmony, good fellowship, and mutual understanding" (96). Heywood's play and other contemporary ballad-inspired histories exemplify a genre Barton calls "comical history," while she argues that Shakespeare's treatment of these same motifs is essentially tragic.

To anyone familiar with the ending of the *Edward IV* plays, this is a problematic contention. The deaths of the Shores and their comrades bring the cycle to a bleak conclusion, while Heywood supplies only the barest hint that Richard will eventually fall. Barton's use of the terms "comical" and "tragical" history is one of the key points with which Richard Helgerson takes issue in *Forms of Nationhood*. He argues that this distinction not only misrepresents Heywood's tone, but carries with it an implicit, and unfair, value judgment in Shakespeare's favor. Helgerson does read the *Edward IV* plays as qualitatively different from the Shakespearean histories, claiming that ballad-inspired histories such as Heywood's reflect the perspective of the subjects rather than the rulers. While they do not support open rebellion, they do "represent [monarchic] power from the point of view of those who suffer its

30 NORA L. CORRIGAN

harshest consequences" (239). The hallmark of this group of plays, in his view, is the prominent presence of a likeable character with populist sympathies who eventually becomes a victim of royal power, suffers greatly as a result, yet remains deeply loyal to the monarch; Heywood's Jane and Matthew Shore exemplify this character type. Helgerson perceives the general political position of Heywood's play as indistinguishable from that of the ballads, which he summarizes as follows:

> [T]he dominant attitude of the play accords with that of Hobs, the tanner of Tamworth. "I am just akin to Sutton Windmill," Hobs tells the disguised King Edward. "I can grind which way soe'er the wind blows. If it be Harry, I can say 'Well fare Lancaster.' If it be Edward, I can sing, 'York, York, for my money.'" Hobs shares the instinctive and indiscriminate loyalty of the balladeers for whom every king, regardless of lineage or personal qualities, is "our king."
>
> (*Forms* 238)

Yet when they are placed in context, and especially when read alongside the ballad from which Heywood drew the Hobs scenes, these lines admit a more cynical and more politically sophisticated reading. If we accept Barton's basic argument about the Michael Williams scenes, Heywood and Shakespeare do not seem so far apart after all.

Heywood's story line about Hobs the Tanner is drawn from a ballad source, but substantially reworked in ways that throw the ballad's ideological position into question. The ballad of "King Edward the Fourth and a Tanner of Tamworth" exists in multiple versions, but Heywood would most likely have known the one printed in London in 1596 by John Danter (*Child Ballads,* V, 81–83). Unlike Heywood's play, this ballad makes no reference to Edward's reputation as a playboy or the broader political context of his reign; any of the other popular ballad kings—Alfred, Henry II, Edward III—would have served the purpose equally well. The unnamed tanner is also a generic figure, unaware of the world outside of Tamworth. He expresses no political opinions, though he speaks bluntly enough when giving his opinion of the king, whom he considers a fool because the king does not recognize a good cowhide when he sees one. Every aspect of the tanner's characterization is classmarked. He is chiefly concerned with his own possessions—he takes great pride in his "good russet coat" and his "mare cost foure shillings"—and his trade (lines 13–15). When Edward insists on changing horses, the tanner first demands payment because he likes his own mare better, and then proceeds to demonstrate his crudeness and ineptitude in a comical riding scene:

> The king tooke the tanner by the leg,
> and lift him up a loft;
> The tanner girded out a good round fart,
> his belly it was so soft.

THE MERRY TANNER, THE MAYOR'S FEAST, AND THE KING'S MISTRESS 31

"You make great waste," said our king,
"your curtesie is but small;"
"Thy horse is so high," quoth the tanner againe,
"I feare me of a fall."

But when the tanner was in the saddle
the steede began to blow and blast,
And against the roote of an old tree
the tanner downe he cast.

(lines 145–56)

The tanner's inability to remain mounted on the king's high horse—or even to recognize that it is a better horse than his own—underscores the apparent "rightness" of social distinctions. The ballad never seriously questions these distinctions, although it introduces elements of comic misrule, culminating in Edward's offer to make the tanner an esquire. In return, the tanner promises the king, "The next time thou comest to Tamworth town, / Thou shalt have clouting-leather for thy shoon" (line 220). Although he has, in a sense, struck up a neighborly relationship with King Edward, he is never in any danger of losing either his present social standing or his comic ignorance of appropriate social behavior. Stephen Greenblatt, writing about peasant humor in the Renaissance, underscores the distinction "between a laughter that levels—that draws lord and clown together in the shared condition of the flesh—and a laughter that attempts to inscribe ineradicable differences"; the humor of the ballad is clearly the latter (17). Finally, and most importantly, the tanner is clearly as unfit to judge the king's policies as the king is to judge a cowhide, nor does he attempt to claim a political and historical voice for the commons by expressing his opinions of the king and the times.

The implication that king and commoner are made of different stuff has vanished from the parallel episode in *1 Edward IV.* Heywood's Hobs may be ignorant of the finer points of court etiquette, but he lacks the crudeness and absence of control over his own body that make the tanner in the ballad the butt of slapstick humor. The scene in the play is also darker and more politically charged. The civil wars, never mentioned in the ballad, are always in the background here. Before the king arrives, Hobs voices his frustration with the political situation: "[B]y my troth, I know not when I speak treason, when I do not. There's such halting betwixt two kings, that a man cannot go upright, but he shall offend t'one of them. I would God had them both, for me" (sc. 11.63–66). Hobs's responses to the disguised king's questions are understandably guarded. The audience cannot assume that he has no opinion about the wars, only that he has a keen sense of self-preservation. Despite the pervading atmosphere of danger and surveillance, a note of protest against current conditions creeps into the conversation from time to time:

32   NORA L. CORRIGAN

King. Pray thee tell me, how love they king *Edward?*
Hobs. Faith, as poor folks love holidays: glad to have them now and then, but to
have them come too often will undo them. So, to see the King now and then, 'tis
comfort, but every day would beggar us. And I may say to thee, we fear we shall
be troubled to lend him money, for we doubt he's but needy.

(13.28–34)

Hobs, then, has definite political opinions but is wise enough to soften his
criticism of the king with compliments. The tanner neatly parries Edward's
subsequent line of questioning, presenting himself as a politically ignorant,
indiscriminately loyal peasant, but by this point the audience knows it is a
pose. His tone remains lighthearted and he quotes a snatch of popular song,
but he seems acutely conscious that identifying himself to a stranger as either
a Lancastrian or a Yorkist would court danger.

King. Say'th whether lovest thou better Harry or Edward.
Hobs. Nay, that's counsel, and two may keep it, if one be away.
King. Shall I say my conscience? I think Harry is the true king.
Hobs. Art advised of that? Harry's of the old house of Lancaster, and that progen-
ity do I love.
King. And thou dost not hate the house of York?
Hobs. Why, no, for I am just akin to Sutton windmill: I can grind which way so
e'er the wind blow. If it be Harry, I can say "well fare Lancaster"; If it be Ed-
ward, I can sing "Yorke, Yorke, for my money." (38–48)

Unlike the tanner of the ballad, Heywood's Hobs is far from naive. One gets
the impression that he may well have strong views about the succession, but
is intelligent and crafty enough to evade a potentially dangerous line of questions. The entire scene, on close reading, reveals a delicate balance between
loyalty and fear.

Hobs becomes more outspoken when the king offers him a monopoly on
his trade: "By the mass and the matins, I like not those pattens. Sirrah, they
that have them do as the priests did in old time: buy and sell the sins of the
people. So they make the King believe they mend what's amiss, and, for
money they make the thing worse than it is . . . Faith, 'tis pity that one subject
should have in his hand, that might do good to many throughout the land"
(75–83). Hobs implies that the holders of patents have deceived the king
about their intentions, and that the commoners are in a better position than
King Edward to know about these abuses. While he avoids criticizing the
king directly, he also makes a powerful argument in favor of popular participation in the government by implying that kings are not always fully informed of conditions in their kingdom. The king's response to this is rather
oblique—"Sayst thou me so, tanner?"—suggesting that he is, perhaps, in less
than perfect concord with these sentiments, although he will later allow him-

THE MERRY TANNER, THE MAYOR'S FEAST, AND THE KING'S MISTRESS   33

self to be ruled in this matter by Jane Shore, who shares Hobs's dislike of patents (84).

Nevertheless, there seem to be no hard feelings; in keeping with the usual conventions of the disguised-king narrative, Hobs invites the king and his companion home for a meal. The fare is simple: "a good barley bagpudding, a piece of fat bacon, a good cow heel, a hard cheese, and a brown loaf" washed down with plenty of "Mother Whetstone's ale" (14.15–16, 88). In this homely setting, the king drops the biggest political bombshell of the play: Henry VI is dead, and with him the Lancastrian line. Hobs's response to the king's anxious question about how the commons will take this news is one part heartfelt insistence on the common destiny of mankind and one part cynical political commentary:

> Well, God be with good king Henry.
> Faith, the commons will take it as a common thing.
> Death's an honest man; for he spares not the king;
> For as one's come, another's ta'en away—
> And seldom comes the better, thats all we say.
>
> (82–86)

The evening's entertainment concludes with a song about England's past:

> *Agincourt, Agincourt, know ye not Agincourt?*
> *Where the English slew and hurt*
> *All the French foemen:*
> *With our guns and bills brown,*
> *O, the French were beaten downe,*
> *Morris-pikes and bowmen.*
>
> (109–14)

Hobs's choice of song provides a rather amusing metatextual moment: a popular ballad about English history is being performed by a character from a popular ballad about English history. The lyrics emphasize the notion that the battle of Agincourt was won by the *people:* the verse quoted is not about the heroic exploits of Henry V, but about "the English" and "our Guns and bills brown." This intensely populist (and jingoistic) view of history underscores the theme of popular patriotism—and popular solidarity—that informs the entire play.

Nevertheless, the type of historical narrative that Heywood's play provides is fundamentally different from that of the popular ballad. The ballads offer a vision of the past that is comforting, idyllic, and above all stable. Not only does Heywood weave the story of King Edward and the tanner into a broader historical context and situate it at a critical moment of dynastic change, but he also draws the audience's attention to the idea of historical change by having Edward remark after his first meeting with Hobs, "I see plain men, by observation / Of things that alter in the change of times / Do gather knowledge" (13.98–100). The times are in flux, and there is at least a hint that these changes may be empowering for men like Hobs: "plain men" are more knowledgeable and more politically aware than they have been in the past. However, the commoners in the *Edward IV* plays are left in the awkward position of having knowledge and opinions but no political agency of their own, except such agency as they can negotiate through their brief and unstable relationships with the king. The episodes that follow Hobs's encounter with the king lead the audience to question whether this is sufficient, even under Edward's relatively benevolent rule; they also introduce some of Heywood's sharpest social commentary.

Laura Caroline Stevenson has noted that several of the financial concerns mentioned in the play, such as Hobs's criticism of patents and his fear that the "needy" king will ask him for money, touch upon abuses common at *Elizabeth's* court rather than Edward's (206 ff.). Shades of the present also creep in when Hobs and his neighbors appear in a follow-up scene with Edward's officials, who are collecting a quasi-voluntary tax called a benevolence. At first glance, the episode does appear benevolent; many of the residents of Tamworth give willingly and generously, while Hobs shames the more reluctant members of his community into contributing. Perhaps this is the payoff from Edward's personalized, commoner-friendly style of kingship. The scene is, however, problematic for several reasons. This method of taxation would have been an odd practice for Heywood to romanticize. Never popular, benevolences were outlawed under Richard III, although later monarchs continued to collect them from time to time; Elizabeth did so in 1599, the year that the *Edward IV* plays were written. The first benevolence, the one dramatized in the play, inspired Holinshed to editorialize, "many with grudge gave great summes toward that newe found ayde, which of them might bee called a Maleuolence" (qtd. in Crupi 234). Heywood transforms this picture of a reluctant populace into a scene in which the grudging are punished and those subjects who give willingly are "rewarded" with the moral high ground, but, as Charles Crupi points out, it is less clear whether they will receive a more practical recompense from the king in return: "[W]e must ask whether the play dramatizes royal willingness to honor the feudal obligations contained in language and represented in ritual. If not, obedience is merely submission and the fantasy of conciliation is accordingly subverted" (232). Because the play raises grave and persistent questions about whether Edward's hearty populist manner is actually *good* for his subjects, the scene takes on a darker tone in context.

In particular, Edward's failure to "requite" generosity in kind will become the defining feature of his relationship with Matthew Shore, an ideal citizen who loses his wife to a less than ideal king. Matthew, whether motivated by humility or by a touch of pride in his own social rank, refuses to be knighted in the aftermath of Falconbridge's rebellion. Instead, Edward promises him, "some other way / We will devise to quittance thy deserts" (10.240–41). As Lena Cowen Orlin notes, Edward's words find a bitter echo toward the end of the play, when Shore resigns his wife to the king and plans to leave the country: "England, fare thou well. / And Edward, for requiting me so well, / But dare I speak of him? Forbear, forbear" (20.94–96). This emphasis on requital, or the lack thereof, colors the resolution of the benevolence episode. Immediately after Shore's exit, the king enters and discusses the excellent yield from the benevolence with Howard and Sellinger. He promises that he "must requite that honest tanner" (21.14) with an invitation to court—but the juxtaposition of the two scenes provides a dark reminder that the king's requitals are not always fair or kind. Even his desire to play host to Hobs seems as much motivated by the promise of "good sport" as a sincere wish to return a favor (16). Both balladeer and playwright invoke the idea of neighborly reciprocity as they explore the relationship between king and subject, but while the ballad's happy ending provides a comforting fantasy of a subject establishing a successful neighborly relationship with the king, Heywood emphasizes Edward's failure to fulfill his end of this social obligation.

The play brings the Hobs story line to a happy, but by no means unproblematic, conclusion. *1 Edward IV* ends as most disguised-king ballads do, with the familiar rite of recognition, pardon, and celebration. Hobs comes to London to plead for his son, who is in jail for robbery, and ends up fearing for his own life when he discovers that he has addressed the king as "plain 'Ned,' mad rogue and rascal" (23.86). Predictably, the king absolves him, pardons his son, and gives him forty pounds, but Hobs remains wary and mildly skeptical of Edward's good faith to the end: "Marry, you speak like an honest man, if you mean what you say" (101–2). Furthermore, Heywood departs from the usual ballad pattern by foregrounding the generosity not of the king, but of the Widow Norton, who voluntarily adds her own "widows mite" to the sum the king originally requested as a benevolence (120). Edward's efforts to help her to a good husband are gently undermined by Hobs and the widow, who have no particular desire to be married off to one another. Thus, while a certain measure of harmony and good fellowship are indeed evident in the Hobs subplot, the third element Barton describes as central to the comical history—"mutual understanding"—remains elusive.

Another perennial feature of the disguised-king ballads, the feast shared by king and subjects, reappears elsewhere in the play and in a more troubling context, when Mayor Crosbie invites the king to the feast where he first sees Mistress Shore. The Lord Mayor is a self-made man, and his characterization has been cited as evidence of Heywood's ideological conservatism and procapitalist stance. Jean Howard and Theodora Jankowski, for example, argue that Crosbie's story of his origins romanticizes the status quo and erases the real obstacles to a penniless foundling becoming a prosperous tradesman, suggesting that poor people who *fail* to pull themselves up by the bootstraps are at fault. Crosbie's initial soliloquy, however, does not celebrate individual entrepreneurship, but rather the network of social obligations that knits London tradesmen together. One salient feature of his rags-to-riches tale is that there are no aristocrats in it. His chief benefactors are a poor shoemaker and the masters of the Hospital of London. Both, in turn, have become the beneficiaries of his good fortune, and he has also established a poorhouse. While actual social realities were, of course, grimmer, it is significant that Heywood imagines private charity as a self-contained, commoner-run success story, based on reciprocity and mutual respect. At the disastrous feast which the king attends, these social virtues break down. Rather than reciprocating the mayor's hospitality, Edward sows discontent in the Shores' marriage and abruptly leaves the table when he can no longer keep his desire for Jane under control. Crosbie is both devastated and bewildered ("My house to cause my Sovereigns discontent?"), while the king does nothing to assuage his distress (16.179). As Stevenson argues, the episode "suggest[s] that Edward's courtly behaviour, unlike the London citizen's loyal conduct, is merely a cover for what in Heywood's plays are consistently the greatest of faults—callousness and ingratitude" (118). While Edward's supper with Hobs has the expected genial good humor and harmonious outcome of the popular ballads, a more complete reversal of these tropes than the mayor's feast cannot be imagined.

This scene also introduces the King Edward / Jane Shore subplot, the site of Heywood's most radical departure from the ballads' ideological position. Because Mistress Shore's name was both familiar and laden with cultural baggage for the Elizabethans, it will be helpful to give a brief overview of her other appearances in sixteenth-century literature, beginning with Sir Thomas More's *History of King Richard III*. More apologizes for including such a lengthy account of a female commoner's character and deeds, conscious that this digression was at odds with his contemporaries' sense of decorum and his own practices elsewhere in the *History*:

> I doubt not some shall think this woman so slight a thing to be written of and set among the remembrances of great matters, which they shall specially think that haply shall esteem her only by that they now see her. But me seemeth the chance so much the more worthy to be remembered, in how much she is now in the more beggarly condition, unfriended and worn out of acquaintance, after good substance, after as great favor with the prince, after as great suit and seeking to with all those that those days had business to speed, as many other men were in their times, which now be famous only by the infamy of their evil deeds. Her doings were not so much less, albeit they be much less remembered, because they were not so evil. For men use if they have an evil turn to write it in marble: and whoso doth us a good turn, we write it in dust, which is not worst proved by her; for at this day she beggeth of many at this day living, that at this day had begged if she had not been.
>
> (57–58)

More justifies his interest in Mistress Shore's life because it emblematizes a larger moral truth. He extrapolates her story into a commentary on the rise and fall of great men—a more fitting subject for historiography, in the eyes of most Renaissance writers. Richard Helgerson considers More's work the first "commoner's history," in large part because this portion of the text suggests that "tragic emotion may not be the exclusive province of the great" ("Weeping" 456). This interpretation, however, obscures the fact that this passage is unique in the *History*. Elsewhere, More appears to sympathize with the commoners as a group—portraying the London citizens as politically savvy and quick to see through Richard's political machinations—but rarely comments on the character and deeds of individuals. Mistress Shore is a remarkable exception in a text where the commons appear, for the most part, as commentators rather than as agents.

The citizen's wife turned royal paramour was an unlikely heroine in a culture that valued female chastity and regarded history making as the province and prerogative of aristocratic males. Nevertheless, Mistress Shore's story captured the popular imagination throughout the sixteenth century.[2] She became a central character in a number of poetic and dramatic texts dealing with Edward's reign, including *A Mirror for Magistrates,* a series of popular poems and ballads, and three history plays, including Heywood's two *Edward IV* plays. Along the way, she acquired a first name—Jane—and a pathetic death scene. As Helgerson has noted, her absence from the stage in Shakespeare's first tetralogy would have been perceived by contemporaries as a conspicuous and deliberate omission; she was as integral to many popular accounts of Edward's reign as the king himself ("Weeping" 462). In Heywood's treatment of the same era, by contrast, she appears at the heart of the story, just where audiences would have expected her to be—but Heywood makes some unprecedented changes to his sources in his treatment of her character.

While More describes Mistress Shore in sympathetic terms and does not stress her wantonness or desire to take a lover above her husband's social station, the popular ballads ascribe these negative traits to her *before* she meets Edward. In *The Garland of Good Will,* Thomas Deloney characterizes her as a willful, spoiled girl: "The only daughter of a wealthy merchant man / Against whose counsel evermore / I was rebelling" (lines 12–14). In an anonymous ballad from the Roxburghe collection,[3] Jane admits she "spread my plumes as wantons do / Some sweet and secret friend to wooe / Because my love I did not find / Agreeing to my wanton mind" (lines 23–26). One version of this ballad substitutes "chaste" for "my" in the third line, further underscoring Jane's sexual transgressions (Chappell 484, n. 7). The same ballad introduces Jane's false friend Mistress Blage, who urges her companion to accept Edward's advances because she considers it "a gallant thing / To be beloved of a king" (lines 33–34). Thus counseled, Mistress Shore embraces her new position at court and "the Joys that love could bring" (line 45). There is no sign of Heywood's tormented Jane in this text; Matthew is the only one who suffers while King Edward is alive. After Jane's fall from influence, the ballads emphasize her physical mortification rather than her repentance and spiritual redemption. She becomes a Cressida-like figure, begging "with clacke and dish" and wearing filthy, vermin-infested rags (Deloney, line 62).

As Helgerson notes, Heywood departs from every known contemporary version of the story by depicting the Shores' marriage as genuinely affectionate and the middle-class household as a "place of value" ("Weeping" 463). Heywood fiercely interrogates assumptions that the ballads take for granted—the king's "right" to a mistress, the transgressive desire for pleasure and power that leads to Jane's fall. Jane shows no sign of excessive social ambition or discontent with her husband in *1 Edward IV,* although Edward attempts to instill these feelings in her when he speaks of her marriage: "You had been a lady but for him" (16.92). Like most of the arguments he uses to persuade her to become his mistress, this ploy proves unsuccessful. Ultimately, Heywood's women are motivated not by lust or ambition, but by an acute sense of their own powerlessness and the dangers of disobeying the monarch. Jane's friend, Mistress Blage, counsels her:

> Believe me, Mistress Shore, a dangerous case,
> And every way replete with doubtful fear . . .
> If you should yield, your virtuous name were soiled,
> And your beloved husband made a scorn.
> And, if not yield, it's likely that his love,
> Which now admires ye, will convert to hate;
> And who knows not, a prince's hate is death?

$$(19.21–27)$$

The pervasive atmosphere of fear, both in this scene and in the episode in *2 Edward IV* where Mistress Blage rejects her friend, renders both women's transgressions more understandable and forgivable.

But in another sense, Mistress Blage's treachery is far more serious in the play than in the Roxburghe ballad: Heywood treats personal loyalty as the fundamental measure of a character's decency. Nowhere is this clearer than in the differing treatments of Jane's middle-class community in the play and in its sources. The Roxburghe ballad makes social isolation part of Mistress Shore's punishment and portrays the loss of friendships and respect among her peers as a natural consequence of adultery: "Thus was I scorn'd of maid and wife / For leading such a wicked life / Both sucking babes and children small / Did make a pastime of my fall" (123–26). Only one friend defies the general condemnation of Jane and ventures to relieve her, and gets hanged for

THE MERRY TANNER, THE MAYOR'S FEAST, AND THE KING'S MISTRESS 39

his pains. The ballad ends, not happily, but with a validation of conventional morality—Mistress Shore repents her sins and urges others not to imitate them. The respectable neighbors who ostracized her are vindicated.

By contrast, in Heywood's play the community at large sympathizes with Jane. The petitioners whose cases she has pleaded risk their lives to help her, and Brakenbury comments that the crowds who witness her disgrace "have their relenting eyes even big with tears" (*2 Edward IV,* 18.113). Mistress Blage and Rufford, characters whom Heywood strongly condemns and portrays as hypocrites, are the sole exceptions. The contrast between their behavior and the ready generosity of Aire, Jockie, Brakenbury, and even Matthew Shore encourages the audience to judge Jane's betrayers harshly, while the royal mistress's own errors seem readily excusable in the light of her friends' forgiveness and her own willingness to extend charity toward Mistress Blage.[4] Moreover, the play ends with the sense that Richard's treatment of Jane is an unrelieved moral travesty. Because Heywood chooses to include only the faintest foreshadowing of the tyrant's fall at the conclusion of the play, readers and viewers are deprived of the neat sense of closure and justice that characterizes the ballads.

Jane's moral transgressions do not go unacknowledged in the play, but the public shame that constitutes her punishment in the ballads has been replaced by an internal sense of guilt. The level of self-awareness and self-condemnation that Heywood's Jane displays, almost from the very moment when she agrees to become the king's mistress, has no parallel in the ballads, in which she shows no sign of repentance until after Edward's death. If her remorse is private, however, her method of seeking atonement is very public; she becomes the king's proxy and link to the people who seek his assistance. More's description of Mistress Shore's "great suit and seeking to with all those that those days had business to speed" is vividly dramatized in a scene in which Jane agrees to help a series of petitioners. Her sympathies clearly lie with the poor against the powerful, and she becomes an eloquent spokeswoman and advocate for the commons. The three petitioners to whom Jane offers assistance become, in a sense, her new community; they will repay her favors in *2 Edward IV,* after her fall from grace. However, a fourth petitioner, a man named Rufford who seeks a license to transport corn (another abuse more reminiscent of Elizabeth's reign than Edward's), incurs Jane's anger: "[You] care not how you wound the commonwealth. / The poor must starve for food to fill your purse, / And the enemy bandy bullets of our lead" (*1 Edward IV,* 22.66–68). This is the second time the play has raised the issue of monopolies. While Crupi argues that Hobs's subversive potential has come to nothing, since Edward's noncommittal response to his tirade against patents "provides . . . no indication of the possibility of reform," this episode picks up on one of the tanner's most important complaints and dramatizes one potential (if impractical) avenue for change: the principled decision of a commoner elevated to a social position where she can influence policy (245). The English people benefit from Jane's elevation to royal favor; but she herself will not be so lucky in the end.

Thus, Heywood's treatment of the relationship between king and subject is diametrically opposed to that of most popular ballads, which use the motifs of the disguised king and the common feast to bring about a happy ending marked by good fellowship between king and commoner. While social distinctions are temporarily set aside or reversed in these episodes, the harmonious ending reasserts their essential rightness and usefulness. In *1 Edward IV*, Heywood deliberately manipulates these ballad conventions in order to blacken the king's character and raise questions about the rightness of social distinctions. Differing treatments of community are central to this transformation. The disguised-king ballads typically have two important characters, the king himself and the subject temporarily deceived by his appearance; their friendship emblematizes a broader vision of cross-class harmony. In Heywood's plays, the commoners' primary relationships are with other commoners, and these social networks are permanently disrupted by the king's actions. By placing Crosbie, Matthew, and especially Jane at the heart of a vital and supportive community, Heywood makes us acutely aware of what these characters—with whom Heywood's original audience would have had much in common—stand to lose through their familiarity with the king.

Notes

1. Prince Hal's boast that he "can drink with any tinker in his own language" (*1 Henry IV*, II. iv. 18–19) is reminiscent of this motif.

2. For background information and more extensive discussion of the numerous literary texts dealing with Mistress Shore, see Beith-Halahmi, *Angell Fayre or Strumpet Lewd;* Harner, "Jane Shore in Literature," and Pratt, "Jane Shore and the Elizabethans."

3. This ballad is titled, in full, "The Woful Lamentation of Mrs. Jane Shore, a Gold-smith's Wife of London, sometime King Edward the Fourth's Concubine, who for her Wanton Life came to a Miserable End. Set forth for the Example of all wicked Livers"; its presentation as a warning for wicked wives emphasizes the domestic rather than the historical implications of Mistress Shore's story.

4. Interestingly, Mistress Blage appears "very poorly, a-begging with her basket and clap-dish" in her final scene on stage (sc. 20, s.d.). This grim image of female penitence is attached to Jane in the ballads.

Works Cited

Barton, Anne. "The King Disguised: Shakespeare's *Henry V* and the Comical History." In *The Triple Bond,* edited by Joseph G. Price. University Park: Pennsylvania State University Press, 1975, 92–117.

Beith-Halahmi, Esther Yael. *Angell Fayre or Strumbet Lewd: Jane Shore as an Example of Erring Beauty in 16th Century Literature.* Vol. 2. Salzburg, Austria: Institut für Englische Sprache und Literatur, 1974.

Chappell, William. *Roxburghe Ballads.* Vol. 1. London: Taylor and Company, 1871. 9 vols.

Child, Francis James. *The English and Scottish Popular Ballads.* Vol. 5. New York: Dover, 1965. 5 vols.

Crupi, Charles W. "Ideological Contradiction in Part I of Heywood's *Edward IV:* 'Our Musicke Runs . . . Much upon Discords.'" *Medieval and Renaissance Drama in England* 7 (1995): 224–56.

Deloney, Thomas. "Shores Wife" from *The Garland of Good Will.* Edited by F. O. Mann. http://www.pbm.com/lindahl/deloney/goodwill.

Greenblatt, Stephen. "Murdering Peasants: Status, Genre, and the Representation of Rebellion." In *Representing the English Renaissance,* edited by Stephen Greenblatt. Berkeley: University of California Press, 1988, 1–30.

Harner, James L. "Jane Shore in Literature: A Checklist." *Notes and Queries* 28 (1981): 496–507.

Helgerson, Richard. *Forms of Nationhood.* Chicago: University of Chicago Press, 1992.

———. "Weeping for Jane Shore." *South Atlantic Quarterly* 98, no. 3 (1999): 451–76.

Heywood, Thomas. *The First and Second Parts of King Edward IV.* Edited by Richard Rowland. Manchester: Manchester University Press, 2005.

Holbrook, Peter. *Literature and Degree in Renaissance England.* Newark: University of Delaware Press, 1994.

Howard, Jean. "Other Englands: The View from the Non-Shakespearean History Play." In *Other Voices, Other Views: Expanding the Canon in Renaissance Studies,* edited by Helen Ostovich, Mary V. Silcox, and Graham Roebuck. Newark: University of Delaware Press, 1999, 135–53.

Jankowski, Theodora A. "Historicizing and Legitimating Capitalism: Thomas Heywood's *Edward IV* and *If You Know Not Me, You Know Nobody.*" *Medieval and Renaissance Drama in England* 7 (1995): 305–37.

More, Sir Thomas. *The History of King Richard III and Selections from the English and Latin Poems.* Edited by Richard S. Sylvester. New Haven: Yale University Press, 1976.

Orlin, Lena Cowen. *Private Matters and Public Culture in Post-Reformation England.* Ithaca: Cornell University Press, 1994.

Palmer, Daryl W. "Edward IV's Secret Familiarities and the Politics of Proximity in Elizabethan History Plays." *ELH* 61 (1994): 279–315.

Porter, Gerald. "Shakespeare and the Ballad." In *Ballads into Books: The Legacies of Francis James Child,* edited by Tom Cheesman and Sigrid Rieuwerts. Bern: Peter Lang, 1997. 165–78.

Pratt, Samuel M. "Jane Shore and the Elizabethans: Some Facts and Speculations." *Texas Studies in Literature and Language* 11 (1971): 1293–1306.

Shakespeare, William. *The Complete Works.* Edited by Hardin Craig. Glenview, IL: Scott, Foresman and Company, 1961.

Stevenson, Laura Caroline. *Praise and Paradox: Merchants and Craftsmen in Elizabethan Popular Literature.* Cambridge: Cambridge University Press, 1984.

Woolf, D. R. "The 'Common Voice': History, Folklore and Oral Tradition in Early Modern England." *Past and Present* 120 (1998): 26–52.

"That which Marreth All": Constancy and Gender in *The Virtuous Octavia*

Yvonne Bruce

IN his study of the influence of French Senecanism on the drama of the Pembroke circle, A. M. Witherspoon effectively dismisses Samuel Brandon's 1598 closet drama, *The Virtuous Octavia*. Calling it "a servile imitation of [Samuel Daniel's] *Cleopatra*"[1] Witherspoon suggests that Brandon chose to dramatize the plight of Octavia because all the good dramatic subjects—namely Antony and Cleopatra—had already been taken by other playwrights. There are compelling reasons for Brandon's choice of Octavia, however—as well as for Daniel's own choice of her as a character in his "Letter from Octavia to Marcus Antonius" and for Fulke Greville's choice of her as a character in "Letter to an Honourable Lady." The Octavia figure, in classical sources as well as in Renaissance representations, epitomizes the long-suffering and long-virtuous wife of a philandering husband, an epitome of direct consequence for the dedicatees of Brandon's, Daniel's, and Greville's works. But Octavia, chosen ostensibly by these poets to exemplify a feminine ideal of Christian Stoic resolve, serves as more than a classical model for a few literary patrons; she is also used to explore the inadequacies Christian Stoicism's hybrid morality presented to women, as this hybrid was popularly understood to exist in late Elizabethan England.

The treatment of Stoicism in this group of writings centers on "the heroics of constancy," to use Mary Ellen Lamb's expression.[2] "Constancy" itself is a vexed term, not only because it resists stable definition, as any abstraction does, but also because its meaning is fluid in both the classical and early modern understanding of Stoicism. For example, Guillaume Du Vair, in *La Philosophie Morale des Stoïques,* translated into English as *The Moral Philosophy of the Stoicks* in 1598, the same year Brandon's drama was registered by the Stationers' Company, follows Seneca in expressing the belief that "the good & happines of man consisteth in the right use of reason, and what is that but vertue, which is nothing els but a constant disposition of will."[3] Seneca describes this "constant disposition" variously, however, as *ratio immutabilis, moderatus, firmitas,* and *constare,* and he distinguishes his Stoicism from "Certain of our school [who] think that, of all such qualities, a stout endurance is not desirable."[4] Joseph Hall, the "English Seneca," writing shortly after the turn of the seventeenth century, identifies "tranquillity" as one of Stoicism's chief virtues, but in his lengthy Christian interpretation of it, he calls it variously "constancy," "controlement," and "composedness of mind."[5] Montaigne, who takes issue with Stoic precepts throughout his essays, defines constancy in "Of Repenting" as a "languishing and wavering dance" and questions the supremacy of reason itself in "Of Constancy."[6] Cicero's *De Officiis,* the least purely Stoic of his philosophical works but the most popular in the sixteenth century, appearing in nearly twenty translated editions or reprints, is, like Du Vair's work, an amalgam of ethical instruction that promulgates the cardinal virtues, glossed in translation as wisdom, justice, fortitude, and temperance, but variously defined and described by Cicero. "Constancy" may correspond either to fortitude or to temperance, but both qualities are interpreted similarly, as states of a soul that holds external things in contempt [quarum una in rerum externarum despicientia ponitur] and controls all its own perturbations [omnisque sedatio perturbationum animi].[7]

The greatest advocate of Stoic constancy and the greatest popularizer of Stoic thought in the 1590s—in England and on the Continent—was the Dutch scholar Justus Lipsius. In his *De Constantia,* available in England in 1594 in John Stradling's translation, *Two Bookes of Constancie,* Lipsius attempts to make Stoic constancy an active Christian quality. *Two Bookes* is cast as a dialogue between the student Lipsius and the constant and virtuous teacher Langius. Lipsius meets Langius as Lipsius is on his way to Vienna, fleeing the civil wars in his "unfortunate and unhappie Belgica."[8] This provokes, in book 1 of the work, a long lecture from Langius on the fruitlessness of flight, for the civil war that Lipsius seeks to flee is in his mind. Languis advises Lipsius to "seek remedie from Wisdome and Constancie," and he continues to discuss at length those external things that cannot be controlled and therefore should have no power over the mind, including the "publicke evils" of civil war. Departing sharply from the Stoic advice given in Cicero's *De Officiis,* Langius exposes the foolishness of patriotic feeling, which is merely the result of popular opinion and custom, and advises Lipsius to submit to divine reason, which alone can distinguish virtue. "The smoake of OPINIONS," claims Langius, "striveth . . . for the body," while "Reason striveth for the soul." Reason, which leads to constancy, springs from the "the mind of the soule," for "albeit the soul be infected and a little corrupted with the filth of the bodie and contagion of the senses: yet it . . . is not without certaine cleare sparks of the pure fiery nature from whence it proceeded."[9] Guillaume Du Vair too warns against the "false opinions" of the affections, which can be banished only by "Wisdome . . . the beginning and end of all vertues." The soul has many "contrarie" parts within it, and those passions "which do

44 YVONNE BRUCE

waxe most mutinous and troublesome . . . doe first arise in the appetible or concupiscible parte.[10]

The Christian Stoicism of Lipsius and Du Vair clearly debases the soul with the body, which makes apprehending reason (and thus achieving a "constant disposition") through the corrupted channels of sense an oppressive task. This Christian Stoic position is one also taken by the Academic Skeptics and, among the Pembroke dramatists, pursued by Greville in his late verse and by Thomas Kyd in *The Spanish Tragedy* (although the idea is too common to Protestant thinking for a shared belief in it to have special significance, it is worth noting that Philip Sidney expresses the same idea in his *Defence of Poesy*). In *Two Bookes of Constancie,* the wise man is advised, in accordance with classical Stoicism, to strive for a kind of Platonic union with universal nature, but the obstacles to this union are well known: not only the inability of the senses to objectively perceive external reality but also the difficulty or even impossibility of the wise man to achieve a state of being that would make him, according to Seneca, different from the gods only in his mortality.[11] Du Vair's Christian conclusion to *The Moral Philosophie* advocates prayer "in invocation of [God's] divine favour," because "our naturall forces can never bee sufficient of themselves to keep us in . . . perfection."[12] In his introduction to *Heaven Upon Earth,* Joseph Hall envies the heathen Stoics their wisdom in treading the path to tranquillity without the benefit of God's guidance, yet he pities them their "Mistris Nature," who has "never performed without much imperfection."[13] It is Christianity's unique (but Skeptical) contribution to Stoicism to insist upon this distinction between nature and God and upon the corruption of the soul in its physical prison so that God's grace and man's free will in choosing faith might be emphasized.

Another difficulty with defining (and thus achieving) Stoic constancy is that "constancy" is frequently glossed as "patient suffering," but this is a wholly Christian construction of the word (both Tudor writers and contemporary scholars are guilty of this Christianization). Classical Stoic constancy is not a Job-like passivity but an active—and largely impossible—achievement of the will, one that comes from the *sapiens'* recognition of the unity of nature, God, and reason. Each is a different name for the same transcendent virtue it is the wise man's duty to obey and manifest. Thus Epictetus notes of one who is "making progress" toward wisdom that "he has got rid of the will to get, and his will to avoid is directed no longer to what is beyond our power but only to what is in our power and contrary to nature."[14] In Cicero's words, "No one who is totally self-reliant, and contains within himself all that he owns, can fail to be completely happy."[15] Seneca advises that, to live the good life, the mind must achieve "a uniform energy . . . and there will thus be born that unerring reason . . . which, when it has regulated itself and has . . . harmonized all its parts, has attained the highest good . . . The highest

"THAT WHICH MARRETH ALL" 45

good is the harmony of the soul; for the virtues will be bound to exist where there is agreement and unity."[16] Justus Lipsius, however, doubts that true constancy can be achieved by the Christian and advocates moderation of the passions rather than the Stoic elimination of them. "[T]he true mother of Constancie is PATIENCE, and lowlinesse of mind, which is *A voluntarie sufferance without grudging of all things whatsoeuer can happen to, or in a man.*"[17] Lipsian constancy seems to spring from Christian humility, which resembles classical forbearance more closely than it resembles Stoic *apatheia.* Unfortunately, Lipsius's attempt to redefine constancy and to link Stoic paradox to the mysteries of faith had a negative impact on, among others, James I, who derided Lipsian constancy as that "Stoick insensible stupiditie"[18] which could very well lead, via a deadening of the emotional and moral sense, to indolence and inconstancy. Neither was insensibility confined to the Stoics, as Gilles Montsarrat points out: "Sometimes Christian patience even comes perilously close to the oft-denounced 'senselessness' of the Stoics"; Montsarrat cites Gabriel Powell's condemnation of Job, who "seemed as it were, to take pleasure in his afflictions."[19] Powell's skepticism toward the exemplar of Christian patience recalls Montaigne's toward the exemplar of Stoic constancy, Cato the Younger. Ruminating on Cato's suicide, Montaigne "cannot believe that [Cato] merely maintained himself in the attitude that the rules of the Stoic sect ordained for him . . . I believe that he felt pleasure and bliss in so noble an action, and that he enjoyed himself more in it than in any other action of this life."[20] Joseph Hall does not see suffering as salutary either. To achieve "tranquillity," which is a "steadinesse of the mind," one needs resolution, and "how can that vessel which is beaten upon, by contrary waves and winds (and tottereth to either part) be said to keep a steady course?"[21] Hall's use of this image is in contrast to it in Lipsius's *Two Bookes:* "let showres, thunders, lighteninges, and tempestes fall round about thee, thou shalt crie boldlie with a loude voyce, *I lie at rest amid the waves.*"[22]

As the descriptions by Montaigne, Powell, James, and others make vividly clear, "constancy" is subject to a variety of often incompatible interpretations, including, as we have seen, inconstancy. The pose of Stoic indifference had a vogue in Renaissance Europe, for example, particularly on the Continent, much like the vogue for melancholy. The ease with which inconstancy, or at least the indolence and amorality feared by James, could be taken for its opposite led Stoic writers themselves to link Stoic behavior with acting—with all acting's debauched connotations—and gave the Tudor stage material for its caricatured figure of the Stoic in the stocks. This ambivalence toward Stoic constancy was exacerbated if the constant figure in question was a woman. While Stoicism has conventionally been considered a doctrine of the disenfranchised, like early Christianity—one may have power over one's reason or faith even if one has no power over anything else—the reputed indif-

46 YVONNE BRUCE

ference of the Stoic is a function of his self-sovereignty, hardly a desirable trait in a sixteenth-century woman. Although the writings of the Roman Stoics tend simply to discount women,[23] the social role and behavior of women were of concern to Tudor Christians writing in a time of religious crisis in France and the Netherlands and, of course, under the reign of Elizabeth.

In instructional texts written and translated throughout the sixteenth century, Christian humanists and Protestant reformers shared some goals in their plans to educate women: while the former emphasized facility with languages and the study of classical texts and the latter emphasized biblical exegesis, both kinds of educators saw this study as a means to a pious end. Women's piety, however, especially for the Protestant reformers, was dependent on its adherence to standards of conduct laid out by men.[24] Female constancy as the primary *observable* element of faithfulness or obedience toward God was measured by faithfulness or obedience toward men—usually their husbands. Because women's constancy was judged first by men and only second by God, judgment was plagued by the same weaknesses associated with constancy: first, the appearance of constancy might not convey true constancy, thus women—being naturally duplicitous—were under greater pressure than men to conform to conventional standards of Christian Stoic behavior (modesty, silence, equanimity), or to both "be and seem," as Elizabeth Cary's motto had it. Second, judgment depended upon the ability of men to apprehend the difference between true and feigned constancy. These weaknesses led to the paradoxical expectations for women's constancy explored in the Octavia characters created by Daniel, Greville, and Brandon.

Of these writers, Samuel Daniel advocates the most classically Stoic constancy, in his epistle "To the Lady Margaret, Countesse of Cumberland." Daniel knew the countess at first hand, tutoring her daughter the Lady Anne Clifford and dedicating an epistle to her; the countess herself, wife of George Clifford, third Earl of Cumberland, was one of the country-house wives whose misfortunes feature so prominently in verse of the period (the inscription on a Laurence Hilliard portrait of her reads "Constant in the Midst of Inconstancy"). Daniel's epistle, far from advocating a meek submission to the comings and goings of monarchs, tyrants, and other emblems of matrimonial power, praises the individual who "of such a height has built his mind" (line 1) that he looks down upon the "lower Regions of turmoyle" (line 13) with a free eye and a "setled peace" (lines 9, 12); the epistle's narrator assumes that a similar spiritual concord is available to the countess:

> This Concord (Madame) of a wel-tun'd minde
> Hath beene so set by that all-working hand
> Of heaven, that though the world hath done his worst,
> To put it out, by discords most unkinde,
> Yet doth it still in perfect union stand

"THAT WHICH MARRETH ALL" 47

With God and Man, nor ever will be forc't
From that most sweete accord, but still agree
Equall in Fortunes inequalitie.

(lines 116–23)[25]

Daniel attributes to the countess a very classical constancy, using a very classical as well as very Elizabethan figure of speech. She is compared to an instrument "wel-tun'd" by the virtuoso "hand / Of heaven." Wordly discordance cannot mar the tuneful concord achieved between the musician and his instrument. Daniel describes a woman who is worthy of both pity and, in the last two lines, profound admiration: despite her tumultuous existence, her equanimity of mind is so complete that she is equal not only to "Fortunes inequalitie" but, as "Equall *in*" suggests, to "God and Man."

Daniel's is a superb exhortation, but the epistolary poem is not an ideal form for exploring the many sides of such complex counsel. Drama is a more suitable medium, and the importation of Cleopatra from continental to English letters, via Mary Sidney Herbert's translation of Robert Garnier's *Marcus Antoine,* led to a dramatic reevaluation of the subtler ethical forces at work on and within the character of Octavia, too, who had not been dealt with before in English letters and who had been positioned in classical literature as a foil to Cleopatra's own voluptuousness. Octavia better exemplified the qualities of the ideal Tudor Englishwoman—she valued her marriage, she was devout, she was chauvinistic; she was, in short, an ideal character upon which to work out the conflicts facing the Pembroke poets as they addressed issues of patronage, succession, and religious and civil war and, possibly, as they strove to take English letters in a Sidneian direction.[26] As poets writing about and inspired by a woman, answerable to her as patron, and answerable ultimately to the woman running the nation,[27] Daniel, Greville, and Brandon were forced to confront the scant opportunities for credible virtuous behavior available to women who desired to be ethically autonomous (the ideal of Stoic constancy) and spiritually obligated to no one but God (an assumption of Calvinist theology). These poets found the most usable dramatic models in the classical past because England saw itself mirrored in the Rome of the early empire, because Queen Elizabeth faced—or so it was feared—the same incompatible claims of personal love and national duty that Cleopatra faced, and because England was not forced to confront in the present the civil and religious strife tearing apart France and the Netherlands, although these issues did anticipate England's own religious wars, and England was involved and interested in resolving these foreign disputes to its best advantage.[28] Of these poets, however, only Samuel Brandon seems to have been alert to the dramatic possibilities in and cultural echoes sounded by Octavia's complex ethical and political situation. And despite the ready similarities between Cleopatra and Elizabeth as monarchs torn between public and private loyal-

48 YVONNE BRUCE

ties, Octavia offered the politically safer and more virtuous likeness. Ironically, however, all the fictional Octavias use the language of classical Stoicism to lament a specifically Tudor Christian lot.

The tone of Daniel's verse letter from Octavia to Marc Antony (1599) differs significantly from the tone in his letter "To the Lady Margaret," primarily because in the longer former epistle Octavia speaks, bitterly reproaching Antony for his inconstancy and the inconstancy to which she herself is doomed as a woman (stanzas 15 and 16). More interestingly, she also addresses the difficulty of her sex to escape the prison of custom and reputation that is excoriated in Lipsius's *Two Bookes of Constancie:*

> I know not how, but wrongfully I know
> Hath undiscerning custome plac'd our kind
> Under desert, and set us farre below
> The reputation to our sexe assign'd:
> Charging our wrong reputed weaknesse, how
> We are unconstant, fickle, false, unkinde:
> And though our life with thousand proofes shewes no,
> Yet since strength saies it, weaknesse must be so.[29]

According to Octavia, Roman men, from their position of political and domestic strength, create external reality. Far from following the evidence of rational nature—as Stoics must—men ignore the "thousand proofes" of women's constancy. Ultimately, Octavia is indicting the very method by which Stoics apprehend reality: those who believe in women's inconstancy are being misled by false impressions, while those who construct "undiscerning" impressions of women according to custom do so in the name of following nature, which is all Octavia herself is claiming to do:

> We, in this prison of our selves confin'd,
> Must here shut up with our owne passions live,
> Turn'd in upon us, and denied to find
> The vent of outward meanes that might relieve:
> That they alone must take up all our mind,
> And no room left us, but to thinke and grieve:
> Yet oft our narrowed thoughts looke more direct
> Than your loose wisdomes born with wild neglect.

(stanza 18)

Here Octavia admits that passion is inevitable, and in order for women to achieve true constancy, this passion must be vented out so that external "meanes" can come in—a *natural* equilibrium between the outside and inside, a concordance with nature. She suggests that women have been impris-

"THAT WHICH MARRETH ALL" 49

oned by men, but that their solitary confinement, as it were, has resulted in the wisdom that comes of long looking inward; her imagery, that is, suggests there are alternatives to Stoic equilibrium as a way to wisdom.

Octavia perceives that Stoic constancy is inadequate to smooth over the messy frailties of human nature. For her, constancy is primarily an action, not a state of mind—this is a crucial distinction between her Stoicism and the classical Stoic ideal. Thus, Octavia blames Antony's infidelities on the general nature of humankind (and on Cleopatra), which makes doing "The lawfull undelightful" (stanza 41), more than on Antony's peculiar weaknesses. Daniel's careful handling of tone suggests that Octavia is aware of her own weaknesses and the lure of the consoling passions for herself: sanctimoniousness, vengeance, self-pity. In stanza 45, for example, Octavia's vow to forgive Antony cannot quite efface, especially in lines 5 and 6, the extremity of the shame she has suffered:

> Yet all this [i.e., public opinion] shall not preiudice my Lord,
> If yet he will but make returne at last;
> His sight shall raze out of the sad record
> Of my inrowled griefe all that is past:
> And I will not so much as once afford
> Place for a thought to thinke I was disgrac'd:
> And pitty shall bring backe againe with me
> Th'offended harts that have forsaken thee.

Unlike Daniel's Octavia, Fulke Greville's unnamed honorable lady does not speak. In Greville's Senecan epistle to her, she is urged to avoid the antistoical passions of fear and hope and to escape her corporal prison through a reliance on divine grace and the cultivation of obedience. The epistle phrases obedience less as wifely submission to her husband's tyranny than as selfmastery through the avoidance of the "mists of opinion"[30] and the moderation of her desires (again, a Christian softening of the Stoic goal) to achieve a "naturall Harmony" (273). Greville uses Octavia as the exemplar of this self-mastery. According to Greville, Octavia might have done many things to attempt to win Antony back because compared with Cleopatra "she was as yong, equall in beauty, stronger in honour"; unfortunately, Octavia was also "*ever the same,* which (she knew) was not so pleasing to [Antony], as the same in others": "[T]o be short, [she] was content, when she could not doe the workes of a well-beloved Wife, yet to *doe well, as becomes all excellent Women.* In which course of moderation, shee neither made the World her Judge, nor the Market her Theater, but contented her sweet minde with the triumphs of Patience" (285–86, first set of italics mine).

Greville's sympathy for the Octavia character is pervasive and subtle. He knows she is the victim of Antony's arbitrary preference for Cleopatra and so offers her his recognition of Antony's inconstancy rather than the mere solace of constancy, "the triumphs of Patience." But Greville's advice to the honorable lady, while extensive and compassionate, is predicated on the lady's inability to effect change or to sustain herself without divine intervention; it is also predicated on the more troubling issue of her sex. Greville takes great pains to demonstrate that women are naturally more constant than men, but he mourns Eve's lapse in the Garden, which means that woman's constant love for men must now, sadly, be reciprocated with the "unconstant proportions of Power, and Will" (260). In other words, Greville's emphasis on self-mastery seems to gesture toward a fully Stoic constancy for the honorable lady, even as it registers the reality of women's inferior social position (273–74), but his final interpretation of Octavia—and of the state natural to women—is one of Christian obedience. This suggests that for Greville both Stoicism and Christianity, universal reason and divine law, share a foundation in male superiority: "Yet Noble Lady! Because you are a Woman, and a Wife; and by the Lawes of both these estates, [you are] in some measure ordain'd to live under meane, and supreame authority" (273). In Greville's letter, a far more lengthy and rhetorically complex analysis of the relationship of gender to ethics than Daniel's, the unnatural, monstrous, tyrannical abuses of power displayed by the lady's husband are not general perversions of the man's humanity, but specifically of his natural superiority as a man, a superiority underscored by Greville's frequent references to humankind's original fall from grace and illustrated through the frequent analogy of man to monarch.

Scholars who characterize the advice given or illustrated by the epistles of Daniel and Greville as Stoic (or Neostoic) are missing the complexities the Octavia character brings to the attempted reconciliation of Christianity and Stoicism. Greville urges the honorable lady to consider all the things Octavia might have done, given her position, to save her "from the barren grounds of Duty" (285) but did not—avenge herself on Antony or pursue political power by allying herself with her brother, for example. Daniel's Octavia acknowledges the difficulty of matching her violent passions to her submissive actions. Both epistles, however, rely on a type of "great chain of being" argument to examine Octavia's position which does not quite correspond to Seneca's Stoic maxim that the wise man is ethically superior to God and which is unsympathetic to an Epictetian elevation of the lower classes via the development of self-mastery. Daniel's Octavia, for example, observes that Antony's class superiority demands concomitant moral superiority: "What doth divide the Cottage from the Throne, / If vice shall lay both levell with disgrace?" (stanza 14).

Once Samuel Brandon places Octavia at the center of a drama, the tensions and inconsistencies between Christianity and Stoicism—especially as they manifest themselves for women—are given free play. Brandon's Octavia shares her dilemma with Daniel's, with Greville's honorable lady, and with the many country-house mistresses to whom these works and others are addressed or dedicated. But Brandon utilizes genre most effectively to illustrate Octavia's moral plight. Without exception, the classical sources for the Octavia story do not exploit the drama of her position in relation to Antony and Cleopatra, and without exception they do not allow Octavia to speak for herself or to initiate action, even when, as Plutarch, Appian, and Dio Cassius do, historians emphasize Octavia's role in averting war between her husband and brother. Brandon, like Greville, ultimately supports a Christian restraint of the passions for Octavia, and advocates her refusal to avenge herself on Antony in the face of reasonable and politically sound advice to the contrary, but we see that none of these virtuous behaviors leads to her peace of mind, which Stoicism is expressly designed to do. Thus by foregrounding Octavia's plight and allowing her to speak for herself, as Daniel's Octavia also does, and by situating her within a context of civil war, as the classical sources do, Brandon ably exploits the implications of, as Lipsius puts it, the civil war of the mind, by pitching Octavia not only between her husband and brother but between Christian virtue and Stoic constancy.

Brandon's drama, to which is appended an exchange of verse letters between Octavia and Antony written in the tone of Daniel's "Letter from Octavia," covers the period between the battle of Tarentum and the deaths of Cleopatra and Antony.[31] It is in some ways an uninspired drama of its type—in its conventional rhetorical flourishes and pentameter filling and its rather plodding march through the events leading to the deaths of the lovers. Senecan closet drama stands or falls on its handling of ideas, however, and it is in this realm that Brandon's drama has been unjustly neglected. There are considerable unexpected touches that deepen interest in Octavia's plight and lay bare the inadequacies of Christian Stoic platitudes, some of them Brandon's invention, some of them odd inclusions from his sources.

I have already mentioned the suitability of the Octavia character for illustrating an ideal English womanhood, an ideal that represents contemporary Christianity and translates a classical model of constancy into New Roman terms. Typically Cleopatra has borne the responsibility of serving as this ideal and its negative, as a warning to fair women (including Queen Elizabeth) and as an example of a woman who has been redeemed by love.[32] Scholarly attention has thus naturally focused itself on the Cleopatra figure because of her political importance to early modern England and because of her inherent fascination. No such fascination attaches to Octavia, although Shakespeare, in his treatment of her in *Antony and Cleopatra,* will draw attention to her marginal status in a quietly enigmatic way that emphasizes her contrast to Cleopatra.

Brandon's drama opens with a monologue by Octavia that begins as a Chaucerian celebration of earth's springtime youth, then segues ironically

52 YVONNE BRUCE

into an observation of the illusory nature of human authority: "we, whom reason named . . . Princes of all the rest that nature framed: / Still subject are to sorrowes tyranny; / Slaves to mischance, vassals of fortunes power."[33] Octavia's initial description of the natural world, before her bitter introduction of human misery, is of a "golden time" (1), which suggests a paradise neither exclusively pagan nor Christian. More importantly, Octavia's reference—and the diction of her lament—suggests a political golden time that is undercut by the brazen personal drama of which she is a part. Like the Lipsius character in *Two Bookes of Constancie,* Octavia seeks to flee a civil war within her mind, but unlike that character, Octavia is the catalyst for peace in the actual civil war between her husband and brother; in other words, Octavia (like Cleopatra) bears a responsibility for family and country that the Lipsius character does not. Brandon highlights Octavia's dilemma with inventive literalness in act 1, when Titius arrives to report that Octavia has halted fighting at Tarentum by appearing on the battlefield "*Minerva*-like" (255) between the two armies: "No womans weapon blindes her princely eye; / No womans weakenesse, hir tongues passage stayes: / Like one, that did both death, and fate defie" (252–54). Because we see Octavia in her private character and in her public character (via the reporting of action, the typical means of communicating events in Senecan drama), we can appreciate the very deep divide between Octavia's outward constancy and her inward turmoil—a divide the works of Greville and Daniel, with their limited perspectives, cannot fully articulate.

Brandon provides the drama's richest irony, however, by linking Octavia with the inspired character Sylvia, "a licentious woman." Sylvia appears in the second half of act 2 (shortly before Octavia's oscillating response to her brother's desire for vengeance on Antony) in conversation with the "Romaine ladies" Iulia and Camilla. As the two latter discuss Antony's behavior, Sylvia attacks the very notion of virtue with an attack on constancy: "Were I Octavia I would entertaine / His double dealing, with as fine a sleight . . . One nayle you see another will expel, / When nothing else can force the same to moove" (755–56). To Camilla's remonstrance that she ought to fear the wrath of heaven, Sylvia replies:

> The wrath of heaven, why no, the heavens are iust,
> And Iustice yeeldes a man his due desert:
> Then sithe I do no iniurie, I trust
> Not I, but he, for both our faults shall smart.
> . . . .
> But tis most strange to see you go about,
> To praise the thing that workes all womens fall.
> Why constancie is that which marreth all
> A weake conceipt which cannot wrongs resist,

"THAT WHICH MARRETH ALL" 53

> A chaine it is which bindes our selues in thrall,
> And gives men scope to use us as they list.
> For when they know that you will constant bide,
> Small is their care, how often they do slide.

(783–91)

Her rhetoric is, ironically, similar to Octavia's at the end of act 4, when Octavia admits that Antony will not change and thus trusts her soul to virtue's superior justice. Clearly, the Stoic maxim that virtue is its own reward does not prompt Sylvia's moral perspective; Sylvia, in fact, crafts a positive ethical system out of the very difficulties that confront Daniel's and Brandon's Octavias—achieving constancy among men who undermine its definition by divorcing it from virtue, as Brandon's Antony does, with taunting disdain, in his letter to Octavia:

> Heere will I shew, I neither am
> Unconstant, nor unkinde:
> For Cleopatra whiles I live,
> Shall me most constant finde.
> Why am I call'd an Emperour,
> If I should subject be:
> And be compeld to leave the thing,
> Which most delighteth me?

(721–28)

What makes Sylvia so inspired a character is not her stock licentiousness but the way she casts into doubt the assured morality expressed by the play's principals. Sylvia is the most Stoic of them all, refusing to be subject to her passions. In this she resembles Anthony (at least as Anthony imagines himself to be), and in her response to Iulia's remonstrance, Brandon uses Sylvia's similarity to Antony to point up the shaky construction of the gender-class-virtue equation:

> Affection, no, I know not such a thought,
> That were a way to make my selfe a slave:
> I hate subiection and will nere be brought,
> What now I give, at others hands to crave.

(865–68)

As Marta Straznicky has pointed out, not only does Sylvia claim the sexual freedom of a man, but she also dares to compare her lot with that of a man of aristocratic birth.[34] Her lengthy musings eventually prompt the spellbound Roman ladies to deride her as unnatural, but Brandon's treatment shifts "unnatural" from Sylvia's licentiousness to the moral and passional emptiness she and Antony share. Over the course of the play, Sylvia becomes increas-

54   YVONNE BRUCE

ingly important to an understanding of Brandon's interpretation of constancy.
Sylvia believes inconstancy to be humankind's usual state of existence and,
in fact, a natural law. Octavia herself briefly disdains constant behavior and
vows revenge upon Antony. As she says resignedly to her brother Octavius:

> I know not what you thinke of woman kinde,
> That they are faithlesse and unconstant ever:
> For me, I thinke all women strive to finde
> The perfect good, and therein to persever.

(1298–1301)

Striving to find this good, Octavia has at times echoed Sylvia in her belief
that inconstant behavior is ordained by nature (line 1699, e.g.), and by the
end of act 4 even one of the Roman ladies will echo Sylvia's explanation
for Antony's continued rejection of Octavia. It is not Antony's fault, decides
Iulia,

> for nature is the cause.
> By nature are we moov'd, nay forst to love:
> And being forst, can we resist the same?
> The powerful hand of heaven we wretches proove:
> Who strike the stroke, and poore we, beare the blame.

(1960–64)

Not until Shakespeare will the emotional complexity attending this historical
period be better shown, nor will there be such a fully realized Octavia. Unlike
Shakespeare's art, however, Brandon's is unequal to his thought, but as Mary
Ellen Lamb puts it, the play presents, "as perhaps a better play would not
dare, the pathology from which the heroics of constancy drew its strength."[35]
   Recall that the passions (or affections, as Lipsius calls them) so dangerous
to Christian reason spring, according to Stoic philosophy, from incorrect
judgments, that is, opinions rather than the things themselves. The true Stoic
ideal does not recognize inner turmoil as natural: "Because passion *is* error
it must be suppressed, and this can be done by rectifying the erroneous judgement, the opinion, which gives birth to it."[36] This certainly describes Sylvia,
whose judgments, we learn, are completely dispassionate: "But I take order
not to perish so," she says, in "endlesse misery"; "He shall care little, that
cares lesse then I" (776–78). Octavia's passions, on the other hand—her patriotism, her devotion to her brother, her love for Antony, her desire to fulfill
her social and political obligations—are inextricably linked to her virtue,
which escapes a pure association with either Christianity or Stoicism. In fact,
every character in Brandon's drama demonstrates more constancy than Octavia, so that it becomes impossible, by the play's end, to link constancy with
virtue. Octavia's two last lines of the play pay lip service to a Christianized

"THAT WHICH MARRETH ALL" 55

patience that will enable her to bear what the heavens have assigned to her on the unhappy world's stage, but the remainder of her closing speech, spoken in response to news of Antony and Cleopatra's deaths, belies this patience with a Job-like lamentation: "But from the very instant of my birth, / Uncessant woes my tyred heart have wasted . . . Successive cares with utter ruine threate me; / Griefe is enchain'd with griefe, and woe with woe" (2266–67, 2275–76). The deaths of Antony and Cleopatra seem to lead her close to emotional despair, and her final lamentation is answered only by the Chorus, which can at most promise that her *reputation* for virtue—that "smoake of opinion"— will live on immortally: this is Brandon's ironic reminder that the gulf between human passion and the ideals of divine reason remains unbridgeable.

Notes

1. *The Influence of Robert Garnier on Elizabethan Drama* (New Haven: Yale University Press, 1924), 112.

2. In *Gender and Authorship in the Sidney Circle* (Madison: University of Wisconsin Press, 1990), 163.

3. Guillaume du Vair, *The Moral Philosophie of the Stoicks,* Englished by Thomas James, ed. Rudolf Kirk (New Brunswick, NJ: Rutgers University Press, 1951), 55.

4. This "constant disposition" is defined in Epistle 66 in *Ad Lucilium Epistulae Morales.* See also Epistle 67, trans. Richard M. Gummere, Loeb Classical Library, 3 vols. (Cambridge: Harvard University Press, 1943), 2:39. In his *Moralia,* however, Seneca distinguishes between the man who, from having become inured to injury by suffering repeated blows, learns to endure it, and the Stoic man, whose very manner discourages others from injuring him and renders their attempts to do so fruitless. See "De Constantia" in *Moral Essays,* trans. John W. Basore, Loeb Classical Library, 3 vols. (Cambridge: Harvard University Press, 1958, rpt.), 1:55.

5. In *Heaven Upon Earth* and *Characters of Vertues and Vices,* ed. Rudolf Kirk (New Brunswick, NJ: Rutgers University Press, 1948), 85–58.

6. "On Repenting," in *The Essayes of Montaigne: John Florio's Translation* (New York: The Modern Library), 725. But note also Montaigne's linking of constancy to obstinacy in "A Defence of Seneca and Plutarke."

7. *De Officiis,* trans. Walter Miller, Loeb Classical Library (Cambridge: Harvard University Press, 1938), 68, 96 (trans. mine).

8. Justus Lipsius, *Two Bookes of Constancie,* Englished by John Stradling, ed. Rudolf Kirk (New Brunswick, NJ: Rutgers University Press), 72.

9. Lipsius, *Two Bookes,* 76, 84–86, 73, 80, 81, 61, 63, 65.

10. du Vair, *Moral Philosophie,* 61, 63, 65.

11. See Epistle 73 in *Ad Lucilium Epistulae Morales,* 2:111. See also "De Providentia" in *Moral Essays,* 1:7 and 1:45, where Seneca compares the wise man favorably with God, because while the former must gain strength by overcoming

56 YVONNE BRUCE

weaknesses and adversities, the latter is "exempt from enduring evil" [ille exta patientiam malorum est, vos supra patientiam].

12. du Vair, *Moral Philosophie,* 129, 128

13. Hall, *Heaven upon Earth,* 85–86.

14. Epictetus, *The Discourses and Manual, Together with Fragments of His Other Writing,* trans. P. E. Matheson, 2 vols. (Oxford: Clarendon, 1916), 2:235 (section 48 of the *Manual*). It is worth noting in this context of Epictetian progress that, according to Jason L. Saunders in his study of Justus Lipsius, nowhere in Lipsius's writing does Lipsius address the notion of the Stoic "who is in a *state of progress* toward wisdom." *Justus Lipsius: The Philosophy of Renaissance Stoicism* (New York: Liberal Arts, 1955), 85, n. 6.

15. "Nemo potest non beatissimus esse qui est totus aptus ex sese quique in se uno sua ponit omnia," in "Paradoxa Stoicorum," section 17, In *De Oratore,* vol. 2, trans. H. Rackham. Loeb Classical Library (Cambridge: Harvard University Press, 1948; rpt.), 266, 267.

16. "Hoc modo una efficietur, vis ac potestas concors sibi et ratio illa certa nascetur non dissidens nec haesitans in opinionibus comprensionibusque nec in persuasione, quae cum se disposiut et partibus suis concensit et, ut ita dicam, concinuit, summum bonum tetigit." "De Vita Beata," in *Moral Essays,* 3 vols., trans. John W. Basore. Loeb Classical Library (Cambridge: Harvard University Press, 1958, rpt.), 2:118–21.

17. Lipsius, *Two Bookes of Constancie,* 79 (1.4)

18. *The Basilicon Doran of King James VI,* Scottish Text Society, ed. James Craigie, 2 vols. (Edinburgh: William Blackwood, 1944–1950), 1:156.

19. Gilles Montsarrat, *Light from the Porch: Stoicism and English Renaissance Literature* (Paris: Didier-Érudition, 1984), 93. Powell quotation same page, from *The Resolved Christian, Exhorting to Resolution* (1600), p. 86. Compare Powell's belief that torture is endurable with Montaigne's in "A Defence of Seneca and Plutarke," 646–52.

20. In "Of Crueltie," in *The Essayes of Montaigne,* 374.

21. Hall, *Heaven Upon Earth,* section 24 (p. 129).

22. Lipsius, 1.6. In Shakespeare's *Antony and Cleopatra,* Octavia herself is described by Antony with identical imagery. After the marriage between Antony and Octavia, as the latter speaks with her brother, Antony remarks in an aside on his new wife's (in)ability to mediate between the two men:

> Her Tongue will not obey her Heart, nor can
> Her heart inform her Tongue: the Swan's Down Feather
> That stands upon the Swell at the full of Tide
> And neither way inclines.

Shakespeare's comparison of Octavia to a feather afloat illustrates in one rhetorical figure the dilemma that emerges from Hall's and Lipsius's imagery in combination: a woman who floats movelessly as "swan's down" upon the surface of the sea, inclining neither way, is identical to one trapped by the equally rough currents besetting her from contrary directions (William Shakespeare, *Antony and Cleopatra* [London: Everyman, 1989], 3.2.47–50). The difference between activity and passivity—and how these states are defined—points to one of the primary differences between Stoicism and Christianity. Gilles Montsarrat discusses this difference and its influence on Lipsius's *De Constantia,* 52–57.

23. See the introduction to *The Paradise of Woman: Writings by Englishwomen of the Renaissance,* 2nd ed., ed. Betty Travitsky (New York: Columbia University Press, 1989), 5–12.

24. See Seneca's "De Constantia": "there is as great a difference between the Stoics and the other schools of philosophy as there is between males and females, since while each set contributes equally to human society, the one class is born to obey, the other to command." In *Moral Essays,* 1:49. See also "Paradoxa Stoicorum," in which Cicero cannot "think a man free who is under the command of a woman, who receives laws from her, and such rules and orders and prohibitions as she thinks fit. . . . For my part I hold that such a fellow deserves to be called not only a slave but a very vile slave." In *De Oratore,* trans. H. Rackham. Loeb Classical Library, vol. 2 (Cambridge: Harvard University Press, 1948, rpt.), 287.

25. Samuel Daniel, *Poems and A Defence of Ryme,* ed. Arthur Colby Sprague (Cambridge: Harvard University Press, 1930), 111–15.

26. My circumspection in this sentence has to do with the great difficulty of defining an entity called "The Pembroke Circle." I use the phrase throughout my essay partly by scholarly convention because of course there is no conclusive evidence that the poets associated with Mary Sidney ever considered themselves a coterie. The makeup of this poetic circle, and indeed the legitimacy of the assumption that certain poets had enough in common—socially, literarily, or ethically—even to be considered members of a group are contentious issues. The extremes of interpretation are represented by two scholars already cited in this essay. A. M. Witherspoon, in *The Influence of Robert Garnier on Elizabethan Drama,* argues that the poets Mary Sidney, Thomas Kyd, Samuel Daniel, Samuel Brandon, Fulke Greville, William Alexander, and Elizabeth Cary are all linked by the influence of Robert Garnier on their prosody. Witherspoon is not interested in the historically verifiable relations between Sidney and poets who may or may not have enjoyed or sued for her patronage; rather, Witherspoon (clearly a critic of an earlier generation) sees a thematic, dramatic, and prosodic similarity between the poetry of the "circle" and Garnier's adaptations of Senecan drama for moral and political purposes. Mary Ellen Lamb, on the other hand, in "The Myth of the Countess of Pembroke: The Dramatic Circle," has a very different argument: "There was no dramatic circle surrounding the Countess of Pembroke, and the idea of reforming the English stage probably never entered her head" (196). Lamb limits Witherspoon's "circle" to those poets whose work "shows the Countess's certain influence . . . Abraham Fraunce, Samuel Daniel, and perhaps Samuel Brandon." See Witherspoon citation, note 1, and Lamb, "The Myth of the Countess of Pembroke: The Dramatic Circle," *Yearbook of English Studies* 11 (1981): 194–202, esp. 197, 200.

27. As demonstrated, for example, by Greville's destruction of his *Antony and Cleopatra* and by Daniel's defense of his *Philotas.* See *The Tragedy of "Philotas" by Samuel Daniel,* ed. Laurence Michel (New Haven: Archon, 1970), chap. 2, esp. 36–46.

28. See Montsarrat, *Light from the Porch,* 1–2.

58 YVONNE BRUCE

29. *The Complete Works in Verse and Prose of Samuel Daniel,* ed. A. B. Grosart, vol. 1 (of 4) (Printed for private circulation, 1885), stanza 15. Further references to this work will appear parenthetically by stanza.

30. *Certain Learned and Elegant Workes* (1633) (Delmar, NY: Scholars' Facsimiles and Reprints, 1990), 269. Further references to this work will appear parenthetically by page number.

31. As Mary Ellen Lamb has noted in "The Myth of the Countess of Pembroke," Ruth Hughey argues that, although Brandon's drama was published in 1598 and Daniel's "Letter from Octavia" in 1599, Brandon was influenced by Daniel's letter, which he saw in manuscript form. Interestingly, however, the earlier version of Daniel's letter, which appears in *The Arundel Harington Manuscript* that Hughey edits, lacks the strong pagan flavor of his final version; the earlier manuscript does not include three stanzas (bemoaning the unequal lot of virtue bestowed by men on women) that distinguish the 1599 version (including stanza 18, quoted on p. 48 of this essay). It remains possible that Daniel's revision was influenced by Brandon's treatment of Octavia.

32. J. Max Patrick, in "The Cleopatra Theme in World Literature up to 1700," discusses Cleopatra's transformation from Augustan-era "threat to 'civilization'" (65) to a comical or baroque figure in late seventeenth-century treatments. Patrick also mentions treatments of Cleopatra that reflect a theme common to the sixteenth century, "heroic death cancels earlier mistakes" (68), a theme Mary Ellen Lamb explores in some detail in *Gender and Authorship in the Sidney Circle* (chapter 3, "The Countess of Pembroke and the Art of Dying"). Patrick, in *The Undoing of Babel: Watson Kirkconnell, the Man and His Work,* ed. J. R. C. Perkin (Toronto: McClelland and Stewart, 1975), 64–76. See also Mary Morrison, "Some Aspects of the Treatment of the Theme of Antony and Cleopatra in Tragedies of the Sixteenth Century," *Journal of European Studies* 4 (1974): 113–25.

33. *The Virtuous Octavia* (1598) (Oxford: Malone Society Reprints, 1909), lines 20–24. Further references to this work will appear parenthetically by line number.

34. "In the choral commentary following this scene [the scene in which Sylvia is chastised by Camilla], Sylvia's monstrous desire is transferred not to Octavia's darker self, as one might expect, but to Antony, who is the only other character in the play to be tagged 'licentious,'" Straznicky, Short title, 121. Both Sylvia and Daniel's Octavia—in their penetrating rhetorical questions and haughty disdain for the double standard—anticipate Salome in Elizabeth Cary's closet drama *Mariam.* Here Salome contemplates the unequal Jewish divorce laws:

> If he [Constabarus] to me did beare as Earnest hate,
> As I to him, for him there were an ease,
> A separating bill might free his fate:
> From such a yoke that did so much displease.
> Why should such privilege to man be given?
> Or given to them, why bard from women then?
> Are men then we in greater grace in heaven?
> Or cannot women hate as well as men?
> Ile be the custome-breaker: an beginne
> To show my Sexe the way to freedomes doore.

Mariam, Fair Queen of Jewry, ed. A. C. Dunstan and W. W. Greg. Malone Society Reprints (Oxford: Oxford University Press, 1914), sig. B3r. Incidentally, even a brief

"THAT WHICH MARRETH ALL" 59

comparison of Salome's speech with the examples of Octavia's speech in Daniel's "Letter" quoted throughout this essay illustrates the rhetorical similarities that justify A. M. Witherspoon's inclusion of both authors in the Pembroke Circle (in *The Influence of Robert Garnier on Elizabethan Drama*).

35. Mary Ellen Lamb, *Gender and Authorship,* 138.
36. Montsarrat, *Light from the Porch,* 16.

"A Fine and Private Place":
Chapman's Theatrical *Widow*

Elizabeth Hodgson

I.

MARVELL underestimates the amorous imagination when he says that "the grave's a fine and private place, / But none . . . do there embrace." In *Bartholomew Fair* Quarlous argues almost the opposite, that suitors must "visit [a widow] as thou wouldst doe a *Tombe,* with a Torch . . . flaming hot."[1] Sex in the cemetery, it seems, is not an impossibility but a positive convention.[2] The eroticized widow, that epitome of the sexual attractiveness of grief and a standby in early modern drama, is rendered still more dramatic when she is encountered in the graveyard itself. Here both setting and role make her a walking social embodiment of the very idea of secret desire. Her veiled disguise, her carefully managed enactment of sorrow, her curiously masked and anomalously public social role, and especially her public sexual secrecy all make her a figure whose private interiority is urgently in question. In Jacobean tragicomedies, this disguised self-dramatization means that the widow in a tomb raises in her most complicated characterizations the same questions about embodied performance that playwrights asked of drama itself. Chapman's play *The Widow's Tears* (ca. 1605) offers fascinating insights into these concerns, as in it Chapman questions the sexual privacy of the tomb and the widow who symbolizes it by creating an extended graveyard-performance within the play itself, one which invents the most extravagantly sexualized widow's grief imaginable while theatricalizing and burying its meaning from the scrutiny of the inquisitorial characters and from the audience.[3] More explicitly and yet more ambiguously than Shakespeare does in *Hamlet,* Chapman's whole play-structure questions whether anything can really be known about a widow's love and grief through its analogy to dramatic performance itself. With a theatrical test more personally enacted than Hamlet's professional players', Chapman's characters stage-manage a test of a widow's loyalty in the charnel-house. In Chapman's hands the "play-memorial" of Shakespeare's revenge-tragedy becomes instead a much more realistically enacted "theatrical fiction," paradoxically much less transparent

60

than *Hamlet*'s staged "images of the occluded truth" (Neill 259). Chapman's play has been particularly elusive of judgment precisely because *The Widow's Tears*' reinvention of a popular widow-narrative so closely interweaves the inscrutability assigned to womanly grief and the inscrutability of a theatrical performance. Reenacting the "Widow of Ephesus" legend which forms his central source and citing the idiom of performance so visible in conduct-books for widows, Chapman engages in but also challenges cultural efforts to locate a widow's meaning by pressing the relationship between her affect and performativity *tout court*.[4]

Francis Barker, Katharine Eisaman Maus, and others have argued for the complex interrelationships between theatricality and different ideologies of inwardness and privacy in the period, and this particular play by Chapman pursues similar questions in relation to the particularly troubling subject of a widowed woman's sexual value and meaning.[5] The double meanings of those theatrical categories which suggest both revelation and concealment ("perform," "act," "show") are invoked in relation to feminine knowability, a question which the play asks on both linguistic and structural levels through the figure of the widow. Chapman is after a more profound question than Hamlet's of how to understand or how to judge widows.[6] Not just a simple satire, either, of womanly constancy or of "the ideal of widowhood,"[7] Chapman's play, through its explicit dramatizations of cemetery-seductions, questions the very meaning of such a "discovery." The impossibility and inadvisability of seeing through the widow's tears, or *The Widow's Tears,* on all of these levels, would seem to be Chapman's point.[8] The misogynist assertion of woman's doubleness[9] and the ideological privileging of inwardness collide with particular force in the presence of the widow's tears, especially as Chapman stages such a direct intersection of theatrical and widowly performativity.[10]

II.

"The Widow of Ephesus," the scandalous classical story behind Chapman's play, is the perfect paradigm of this fixation with a widow's performance of grief. Chapman was hardly the first to rewrite this source-narrative; Petronius's and Phaedrus's versions of the Ephesian-widow tale were enormously popular in late medieval and early modern European literature.[11] Petronius' classical version of the story (the Latin text of which is Chapman's central source) is perhaps the most understated and ambiguous, though, the one most conducive to the challenge of interpretation which Chapman's play offers.

Petronius's Latin tale describes an intensely performative world, in which acting, enactment, show, and disguise are all crucial elements. The story is this: an Ephesian widow famous for her devotion to her husband follows him not just to the cemetery but into his tomb, vowing publicly to remain there and weep herself to death. Meanwhile, a soldier is sent to the same graveyard to guard the criminals' bodies on their crucifixes (lest their families try to remove the bodies for decent burial). The soldier discovers the now-solitary weeping widow and offers her comfort: first food and drink, and then love. She resists, but only at first, and they engage in a sexual adventure in the privacy of the sepulchre. Meanwhile, the families of the criminals have noticed the soldier's absence, and they steal one of the bodies down from its crucifix. The soldier faces death as the penalty for his neglect, but the widow (unwilling to lose her lover so soon) offers to put her husband's body on the cross in the criminal's place, a switch in casting which causes no small confusion among the Ephesians.

In Petronius's version this story is greeted with laughter, but one auditor viciously condemns the widow.[12] The widely circulated medieval versions of the story pick up on this hostility, embellishing the tale by intensifying both the first husband's uxoriousness and the widow's macabre and callous independence of him.[13] In these versions, the widow is stage manager both of her grief and of her previous husband's new role as understudy to a criminal: she helps to carry her husband's corpse to the cross, and in several she maims his body to match the missing criminal's (knocking out his teeth, ripping out his hair, breaking his arm), all of which the soldier himself refuses to do. The *Seven Sages* collection is framed as a series of accounts of faithless women, and these versions tend to embellish the widow's perfidy. (In several, her husband has died of grief because he accidentally nicked her thumb or her arm.)[14]

The story in its various versions is intended to highlight (and often critique) the widow's remarkable conversion from public mourner to private lover, emphasized by the rapidity of her switch in allegiance and her desire to conceal that switch in roles, by her apparent lack of concern for the uncongenial surroundings for her romantic tryst, and by her willingness to make her husband a Girardian scapegoat, subjecting his body (and thus clearly his honor, reputation, and social after-life) to both misrepresentation and public humiliation in order to secure her new lover's safety. The story also demonstrates the widow's masculinized authority and transgendered social role, as she becomes, in this liminal space, an agent and actor, the initiator of quite politically charged actions in pursuit of her own desires as mourner and lover.

Both the question of masculine value inherent in widowly constancy and the uncovered woman's potential for social disruption are connected in the bodies in this Ephesian tomb, as the widow's choices change the meaning of her first husband and her first marriage. The story attempts, but fails, to explain how and whether womanly affection (and thus masculine value) can be knowable and testable and therefore also how the liminal independence of a "femme decouvert" can be managed. In a tale which offers a kind of revelation of how untrustworthy women's affections are, her devotion to her new lover seems simultaneously obvious and inexplicable, as the many different responses it elicits confirms. As in Chapman's *The Widow's Tears,* the story of feminine inconstancy does not function as such an absolute ethical or essentialist sign as it might seem at first to do. Each version of the story seeks to discover how to read the widow's actions: as humoral transformation, minor human folly, natural desire, unnatural betrayal, womanish weakness, social disruption, social continuity, or calculated self-interest. Jeremy Taylor simultaneously excuses the widow's lust as a natural humoural process and critiques it as an example of social lawlessness; John Taylor enjoys the male fantasy that widows are *all* looking for a man "provided like a Souldier, never not with standing, but in a centinell posture, . . . cocked bolt upright, and ready to do execution."[15] John Taylor's phallic pointing toward the Ephesian widow with her soldier, and Jeremy Taylor's acceptance of her transformation and fear of her unruliness, suggests the multiplied interpretive potential of this narrative.

Juan Luis Vives's famous and influential 1538 manual on female conduct makes this same argument about the theater of widows, fixating on this problem of the readability of the widow's bodily signs and actions, though in widows with perhaps less-flamboyant predilections than the Ephesian widow's. The chapters on widows in his extremely influential *The Instruction of a Christen Woman* display considerable anxiety over the social management of an "uncovered" woman, precisely because her private self seems to be, like the Ephesian widow, symbolically significant but fundamentally unreadable.

For Vives, a widow's displays of grief indicate and define a husband's memorial afterlife. Vives seems to claim that this test is reliable; he argues for instance that such a reading of a dead man through his widow is fruitful, as her ungoverned status gives her no reason to dissemble: "than shall it be knowen, what nature or condition a woman is of, whan she may do what she wyll. . . . often tymes wydowes do shewe, what they have bene in mariage, and under the lybertie of wyddowheed, open and shewe that whiche they kepte in before for feare of theyr husbandes."[16] A widow's active mourning, her tears, are an even more emphatic sign for Vives. He declares confidently that an unmoved widow provides an "evident sygne of but colde love. . . . Hit is the greattest token that can be of an harde harte and an unchast mynde, a woman nat to wepe for the dethe of her husbande."[17]

This is the paradox with which Vives negotiates. In every case he sees the widow as a particularly transparent sign (because she is "under the lybertie of wyddowheed") of her own and her husband's merit. But this signification is profoundly performative rather than ontological. "Then shall it be knowen," he says; then shall they "open and shewe"; this shall be a "token."

And Vives duly notes how easily this performance is false theater: "for they seme to lyve in the syght of those that se them eate and drynke, and go, and speke, and do other workes of lyfe. But and one coulde perse with his syght in to them, or entre with in the secretes of their myndes and thoughtes, he shulde se that poure synfull soule, how it is put from god, and spoyled and deprived of his lyfe."[18] So the transparency which he declares is the mark of an "uncovered woman" and the crucial social signifier which is her unforced weeping are both also inherently unreadable, unprovable, and unknowable.

Vives's widow must perform miracles, then, to construct a reputation while simultaneously remaining private. She must be seen to be tearful, but she must also do her weeping in privacy, without display ("a chaste woman desyreth secretnes," he says).[19] Her public privacy is what matters most. Her physical display of grief must be known but not seen, a coterie performance which is disseminated by others who tell of it and through which both her own reputation and her husband's are safeguarded. "A woman had nede to worke more warely, when bothe the disprayse of vices and the prayse of vertue is imputed to her selfe" alone.[20] Her "wariness" or secret self-management is directly in relation to her widow's vulnerability to the public gaze. Vives describes how easily she can acquire "an yll name,"[21] clearly as great a hazard as ill deeds, especially as evidenced in his list of widowly virtues: "chast, honest, of good fame, and vertuous."[22] He conjures up the fragility of a widow's reputation in a second marriage as a particular disincentive: "if thy stepson be sicke, or his heed ake, thou shalte be diffamed for a witche . . . if thou gyve [him meate] thou shalt be called a poysoner."[23] This threat of demonization has everything to do with what she will be "called." As Maus argues in another context, "in such cases the difference between fact and reputation is obscure, so that fact can seem nothing more than a particularly convincing form of reputation."[24]

Vives attempts to resolve his two concerns, over her tears' performative meaning and over a widow's anomalous status, by the fantasy of perfect surveillance which Shakespeare conjures up in *Hamlet* and which Chapman will literally fulfill in his play: "let her take [her dead husband] for her keper and spy, nat only of her dedes, but also of her conscience. Let her handell so her house and householde, and so bryng up her children, that her husbande maybe glad."[25] Vives's solution to both the representational problem of a widow's tears and the problem of an independent woman is to revivify the husband to both test her loyalty and perpetuate her servanthood.[26] The punitive nature of this fantasy is clear: "let her nat behave her selfe so, that his soule have cause to be angry with her, and take vengeaunce on her ungratiousnes."[27]

This striking anxiety about widows, with their anomalous gendered status and their problematic role as unbondable guarantor of a vulnerable male patrilineage, is as pervasive in Vives's text as they are in the Ephesian-widow tale and in many others of the period. Vives's concerns are added to and explained by the Ephesian-widow tale, as that ancient story both crucially illustrates and provokes the anxieties over the testable performance of feminine grief to which Vives's text bears such witness and which Chapman's play will reanimate. What makes Chapman's play so fascinating is its persistent analogy between theatrical performativity and widows' performatively private grief. By associating the two cultural questions so closely, Chapman makes both the stage and the widow images of one another's private show.

III.

Chapman's *The Widow's Tears* provides a local habitation and a name to this performative question of a widow's private truth. It dramatically reenacts the optic in Chapman's 1595 *Ovid's Banquet of Sense* which shows, at a distance, a woman's face weeping, the image of which disappears at close range.[28] In its intensely theatrical structures, its dramaturgical re-creation of Quarlous's fantasy of the widow's tomb, *The Widow's Tears* proves that what a widow embodies is distinctly unlocatable, an assertion which involves a dismantling of her trustworthiness but also a dismantling of that same trust in revelation, in "show." Chapman both appropriates and challenges the misogynistic truism of woman's evasive privacy by replicating his widows' unknowability in the drama's persistently enigmatic situations and conclusions. Like the widows of the plot, the play challenges the very idea of evidence by being, very self-consciously, all theatrical "show" and no "tell."

The Widow's Tears (ca. 1605) is in several respects a cultural archive of suspected grief. With its extensive borrowing from Petronius's version of the legend of the widow of Ephesus, as well as its echoes of Homer's Penelope and Ulysses, Shakespeare's *Twelfth Night* and *Hamlet* (and possibly *Othello*),[29] its fascination with suspicion and constancy also looks toward the tragicomedies of Beaumont and Fletcher. This referentiality makes it all the more interesting as a staging of embodied female secrets. Weidner argues that Chapman often uses "complexly conceived masks and 'shews' . . . to oppose the naive action of shallow absolutists";[30] *The Widow's Tears* is just such a theatrical demonstration, though it interrogates the very possibility of scrutiny itself as well. While critics like Albert Tricomi argue that the play is all about the discovery of corruption, the "revelation that religious and ethical values exist everywhere only in illusion and hypocrisy,"[31] such cynical pleasures are also seen in the text as themselves illusory and untrustworthy. Jackson Cope suggests that Chapman's neoplatonism makes this a play in which "not action, but interpretation, is all."[32] And as Lee Bliss compellingly claims, the play's structure undermines its own satirical and cynical first half, leaving both trust and suspicion as hazardous territory.[33] But neither one of these explanations addresses how (or why) Chapman uses widows to embody his skeptical theatricality, or how he uses theatrical performativity to challenge masculinist skeptics, in the double optic which is *The Widow's Tears*.

The story of the *Widow's Tears* is an explicit retelling of the Ephesian-widow narrative, with several variations and a secondary plot added. In the secondary plot, Tharsalio, an impoverished gentleman-rogue, wins the hand of Eudora, a widowed countess, by assuming correctly that her desires are far stronger than her grief, her vows of chastity, or her pride. In the subsequent, "Ephesian," plot, Tharsalio's wealthy older brother Lysander stages and scripts his own "death" to test his wife's vow of eternal faithfulness. Like the widow of Ephesus, his wife/widow Cynthia proves vulnerable to seduction despite her vows. In Chapman's version, though, Lysander himself woos his "widow" in the disguise of the soldier who has killed her beloved husband; like Vives's fantasy of the husbandly ghost, Lysander tests and judges his own widow's loyalty. Tharsalio, the trickster brother, and Lysander, the jealous husband, resist the idea of the widow's independence and distrust the widow's quintessentially feminine affect of grief, and both find themselves in the same dilemma to which Vives and the Ephesian-widow tale attest. "The very unreadability that seems so attractive in one's (male) self seems sinister in others; one man's privacy is another woman's unreliability. The female interior encloses experiences unappropriable by an observer."[34] Chapman's play amplifies this theme by extending this incapacity to know to his readers and audience as well. Chapman establishes in both of his plots (the first farcical, the second tragicomical) that a woman's sorrow cannot be read, suggesting however that this is not evidence of women's perfidious impermeability but rather a symbiotic reading of the links between performance and evidence. The staging of Lysander's play, in his family-sepulchre, renders this paradox of secrecy all the more apparent.

Characters in the play consistently use explicitly theatrical metaphors of performance to suggest that widows' inconstancy can be truly seen. Tharsalio insists upon the trope of deceitful performance to describe a widow's sorrow: "[I] judge of objects as they truly are, not as they seem, and through their mask . . . discern the true face of things. [I know how] short-lived widows' tears are, that their weeping is in truth but laughing under a mask, that they mourn in their gowns, and laugh in their sleeves."[35] Tharsalio claims that a widow has both a "mask" and a "true face," like an actor, and that it is possible for some (men) to know both. Tharsalio also offers a theatrical analogy for his assertions about female grief: "These griefs that sound so loud prove always light, / True sorrow evermore keeps out of sight. / This strain of mourning . . . like an overdoing actor, affects grossly, and is indeed so far forced from the life, that it bewrays itself to be altogether artificial."[36] The very traceability of her sorrow makes it unreliable, as if "true" acting is the kind which only *hides* its artificiality. Like Vives, he also argues that the outward sign proves the absence of the inward grace, as if true acting were not acting at all.

Characters *really* acting, playing a part, are treated in the same way as women in mourning: "didst act the Nuntius well?" Tharsalio asks Lycus, the messenger sent to tell of Lysander's supposed death, but he comments on Cynthia's responses as well: "Then was her cue to whimper."[37] "Forget not to describe her passion at thy discovery of his slaughter. Did she perform it well?" The "discovery" here is multiple: Lycus performs sorrow, Lysander performs death, and Cynthia, Tharsalio is convinced, performs the grief of a dis-covered woman. He calls her grief a "sleeping mummery," doubly deceptive.[38]

Along similar lines, *The Widow's Tears* also questions the possibility of reading women, their words or their actions, as if they are published texts with the imprimatur which can "force belief."[39] The impossibility of access to a kind of divine assurance, the readability of the grieving widow, is a substratum of the play's discursive play-language. This correlation is clear in an early description of Eudora's trustworthiness: " 'Twere a sin to suspect her. I have been witness to . . . many of her fearful protestations to our late lord against that course; to her infinite oaths imprinted on his lips, and sealed in his heart with such imprecations to her bed if ever it should receive a second impression."[40] The witness to her imprinted, sealed vows promises ironically that she is the book with no "second impression," as if she can only be published once and never revised, and that her husband is the book upon which her text is "imprinted." But even this description allows for several kinds of ambiguity. Are her "fearful" protestations "in fear" or "frightfully strong"? The oaths are imprinted on "his" lips and "sealed in his heart"; does that mean they die with him? Tharsalio suggests as much: "well, for her vows, they are gone to heaven with her husband, they bind not upon earth."[41] She will curse "her bed" if it ever receive "a second impression"; does this deflect blame in a metonymic gesture? Women are, says Tharsalio, but "weak paper walls thrust down with a finger";[42] his sexually charged image suggests that widows' bodies are a particularly permeable page, just as their "widow-vows" are[43]—just as "weak" as the play-text's paper walls.

The interesting twist in this suspicion of "show," play-text or womanly, is that it appears not to be the final resting-place of the drama (Chapman's or Lysander's). Lee Bliss argues that the play shifts genres from the cynicism of farce to the critique of suspicion which governs the tragicomedy in the second half; belief in a widow's grief, he argues, becomes in the later part of the play a kind of necessary corollary for social stability.[44] This is part of the dynamic of the play, but Chapman also sows the seeds of doubt over these characters' own cynical confidence throughout the drama.

Even Tharsalio, as the spokesman for such modes of theatrical and spiritual skepticism, finds it difficult to define a reliable source for his convictions.

68 ELIZABETH HODGSON

Tharsalio insists on the performativity of a widow's grief, but he can only apply general principles ("monopolies are cried down";[45] "he that believes in error, never errs";[46] "true sorrow evermore keeps out of sight"[47]), and examples and analogies (Niobe, Dido, Penelope[48]) to the widows whose performance he claims to understand, for by his own declaration they are natural performers and expert deceivers. The very performativity he attributes to them undoes his triumph. His general skepticism is no more specifically insightful than Leonato's general idealism. Tharsalio can never know that a woman *is* true or loving; he can only prove (or rather, she can prove by actions) that she is *not* true or loving. He must still read her, and he can only read her negatively, never positively. In Tharsalio's view, women are mirrors of the men who "own" them, and so there is nothing predictably existing behind the image of themselves which men perceive, however much he himself claims to see beneath the mask. His own actions are "scenes" for which he desires "spectators";[49] he cannot and does not ask what this means for his reading of others' performances.

It is certainly possible to argue that Tharsalio's vulnerable arguments about widowly performance are irrelevant, since both widows in the play prove his point through their willingness to take new lovers. In spite of this evidence, though, *The Widow's Tears* consistently disguises from the audience the meaning of feminine sexual acting. Both women are allowed a certain degree of privacy surrounding their desires. The Countess Eudora's lust for Tharsalio is never directly voiced by her; unlike *Twelfth Night,* Chapman's play does not display her transformation or permit her to declare either her previous vows or her present desires in any interpretable fashion. We hear it all "reportingly"; the marriage is only revealed in theatrical terms, when Tharsalio appears onstage in the new costume of a wealthy husband and when the couple is introduced through a hymeneal masque-performance.

Cynthia's Ephesian-widow actions are more transparent, as this "widow" makes her vows of undying loyalty explicitly and publicly. Cynthia fears for Lysander's safety, engages in anticipatory mourning when Lysander departs, and in her own words resists consolation when it is preferred by her maid at the tomb. She too, however, expresses her first flood of grief only reportingly; an actor acting grief describes her act of grief. She also declares herself a virtuous thing which "in itself, perhaps, is spotless."[50] The qualifying term "perhaps" says it all. Ero notes that Cynthia's sexual capitulation to her soldier-lover is wordless: "she is silent, she consents,"[51] and Cynthia is equally silent about her own feelings throughout the final act as well. The play refuses to stabilize the meaning of a woman's tears or desires, even when her actions would seem to make such meaning incontrovertible or obvious. Cynthia performs her capitulation in such a way that her true motives or self-justifications are not available, either to her husband or to the reader. She admits to nothing. The play's final line, "think you have the only constant wife," implies

"A FINE AND PRIVATE PLACE": CHAPMAN'S THEATRICAL *WIDOW*   69

precisely the impossibility of knowing which Chapman seems to be suggesting and, perhaps, defending. Preussner argues that "the tomb and its empty casket have emerged as fully realized symbolic correlatives to the hollow, apparently irretrievable relationship of Lysander and Cynthia themselves,"[52] but these are far more convincing symbols of the absence of certainty in Cynthia and in the performativity of the play as a whole.

Lysander, Cynthia's husband, is Chapman's central illustration of the connection between grief and performance. Through his elaborate staging of his own death, he comes, like Tharsalio, to trust in disguise more than he trusts in "truth." As he dresses up as the soldier, Lysander becomes almost enamored of the very idea of theatricality: "Come, my borrowed disguise, let me once more / Be reconciled to thee, my trustiest friend . . . / Assist me to behold this act of lust; / Note . . . a scene of strange impiety."[53] He sees his own mask as now a person rather than a persona, an important sign of his move beyond even a Tharsalio-like theatrical cynicism. The capacity to stage-manage the meaning of "act" and "disguise" and "scene" is beyond him, however. When Lysander seduces Cynthia, is the "act of lust" here a "deed," or a "performance"? Even as he has arranged it, it must be both and neither. Lysander imagines that he can control and interpret the performance he has begun, but he cannot, as he finally acknowledges: "put women to the test; discover them; paint them, paint them ten parts more then they doe themselves, rather then looke on them as they are."[54] His confused rant can see now no difference between testing women, "discovering" them, and disguising them in greasepaint.

Lysander's incapacity to understand the impossibility of certainty is understood both in terms of this ironic belief in theatrical masking and in terms of the disinterring in which he is so bizarrely engaged. He meets his wife at the family tomb, in the cemetery, and there engages, like Actaeon,[55] in a necessarily "destructive search for certainty."[56] The disemboweling this provokes is virtually his own: "it was a strange curiosity in that Emperor that ripped his mother's womb to see the place he lay in."[57] Lysander's opening of the tomb in "mother earth" to "see the place he lay in" is just such an act of self-dismemberment. Cynthia accuses her husband of destroying himself by wanting to "assure himself of what he knew";[58] the sexual implications of his "knowing" here are explicit. Lysander "claims to be uncovering brute material facts, but discoverer and discovered, prestigious examiner and denuded examinee, always seem perilously close to switching places."[59] Lysander-the-cuckold thus becomes a "chimaera,"[60] or more tellingly still a cross-gendered "transformed monster."[61] His rapacious scrutiny makes him "[lose] the shape of a man,"[62] like the Ephesian soldier in Petronius's story; his suspicion is a "strange conception,"[63] a "whelp . . . [licked] into full shape"[64] like a beast to which he has given birth. In both of these images it is Lysander's gender-role, not Cynthia's, which is under scrutiny—his

70   ELIZABETH HODGSON

"transformed . . . shape" is "monstrous," to be dissected and displayed like
the strange conceptions of the widow's desire in Petronius's legend. He,
rather than Cynthia, feels "much fear of . . . discovery,"[65] then, as the far
greater deceiver. In fact, he becomes both the performative widow and the
corpse he has scripted, the one who will "lie and grieve"[66] in the family
tomb.

The cemetery itself is the locale for the last two acts of the play as a whole,
and its iconic role as the keeper of secrets is prominent in Chapman's text.
The tomb is the ultimate private place, even more private than a bedroom;
Ero compares the lovers in the sepulchre to "Dido and Aeneas . . . in the
cave."[67] Tharsalio and Lysander both go further and make the standard
womb-tomb comparison, only with an ironic double face: "Sister? you hear
me well, paint not your Tomb without; we know too well what rotten carcases
are lodg'd within."[68] The grotesque metaphor Tharsalio uses continues
throughout the mock *quem quaeritis* drama of the last act, confusing Cynthia's sexual privacy with Lysander's missing corpse by making both mysteries the object of ribald speculation. The characters who know about
Lysander's staged death declare his corpse "a mere blandation; a *deceptio
visus*. Unless this soldier for hunger have eat up Lysander's body. Why, I
could have told you this before, Captain; the body was borne away peece-
meal by devout Ladies of Venus' order. . . . and yet I heard since 'twas seen
whole at th'other side the downs . . . betwixt two huntsmen, to feed their dogs
withal."[69] These fantasies of mutual dismemberment and consumption both
reveal and hide the secrets of the drama.[70] The threatened opening of the cof-
fin to discover who murdered Lysander, and the threatened revelations of
Cynthia's adultery, also become conflated in the search for Lysander's own
true status (alive or dead, husband or soldier?). Lysander hunts out "obscure
nooks for these employments,"[71] both sexual and vengeful, but he himself is
then chased into "a blind corner of the Tomb" when he hides from the soldiers who hunt him.[72] Like the tomb itself, Lysander's and Cynthia's behaviors lead the captain to declare: "mischief in this act hath a deep bottom; and
requires more time to sound it."[73] Truth, guilt, virtue, material objects and
facts, reputations, and identities, are all hidden in this mysteriously open secrecy of the tomb. When the Governor declares at the end of the play that he
will "cut off all perished members" and "cast out these rotten stinking carcases for infecting the whole City,"[74] it is no longer clear whether the play
admits of any difference between the living and the dead, burying or disinterring, killing or anatomizing. The Governor declares these edicts while he is
standing in the cemetery, as if "th'Antipodes"[75] cannot be distinguished from
the public center of the city.

When the Governor at the end of the play dismisses "fending and proving,"[76] then, he unconsciously rebukes Lysander for his self-destructive efforts to "discover" truth; when the Governor says he "[knows] no persons,"[77]

"A FINE AND PRIVATE PLACE": CHAPMAN'S THEATRICAL *WIDOW*

he proclaims both his own ignorance and the truth Lysander has been compelled to admit. As Cope notes, the play "closes under the auspices of the blind."[78] The play and the widow are both thus, of necessity, inscrutable, as the play's ambiguous ending suggests. Parrott suggests that Chapman has "simply burked" the play's ending,[79] but that sidestepping is, I would argue, deeply symbolic. Whatever or whomever the characters embrace, the widow's privacy, her bodily absences, and her inscrutability, are both complete and impermeable. Chapman has proven that the fine and private place, both play and widow, is absolutely not knowable, either to the characters or to the audience.

Widows, and their attitudes and feelings, are thus in Chapman's world as liminally unknowable as the purgatorial dead had been in pre-Reformation England. That this metaphor of inscrutability should apply particularly to sexual matters is hardly surprising, nor is its adhesion to women's sexual bodies unexpected; in this period "sexual experience becomes a *topos* of unknowable inwardness."[80] But more critical still is Chapman's elision of theatrical show and the performative display of female tears. The slide between love and lust in the Ephesian-widow tale, with its various explanations and interpretations, is mirrored by the confusion of fact and reputation, privacy and public identity, in Vives's conduct-book, and both are reenacted in the curiously hidden motives, reasoning, and ethical value of the widow's bodies and desires in Chapman's play—and of the play itself. In both cases, their actions may lie open to all, but their secret meaning is still assured. "The surfaces of the body are always capable of being theatricalized, so that while they can be made to seem absolutely trustworthy, they are never actually so";[81] this says as much about theatricality as about the female body, external or internal. The whore Ecclesia in Donne's sonnet who is "most trew, and pleasing to thee, then / When she'is embrac'd and open to most men,"[82] is revived by the Governor: "it shall be the only note of love to the husband to love the wife":[83] the double transference of love and faithfulness in both *sententiae* captures the paradox of knowledge as it attached to women's affective sorrow, to the death which engendered it in Chapman's culture, and to the "noting" and "showing" of performance itself. Chapman's widows, both Eudora and Cynthia, are symbolic of the banal but also ultimate secrets, here of sex and death, which his drama can only mirror. As Marvell imagines a performance of death, as Lysander tries to enact it, both discover nothing but a private place. Whether they mean Hamlet's "nothing" or Ophelia's by it, Chapman's text will not reveal.

Notes

1. Ben Jonson, *Bartholomew Fair,* ed. E. A. Horsman, Revels Plays (London: Methuen, 1965), 1.3.73–75.

72   ELIZABETH HODGSON

2. *Romeo and Juliet* provide an early dramatic version; there are several in the prose-romances of the period.

3. George Chapman, *The Widow's Tears,* edited by Akihiro Yamada (Manchester: Manchester University Press, 1975). All subsequent citations are from this edition.

4. Juan Luis Vives, *The Instruction of a Christen Woman,* ed. Virginia Walcott Beauchamp et al. (Chicago: University of Illinois Press, 2002). All subsequent citations to Vives are from this edition.

5. Barker, *Tremulous Private Body,* 22–26; Katharine Eisaman Maus, *Inwardness and Theater in the English Renaissance* (Chicago: University of Chicago Press, 1995), 1–35, 128–81.

6. Renu Juneja, "Widowhood and Sexuality in Chapman's The Widow's Tears," *Philological Quarterly* 67 (1988): 157–75, reads the play thus.

7. Albert H. Tricomi, "The Social Disorder of Chapman's *The Widow's Tears,*" *Journal of English and German Philology* 72, no. 3 (1973): 354.

8. Cope, *Theatre and the Dream,* 30. Cope sees Chapman's interest as stemming from the idea of "mystery" within neoplatonism (Ficino's neoplatonism in particular).

9. Maus, *Inwardness and Theater,* 191.

10. This homology depends upon the metaphors of privacy and concealment surrounding the female body. "As the great sixteenth-century French physician Ambroise Paré says, 'that which man hath apparent without, that women have hid within.'. . . . both men and women have 'secret parts,' but women's are genuine secrets:" Maus, *Inwardness and Theater,* 190. "The woman's body, in other words, incarnates in risky but compelling ways some of the particular privileges and paradoxes of Renaissance subjectivity . . . her interior 'difference,' her lack of visibility, can enable a resistance to scrutiny, since possibly her inner truth is not susceptible to discovery or manipulation from the outside" (ibid., 191–92). As Michael Neill puts it, "the scandalous interrelation of these apparently conflicting ideas of the private—that which is at once so valuable . . . that it must be shut away and protected; and that which is so shameful, that it must be buried from view—is reflected in the culture's contradictory attitudes towards bodily secrets, especially those of the female body." Michael Neill, *Issues of Death: Mortality and Identity in English Renaissance Tragedy* (Oxford: Clarendon, 1997), 178.

11. Editions of Petronius's *Satyricon,* in which the Widow of Ephesus story appears, were scarce in England until the last decade of the sixteenth century: Johanna H. Stuckey, "Petronius the 'Ancient': His Reputation and Influence in Seventeenth Century England," *Rivista di Studi Classici* 20 (1972): 146. Prior to the performance of *The Widow's Tears* ca. 1605, three successive editions of the *Petronii Satyricon* were published in Leyden (1594, 1596, 1604), and one of these editions was reprinted four times in Paris in 1901: Stephen Gaselee, "The Bibliography of Petronius," *Transactions of the Bibliographic Society (of London)* 10 (1909): 148, 214. Three editions of Phaedrus's fables also appeared in western Europe in the same time period: Leon Hermann, *Phedre et Ses Fables* (Leiden: E. J. Brill, 1950), 160.

The classical fable was also reworked in a wide array of French and Italian romances and novellas in the fifteenth and sixteenth centuries and included in the popular *Seven Sages* collections in Latin, French, and English, among other languages, which date back to 1493 and appear in ballad-form, in editions annotated by Erasmus, and in James I's schoolbooks. Hans R. Runte, J. Keith Wikley, Anthony J. Farrell, eds., *The Seven Sages of Rome and the Book of Sinbad: An Analytical Bibliography,* Garland Reference Library of the Humanities (New York: Garland, 1984), 38ff.; Stuckey, "Petronius the 'Ancient,'" 149. Vernacular versions of the Ephesian-widow story date back to Caxton, forward to lost play-texts by Dekker in 1600, and on through the seventeenth century, with the first English translation of the *Satyricon* appearing in 1694: Hans R. Runte, "Translatio Viduae: The Matron of Ephesus in Four Languages," *RLA: Romance Languages Annual* 9 (1997): 114; Runte, Wikley, Farrell, *Seven Sages;* Gaselee, "Bibliography of Petronius," 180–81.

12. "[H]e shook his head angrily and said: 'If the governor of the province had been a just man, he should have put the dead husband back in the tomb, and hung the woman on the cross.'" Petronius, *Satyricon,* trans. Michael Heseltine (Cambridge: Harvard University Press, 1961), 235.

13. A succinct comparison of these embellishments in the several Old French recensions of the *Seven Sages* appears in Hans R. Runte, "The Matron of Ephesus: The Growth of the Story in the Roman Des Sept Sages de Rome," in *Studies on the Seven Sages of Rome and Other Essays in Medieval Literature,* ed. H. Niedzielski, H. R. Runte, and W. L. Hendrickson (Honolulu: Educational Research Associates, 1978), 109–18.

14. In the following medieval and Renaissance English editions of the *Seven Sages* the husband dies in this way, and the widow maims his corpse in all but Caxton's edition. In all of these editions, the wife helps to carry her husband's corpse to the cross. R. T. Lenaghan, ed., *Caxton's Aesop* (Cambridge: Harvard University Press, 1967); Karl Brunner, ed., *The Seven Sages of Rome (Southern Version),* Early English Text Society (London: Oxford University Press, 1933); *Here Beginneth Thystory of the Seuen Wyse Maysters of Rome Conteynyng Right Faire and Ryght Ioyous Narracions, and to the Reder Ryght Delectable* (London: William Copland, ca. 1555); John Rolland, ed., *The Seuin Seages Translatit Out of Prois in Scottis Meter by Iohne Rolland in Dalkeith, with Ane Moralitie Efter Euerie Doctouris Tale, and Siclike Efter the Emprice Tale, Togidder with Ane Louing and Laude to Euerie Doctour Efter Hos Awm Tale & Ane Exclamation and Outcrying Upon the Empreouris Wife Efter Hir Fals Contrusit Tale* (Edinburgh, 1578); *The Hystory of the Seuen Wise Maisters of Rome, Now Newlye Corrected with a Pleasaunt Stile, and Purged from All Old and Rude Words and Phrases, Which Were Very Loathsome and Tedious to the Reader* (London: Thomas Purfoote, 1602).

15. Quoted in Jennifer Panek, "'My Naked Weapon': Male Anxiety and the Violent Courtship of the Jacobean Stage Widow," *Comparative Drama* 34, no. 3 (2000): 323–24.

16. Vives, *The Instruction of a Christen Woman,* 170.

17. Ibid., 161.

18. Ibid., 169.

19. Ibid., 174.

20. Ibid., 170.

21. Ibid., 172.

22. Ibid., 174.

74 ELIZABETH HODGSON

23. Ibid., 177.

24. Maus, *Inwardness and Theater,* 140.

25. Vives, *The Instruction of a Christen Woman,* 168.

26. Barbara J. Todd aptly names this argument of Vives's "patriarchal spiritualism." See her helpful discussion of Vives's struggle to deal with his own contradictory advice: "The Virtuous Widow in Protestant England," *Widowhood in Medieval and Early Modern Europe,* ed. Sandra Cavallo and Lyndan Warner (Harlow: Longman, 1999), 66–84: 69.

27. Ibid., 168.

28. Jonathan Hudston, ed., *Plays and Poems,* by George Chapman (New York: Penguin Books, 1998), xvi.

29. Henry M. Weidner, "Homer and the Fallen World: Focus of Satire in George Chapman's The Widow's Tears," *Journal of English and Germanic Philology* 62 (1963): 521.

30. Weidner, "Homer and the Fallen World," 531.

31. Tricomi, "Social Disorder," 356.

32. Cope, *Theatre and the Dream,* 63.

33. Lee Bliss, "The Boys from Ephesus: Farce, Freedom, and Limit in The Widow's Tears," *Renaissance Drama* 10 (1979): 161–83.

34. Maus, *Inwardness and Theater,* 192–93.

35. Chapman, *Widow's Tears,* 1.1.138–43.

36. Ibid., 4.1.103–8.

37. Ibid., 4.1.50,63.

38. Ibid., 5.3. 140.

39. Ibid., 3.1.198.

40. Ibid., 2.4.21–25.

41. Ibid., 2.4.36–37.

42. Ibid., 3.1.98.

43. Ibid., 3.1.92.

44. Bliss, "Boys from Ephesus," 179.

45. Ibid., 1.1.123–24.

46. Ibid., 5.1.80.

47. Ibid., 4.1.104.

48. Ibid., 1.1.151.

49. Cf. Cope, *Theatre and the Dream,* 59.

50. Chapman, *Widow's Tears,* 1.138–39.

51. Ibid., 4.3.70–71.

52. Preussner, "Anti-Festive Comedy," 264.

53. Chapman, *Widow's Tears,* 5.4.1–2, 9–10.

54. Ibid., 5.3.207.

55. Preussner, "Anti-Festive Comedy," 369ff.

56. Cope, *Theatre and the Dream,* 56.

57. Chapman, *Widow's Tears,* 3.1.3–4.

58. Ibid., 5.5.82.

59. Maus, *Inwardness and Theater,* 140.

60. Cope, *Theatre and the Dream,* 69.

"A FINE AND PRIVATE PLACE": CHAPMAN'S THEATRICAL *WIDOW*   75

61. Chapman, *Widow's Tears,* 5.5.81.

62. Ibid., 5.3.140.

63. Ibid., 2.3.170.

64. Ibid., 2.3.68.

65. Ibid., 5.5.20.

66. Ibid., 5.5.90.

67. Ibid., 5.1.77.

68. Ibid., 5.3.138.

69. Ibid., 5.5.144–48.

70. Note Wendy Wall's fascinating discussion of this notion of theatrical dismemberment in *Staging Domesticity: Household Work and English Identity in Early Modern Drama* (Cambridge: Cambridge University Press, 2002), p. 191ff.

71. Ibid., 5.5.24.

72. Ibid., 5.5.139.

73. Ibid., 5.5.150.

74. Ibid., 5.5.217–19.

75. Ibid., 5.2.10.

76. Ibid., 5.5.193.

77. Ibid., 5.5.209.

78. Cope, *Theatre and the Dream,* 73.

79. Thomas Marc Parrott, ed., *The Plays and Poems of George Chapman: The Comedies* (London: Routledge, 1910).

80. Maus, *Inwardness and Theater,* 131, n.1.

81. Ibid., 130.

82. John Donne, "Show Me Deare Christ," in *The Divine Poems,* ed. Helen Gardner (Oxford: Clarendon, 1982), lines 13–14.

83. Chapman, *Widow's Tears,* 5.5.250–51.

Bibliography

Barker, Francis. *The Tremulous Private Body: Essays on Subjection.* London: Methuen, 1984.

Bliss, Lee. "The Boys from Ephesus: Farce, Freedom, and Limit in The Widow's Tears." *Renaissance Drama* 10 (1979): 161–83.

Brunner, Karl, ed. *The Seven Sages of Rome (Southern Version).* Early English Text Society. London: Oxford University Press, 1933.

Chapman, George. *The Widow's Tears.* Edited by Akihiro Yamada. Manchester: Manchester University Press, 1975.

Cope, Jackson I. *The Theatre and the Dream: From Metaphor to Form in Renaissance Drama.* Baltimore: Johns Hopkins University Press, 1973.

Donne, John. "Show Me Deare Christ." In *The Divine Poems,* edited by Helen Gardner, 15. Oxford: Clarendon, 1982.

Gaselee, Stephen. "The Bibliography of Petronius." *Transactions of the Bibliographic Society (of London)* 10 (1909): 141–233.

Here Beginneth Thystory of the Seuen Wyse Maysters of Rome Conteynyng Right

76 ELIZABETH HODGSON

Faire and Ryght Ioyous Narracions, and to the Reder Ryght Delectable. London: William Copland, ca. 1555.

Hermann, Leon. *Phedre et Ses Fables.* Leiden: E. J. Brill, 1950.

Hudston, Jonathan, ed. *Plays and Poems* by George Chapman. New York: Penguin Books, 1998.

The Hystory of the Seuen Wise Maisters of Rome, Now Newlye Corrected with a Pleasaunt Stile, and Purged from All Old and Rude Words and Phrases, Which Were Very Loathsome and Tedious to the Reader. London: Thomas Purfoote, 1602.

Jonson, Ben. *Bartholomew Fair.* Edited by E. A. Horsman. Revels Plays. London: Methuen, 1965.

Juneja, Renu. "Widowhood and Sexuality in Chapman's The Widow's Tears." *Philological Quarterly* 67 (1988): 157–75.

Lenaghan, R. T., ed. *Caxton's Aesop.* Cambridge: Harvard University Press, 1967.

Maus, Katharine Eisaman. *Inwardness and Theater in the English Renaissance.* Chicago: University of Chicago Press, 1995.

Neill, Michael. *Issues of Death: Mortality and Identity in English Renaissance Tragedy.* Oxford: Clarendon, 1997.

Panek, Jennifer. "'My Naked Weapon': Male Anxiety and the Violent Courtship of the Jacobean Stage Widow." *Comparative Drama* 34, no. 3 (2000): 321–44.

Parrott, Thomas Marc, ed. *The Plays and Poems of George Chapman: The Comedies.* London: Routledge, 1910.

Petronius. *Satyricon.* Translated by Michael Heseltine. Cambridge: Harvard University Press, 1961.

Preussner, Arnold W. "Chapman's Anti-Festive Comedy: Generic Subversion and Classical Allusion in *The Widow's Tears.*" *Iowa State Journal of Research* 59, no. 3 (February 1985): 263–72.

Rolland, John, ed. *The Seuin Seages Translatit Out of Prois in Scottis Meter by Iohne Rolland in Dalkeith, with Ane Moralitie Efter Euerie Doctouris Tale, and Siclike Efter the Emprice Tale, Togidder with Ane Louing and Laude to Euerie Doctour Efter Hos Awm Tale & Ane Exclamation and Outcrying Upon the Empreouris Wife Efter Hir Fals Contrusit Tale.* Edinburgh, 1578.

Runte, Hans R. "The Matron of Ephesus: The Growth of the Story in the Roman Des Sept Sages de Rome." In *Studies on the Seven Sages of Rome and Other Essays in Medieval Literature,* edited by H. Niedzielski, H. R. Runte, and W. L. Hendrickson, 109–18. Honolulu: Educational Research Associates, 1978.

———. "Translatio Viduae: The Matron of Ephesus in Four Languages." *RLA: Romance Languages Annual* 9 (1997): 114–19.

Runte, Hans R., J. Keith Wikley, Anthony J. Farrell, and The Sociey of the Seven Sages (Dept. of French at Dalhousie University), eds. *The Seven Sages of Rome and the Book of Sinbad: An Analytical Bibliography.* Garland Reference Library of the Humanities. New York: Garland, 1984.

Stuckey, Johanna H. "Petronius the 'Ancient': His Reputation and Influence in Seventeenth Century England." *Rivista di Studi Classici* 20 (1972): 145–53.

Tricomi, Albert H. "The Social Disorder of Chapman's *The Widow's Tears.*" *Journal of English and German Philology* 72, no. 3 (1973): 350–59.

Vives, Juan Luis. *The Instruction of a Christen Woman.* Edited by Virginia Walcott Beauchamp et al. Chicago: University of Illinois Press, 2002.

Weidner, Henry M. "Homer and the Fallen World: Focus of Satire in George Chapman's *The Widow's Tears.*" *Journal of English and Germanic Philology* 62 (1963): 518–32.

Articles

Playing in the Provinces: Front or Back Door?

Barbara D. Palmer

BECAUSE it cast the mold for centuries of perceptions about provincial playing, an excerpt from the June 29, 1572, "Acte for the punishement of Vacabondes and for Releif of the Poore & Impotent" is worth repeating, yet again, as a headpiece to this reevaluation of playing in the provinces. The familiar extract reads that

> [a]ll and everye persone and persones beynge whole and mightye in Body and able to labour, havinge not Land or Maister, nor using any lawfull Marchaundize Crafte or Mysterye whereby hee or shee might get his or her Lyvinge, and can gyve no reckninge howe he or shee dothe lawfully get his or her Lyvinge; & all Fencers Bearewardes Comon Players in enterludes & Minstrels, not belonging to any Baron of this Realme or towardes any other honorable Personage of greater Degree; all juglers Pedlars Tynkers and Petye Chapmen; whiche seid Fencers Bearewardes Comon Players in Enterludes Mynstrels Juglers Pedlers Tynkers & Petye Chapmen, shall wander abroad and have not Lycense of two Justices of the Peace at the leaste, whereof one to be of the Quorum, when and in what Shier they shall happen to wander . . . shalbee taken adjudged and deemed Roges Vacaboundes and Sturdy Beggers.[1]

Two other formative edicts contributed to earlier perceptions of provincial playing. On May 10, 1574, Elizabeth issued a patent to Leicester's Men licensing them to play "for and during our pleasure. And the said Commedies, Tragedies, Enterludes, and stage playes, to gether with their musicke, to shewe, publishe, exercise, and occupie to their best commoditie during all the terme aforesaide, aswell within oure Citie of London and liberties of the same, as also within the liberties and fredomes of anye oure Cities, townes, Bouroughes &c whatsoeuer as without the same, thoroughte oure Realme of England."[2] This patent giving Leicester's Men the right to perform anywhere in the country locked in the notion that authority to play emanated exclusively from the Court, which may have been true in law but certainly was honored more in provincial breach than in practice. Further, on February 9, 1597/98, the 1572 Act for punishment of rogues, vagabonds, and sturdy beggars was "utterly repealed," to be replaced by an edict which took away, by omission, the power of justices to license traveling players. Chambers notes that "[t]he right of noblemen to protect their servants was not interfered with" and concludes that it "indeed must now have become even more important, as they acquired a monopoly; but it must be exercised under hand and seal and, although this point is not dealt with in the statute, must presumably be endorsed by the Master of the Revels."[3] Collectively these three, of the many, regulatory edicts on playing concretized later perceptions and characterizations of provincial playing.

In 1910 John Tucker Murray neatly parted the early modern dramatic sea into "London Companies" and "Provincial Companies," a divide which has endured, more or less, for the century since. The note which he appends to his preliminary essay on provincial dramatic companies well serves this present endeavor: "As the examination of the material connected with this subject is still going on with a view to the publication of a history of the dramatic companies, I wish it to be understood that the opinions expressed in this article are more or less tentative."[4] Prescient in many ways, Murray was not unaware of the inadequacies of his data, particularly "the danger of attempting to write the history of the London companies, while ignoring the provincial companies."[5] Chambers's understanding of provincial playing was largely based on Murray, without Murray's "tentative" qualifiers. Chambers concludes that "[t]he most important of the provincial companies which did not come to London also bore the names of noblemen, and although many others were entertained by mere knights and gentlemen, it is probable that, at any rate after 1572, these did not range very widely from their head-quarters," an assertion he buttresses from Murray: "The list of small travelling companies in Murray, ii. 77, 113, includes 14 belonging to knights and 3 to gentlemen in 1558–72, and 8 belonging to knights and 2 to gentlemen in 1573–97; also 7 companies under the names of their towns only in 1558–72 and 11 in 1573–97."[6]

Where Murray saw examples, Chambers saw surveys and polls. Whether by inclination or geography, both men's research was limited to London archives and whatever provincial materials were in print from antiquarians, local historians, and county record societies. Both scholars were exemplary trawlers in London muniments and libraries but somewhat misguided on practical matters of provincial playing. The difficulties of tracking professional players through erratic and ambiguous documentation are enormous, then and now. The "London companies" are bad enough, long familiar as much of their documentation has been; the "provincial companies" are worse, in part because much of their documentation still is coming ashore. Enough documentation exists, however, to argue that the model established by Collier, Fleay, Greg, Murray, Chambers, Bentley, Gurr, and the many others who followed is an inadequate analytical tool. In broad outline, their model pitted Column A against Column B: London versus provincial, A-list versus B-list, proficient versus mediocre, cutting edge versus musty, fixed theaters versus rural waysides, professional players versus ragtag vagabonds, a bipolar model which no longer can be stretched to fit the evidence.

Time has eroded the bipolar model of London playing versus provincial playing, not by invalidating the extraordinary discoveries of those theater history pioneers but by validating both a broader haul of provincial data and also an expansive context of approaches to understanding them. Central to this expansion both of data and approach has been the Records of Early English Drama (REED) project. When the REED project was conceived over a quarter century ago, its initial energies were focused toward urban centers and civic drama, particularly the great Corpus Christi cycles—York, Chester, Newcastle-on-Tyne, Norwich, Coventry. Likewise at that time, social history as a discipline was in its tottering infancy, overshadowed by the monuments of great men, great wars, great dates. Happily, over this past quarter century both REED and sociocultural history have come to complement each other in the broader examination of social and domestic fabrics, of the relationships and activities which constitute daily life. Accompanied by scholarly strides in material culture; feminism; and economic, architectural, and art history, REED editors increasingly have drawn on the interdisciplinary tools needed to craft raw household materials into a fit dwelling.

One of the more significant recent dimensions of the REED project has been the growing revelation of entertainment activity in the houses of those who were born great, those who achieved greatness, and a few who had greatness thrust upon them. As the domestic entertainment data have burgeoned, they have invited new tenets about provincial playing, tenets quite different than those which were inferred from Elizabethan edicts and London performance records. From a northern, provincial body of payment records to players (see appendix A), as I have argued before, four major points can be made.[7] First, these data, which I believe to be representative when sufficient records spanning sufficient time survive, argue that provincial tours were a given mode of economic survival and profit for the professional company, whether based in the provinces or in London. Second, traveling professional players, at least in this part of the country, played towns and great houses with nearly equal frequency (the slight shortfall in house visits can be dismissed as household stewards' occasional "*hoc anno*" lump sums). Third, they actually could plan for playing in these towns and great houses: repeat visits are regular and the turn-away rate at most 10 percent, in only one instance without significant payment "not to play." Fourth, they could count on playing "their exits and their entrances" on a very familiar world's stage: the rectangular great hall, some larger, some smaller but all about twice as long as wide, well-lighted, heated, roofed, often paneled, painted, and decorated with wall hangings.

If these four points shape a new paradigm of provincial playing, then they also shape a redefinition of provincial players' status, which in turn invites a re-evaluation of provincial performance conditions, which is the focus of this present study. More simply put, in the face of these new data we cannot have it both ways. Either provincial players are rogues, vagabonds, and sturdy beggars, semi-articulate fugitives skulking through hedgerows, mumbling fragments of bad quartos, and shooed to the great house back door for alms; or they are guests, often anticipated, sometimes not, who are shown through the front door into the great hall and welcomed by the household steward. And once the majority of provincial players are acknowledged to be "straungers in the hall" rather than rascals in the scullery, that status dictates their treatment by the rules of hospitality and reopens all dimensions of their professional lives to scrutiny, starting with the nature of these "provincial troupes."

This study broadly defines a provincial troupe as any professional company of players playing elsewhere than London, a definition which may seem inclusively useless to many readers but at least covers the extraordinary variations in their documented travels. Even the great London companies seem to raise more questions than answers when they are on the road, questions of multiple troupes and multiple routes rather than the simple formula of being driven from their London playing houses by the plague or Puritans.[8] In the fifteenth and early sixteenth centuries, traveling companies were small, averaging three or four players;[9] from the 1570s well into the seventeenth century their numbers swelled to between six or eight and eleven to fourteen. The average company size represented in the comparative payments table (appendix A), when numbers are recorded in the accounts, is 11.6 players, slightly smaller than a London company but well able to "play twenty to forty speaking roles."[10] Traveling troupes after 1600 were about the same size as in London—14 for the Earl of Derby's company in 1611; 12 for Queen Anne's players in 1612, 15 for "the late Queen's men" in 1619; Lord Mounteagle's company at 11; consistently 16 for Princess Elizabeth's troupe, 14 for her father the King's Men, 14 for Prince Charles's. There also is some evidence that on occasion touring players were augmented by household entertainers, a subject discussed below.

One should add the caveat that the term "players" by no means defines performers' activities as dramatic. Terminology in the records varies from household steward to steward, town clerk to clerk, and unless the account specifically records payments for plays or names a recognized stage player as group leader, one cannot rule out musical performers.[11] As slippery a term as "players" in these records is "men" or "company," where identification can be guided only by such contextual factors as the number of men; similar visits by similar numbers; knowledge of which gentry maintained players, which maintained musicians, and which both; comparative amounts of rewards paid; and the accounts' section in which the rewards are grouped. Sometimes, of course, the records are quite clear: "feats of activity" means rope dancing, tumbling, or other physical spectacles; and Murray cites such

PLAYING IN THE PROVINCE: FRONT OR BACK DOOR? 85

unambiguous payments as those "To Lord Haworth's players and musicians," "To My Lord Dacre's players and musicians," and "to L of Darby's musicians and Earl of Worcester's players."[12] Musicians frequently are listed as "musicians," "the musick," or by their instruments—"fiddlers," "a trumpeter," "the virginals player," which somewhat trims the confusion.

Chambers is but one of the many who have not recognized the pitfalls of terminology as he cites the August 3, 1581, will of Alexander Hoghton of The Lea in Lancashire:

> "Yt ys my wyll that Thomas Houghton of Brynescoules my brother shall have all my instrumentes belonginge to mewsyckes and all maner of playe clothes yf he be mynded to keppe and doe keppe players. And yf he wyll not keppe and maynteyne players then yt ys my wyll that Sir Thomas Heskethe Knyghte shall haue the same instrumentes and playe clothes. And I moste hertelye requyre the said Syr Thomas to be ffrendlye unto Foke Gyllome and William Shakshafte now dwellynge with me and ether to take theym unto his servyce or els to helpe theym to some good master". Was then William Shakshafte a player in 1581?[13]

Lancashire REED editor David George cautions that "[t]he term 'playe Clothes' (p 156, 1.20) notwithstanding, it is impossible to be certain that these 'playeres' (p 156, 1.21) were really actors and not musicians. The fact that there were only two of them is puzzling, because such a small band could not have acted a typical Elizabethan play; if they were actors, we must assume that Hoghton did not single out the other members of the troupe."[14]

As one can see from the preceding document, how provincial troupes were organized and under whose authority they traveled is perhaps the most complex and murky dimension of the many which await far greater attention than has been paid. Chambers wrestles manfully with the numerous perplexities of multiple London companies apparently on multiple tours, finally blaming "[t]he system of patents [which] lent itself to certain abuses by travelling companies," something of an understatement which does not address quite imaginative provincial permutations of licensing regulation.[15] The number of provincial troupes has been grossly undercounted; the various regulatory edicts were not enforced top down; and the simplistic division that provincial troupes either were linked to London companies in ways licit or illicit or else were wandering vagabonds has obscured some richly creative "licensing" practices.[16] Again, terminology creates problems as

> company designations—Revels, Queen's, Queen's Revels, King's, King's Revels, Queen's Children, Children of the Revels, Prince[']s[s] (Prince's or Princess?), etc.—provide much occasion for confusion[,] . . . exacerbated by the fact that some companies carried papers displaying the King's hand or signet or authorization from the Master of the Revels, whether or not they were a "King's" or "Revels"

86 BARBARA D. PALMER

company. In addition there was a tendency for the players to sometimes make a single patent or license provide authorization for more than one company.[17]

One of the more egregious cases of the "exemplification or duplicate of his Ma*iestes* Letters paten*tes*" is the infamous June 4, 1617, warrant from William, Earl of Pembroke and Lord Chamberlain to the sorely tried governors of Norwich. Thomas Swinnerton and Martin Slaughter of the Queen's Men; William Perry of the Queen's Revels; Gilbert Reason of the Prince's Players; and Charles Marshall, Humphrey Jeffes, and William Parr of the Prince Palentine's Players, Pembroke informs the mayor, used break-away licenses to create their own companies, and Pembroke wants the "seuerall exemplifications or duplicates or other ther warrantes" confiscated immediately.[18]

Household stewards and civic clerks often were aware of the duplicity, as their tone and diction reflect, but suspect documentation seems not to have impeded the players' welcome. In some instances, livery or the proper badge confirmed authority.[19] In others either the players had papers or the steward recognized them. The Cliffords' Londesborough steward faced a most extraordinary week, July 18–25, 1618, when on July 18, twelve "Children of the Revels" received 30s, dinner, supper, and breakfast for one play; on July 23–24, 1618 fourteen of the Prince's players, "men and boys," were fed supper, dinner, and supper in their two-day stay (for which the playing reward is missing); and on July 24–25, 1618, fourteen players "pretending to be Lady Elizabeth's" received £4, dinner, supper, and breakfast for four plays during their two-day stay. No less astute by 1624, the Londesborough steward pays "a Companie of Players goeing by the name of the kinges Players" £3 for "three times." Clifford's Skipton stewards were no fools either. On January 4, 1633/34 the Skipton steward paid "Certeyne men which came to Act a play & did" 13s.4d; two weeks later he paid "Certeyne players Itinerantes" 20s. On February 10, 1635/36, a "certeyne company of Roguish players" received £1 to play "A new way to pay old Debtes."[20] The slightly arch diction but consistency of payment suggests licensing to be more of a London than a provincial fixation.

Another dimension of provincial playing which has been grossly neglected, underestimated, and misunderstood is the professional entrepreneur who seized opportunities, exploited advantages, dodged disasters, invested wisely, and generally profited from a shrewd sense of the market. "London" entrepreneurial examples abound—Henslowe, the Burbages, Alleyn, Shakespeare—although earlier gentlemen-scholars sometimes were reluctant to acknowledge that their artistic success may have owed something to the taint of filthy lucre.[21] What also has not been acknowledged—or perhaps not even recognized—is that "provincial" professional entrepreneurial examples abound as well, men who constructed long and presumably satisfactory careers playing from town to town, great household to great household, and,

PLAYING IN THE PROVINCE: FRONT OR BACK DOOR?

on occasion, from company to company, patron to patron. Their careers can evidence all variants of company size and organization. If household stewards' or civic clerks' formulae are to be credited, a matter over which one has little choice, these provincial entrepreneurs played alone; played as senior sharers or actor-managers of companies with noble or gentry patrons; played as heads of their own companies; joined their company to another company for a joint performance; and played star turns with other professional troupes. Some of these men, I think, were models of what we now term "upward mobility," skilled professionals who knew when to hold 'em and knew when to fold 'em, knew when to walk away, knew when to run. If, however, theater historians continue to restrict the "norm" for professional achievement to a senior sharer's long-term residency in a fixed London theater, interrupted only by such Acts of God as plague, Puritans, coach-parking regulations, or incendiary thatch, small wonder that provincial entrepreneurs have flown under the radar. They have not been acknowledged because, in the myopic context of "London companies," no one suspected their existence, let alone the value of tracking them or how to evaluate what they were doing. For illustrative purposes here, I have selected but two of these provincial entrepreneurs for resurrection—Richard Bradshaw and "Disley the player"—though many more of their fellows invite future study.[22] First, however, a summary of why Bradshaw and Disley went dead or missing might be instructive to future resurrectionists.

Content to dismiss provincial players as "unlicensed vagrants" wandering the provinces cheek by jowl with "the protected servants of noblemen," Chambers does not even index these men under their own names.[23] "Richard Bradshaw" is subsumed under "Actors" and referenced only under "Dudley, Edward, 4th Lord": "Edward, Lord Dudley's (provincial), 1595. He was Gabriel Spencer's 'man' in 1598, and concerned in financial transactions with Henslowe during 1598–1601. He may be the same Richard Bradshaw who had a provincial company, with a licence to which his title was dubious, in 1630–33 (H[enslowe's *Diary*]. ii. 245; Murray, ii.42, 106, 163)."[24] Chambers's only other citation indexed to Edward, Lord Dudley, the players' patron, is iv.92, which in fact fetches up 1576 and Robert Dudley, Earl of Leicester. "Disley," however spelled, fails to appear in any of the four volumes of *The Elizabethan Stage,* an omission no doubt owing in part to Chambers's characterization of touring as fraught with "the 'intollerable' charge of traveling with a great company and the danger of 'division and separacion,'" to say nothing of the unreliability of "provincial records, subject to the confusion of company nomenclature already noted."[25]

Murray identified some of the players, and he clearly suspected that some of their careers were long, varied, and perplexing. He first places Richard Bradshaw as one of Lord Dudley's lead players based on Dudley's February 16, 1595, warrant "'to Francis Coffyn and Rich. Bradshaw, his servants, to

88 BARBARA D. PALMER

travel in the quality of playing and to use music in all cities, towns and corporations.'—to use 'the Town Hall or other place and countenance' and to play 'except during time of Divine Service.'" By 1610 Murray surmises that Bradshaw left Dudley's company because "one Distle or Distley is mentioned in the Shuttleworth accounts of Gawthorpe and Smithils in Lancashire, as the head player of a company which in 1612 is spoken of in the same accounts as Lord Edward Dudley's."[26] Between 1610 and 1630 when Bradshaw shows up in Reading with "licens and company," Murray has no record, until Bradshaw's players run afoul of the Banbury authority in 1633. Based on the players' testimony about their and Bradshaw's whereabouts, past, present, and future, Murray constructs an otherwise undocumented itinerary which includes their playing at Nottingham, Leicester, Market Bosworth, Stanton, Solihull, Meriden, Stratford "at Sir Thomas Lucy's," Coventry, Kineton, "in Cornwall," Bristol, "at Sir William Spencer's [Wormleighton]"— with plans to visit Marlow, Buckinghamshire, and Thame, Oxfordshire.[27]

Murray hardly can be blamed for records which neither he nor anyone else yet had found, but his tentative Bradshaw biography has at least three other serious flaws. First, the date on the "warrant for a Company of players to passe & play by from Ed*ward* Lord dudley 41 QE. 1595," a date which is repeated at the end of the warrant as "the 16 of febuary in the 41th yeare of her maiesties 1595," is mystifyingly wrong in one respect or another: Elizabeth's forty-first regnal year spanned November 17, 1598, to November 16, 1599. Either the date of the warrant is February 16, 1594/95, or it is February 16, 1598/99, which makes something of a biographical difference given the London records to Bradshaw as Gabriel Spencer's "man" (see appendix B). Second, Murray apparently was unaware of the November 11, 1602, endorsement by Chester mayor Hugh Glaseour on the back of this warrant:

> Mem*orandum* that francis Coffen & others within named who were licenced to play as the lord dudleys seruants did repayre to this citty for that purpose 10 no*uember* 1602 & for as much as I am Credbly enformd the lord dudly had long since discharged the sayd Coffen & licensed certayn others with words of reuocation of this warrant w*hi*ch was shewed vnto me I haue therfore taken the same from them giuinge them admonitions nether to play in this citty nor els where opon payne of punishment accordinge to the lawes & statutes in that Case pro*v*ided.[28]

Third, Murray uses the testimony of the Bradshaw players detained in Banbury to construct the company's 1633 itinerary, which is a tempting but high-risk research method. No independent documentation of their asserted visits to Nottingham, Leicester, or Bristol has yet been found, and the remainder of their purported itinerary thus falls under query as well.[29] What I find unquestionable, however, is Murray's sense that Richard Bradshaw was a most durable player from something like 1595 until at least 1633. That Bentley, following Murray, was so bonded to his notion of provincial actors' travails and transiencies that he split "Richard Bradshaw" into two players of the same name defies documentation, and his characterization of Bradshaw's 1633 company as "six suspicious strolling actors" sounds like a Dorothy Sayers' title.[30]

Elsewhere I have traced the secondary materials on the elusive Disley, whose continued elusiveness generated my "errata" note in this present piece (n. 22).[31] To date, I have found twenty-one entries to Disley as a named player under the variant surname spellings of "Distley," "Distle," "Dishley," and probable further manuscript orthography which printed sources tend to regularize; his Christian name has not surfaced, and only one record thus far dignifies him as "M*aster*."[32] Disley's named entries span 1601 to 1633, throughout the Midlands and North, from Lancashire to Londesborough, with a low reward of 5s to a high of 30s. To repeat myself, "over his thirty years of professional playing, Disley seems to have experienced almost all variants of company size and organization. He played alone; he played as the senior sharer or actor-manager of a company with at least two separate noble patrons, one of them twice; he played as the head of his own company; and on two occasions he seems to have played a star turn with other professional troupes."[33]

Disley's origins are unknown, but by 1612 and perhaps earlier he heads Lord Dudley's players. Bradshaw's playing origins place him through the 1590s in London as Gabriel Spencer's "man," who is documented first with Pembroke's and then with the Admiral's Men. In either 1595 or 1598/99, depending on the document's rightful date, Bradshaw and Francis Coffyn are authorized to head Dudley's players, through a Chester warrant which by 1602 Dudley had revoked and assigned to other players. In 1600 and 1601, Henslowe's records suggest Bradshaw on tour but a London resident between tours. By 1612 Disley headed Dudley's players; by 1617 Bradshaw headed Derby's players. By March 1617/18 Disley's company patron was the Earl of Shrewsbury, but by September 1619, Disley's company again was under Dudley's patronage. By 1625, Bradshaw and his company played in Doncaster as the King's Players, a patronage which has thus far gone unremarked. He and his company were licensed for Reading in 1630 (according to Murray); and the 1633 trouble in Banbury is his last known appearance in the records. Disley's final known engagement was also 1633, in York.

Appendix B documents as many records to the fifteenth Earl of Derby's players, the fifth Lord Dudley's players, the eighth Earl of Shrewsbury's players, Disley, and Richard Bradshaw as I have found in the published REED volumes (listed in the appendix B tables under "Source" by collection name and page); the unpublished REED collections of the West Riding, Derbyshire, Leicestershire, and Nottinghamshire; the Malone Society *Collections;* and secondary sources.[34] I have boldfaced those entries which

90   BARBARA D. PALMER

definitively link Disley or Bradshaw to a specific patron. At various points
"Disley's Players" and "Bradshaw's Players" seem likely to have inter-
sected, either as competitors or as colleagues, although I have found no proof
of their meeting. Striking in these records, however, is how closely one company seems to follow another, particularly in the festive seasons of Christmas
and Shrovetide but also throughout the year. To assume that provincial
troupes were ignorant of each other's business—itineraries, texts, players,
costumes, devices, reception—is naive, as the set of entries at Londesborough for 1597/98 suggests.[35] Bradshaw and Disley were businessmen, successfully plying their trade through the North and Midlands for over three
decades from the 1590s until at least 1633. That they themselves were proficient actors, able to recruit and manage other proficient actors, is a reasonable
assumption: their audiences, the source of their long-lived income, were not
rustic fools amused by ineptitude—or at least not repeatedly. Competition
among touring companies was stiff, judging from their numbers alone, and
these "provincial" companies—Bradshaw's, Disley's, Simpson's, John Wilson's, John Ledy's, among the many—went head to head, year after year,
with the touring London companies—Admiral's, Lord Chamberlain's,
Queen's, Pembroke's, King's, among the many. The conclusion is not much
of a stretch: provincial and urban alike, these were all Men of the Theater and
professional entrepreneurs.

Hamlet's question of why the players chance to travel evades the basic
questions of how far, when, and by what means they traveled; the evidence
on provincial troupes' traveling conditions, although not abundant, is yet another dimension which has been underestimated and misconstrued. As should
be evident from the Disley and Bradshaw tables, long distances were no impediment to playing engagements, although the assumption long has been
that provincial troupes played only close to home. Intuitive as Murray was on
the potential importance of these provincial players, his sense of northern
geography seems to have been a bit dim, as is evident from the frontispiece
map to *English Dramatic Companies*. Although one tends to leap directly
into Murray's index or alphabetized entry, the map deserves hard scrutiny.

If one locates Newcastle-upon-Tyne at the top of Murray's map and drops
slightly down to the southwest, one finds a semicircular grouping of playing
places for which Murray had located published records. Clustered in a compelling and attractive tour itinerary are Skipton Castle, Hazlewood, Londesborough, Gawthorpe Hall, and Smithils. Of this group, only Skipton Castle is
approximately where it belongs, over the West Riding moors in Craven. Both
Gawthorpe and Smithils [Smithills] are in Lancashire to the southwest of
Skipton; Hazlewood is in the West Riding slightly southwest of York on the
modern A64, and Londesborough is in the East Riding about halfway between York and Beverley.[36] However whimsical the Harvard professor's
northern England cartography, these misplacements are serious matter, in

PLAYING IN THE PROVINCE: FRONT OR BACK DOOR? 91

that Murray's cluster creates a visual image of the provincial tour circuit as narrow, isolated, and limited to households. Additionally, the map's omission or inconsistency of such topographical features as roads, waterways, and moors or dales impedes any sensible reconstruction of travel routes. When the map's locations and proportions are corrected, however, numerous wider-ranging tour circuits are visible, circuits which include such towns as Doncaster, York, Nottingham, Newark-upon-Trent, Leicester, Coventry, and elsewhere for which records are extant.

Travel distances seem fierce, although even Elizabethan gentry traveled at a daunting pace.[37] John Wilson and his players repeatedly trek from Kirkby Stephen and Natesby in Westmorland to the Cliffords at Londesborough in the East Riding of Yorkshire, a journey of over a hundred miles if roads were direct. Licensed town waits were remarkably mobile over large geographic areas, and there is no reason to think players less so.[38] The seven waits of Stamford, deep in Lincolnshire, regularly played at Burghley House near Stamford; but in March 1634 were paid £6 13s 4d to play at Londesborough when Richard Boyle, Lord Dungarvan and fiancé of Lady Elizabeth Clifford, was in residence. Lady Elizabeth, her wedding trunks, and the Stamford waits departed for Skipton in mid-April, but the wedding was delayed until July 3. "Because of the delayed ceremony, the waits of Stamford had been retained for a further nine weeks, for which they were paid £15, Earl Francis giving them 10s when they departed after at least three months' continuous service."[39] That length of stay for waits licensed by a town is unusual, but certainly weeklong engagements either for a holiday season or for a special occasion are not rare.

The length of traveling players' stays varies from overnight stops to several days to the 1597/98 Shrovetide week when some or all of Derby's Men played at Londesborough or September 5–11, 1596, when "certain of the Queen's players" were at Hardwick. How long, on average, players stayed at a great house is central to assessing the average size of their touring repertory, but the figures are hard to come by. Although the household steward's accounts often list both the reward and how long the musicians' visit ("for this Christmastide past"), all they usually reveal about the players is their reward and departure date. Unless pantry accounts survive and the pantry steward tallies strangers in the hall by meal, number, and occupation ("13 players d[inner]"), the only way to guess length of stay is from the payment amount divided by the "normal" payment per play, which is not a very reliable measure. At best one might approximate the number of performances but not the span over which they were played. Where hard data survive, however, the players' average stay at a great house is between two and three days, with a week's visit not unusual. Whether players stayed longer at great houses where accommodation was free than in towns where they had to pay is yet another unanswered question about touring conditions.

92 BARBARA D. PALMER

Neither is it possible to say much about a "typical" calendar for touring except that the weather does not seem to be any more of a deterrent to travel than distance. Past scholars have taken the London-outward approach in trying to calculate a travel calendar, starting with the known London plague outbursts, mandated restrictions on playing, Lent, and documented appearances at Court. The remnants were thought to constitute provincial tours. As J. Leeds Barroll calculates the London playing season, "excepting the time of plague, one might expect a full autumn, one or two months after New Year's Day, depending on when Lent began, and then a short spring schedule until probably the end of the Easter law term. At this time the companies would begin travelling in the provinces."[40] If, however, one privileges provincial rather than London data, the picture seems quite different and a great deal more complex. Of the 256 provincial visits recorded in appendix A, 214 mark the performance month. Granted that the sample is small in the face of the London data heap and the professional performers a mixed lot of provincial and London troupes, but the numbers do not support summer as the provincial touring season of choice or of necessity. Between 1570 and 1642 in this Yorkshire-Derbyshire sample, "summer" shows 46 visits (June, 11; July, 17; August, 18), "autumn" 46 visits (September, 22; October, 15; November, 9), "spring" 36 visits (March, 18; April, 10; May, 8), and "winter" a confounding 86 visits during the blasts of Yorkshire moors and Derbyshire peaks (December, 19; January, 32; February, 35).

And how did the players negotiate those icy moors and peaks? The question of transportation would seem to be answered easily, but hard evidence on feet, horses, or wagons is sparse. The Sussex and Kent REED records show several early payments to "foot plays" and "foot players." In 1518–19 at Rye, 20d is expended "At Iohn Wynters At dyuerse tymes When the foot pleys Were pleid there" and in 1519–20 at Rye 3s 1d "gevyn to thre foot pleys that pleyd At wynters & hunfrys"; in 1525 at Lydd, Kent, 15d is "paide to the foote players of Essex ij tymes at grenewaies house" and in 1529 "ij Companyes of foote players at ij tymes" receive 15d."[41] REED *Sussex* editor Cameron Louis thinks that "foot pleyes . . . were probably dances" and allows that "'foot plays' may not be related to 'foot players' at all, as the former term may refer to the nature of a performance, while the latter may only be a characterization of the players' form of transportation." REED *Kent* editor James M. Gibson thinks that his Lydd foot players "were probably dancers." Both editors note Suzanne R. Westfall's implication that such entries refer to players who travel on foot rather than by horse and cart, but Gibson observes that "among the thousands of travelling players in Kent and Sussex it is difficult to believe that these were the only players travelling on foot and equally difficult to explain why among all the players only these four groups at Lydd and Rye should be singled out for identification by their mode of transportation."[42]

PLAYING IN THE PROVINCE: FRONT OR BACK DOOR? 93

Horses also are seldom singled out in the records as transporting players, although to investigate every horse reference indexed in the REED volumes invites madness. The Kent collection alone fetches up horses for civic processions; for the New Romney passion play; to carry the pageant of St. Thomas; to lead the cart "whan Iohn martyns wiff [d] was in troble"—i.e., carting (2:598); to transport various knights, ambassadors, and masters of horse; to be shoed; to be hired; to be fed; to carry messengers; and to service numerous civic errands such as 12d paid "for A horse for .william. atkins for to goe by chekins then" in 1580 when Lord Cobham was at Dover (2:473)—but not a single entry which documents professional players traveling by horse. The two records of which I am aware—and the Simon Jewell document, below— reveal the unusual rather than the norm. At Coventry in March 1615 fourteen of the Lady Elizabeth's players, men and boys, with ".5. Horses in the Company," intend to play but run afoul of Sir Edward Coke, then the city recorder, when one of the company threatens to cut Coventry citizens' throats for being peevish. The players' names and the five horses are listed only as part of the misdemeanor, in consequence of which Coke forbade the company to play in Coventry.[43] Second, in the Shrovetide 1597/98 Londesborough scenario outlined in note 35, one Thomas Tomes is paid 3s 8d for my Lord of Derby's players' "horssmeayte 3 nyghtes and laiding." The going 1597 rate for horsemeat was a shilling a day, which suggests one horse away from Londesborough's gratis lodgings for the three nights and further suggests, or so I have speculated, one Derby player's temporary departure perhaps for a Shrove Tuesday engagement.[44] How five horses were apportioned among fourteen Lady Elizabeth's players or one horse among twelve or more Lord Derby's players is something of a mystery, but at least some provincial players provably had horses.

Wagons are quite another matter, although they are assumed to be a fixed appointment for traveling players and their gear. In fact, I have found only six records of wagons, and two, although fascinating, are aside from our topic here. On January 25, 1588/89, Sir Francis Drake requests that the six Norwich waits "may be sent to hym to go the new intendid voyage," and the Council hires a wagon "to carry them and their instrumentes" to Sir Francis's ship, which sailed from Plymouth in April 1589.[45] On September 11, 1638, William Sandes of Preston, Lancashire, bequeaths his "Shewe called the Chaos, the Wagon, the Stage," and all the joiner's tools and other implements belonging to the said show to his son, John Sandes. The wagon here seems to be the vehicle for a marionette or puppet show of the Creation, what Jonson and Shakespeare called "a motion."[46]

The remaining four records to players' wagons of which I am aware are not transparent. The 1576–77 Exeter Receivers' Account Rolls contain a 20s payment "to the plaiers with the waggen," an entry grouped in a six-entry set of "extraordinary expenses" for entertainment. "Certain players" receive

94   BARBARA D. PALMER

6s 8d for "their play," the Earl of Leicester's players are paid 13s 4d, a bear-baiter in the mayor's presence 10s, then "the players with the wagon," followed by 6s 8d to Lord Mountjoy's players, and concluding with 13s 4d to Lord Strange's players.[47] The entry in context is problematic: did other troupes have no wagon or did the clerk, for some reason, not remember the troupe's name but remember their wagon? Regardless, quite interesting is that this unnamed troupe with its wagon received the highest reward of this players' grouping.

Second, on August 19, 1592, Simon Jewell, a London player, notes in his will that among the debts owed to him "from my fellowes the sixth parte of thirtie seaven pounde wch amounteth to six pounds three shillinges fouer pence, and [that I] haue paide my share for horses waggen and apparrell new boughte." He bequeathes "Roberte Nicholls all my playenge thinges in a box and my veluet shewes, And as for my horse and all the reste of my goodes are p[resen]tlie to be solde for my buriall." Mary Edmond discovered this "unnoticed registered will" and postulates Jewell to be one of Pembroke's Men, but Scott McMillin connects him instead with the Queen's Men.[48] This unique document tells us much and hides much. Apparently in 1592 six sharers of either Pembroke's or the Queen's Men contributed equally to the purchase of a wagon, horses, and ready-made new costumes; Jewell owned his own horse, which might have been his transportation on the road; and he traveled lightly, all of his "playing things" fitting into a box. If McMillin is right, "[b]y 1592 the Queen's men could have been what the will implies—a troupe of six sharers, none of them famous and all of them laying out cash for a provincial tour"; a further possibility is that if the "six sharers in Jewell's touring company . . . were the Queen's Men, the original company of twelve was divided exactly in half for touring in 1592."[49] One tour is documented by the Queen's players' reward of £3 6s 8d—a sum which suggests three performances—in York on July 24, the month before Jewell's will was proved.[50]

Third of the four references to players' touring wagons is found in the 1597–98 Faversham, Kent, Chamberlains' Accounts, specifically the account of Nicholas Turner, serjeant at mace, who has collected fines from individual miscreants with which to reimburse the chamberlains' earlier reparation: "Item hee [Nicholas Turner] ys chardged withe the some of xv s. ix d. for money resceived bye him for the misdeameanoure of certen persons done in the same Towne vppon misvsage of a wagon or Coache of the Lord Bartlettes players."[51] The vandalism seems substantial, its repair almost equaling the pound which they received for playing. The troupe probably is that of Henry, seventh Baron Berkeley, whose principal residences were at Yate Court, Gloucestershire, and Caludon Castle, near Coventry, Warwickshire; his players traveled widely in the provinces, but a record of the troupe's size or other playing particulars has not yet surfaced.[52]

PLAYING IN THE PROVINCE: FRONT OR BACK DOOR? 95

The fourth wagon reference is a 1610 Stourbridge, Worcestershire, entry on Lord Eure's players, snagged by Leslie Hotson in one of his fortuitous trawls through the Star Chamber accounts in the Public Record Office and heralded as follows:

> It would be naive to suppose the better Elizabethan touring companies unable to afford more than a single play-wagon. The players of Lord Eure, for example, were certainly not a company at all comparable either in rank or means with the King's men or the Admiral's men. But even this minor troupe, when I find them at Stourbridge in Worcestershire early in 1610, had "cartes & waggens" which are not mentioned as anything exceptional: "the plaiers with theire apparell drumm & trumpettes cartes & waggens being then at theire said Inne [vizt the Crowne]." Here we have the actors with their play-wagons or removable stages—not "boards and barrel-heads"—and not presumed but actually reported in the inn-yard of the Crown at Stourbridge.[53]

Although Hotson's thesis that pageant wagons served as portable stages in yards is a few loads short of proof, his quest also yields Dekker's *Satiromastix* reminder to "'Horace' (*i.e.,* Ben Jonson), 'Thou hast forgot how thou ambledst . . . by a play-wagon in the high way, and took'st mad Ieronimoes part.' And Middleton's Sir Bounteous Progress [in *A Mad World, my Masters*], asking the strollers 'Where be your boys?', is assured that 'They come along with the waggon, sir.'"[54]

The size and appearance of a play-wagon are as elusive as the records to them with part of the problem being terminology: in the few references above, players have a "waggen," "a wagon or Coache," and "cartes & waggens," while the *OED* offers such further nomenclature as wains, cars, carriages, tumbrels, and chariots. In general, however, a wagon has four wheels and is larger than a two-wheeled cart, although both can carry heavy loads; a four-wheeled coach often is closed, has seats inside, and connotes its occupants' higher social status. The vehicle obviously affects the speed of travel with a horse pulling a cart or horses pulling a wagon faster than horses pulling a coach—and players on horseback outdistancing other means. I am unaware of evidence that players traveled by internal waterways, although entertainment traffic between England and the Continent certainly went by sea. The absence of references to water travel may reflect an absence of the mishaps which result in such legal records as coroner's inquests or trials rather than an absence of water travel.

Whatever their mode of transportation, players somehow reached the provincial great houses, which from a London viewpoint often have been assumed to be as shabby as the players. If the vagabond players were sent to the back door, provincial gentry houses were presumed not to have a front door. To be banished from the Court for Elizabeth's displeasure or sent to one's county seat for Christmas at James's public relations' whim is seen as

96   BARBARA D. PALMER

dreadful punishment, a portrait of the provinces which owes more to Henry
Fielding than Sir Anthony van Dyck. A London wit in 1631 satirically describes "a gentleman's house in the country" as

> the prime house of some village, and carryes gentility on the front of it. . . . At
> meales, you shall have a scattered troup of dishes, led in by some black puddings,
> and in the Reare some demolish'd pastyes, which are not yet fallen to the Serving-
> men. Between meales there be bread and Beere for all comers, and for a stranger a
> napkin and cold meate in the Buttery may be obtained. All the roomes smell of
> Dogges and Hawks, and the Hall beares armes, though it be but a muskitt and two
> Corsletts. . . . The master of the house is ador'd as a Relique of gentility . . . his
> house is the seat of hospitality, the poore man's Court of Justice, the Curate's Sun-
> day ordinary, and the only Exchequer of Charity.[55]

Sir Henry Wotton saw the great house rather differently in 1624 when he
wrote of it as "[e]very Man's proper Mansion House and Home, being the
Theater of his Hospitality, the Seat of Selfe-fruition, the Comfortablest part
of his own Life, the Noblest of his Sonnes Inheritance, a kinde of private
Princedome."[56]

The great house was the measure of a man's worth, his material, social,
and cultural context; and in that context traveling players are one of many
symbols of status. Gentry households were highly organized, as numerous
household ordinances detail; particularly in the great hall or, by the sixteenth
century, in the great chamber above it as well, a place was prescribed for
everyone and everything. Seating in the hall was by rank from the dais down
to the screens end with status further defined by whose "board" one occupied—e.g., master's, mistress's, steward's, knight's, or marshall's—and how
many shared a mess. As Felicity Heal notes, "[I]n modified form the insistence on careful ordering at meals survives in household ordinances well into
the seventeenth century."[57] Maintaining household order falls to the household steward; maintaining the order of the hall falls to the head usher, among
whose duties is "diligently to have good regard of every person that comes
into the hall, to the end that if they be of the better sort, notice may be given
to the master, or some head officer that they m[a]y be entertained accordingly. If of the meaner sort, then to know the cause of their coming . . . provided always that no stranger be suffered to pass without offering him to
drink, and that no rascall or unseemly person be suffer'd to tarry there."[58]

To determine the size of a gentry "household in ordinary"—and size matters if one is trying to estimate provincial great house play audiences—
requires the fortuitous survival of certain types of records, namely pantry
accounts and the household steward's quarterly wage accounts. Both types of
records are idiosyncratic, and comparisons indeed are odorous, but up to
eighty in ordinary would not be exceptional. Heal suggests that "an 'average'

size for the noble household at the end of the medieval period [ca. 1485] was around 150 persons, while about sixty-five was average for a gentry establishment[,]" numbers which did not decrease in the following two centuries.[59] As early as 1520 Henry, Lord Clifford moved his peripatetic household of fifty or sixty "from Skipton to Barden, Appleby, Brougham, Brough and the Court at Westminster"; and in 1608 Francis, Lord Clifford's traveling household—usually between Londesborough and Skipton—still numbered nearly sixty.[60] By August 1628 there were sixty-six in ordinary at Skipton Castle and in May 1629 some eighty in ordinary at Londesborough; while at Wollaton Hall, Sir Francis Willoughby maintained between seventy-five and eighty between 1572 and 1580.[61] When the friends, visiting family, neighbors, and other guests which constitute "the extraordinary" are added, particularly for a special event like visiting players or musicians, an audience of well over a hundred would not be abnormal: for a two-week period in August 1609, Francis, Lord Clifford was joined at Skipton "by lord [Henry] Clifford, down from Christ Church, Oxford[;] Roger Manners, 5th earl of Rutland[;] his brother Sir George Manners[;] Sir John Savile of Howley[;] Sir William Ingleby of Ripley[;] Sir Thomas Metcalfe of Nappa[;] Sir Stephen Tempest of Broughton[;] and 'great Companie of about 140 persons dayly.'"[62]

Overseeing the orderliness and dignity of this large establishment was the household steward, a position of enormous responsibility, power, and opportunity. "According to one Elizabethan list of regulations, written for 'the household of an Earl' by the anonymous author 'R.B.,' the chief officers were to be 'not only well borne and of good livings, but also grave and experienced, not proud and haughty, neither too affable and easy. . . .'"[63] The "office and authority" of a household steward are broad of scope, as Anthony, Viscount Montague outlines in 1595. Montague expects his steward to secure all gross provisions; see to all repairs of house, property, and grounds; pay all servants' wages and bills for staff supplies; and disperse money to such other household purchasers as the clerk of the kitchen or gentleman of his horse. Additionally, Montague expects his household steward to be his chief officer, assist him with sound advice, and faithfully keep his secrets. He is held superior over all domestic officers, servants, and attendants, responsible for their civil behavior and distributor of any gratuities given by guests. All inventories—wardrobe, plate, silver, gold, pewter, kitchen, cellar, buttery, pantry, bakehouse, laundry, scullery, larders, porter's lodge, brewhouse—and current checkrolls of both domestic personnel and retainers fall under his oversight, as do regular audits. He is expected to take his meals in the Hall and to maintain his own table (called the "steward's board" in Clifford pantry records) accompanied by "gentlemen and strangers of better account."[64]

And, most central to our topic here, the household steward is responsible for the household entertainment, both the internal entertainers who are part of the household and the external performers who arrive at the gatehouse.

The household steward then is not only the filter between traveling players and the master or mistress of the great house but he also is somehow the liaison between external and internal performers, a dimension which has received next to no attention because the evidence is so sporadic and so difficult to unravel. Household musicians frequently are listed simply by their names as gentlemen of the household, and they often are tallied in pantry accounts as "officers." Only a chance reference—e.g., Martin Otto's asking the Earl and Countess of Shrewsbury in 1606 if he could take his chest of viols with him when he left their employ—reveals their entertainment roles. Even where to look for evidence of household entertainers is not always clear: the Londesborough pantry accounts sometimes list household musicians in the ordinary and sometimes as "straungers in the hall," while John Addison, the household dancing master, always is counted in the extraordinary even though he is at Londesborough for weeks at a time. When traveling players, musicians, and waits are listed as extraordinary in pantry accounts, their presence, length of stay, and numbers are evident; but they sometimes may be buried in the ordinary. Had a December 24, 1612, Skipton Castle record that "This day the v: musitions of Barton Came hither & are for this Christmas to be entered in ordinary" not survived, the consequent pantry accounts would swallow their presence.

Although household entertainment personnel can be difficult to identify, one errs in assuming that provincial great houses were entirely dependent on traveling players for their culture. Some had their own liveried players, many produced their own revels or masques, and almost all maintained household musicians. Surviving household accounts bulge with purchases of lute strings, music books, viol chests; payments to waits, singers, French musicians, dancing masters, music tutors; repairs to virginals, tuning of the organs, an instrument which Sir Arthur Ingram seems to have transported from one of his Yorkshire houses to another. By the late sixteenth and early seventeenth centuries, the Cliffords had between four and five musicians in residence, including their "renowned organist, John Hingeston"; Sir Gervase Clifton, who married, among six other wives, Lady Frances Clifford, had six musicians.[65] Among his ordinary household Francis Willoughby counted "Edward Edlin, a lute player, and a Mr. Astell, who played the virginals"; Willoughby's ca. 1565 notebook of lute music survives, and he regularly wrote "to his sister at Court to ask for her help in finding players and singers."[66] Philip, Lord Wharton, at Healaugh, West Riding maintained between six and twelve players for many years; Sir Richard Cholmley at Egton, North Riding, maintained a troupe which at one point numbered fifteen. Tempting as it is to envision household and traveling entertainers playing nicely together, the little evidence which survives is too fragmented to argue that they regularly performed as a larger group.

Four documented exceptions provide more questions than answers. The

February 10, 1635/36, Skipton Castle performance of *A New Way to Pay Old Debts* is played by a "certeyne company of Roguish players"; on the same date Adam Gerdler of York is paid 5s to play a part in *The Knight of the Burning Pestle* and the York waits are paid £5. Presumably the rest of the *Burning Pestle* parts are filled either by the roguish players or by household members and guests—who, with the steward's tongue-in-cheek entry, may be one and the same. Second, for Shrovetide 1597/98, Lord Derby's players, player John Wilson of Westmorland and two musicians, the Clifford musicians, the dancer John Addison, and perhaps Lord Wharton's players all seem to be in residence at Londesborough. Third, in August 1619 at least three groups of musicians—two from the Court and one from the Loire—seem to be at Hardwick at the same time, presumably in addition to William, Lord Cavendish's own musicians. Fourth, for the July 1634 wedding of Lady Elizabeth Clifford to Lord Dungarvan, music was provided by household organist John Hingeston, the Clifford musicians, French musicians, a singer, and the Stamford, Lincolnshire waits.[67] How these discrete groups come together, determine the program, rehearse, and perform effectively remains somewhat mysterious.

However the players met and made merry, they did so in a fairly predictable performance venue, the great hall or, later in the sixteenth century, the great chamber. As I have written elsewhere, players on tour could count on a large rectangle, which for the sake of argument let us "average" at twenty-five feet wide by fifty feet long; with maximal lighting from daylight (if the play were after late-morning dinner), large windows, fireplace(s), wall sconces, other candlelight, and torches; several doors, a screen, a screens passage, an elevated gallery, a "below" under the gallery, gallery columns, and other potential features for exits, entrances, concealment, and blocking; and, perhaps, performance bonuses such as the "decorative" elements of hangings, carvings, plaster ceilings, friezes, and the dais with its "settings."[68] Clearly not every great hall or chamber featured all of these appointments—a dais at the high end was universal, a gallery markedly less so—and architectural fashions changed significantly between the fifteenth and seventeeth centuries, but the concept of the great hall with its hierarchical layout did not. As Cooper concludes, "The hall expressed the organisation of the household in the same way that the outside of the house had done. In an age which jealously observed distinctions of rank, the decoration of the hall gave greatest honour to those areas that were used by the lord on formal occasions and represented his dignity when he was not there in person to preside over the community."[69]

Knowing the general outline of the great hall venue still leaves numerous questions about how it functioned as a performance space. Its furnishings are difficult to determine from inventories, which tend to catalogue items not stored in the hall. The 1595 inventory made by his Skipton Castle steward for George, Earl of Cumberland, then living in London, documents that "[t]he great hall was virtually empty but for forms [benches], cupboards and red hangings"; the predominantly green silk or cloth of silver high drawing chamber above contained "three chairs of state and cushions[,] . . . a fringed green table cloth five yards in length, much turkey work, five pieces of Arras work worth £30 which had been bought from Mr [Sir John?] Yorke of Gowthwaite, a bellows, chimney cloth and a pair of playing tables." The "'High Great Chamber' . . . held tables, buffets, forms and cupboards—all used for dining—and was hung with six pieces depicting the story of the the Trojans and had tapestry table cloths."[70] Neither the 1550 nor the 1585 inventory of Wollaton Hall made for Sir Francis Willoughby includes great hall furnishings, although his 1572 list of household regulations marks the great hall as the hub of the household. The inventories, however, do furnish the family's great chamber with "a bedstead, folding table, forms (that is, benches), and a cupboard (presumably for the display of plate), while the dining chamber contained two long tables, two trestle tables, two turned stools, a cupboard, a chest, and an old clock."[71] In 1537 the Whalley Abbey dining hall, which saw numerous entertainers prior to Dissolution, was furnished with a cupboard, long settle, two chairs, three carpets to put on the tables, a dozen cushions, and a hanging candlestick in the middle of the chamber.

Documentation on great hall performance lighting is hard to come by but what little I have found to date suggests that Richard Southern is quite wrong to describe it as "quite strikingly dim," a "comparative darkness." Although "[a]t court a glittering profusion of candles might have been within the range of the Revels' expense account," Southern is certain that "in a normal country householder's home it was not," the lights "few and flickering"—as he illustrates with his own drawing of "the dimness of a torchlit hall."[72] Southern has mistaken the late morning dinner hour for evening dining, which would place most daylight-deprived performances at night; he also is not aware of the ever-frustrating pantry and household accounts which tally candles, a subject discussed below under players' keep. In at least some instances there is no reason why the lighting which Irwin Smith postulates for Blackfriars—candles held in branched candelabra "suspended from above, necessarily by cords or wires running over pulleys, so that they could be lowered for 'mending,' lighting, and extinguishing"—could not have been effected for the provincial great hall performance.[73]

That the great hall floor, the players' stage, was covered with rushes seems likely, but, again, definitive proof has not appeared. Smith writes that "[t]he floor of the Blackfriars stage, like the floors of contemporary cottages and palaces all over England, was strewn with rushes. In Elizabethan and Jacobean homes, moist green rushes served primarily to lay the dust. . . ."[74] Alan C. Dessen and Leslie Thomson cite "strewers of rushes" in *2 Henry IV;* a figure who "sits on the rushes, and takes out a book to read" in *Fair Favour-*

PLAYING IN THE PROVINCE: FRONT OR BACK DOOR?

ite; and "servants with Rushes, and a carpet," a "Rush-wench," and a "Rush-maid" in *Gentleman Usher.*[75] Rush mats and carpets eventually replace loose rushes, but in the sixteenth century carpets seem as likely to be on the tables than under them. In *The Taming of the Shrew* Shakespeare provides both in describing the great house welcome which Kate is not going to receive:

> Where's the cook? Is supper ready, the house trimmed, rushes strewed, cobwebs swept, the servingmen in their new fustian, the white stockings, and every officer his wedding garment on? Be the Jacks fair within, the Jills fair without, the carpets laid, and everything in order? . . . Call forth Nathaniel, Joseph, Nicholas, Philip, Walter, Sugarsop, and the rest. Let their heads be sleekly combed, their blue coats brushed, and their garters of an indifferent knit; let them curtsy with their left legs, and not presume to touch a hair of my master's horsetail till they kiss their hands. Are they all ready?[76]

One central question which this study hoped (and has failed) to answer is how the great household "audience" was physically situated for the performance. Folks were invited to hear the play or plays, they traveled significant distances under dubious weather conditions to attend, the "audience" could number well over a hundred, and how they were positioned to hear the play remains indeterminate. The anonymous highly unusual painting usually cited as *The Wedding Feast of Sir Henry Unton* (ca. 1596) is less informative than at first glance it might seem.[77] Actually a *memento mori* to Sir Henry's life and death commissioned by his widow, the "wedding feast" (which with only ten guests looks more like an elopement) is a selective, compressed narrative of a household entertainment, representative rather than representational. The scene highlights Sir Henry as host of his great chamber, presiding over a banquet which has been followed by a masque of Mercury and Diana. The masquers are ascending and descending foreshortened stairs cut away from the great hall below, which is furnished with one long and one shorter bench. Inside the masquers' circle are six musicians sitting on stools in something like a pit below the dining level above, which may be the artist's representation of a dais. On the same level as the high table guests, who are seated on cushioned stools with the household officers standing behind, are a drummer and a fool twirling a plate on a long rod. Although fascinating, the painting provides little hard information on where and how household entertainment audiences were accommodated.

Richard Southern speculates that "if a meal were served in the hall at some special feast, with many guests and their retainers present, then there might not be space for all to find seats, and so a lesser or greater number would have to stand, which was quite customary." In further neglect of the rigid Elizabethan rules on normal dining decorum, he imagines an "eagerly-watching throng" clustered at the screens end and blocking the actors' entrances,

102 BARBARA D. PALMER

who have to shove their way through shouting "Give way."[78] I am aware of only one instance which approaches Southern's scenario, namely the tumult at Gowthwaite Hall in Christmastide 1609/10 when the law descended on a recusant play performance. Depositions reported that numerous unruly people thronged outside the hall entrance unable to get in, an impediment which the same unruly people later gave as their defense for knowing nothing about nor having seen the play. Without hard evidence to date, perhaps one might employ Ockham's Razor. Since the great hall long had served multiple functions—reception area, sleeping area for male servants on palettes, dining, supping, entertainment—its furniture perforce was portable. If the tables are not removed, either the size and comfort of the audience or the size of the playing space is significantly reduced. Trestle tables are easily taken down, leaving benches, stools, and cushions, whose occupancy no doubt was sorted out by the household steward and hall usher along the timeless audience rules of rank, status, wealth, age, health, height, vision, hearing, and gender. Although *Mankind* probably played to academics and is a late fifteenth- century text, Mercy's address to "ye soverens that sitt, and ye brothern that stonde right uppe" still may not be far off the great household audience mark. A three-sided standing and sitting audience's attention easily would be drawn to the screens end for entrances and exits but otherwise as easily focused on playing in the round. If a money collection were taken of the guests—which certainly happens in *Mankind* and may have happened at Skipton Castle—a three-sided audience makes it easier to work the hall.[79]

A further puzzle is how much space the full sail of Elizabethan female regalia—farthingales, bumrolls, kirtles, gowns, puffed sleeves—would occupy, whether seated or standing. Smith calculates for the first Blackfriars playhouse as follows:

> In modern theatres and stadia, the usual space allowance for each seated spectator is 18 to 22 inches from side to side by 30 inches from front to back. But the playgoer of Elizabethan times needed more breadth than that. His was the period of greatest extravagance in English dress. Both he and his lady wore elaborate and voluminous costumes; she wore a farthingale and puffed sleeves and a ruff, and he wore a slashed doublet and cape, and a sword at his side. . . . I therefore base my estimates of seating capacity upon the supposition that each spectator occupied a space 2½ feet deep from front to back, and a full 2 feet wide. On this basis, after reasonable allowances have been made for aisles, a pit of the dimensions indicated [33 feet in length by 26 feet in breadth] would accommodate 120 to 130 persons.[80]

If a great hall measures roughly twenty-five by fifty feet, Smith's estimate of nearly five square feet per spectator allows a maximum of 250 people, a number which when shrunk by the dais, the high table, the playing area, and the screens begins to approximate the size of many great house audiences who came to hear a play.

PLAYING IN THE PROVINCE: FRONT OR BACK DOOR?

What plays they heard is a project-in-progress whose end will not be reached for many years. In 1980 David Galloway paused in the midst of a venomous attack on Murray to bemoan that "the clerks of provincial towns and cities seldom, apparently, recorded the names of plays which visiting companies performed" but went on to urge that "we should not abandon hope of finding some names—even, perhaps, the names of some of Shakespeare's plays—until the records of REED are complete."[81] Galloway's hope gradually is being realized as the names of characters and titles of plays—mainly lost texts but a few extant—continue to emerge; and earlier notions that traveling troupes played "bad" quartos, inferior touring texts, have been put to rest by such scholars as McMillin and MacLean.[82] The records, however, have been frustratingly silent on touring repertories, with an exception which I would like to treat here as a speculative touring paradigm.

This one known repertory contains four plays from four genres—a saint's play, a comedy, a tragedy, and a romance; the number seems appropriate for a several-day engagement, the length of stay most often reflected in pantry accounts, and the variety allows choice to the host. The account comes primarily from PRO STAC 8/19/10 with additional depositions in British Library Harleian MS 1330 and in Northallerton QSM 2/2, North Riding quarter sessions records, which are in print.[83] During Christmastide 1609/10, Sir Richard Cholmley's troupe, led by the Simpson brothers, toured, as usual, from their North Yorkshire base at Egton through the North and West Ridings, playing primarily at recusant great houses. Fortunately for my purposes here, they were apprehended at Sir John Yorke's Gowthwaite Hall in the West Riding, whose records John Wasson and I are editing for REED.[84] Cholmley's company numbered fifteen and at this 1609 Christmastide they offered Sir John a choice of four plays: *The Travailes of The Three English Brothers* (first performed by the Queen's Men in 1607, first published in 1607); *Pericles* (1608 at the Globe with a 1609 quarto), *King Lear* (1605 at the Globe and Court with a 1608 quarto), and *The Play of St. Christopher,* which is what drew the attention of Sir Richard's arch enemy Sir Thomas Posthumous Hoby, son of Lady Russell, famous "not-in-my-backyard" opponent of Blackfriars.

The St. Christopher text is lost but between the transcription of Sir John Yorke's Star Chamber trial, which droned on for years, and the *Legenda Aurea*'s "Life of St. Christopher," a performance outline can be cobbled together, which is not a recommended method for detailed literary analysis. The trial's short version is that when Cholmley's troupe played recusant houses the St. Christopher play allegedly featured a dispute between a "popish priest" and an "English minister," ending with devils taking the pastor to hell and angels the priest to heaven. Or maybe not: of the ninety-some people who testified in the Star Chamber trial, fifty swore such a play never was performed, thirty offered hearsay evidence, several said that it was another

104   BARBARA D. PALMER

play, and only eight allowed they had seen it, two of whom most inventively testifying that they had seen nothing at Sir John Yorke's but had heard that the plays were performed at Sir Stephen Procter's house, Procter being the locally hated Puritan who pulled down Fountains Abbey and used the stones to build his opulent new house. The damning testimony, and fullest account of the St. Christopher performance, came from Thomas Pant, one of the troupe's two boy actors. In 1607, when he was twelve, little Thomas was taken on as a shoemaker apprentice to Christopher Simpson but he grew morally troubled that the Simpsons never taught him to make shoes "but hath been trayned up for these three yeres in wandering the country and playing of Interludes," presumably in gowns and with a beard coming.

The table below lists the four plays apparently on offer that 1609/10 Christmastide and, down the side, the costumes, hand properties, larger properties, and special effects called for in the texts and testimonies. The performance demands of *King Lear* and *Pericles* of course are familiar, with those of "St. Christopher" and *The Three English Brothers* less so. Before his conversion to Christopher, Reprobus (whom Thomas Pant calls "Raphabus" in his testimony) wears greenman apparel, the priest and minister are in black, and the most memorable part of the performance seems to have been the devils' horrible noises, clamor, farting, evil gestures, and casting about flashes of fire. What exactly the trial description of "three strange fellows in painted coats having a chain of iron about them click up another man and held him aloft and letting him down again pulled off his coat" reports is hard to discern: perhaps three devils hoisting the English minister? In this Gowthwaite Hall performance Christopher is reported as carrying Christ over the water; since the play account follows *The Golden Legend,* we probably can assume that the miracle of the flowering staff was represented as well. Whether Reprobus/Christopher approached anything like the "prodigious size, being twelve cubits in height [seventeen to twenty-one feet], and fearful of aspect" described in *The Golden Legend* no witness reveals.

The Three English Brothers' properties and effects are fairly clear from the extant text, as indicated on the table. It, too, seems to have been an exceptionally noisy play, as are *Lear* and *Pericles.* Although the Prologue tells us that the story has been cut to fit the stage and the audience's attention, the action nevertheless is far-ranging and physically energetic. Full of battles, confrontations, captures, releases, tortures, intrigues, exits, and entrances, the text asks space both for definition of locale as well as for display of arms and audience safety. The most extraordinary entrance in the play, however, is that of Will Kempe as an English traveling player with two plays on offer (Adam and Eve naked or Englands Joy). Will's entrance is preceded by a scene esssentially borrowed from *Merchant of Venice* and followed by the entrance of an Italian "Harlaken" player and his wife, who also offer a play. Sir Anthony Shirley asks Kempe to play a part with the Harlaken players, bawdy jests

PLAYING IN THE PROVINCE: FRONT OR BACK DOOR? 105

follow, and we then elide into *Merchant of Venice* echoes of Jew, ducats, and the bond for the jewel.

If we look at these four plays as a properties' list, we have a notion of what Cholmley's players needed to tour Yorkshire in winter: playing clothes for females, clerics, Turks, Venetian Jew, English gentlemen, the fool's gear, "dirty" garments, "clean" robes; shields, swords, armor, some battered and rusty; severed heads; chains; stocks; and the ingredients for making ferocious storms with thunder, lightning, smoke, rain, wind, fire flashes.[85] The list provokes several observations: first, these four texts—saint's play, comedy, tragedy, and romance—are not all that different when compared for staging or performance demands. If a troupe can make one storm, it can make them all. Second, the majority of properties are small, requiring a road manager with a terrific eye to detailed inventory but not taking much space to transport. Third, and with no evidence but common sense, one wonders if a traveling repertory was selected, in part, because the plays' staging requirements were

REPERTORY ON OFFER AT GOWTHWAITE HALL, CHRISTMASTIDE 1609/10
[PRO STAC 8/19/10, et al., transcriptions © Wasson & Palmer/REED]

	St. Christopher	*Three English Brothers*	*King Lear*	*Pericles*
COSTUMES	green apparel, green ivy garland, high-collared black gown, cornered cap, black cloak, Lucifer, angel in white, a Clowne, 3 painted coats [devils?]	Prologue attired like Fame, "Turkes habits," Pope, cardinals, a Venetian Jew, Will Kempe, Harlequin, H's wife, "English Christians," female apparel	a Clowne with coxcomb, mad apparel for Edgar (grimy face, blanketed loins, knotted hair), Lear's storm garments, Lear's clean garments, female apparel, white beard	a Clowne, bride's apparel like the spring, P's wet apparel, cloak, fishing net with P's rusty armor entangled, pleated skirts attached to doublets, 5 sets armor & painted shields, victory wreath, Marina's apparel, P's rough apparel, long hair, beard, P's fresh robes, silvery Diana
HAND PROPERTIES	large yellow wooden cross carried on hermit's shoulder, chain of iron & hoisting device, book like a Bible, ?Christopher's great staff [with magic leaves & fruit?]	drums, colors, 7 suits shabby armor, severed heads on swords, various bonds, bands, irons, chains, a warrant paper, a key, swords, stones for weapons, a jewel, severed head like one of the brothers, 3 "prospective glasses," newborn baby	coronet, map, letter, key, egg, swords, drums, colors, Kent's ring, money purse, straw, torch, cushions, jointstool, a litter, bonds, chair, bowl with "flax & whites of eggs," bandages, Goneril's favor to Edmund, "a tree," face coverings	suitors' heads, pistol, poison, gold/money, sealed commission, banquet display, standing wine bowl & cups, torches, newborn baby, coffin, spices, ink, paper, casket & jewels, vial of restorative, basket of flowers, pillows, ?painted cloth of ship
LARGER PROPERTIES	?perhaps the hoisting/ torture device	leg stocks, hoisting/ torture device, Peter's chair with ascending stairs	leg stocks, "a hovel"	monument hung with golden epitaphs, pavilion
SPECIAL EFFECTS	devils casting fire, flashes of fire, farting, roaring, Christopher carrying Christ over water, capacity to ascend, thunder, lightning	alarums, flourishes, banquet music, noises off pulling up anchors & casting off ships, several dumbshows, fire, smoke, chambers shot off	trumpets, a storm (wind, water, thunder, lightning), blood, sennets, alarums, music	thunder, wind, music, dumbshows, fire, vision of Diana

106 BARBARA D. PALMER

compatible. Fourth, a touring company on regular circuits may have borrowed some particulars, like armor or stocks (or musical instruments), from their great house hosts.

Such properties, costumes, and instruments, like the household musicians, were readily available in a provincial great house, which is not to say that touring players appropriated them. A 1568 probate inventory of Thomas, Lord Wharton of Healaugh lists "Apparell for the Revells" as including long gowns, fools' coats, paper hats, bishops' miters, friars' caps, wooden swords, beards, and various masking items worth a total sum of £3 6s 8d.[86] As noted above, the Hoghtons of Lancashire kept players and play clothes; a 1620 inventory of what were probably Alexander Hoghton's musical instruments includes viols, violin, virginals, various wind instruments, a flute in a velvet case, taber pipes, a chest for some of the viols, and a chest with music books for a total appraised value of £13 16s 8d.[87] In 1572 the Skipton Castle long gallery stockpiled in its various chambers 37 battle-axes, 40 Flanders corslets, 45 spears, armor for 120 men, and "old armour" for another ninety, along with an arsenal of other weapons and fighting gear. In the seventeenth century the Cliffords produced at least six masques at Skipton and Londesborough, leaving purchase records of masking materials and properties— gloves, pumps, ribbons, tinsel, pasteboard, canvas—as well as payments to Arthur, the Knaresborough joiner, and to Henrick de Kesar, "the in-house Dutch painter patronized by Clifford."[88] Master de Kesar receives £3 "for part of his charge & reward in working the scene of the maske"; and Arthur the Joyner 5s "for making the pollyes for the Candlesticks & taking downe the Scene."[89] That various entertainment materials, costumes, properties, and personnel were available at provincial great houses is evident, but whether traveling players borrowed them seems quite doubtful. One is reminded of Simon Jewell's "playenge thinges in a box and [his] veluet shewes," a reminder of the uncertainties of touring conditions and the reassuring certitude of his own playing things in their box. Professional players may have borrowed materials at the great houses, but it seems quite unlikely that they would have counted on doing so when planning a lengthy tour with diverse playing conditions.

In contrast to the abundant unknowns about audience, repertory, and performance conditions, how the players were accommodated is easier to determine, at least when details of their "keep" can be teased from the limited number of extant pantry accounts. At Londesborough and Skipton, players ate in the hall—that is, not in the parlor with the intimate family nor below stairs with inferior servants but with other respectable "straungers," gentlemen, and visitors. Although by the sixteenth century "the lord, his family, and the officers who served him at table . . . withdrew into their more private great chambers or 'dining chambers,'" the hall continued in use for feasts, special occasions, and entertainments.[90] The hall also continued in use by custom and symbolic value. As he became more disabled and dined in his chamber with family and friends, Sir William Cecil did not relinquish maintenance of the

> "honorable table, for Noblemen and others to resort to . . ." which was constantly set in his parlour, and his hall, which . . . "was ever well furnished with Men, served with Meate, and kept in good Ordre." . . . [I]n her old age at Brougham Castle, Westmorland, [Lady Anne Clifford] rarely sat publicly among her guests, but always insisted that "her folk" maintain a formal table in "the painted chamber." . . . The hall, although it had long since ceased to be the exclusive focus of eating and sociability, still provided the central stage on which the drama of commensality could be enacted.[91]

For gentry and aristocratic households, dinner occurred at eleven in the morning and supper between five and six in the evening, perhaps extended by "banquets" on special occasions.[92] Players normally are provided with dinner and supper (abbreviated "ds" in the pantry accounts), although the Cliffords often feed them breakfast as well. When they arrive, several of the players on occasion either eat at or are accounted to the steward's board, which may suggest some conference among senior players, troupe road manager, and household steward. The steward also provides them with the occasional special dish in addition to the regular "messes" served in the hall; and these three factors—being counted in the hall "extraordinary," either eating at or being accounted to the steward's board, and receiving additional fare on the steward's tab—make it quite clear that the players have come in the front door as welcome guests.[93]

Trying to calculate what the players' food costs would amount to is difficult, because they are eating higher on the great household hog than they most likely would purchase for themselves in a town, rather the difference between an expense account and one's own pocket. Andrew Gurr provides one approach to reckoning when he writes that "the Tudor soldier's daily food allowance was 24 ounces of wheat bread and two-thirds of a gallon of beer, each costing a penny; 2 pounds of beef or mutton (cod or herring on fish days), at a cost of $2d.$; half a pound of butter, and a pound of cheese. The cost of this diet under Elizabeth was about $6d.$, but food prices never recovered from the seven successive bad harvests at the end of the century, and rose by about 25 per cent [sic] in the early seventeeth century[,]" but a Tudor soldier's diet does not approximate even modest great hall fare.[94]

Breakfast "often was omitted" as unhealthful, but "when eaten, it usually consisted of bread and beer. . . . Breakfast in the household of Henry Percy, ninth earl of Northumberland, according to the household accounts from 1564 to 1632, for the earl and his lady on a 'flesh day' was 'a loofe of bred in trenchors, 2 manchets, 1 quart bere, 1 quart wyne, a Chyne of Muton or

Chyne of Beef Boilid'"; the two older sons had "'2 loaf of household Breid, a Manchet, 1 Potell [two quarts] of Bere, a Chekynge [chicken] or ells 3 mutton Bonys boyled."[95] The Cliffords' breakfast menu, fed to the players, is close to the Percys'.

Dinner consisted of three courses, the first of boiled dishes (e.g., salt beef with mustard, capon with leeks, mutton stuffed with garlic, boiled cabbage, boiled turnips), the second of roast meats (e.g., chickens, meat pies, venison pasty, shoulder of veal, a capon, a turkey cock, blackbirds, larks, woodcocks, partridges, loins of hare with black sauce), and third the desserts—fruit, such as roasted pears or apples, tarts, egg pies, cheese, and cakes. Robert May's "very modest six-dish courses . . . small menu" for February includes in the first course "'Eggs and Collops [bacon], Brawn and mustard, A hash of Rabbits, A grand Fricase, A grand Sallet, A Chine of roast Pork.' The second course is 'A whole Lamb roast, Three widgeons [a kind of small crane], A Pippin Pie, A Jole of Sturgeon. A Bacon Tart. A cold Turkey Pie.' For the banquet or dessert dishes he adds 'Jellies and Ginger-bread, and Tarts Royal.'"[96]

Even more startling is what Gervase Markham describes as "'a more humble Feast of an ordinary proportion, which any good man may keep in his Family, for the entertainment of his true and worthy friends[;] it must hold limitation with his provision, and the season of the year.'" His "humble" first course includes sixteen dishes—a shield of brawn with mustard, a boiled capon, a boiled piece of beef, a chine of beef roasted, a neat's tongue roasted, a roasted pig, baked chewets, a roasted goose, a roasted swan, a roasted turkey, a roasted haunch of venison, a venison pasty, a kid with a pudding in its belly, an olive-pie [of little meat rolls], a couple of capons, a custard or small tarts. But we are not done: "'Now to these full dishes may be added Sallets, Fricases, Quelquechoses, and devised paste, as many dishes more as will make the full service no less than two and thirty dishes[,] . . . as many as can conveniently stand on one Table . . . and after this manner you may proportion both your second and third course, holding fullness in one half of the dishes and shew [for example, pies empty of meat] in the other, which will be both frugall in the spender, contentment to the guest, and much pleasure and delight to the beholders.'"[97]

Supper was a rather more simple meal, one hopes, of bread, beer, and one course of dishes, sometimes the dinner leftovers which constitute a "scramble supper." The bread in the hall either was manchet, wheaten, or cheat: the quantities consumed can be determined from the Clifford pantry accounts but not by whom. In August 1593, from the Assize of Bread regulations, the approved weight for a penny wheaten loaf was 22 ounces; a half-penny white loaf weighed 24½ ounces in the 1540 Assize of Bread.[98] In addition to the three hall meals, the players also shared on occasion dishes of "butter and eggs," chalked up to the steward's board. Contemporary recipes for butter

PLAYING IN THE PROVINCE: FRONT OR BACK DOOR? 109

and egg dishes are plentiful: in "A Breviate touching the order and government of a Nobleman's House," ca. 1605, "butter and eggs, occasionally roasted, are on all the fish-day menus" and "Robert May gives more than seventy-five ways of 'Dressing Eggs.'"[99]

Finally, should players be unfortunate enough to miss dinner or supper, the Cliffords went out of their way to be hospitable. On December 22, 1575, at either Skipton Castle or nearby Barden Tower, the pantry steward records that "this daye was the players of otlaye . . . before din*ner* who dranke & had Rewarde & went ther wayes."[100] The Otley players, some fifteen miles from home and on their way over the moors either to a Christmastide engagement elsewhere or returning home for the holidays, nevertheless stop at Skipton to quaff their thirst and receive money, apparently without a formal performance. On June 6, 1594, at Londesborough, the Cliffords' East Riding seat, the steward records "that the musitions viz hewit and his men who came after Sup*per* had a kidde pie to there su*per* by my La: comandem*ent* 6 p*er*sons."[101] The steward's scrupulous attribution of this generosity to Lady Clifford is because "kid was a delicacy; in cookbook bills of fare it appears only on feast menus. When the Fairfax family entertained the earl of Rutland in 1579, and later in the year when they were entertaining the archbishop of York, roast kid was served to 'their lordships' tables,' as well as to the guests of somewhat lower rank 'at the board's end,' but it was not served to the guests' retinues."[102]

The Clifford and Cavendish accounts do not yield specifics on where the players slept, except that in the entry below they were housed indoors in "the chamber," for which a pound of candles is provided. As noted above, male servants might sleep on pallets in the great hall or in other lodgings separate from the building; the household steward sometimes lived over the kitchens in a separate chamber or in lodgings apart. If this Clifford pantry record represents a housing norm, the players most likely are accommodated indoors at the low or screens end of a great house. Thus far the candle entry is unique and, as often in pantry accounts, the totals do not seem to add up:

Ewry   Candles   iiij^{li} viij^{li} ds
In parler of 4^{li}—iiij my la. chamber i. of 8^{li} parler ij my la chamber j [?]
j mrs herds chamber j the hall i mrs constables chamber i mr denton j
of 12^{li} [?mr] j wardrop stares ij the hale 4 the players 3 kitchen 4
falk chamber j players in the chamber i dresser j butery seller & pantry iiij^{103}

Of the Londesborough ewery account for February 1, 1600/01, four pounds of candles are used for the hall; four for the kitchen; four for the buttery, cellar, and pantry; and a total of four for the players, perhaps three to light the performance and one to light their sleeping chamber. Regardless of how the candles were apportioned, the players do not seem to have lacked light, and the 1595 Skipton Castle inventory shows twenty-six casks of wax stored in the "great well chamber."[104] For a 1636/37 masque at Skipton the Clifford steward records 10s 6d "ffor Torches & wax candles," 5s 6d "ffor 4 branch Candlesticks making," 4s "ffor lattin for the Candlesticks," and 10s 6d total to Arthur the joiner for making the four-branch candlesticks, covering them with the sheets of latten (which probably also were fashioned into shields to catch the drip and increase reflected light), and rigging them on pulleys so that the candles could be changed out.[105] From formulae calculated by Roger Fouquet and Peter J. G. Pearson, a pound of tallow candles in the 1590s would have cost £1.15s.0d.[106] Usually sold by the pound in bundles of eight, ten, or twelve, everyday candles were made of animal fat, tallow, usually from mutton or cows, which produced a dark yellowish color; wax candles were far more expensive and burned more brightly. The Cavendish accounts also contain numerous payments for candles, which when culled should yield more precise costs.

A second yet unique Clifford entry, with equally baffling arithmetic, for January 26, 1612/13, provides three bushels—presumably 180 pounds—of coal for the players, here almost certainly to heat their chamber:

```
Coles
       Dicke moslar   2 ---------- 0 ---------- 0
       grate          3 --------------------- 3
       Tho:Catterson  5 --------------------- 0
       Laundry        2 --------------------- 0
       halle          2 --------------------- 0
       for the players 0 --------------------- 3
       kitchinge      5 --------------------- 2
              xxj bz[107]
```

England was in a timber crisis as early as the end of the twelfth century; by the fourteenth century iron industries in some parts of northern England— namely the Forest of Knaresborough and the Forest of Craven, near Skipton—had to close down for lack of fuel, which may explain why the Cliffords were using their coal rather than their wood resources. According to geologist Richard Cowen,

> In Elizabethan and Stuart England, prices for wood and charcoal grew faster than for any other major commodity. The Countess of Rutland (or her corrupt manager) apparently made a lot of money by obtaining Royal permission to take timber from Sherwood Forest to repair her castles and mills, then selling the timber on the black market. William Cecil, Lord Burghley (the Lord Treasurer) wrote to her in 1594, furious at this "very foule deceit and abuse toward mee and wrong to hir Majestie, which shall make mee more careful both in granting my warrants hereafter and in seeing them imployed to the use they are granted for." Every economic indicator

PLAYING IN THE PROVINCE: FRONT OR BACK DOOR?   111

suggests that the timber crisis was most acute in England from about 1570 to 1630. It is at this time that we see an unwilling but dramatic change to coal as the nation's industrial fuel.[108]

That charcoal prices were outrageous is documented by the Cavendishes' thriftily buying five dozen charcoals (presumably of fair size rather than the modern barbecue fuel) before they set out from Hardwick to high-street London in October 1605: "To Noble . . . makeinge 5 dozen of Charcole at v[s] per doson xxv[s]."[109]

Besides the players' room and board, whatever horses they brought to a great house also were accommodated, at a rate worth at least a shilling a day were they boarding the horses in a public stable: "Item more paid to thomas tomes for ther horssmeayte 3 nyght*es* and laiding [hay or straw bedding] iij[s] viij[d]."[110] Various recipes for "horsemeat," "horsebread," and "hogman" seem to involve various combinations of bran, ground peas, beans mixed with liquid, and oats, which then are baked as loaves in the household ovens. Additionally, some marshalsea accounts record daily horse provinder of a half-bushel or bushel of oats and armsful of hay.[111] Besides lading, the players' horses also could freeload tackle repairs, blacksmith repairs, shoeing, and veterinary care when necessary, which called for such palliatives as fat or grease, tallow (often applied to the legs and feet), honey, butter, wort (unfermented ale), lard, garlic, olive oil, plasters, or pills.

The astute reader by now will have noticed that despite the Cliffords' four-branch reflecting candlesticks, torches, and wax candles, this paper sheds little light on actual provincial performances as contrasted with potential performance conditions. As often is the case in social history studies, surviving primary documents record what went wrong rather than what went right. If memory serves, Richard Altick labeled the resultant imbalance "the Old Bailey" method of research, which means that among the heap of Clifford and Cavendish entertainment accounts the fourteen records of payments "not to play" may attract more interest than the hundreds of uneventful performances. The Cholmley players' repertory survived as a recusant trial record, not as a commendation of their acting abilities. Thus we know when something misfired in the elaborate arrangements which always constitute touring—the plague (or a sudden awareness of Lent) erupts, Lord Clifford unexpectedly must travel, the players go to Hardwick but Bess is at Chatsworth, a second troupe arrives at Londesborough claiming to be the same troupe already in residence—with its inevitable risks of bad information, bad timing, bad luck, and bad roads.[112] On the overwhelming majority of occasions, however, matters went smoothly. Traveling players came into the great hall by the front door, not the back. They and their horses were welcomed, fed, warmed, lighted, repaired, stabled, bedded, paid, and appreciated by these provincial great households, in the progress of their travels weaving a rich strand through the tapestry of early English drama.

Notes

1. E. K. Chambers, *The Elizabethan Stage* (Oxford: Clarendon, 1923), 4:270.
2. Chambers, *The Elizabethan Stage,* 2:87–88.
3. Chambers, *The Elizabethan Stage,* 4:324–25; 1:299. Richard Dutton, *Licensing, Censorship and Authorship in Early Modern England: Buggeswords* (New York: Palgrave, 2000), 8, notes that the February 1597/98 act's removing the right of justices of the peace to authorize playing meant that "[p]atronage was restricted exclusively to the peerage, while the penalties against masterless men were made even more draconian." A helpful overview of county governance complexities is Candace Gregory, "Sixteenth-Century Justices of the Peace: Tudor Despotism on the County Level," *The Student Historical Journal* 22 (Chicago: Loyola University, 1990–91), available online at http://www.loyno.edu/history/journal/1990–1/gregory.htm.
4. John Tucker Murray, "English Dramatic Companies in the Towns outside of London, 1550–1600," *Modern Philology* 2 (1905): 559.
5. Murray, *English Dramatic Companies 1558–1642* (London: Constable & Co., 1910; rpt. New York: Russell & Russell, 1963), 2:110.
6. Chambers, *The Elizabethan Stage,* 1:280 n. 2.
7. The payments' table (Appendix A) was compiled for my study "Early Modern Mobility: Players, Payments, and Patrons," *Shakespeare Quarterly* 56, no. 3 (Fall 2005): 259–305; the data also are reproduced in "On the Road and on the Wagon," *Locating the Queen's Men: Material Practices and Conditions of Playing* (Aldershot: Ashgate Publishing, forthcoming 2008). Further raids for this present study have pillaged "Star Turns or Small Companies?"—*"Bring furth the pagants": Festschrift in Honor of Alexandra F. Johnston,* ed. David Klausner and Karen S. Marsalek (Toronto: University of Toronto Press, 2007), 9–40; "'The husbandry and manage of my house': Teaching Women's Studies from the Records of Early English Drama Collections," *Teaching with the Records of Early English Drama,* ed. Elza C. Tiner, Studies in Early English Drama (SEED) series (Toronto: University of Toronto Press, 2006), 142–53; and "Great Halls . . . and the Renaissance Center," *The Massachusetts Center for Renaissance Studies Newsletter,* Autumn 2006: 18–19.
8. See Scott McMillin and Sally-Beth MacLean, *The Queen's Men and their Plays* (Cambridge: Cambridge University Press, 1998), 37–83 for a detailed analysis of a prominent London company on regular rather than intermittent tour.
9. John Wasson, "Professional Actors in the Middle Ages and Early Renaissance," *Medieval and Renaissance Drama in England* 1 (New York: AMS Press, 1984), 4.
10. Palmer, "Mobility," 276 and n. 63; McMillin and MacLean, 108.
11. Terminology ambiguities long have haunted early drama studies: Glynne Wickham in *Early English Stages* and, after him, Suzanne Westfall in *Patrons and Performance: Early Tudor Household Revels* conflate the Selby Abbey entertainment terminology of *ministrallus, mimus, histrio, ludo, ludus, lusor, iocus,* and *ioculator* into the English "players." Palmer, "Early English Northern Entertainment: Patterns and Peculiarities," *Research Opportunities in Renaissance Drama* 34 (1995): 171.
12. Murray, "English Dramatic Companies," *Modern Philology,* 551, citing the published records of Nottingham, Doncaster, and Shrewsbury.
13. Chambers, *The Elizabethan Stage,* 1:280 n. 2.

PLAYING IN THE PROVINCE: FRONT OR BACK DOOR? 113

14. David George, ed., *REED: Lancashire* (Toronto: University of Toronto Press, 1991), 350. He further notes that no evidence proves "William Shakshafte" to be William Shakespeare "and the name 'Shakeshaft' is common in Lancashire even today."

15. Chambers, *The Elizabethan Stage,* 1:304–7.

16. See Palmer, "Star Turns," 19–20, on provincial licensing as "a cottage industry by duplicating royal letters patent for spin-off troupes."

17. I am grateful to William Lloyd for sharing with me his preliminary notes on "King's or No King's," his in-progress study of player William Perry's career.

18. David Galloway, ed., *REED: Norwich 1540–1642* (Toronto: University of Toronto Press, 1984), 151–52. See 142–52 ff. for an astounding succession of players and patents assaulting the Norwich council within a relatively short time.

19. The York clerk on September 9, 1587, notes that the Queen's Men came in her majesty's livery, rewarding them £3 6s 8d for playing in the Common Hall. See J. Leeds Barroll, "Drama and the court," *The* Revels *History of Drama in English* (London: Methuen, 1975), 3:6–8 for the 1572 statute on retainers, livery, and badges.

20. Palmer, "Mobility," 300–302, drawn from the Clifford accounts now at Chatsworth; manuscript descriptions, folio numbers, and bibliographic annotation will be available when the complete West Riding–Derbyshire collections have been checked and prepared for REED publication.

21. Such modern scholars as R. A. Foakes, Roslyn L. Knutson, Susan Cerasano, Herbert Berry, William Ingram, and others have redressed earlier neglect of the economics of playing and the role of London theater entrepreneurs.

22. As noted above (n. 17), William Lloyd presently is tracking William Perry, but Ellis Guest, Thomas Swinerton, and dozens of other "provincial" troupe leaders are well worth renewed scholarly pursuit, however humbling the chase. Disley's path through the records is particularly full of brambles, which is why I am correcting here for the record my errata in the "Mobility" and "Star Turns" appendix tables. Erratum in "Early Modern Mobility": p. 297, entry for 4.21.1601, Londesborough: delete "Lord Shrewsbury." Errata in "Star Turns": appendix 2, "Disley the player and his company," p. 28. Entry for "7.25.1621": date should be changed to "b/wn 7.25–9.22.1620" and the entry moved up to follow the entry for "9.9.1619." Entry for "6.11.1625": date should be changed to "7.27.1625" and the note "[apparently with Perry & company]" deleted. Entry dated "February 1627/8": date should be changed to 2.23.1626/7 and the date of Shrove Tuesday in the note should be changed to 2.21.1626/7.

23. Chambers, *The Elizabethan Stage,* 1:304. One eventually locates the Simpsons not under their own names nor even under that of Sir Richard Cholmley, their patron, but under Sir John Yorke, and then as footnotes (1:304–5, 328) to a discussion of warrants, patents, and licensing which concludes that "in the provinces the patented companies had no monopoly; side by side with them still wandered both unlicensed vagrants and the protected servants of noblemen."

24. Chambers, *The Elizabethan Stage,* 2:303–4.

25. Ibid., 2:120, 124.

26. Murray, *English Dramatic Companies,* 2:42–43, 106–10.

27. Ibid., 2:163ff.

28. Elizabeth Baldwin, Lawrence M. Clopper, and David Mills, eds., *REED:*

Cheshire including Chester (Toronto: University of Toronto Press, 2007), 1:293; and C. R. Cheney, *Handbook of Dates* (London: Royal Historical Society, 1978), 25.

29. My skepticism at basing itineraries or any other theater history on the defendants' court testimony alone stems from accounts by Sir Richard Cholmley's players (Simpson's troupe), the putative audience members, and Sir John Yorke's family, friends, neighbors, enemies, and household, immortalized in the Star Chamber and North Riding Quarter Session records and to be published in REED: West Riding. A more inventive, chatty, and hilariously amusing group of folks I cannot imagine as they recount what they may or may not have seen, what may or may not have been played, who may or may not have been there, who may or may not have played it, and where or where not they themselves may or may not have been. I see no reason to assume Bradshaw's players any less self-protective in their testimony.

30. G. E. Bentley, *The Jacobean and Caroline Stage* (Oxford: Clarendon, 1941), 2:387–88. Bentley sounds bemused as he notes Nungezer's 1590s-1600s' citations to Bradshaw and concludes that "[t]he Richard Bradshaw of 1630 and 1633 must have been a different actor, for it is unlikely that a man could have been acting for twenty-five years in the provinces without leaving another record. Yet it is curious that a second actor of the name should also have performed in the provinces only. The Lord Dudley's player of 1595 was probably at least thirty, since he was a leader of the troupe; surely he would not have been still dashing about the country at the age of sixty-eight. On the whole it seems to me more probable that there were two Richard Bradshaws, provincial actors."

31. See Palmer, "Star Turns or Small Companies?", which cites for Disley references Murray, *English Dramatic Companies 1558–1642,* 2:42–44; Edwin Nungezer, *A Dictionary of Actors* (New Haven: Yale University Press, 1929), 116; Bentley, *The Jacobean and Caroline Stage,* 2:423; George, *REED: Lancashire;* H. Maxwell Lyte and W.H. Stevenson, eds., "Extracts from Household Accounts," *HMC Report on the Manuscripts of the Duke of Rutland Preserved at Belvoir Castle* (1905), 4:464; John Wasson, "Elizabethan and Jacobean Touring Companies," *Theatre Notebook* 42 (1988): 51–52; Alan C. Coman, "The Congleton accounts: further evidence of Elizabethan and Jacobean drama in Cheshire," *Records of Early English Drama Newsletter* 14, no. 1 (1989): 7. Lawrence Stone cites Murray's and Bentley's 1610 start date for Disley but adds the 1617–19 Londesborough records (Malone Society *Collections* V, 28, n. 21).

32. Based on the Dulwich papers, Chambers states that "Mr" designates a sharer and the title's omission a non-sharer; that dividing line may apply to London companies, but terminology for provincial players seems to be more flexible, variable, and ambiguous (*English Stage,* 2:125–26). See appendix B.

33. Palmer, "Star Turns," 16.

34. Palmer and John M. Wasson are coediting the West Riding and Derbyshire collections for REED; their unpublished records included here acknowledge the kindness of the Dowager Duchess, the late Duke of Devonshire, and the Trustees of Chatsworth Settlement. I am indebted to Sally-Beth MacLean for allowing me to consult John Coldewey's work on Nottinghamshire and the late Alice Hamilton's extensive work on the Leicestershire collection, both on deposit at the REED Office in Toronto.

35. In a very complicated scenario which I have laid out in "Star Turns," during the week of Shrovetide 1597/98 the Cliffords saw at Londesborough the household musicians; a professional dancer; John Wilson, the lead player of a professional troupe from

PLAYING IN THE PROVINCE: FRONT OR BACK DOOR?   115

Kirkby Stephen, Westmorland; two Kirkby Stephen musicians; some or all of Derby's dozen players; some or all of Wharton's players; and a company claiming to be Derby's players. I am highly tempted to speculate that Disley and Richard Bradshaw could be somewhere in that "Derby/not-Derby" mix. Bradshaw's London master, Gabriel Spencer, was imprisoned in July 1597 for his role in *The Isle of Dogs'* dustup. The Chester warrant for Bradshaw's and Coffyn's heading up Dudley's players is dated either February 16, 1595/96 or February 16, 1598/99, (see above), which may mean that around 1597 Bradshaw wisely turned his eyes north while not severing his London ties. Although Disley is not identified in the records as the head of Dudley's players until 1612, Disley had a company by 1601, a date within the time frame to reflect Dudley's shift of players by 1602. These musings are tentative, to echo Murray, but sufficiently documented to include the various Derby and Dudley records in appendix B.

36. If Hazlewood is misplaced in Murray's map, it is misowned in Lawrence Stone's "Companies of Players Entertained by the Earl of Cumberland and Lord Clifford, 1607–39," Malone Society *Collections* V (Oxford: Oxford University Press, 1959/60), 17–28. Stone gives Hazlewood to the Cliffords ("Francis, 4th Earl of Cumberland, who resided mostly at Londesborough, with occasional removals to Hazelwood [*sic*]"), a transfer which no doubt would have discomforted the powerful Vavasours, owners of Hazlewood since the thirteenth century.

37. Palmer, "Mobility," 287–88.

38. Ibid., 280–81.

39. Richard T. Spence, *Skipton Castle and Its Builders* (Skipton, Yorkshire: Skipton Castle, 2002), 106. How to reconcile the Stamford waits' protracted absence with their civic responsibilities is puzzling. The August 14, 1615 Coventry regulations are typical: "At this day it is agreed that Edward Man, Roger Newland, Iohn Ielfes, [&] Iohn Hill, & Will*iam* Holsworth, shall goe to play w*ith* the waytes about the Cytie according to the ancient Custom of the said Cytie, for w*hich* they are to haue seven pounds by the yere in money and quarteridg, . . . so that they play orderly as thei should, out of w*hich* allowance they are to furnish them selues w*ith* comely and sufficient Cloakes for the cr*ed*it of the place, they are also to play at all solom ffeast*es,* at Mr Maiors commaund and not to goe forth of the Cytie with out licence obtained therof the s*aid* Mr Maior." R. W. Ingram, ed., *REED: Coventry* (Toronto: University of Toronto Press, 1981), 393.

40. Barrell, *Revels History,* 3:36. See also his table I: Court Performances and table 2: Performances, 3:49–94; Barroll, *Politics, Plague, and Shakespeare's Theater: The Stuart Years* (Ithaca: Cornell University Press, 1991); and F. P. Wilson, *The Plague in Shakespeare's England* (London: Oxford University Press, 1927; rpt. 1963).

41. Cameron Louis, ed., *REED: Sussex* (Toronto: University of Toronto Press, 2000), 90, 91; and James M. Gibson, ed., *REED: Kent: Diocese of Canterbury* (Toronto: University of Toronto Press, 2002), 2:681, 683.

42. Louis, *Sussex,* 273; and Gibson, *Kent,* 3:1348, citing Suzanne R. Westfall, *Patrons and Performance: Early Tudor Household Revels* (Oxford: Oxford University Press, 1990), 145.

43. Ingram, *REED: Coventry,* 393–95, 596.

44. Palmer, "Star Turns," 22–23.

45. Galloway, *REED: Norwich,* 93. Under the command of Drake and Sir John

Norris, "[t]he expedition, divided in its command and in its objectives, failed. Among the heavy casualties were three of the Norwich waits." (396).

46. George, *REED: Lancashire,* 87, 334.

47. John M. Wasson, *REED: Devon* (Toronto: University of Toronto Press, 1986), 156.

48. Mary Edmond, "Pembroke's Men," *RES,* n.s. 25 (1974): 129–36; Scott McMillin, "Simon Jewell and the Queen's Men," *RES,* n.s. 27 (1976): 174–77; and McMillin and MacLean, *Queen's Men,* 61–62. I am grateful to Roslyn L. Knutson for drawing the Edmond and McMillin articles to my attention.

49. McMillin, "Simon Jewel," 177 ; and McMillin and MacLean, *Queen's Men,* 62.

50. Alexandra F. Johnston and Margaret Rogerson, eds., *REED: York,* 2 vols. (Toronto: University of Toronto Press, 1979), 1:449.

51. Gibson, *REED: Kent,* 2:563, who notes that "[t]he mayoral and civic accounting year in Faversham began and ended at Michaelmas" (1:cxxviii). Murray, *English Dramatic Companies,* 2:274 also cited the record, which he found in J. W. Cowper, *On Some Tudor Prices in Kent and Notes from the Records of Faversham* (1871), 26–27.

52. Peter H. Greenfield, "Entertainments of Henry, Lord Berkeley, 1593–4 and 1600–5," *REED Newsletter* 8, no. 1 (1983): 12–24. In addition to this Lord Berkeley, for whom REED lists alternative spellings of "Barlett" and "Bartley," Murray, *English Dramatic Companies,* 2:397 cites Sir Richard Bartlett as a patron in 1576–77, a date incompatible with the wagon incident.

53. Leslie Hotson, *Shakespeare's Wooden O* (New York: Macmillan, 1960), 70; cited by Glynne Wickham, *Early English Stages 1300 to 1660,* 2 vols. (New York: Columbia University Press, 1963), 2.1:189, who in turn is quoted by David Gallaway, "Records of Early English Drama in the Provinces and what they may tell us about the Elizabethan Theatre," *The Elizabethan Theatre* 7 (1980): 97. The entry is not contained in *REED: Herefordshire/Worcestershire,* ed. David N. Klausner (Toronto: University of Toronto Press, 1990), probably because of the way Star Chamber cases are indexed at what is now the National Archives at Kew. Hotson does not reveal what the case was about but his note to "Ralph third Lord Eure, of New Malton, Yorkshire" (70, n. 1) suggests that Star Chamber 8/307/14 may be indexed under Yorkshire rather than either Worcestershire or Shropshire, where Eure in fact maintained his official residence at Ludlow Castle. My thanks to William Lloyd for tracing this wagon reference.

54. Hotson, 64.

55. Nicholas Cooper, *Houses of the Gentry 1480–1680* (London: English Heritage, 1999), 18, quoting Wye Saltonstall, *Picturae loquentes* (London: Luttrell Society, 1946; written 1631), 26.

56. Cooper, 11, quoting Henry Wotton, *Elements of Architecture* (London, 1624), 82.

57. Felicity Heal, *Hospitality in Early Modern England* (Oxford: Clarendon, 1990), 32.

58. HMC *Report on the Manuscripts of Lord Middleton Preserved at Wollaton Hall, Nottinghamshire* (London: His Majesty's Stationery Office, 1911), 538–39. Alice T. Friedman, *House and Household in Elizabethan England: Wollaton Hall and the Willoughby Family* (Chicago: University of Chicago Press, 1989), 41, claims that these "are the only set of regulations to survive for an upper gentry household,"

PLAYING IN THE PROVINCE: FRONT OR BACK DOOR?

which may or may not still be valid but there is no shortage of information on orderly household governance. For other contemporary household ordinances, see Heal's bibliography in *Hospitality;* Mark Girouard, *Life in the English Country House: A Social and Architectural History* (New Haven: Yale University Press, 1978); and http://elizabethan.org.

59. Heal, *Hospitality,* 47, citing Kate Mertes, *The English Noble Household, 1250–1600* (Oxford: Blackwell, 1988), app. C.

60. Spence, *Skipton Castle,* 70, 91.

61. Spence, *Skipton Castle,* 102; Palmer, "Mobility," 276; and Friedman, *Wollaton,* 41.

62. Spence, *Skipton Castle,* 92.

63. Friedman, *Wollaton,* 44, who also notes that Sir Francis Willoughby's household steward was his relative Henry Willoughby, who was paid the highest stipend of the Wollaton staff, £1 13s 4d the quarter, in 1572. Shakespeare creates at least eight household stewards or characters who function as household stewards in his plays, the most complex of which are Malvolio and Polonius—a subject which awaits another opportunity than the present.

64. S. D. Scott, ed., "A Book of Orders and Rules of Anthony Viscount Montague in 1595," *Sussex Archaeological Collections* 7 (1853–54): 173–212. Maggie Secara's edited, modernized version can be accessed at http://www.elizabethan.org.

65. Spence, 106, identifies Hingeston, with a portrait reproduced by permission of the Faculty of Music, University of Oxford, on facing page 107. The rest of the Clifford musicians are very much a work-in-progress for the REED West Riding collection.

66. Friedman, *Walloaton,* 29, 20, and n37.

67. Palmer, "Mobility," 275–77, 285; and "Star Turns," 20–24.

68. See Palmer, "On the Road and on the Wagon" and "Great Halls . . . and the Renaissance Center." For numerous examples of great halls, see the REED "Patrons and Performances Web Site" with REED Executive Editor Sally-Beth MacLean's detailed images and explications of documented performance venues (http://eir.library.utoronto.ca/reed).

69. Cooper, 275. His unit in *Houses of the Gentry* on the hall, 275–89, is a well-documented primer.

70. Spence, *Skipton Castle,* 81–83.

71. Friedman, *Hospitality,* 40.

72. Richard Southern, *The Staging of Plays before Shakespeare* (New York: Theatre Arts Books, 1973), 53–54 and plate 1.

73. Irwin Smith, *Shakespeare's Blackfriars Playhouse, Its History and Its Design* (New York: New York University Press, 1964), 301.

74. Smith, *Blackfriars,* 318.

75. Alan C. Dessen and Leslie Thomson, *A Dictionary of Stage Directions in English Drama, 1580–1642* (Cambridge: Cambridge University Press, 1999), 186.

76. William Shakespeare, *The Taming of the Shrew,* 4.1.40–45, 79–85, in David Bevington, ed., *The Complete Works of Shakespeare,* 5th ed. (New York: Pearson Longman, 2004).

77. The painting is in the National Portrait Gallery: see http://www.npg.org.uk and search under "Sir Henry Unton."

78. Southern, *Staging,* 53.

79. Spence, *Skipton Castle,* 109, who notes that players' rewards are increased by "hospitality thrown in and [Clifford's] friends showing their own appreciation." In calculating players' payments at great houses I had not weighed this potential profit factor but will do so, as the documents allow, when preparing the West Riding and Derbyshire collections for REED publication.

80. Smith, *Blackfriars,* 147.

81. Galloway, "Records of Early English Drama in the Provinces," 93.

82. McMillin and MacLean, *Queen's Men,* 108.

83. In dismissing this rich episode as Sir John Yorke's "encouraging some vagrant players to perform an interlude in favour of the Popish religion," Chambers, *Elizabethan Stage,* 1:328, cites Harl. 1227, which he read in J. S. Burn, *The Star Chamber* (London, 1870), 78; and the North Riding Quarter Session Records as further evidence of "the workings of the Vagabond Acts" (1:304–5).

84. In the mid-1980s John L. Murphy (*Darkness and Devils*) generously brought the 131-folio scrawl which is PRO STAC 8/19/10 to John Wasson's attention.

85. Controlled pyrotechnics, indoors and out, long have been standard spectacle in English drama: see Philip Butterworth, *Theatre of Fire: Special Effects in Early English and Scottish Theatre* (London: Society for Theatre Research, 1998).

86. Yorkshire Archaeological Society, Leeds, MS 707, mb 4–5.

87. George, *REED: Lancashire,* 153.

88. Spence, *Skipton Castle,* 110, makes this identification of Hendrick de Keyser the younger, which I have not yet been able to confirm independently.

89. Chatsworth, Bolton Abbey MS 175, fols. 182, 182ᵛ˙ Spence misreads "scene" as "screen." With 12s 7d of "Tinfoyle & diuerse cullers," Hendrick painted the masque scene on the "diuerse yard*es* of Canvas for the Scene"; the joiner probably framed or stabilized the scene with wood and then unassembled it after the masque.

90. Peter Brears, *Tudor Cookery: Recipes and History* (Swindon: English Heritage, 1985; rev. ed. 2003), 75.

91. Heal, *Hospitality,* 153–58.

92. Brears, *Tudor Cookery,* 77.

93. The Cliffords seem to have set at least three boards: the lord's, the lady's, and the steward's. For further discussion of players either at or accounted to the steward's board, see Palmer, "Mobility," 275; and "Star Turns," 20–24, 30–33.

94. Andrew Gurr, *The Shakespearean Stage 1574–1642,* 3rd ed. (Cambridge: Cambridge University Press, 1992), 12–13.

95. Madge Lorwin, *Dining with William Shakespeare* (New York: Atheneum, 1976), 151–52.

96. Lorwin, *Dining,* 156, quoting Robert May, *The Accomplisht Cook, or the Art and Mystery of Cookery* (London, 1660).

97. Lorwin, *Dining,* 157, quoting Gervase Markham's *The English Hus-wife* (London, 1615).

98. Lorwin, *Dining,* 314.

99. Lorwin, *Dining,* 252, citing "A Breviate touching the order and government of a Nobleman's House," Sir Joseph Banks, ed., *Archaeologia* 13 (1800); and Robert May, *The Accomplisht Cook.*

PLAYING IN THE PROVINCE: FRONT OR BACK DOOR? 119

100. Chatsworth, Bolton Abbey MS 13, f 75.

101. Chatsworth, Bolton Abbey MS 13a, f 14.

102. Lorwin, *Dining,* 208.

103. Chatsworth, Bolton Abbey MS 39, f 1v.

104. Spence, *Skipton Castle,* 83.

105. Chatsworth, Bolton Abbey MS 175, f 181v. Strong lighting also illuminates the Sir Henry Unton painting with the masquers carrying lighted tapers and light streaming through the great chamber windows. In 1568 the Newcastle Chamberlains spent 2s in four links (torches) "to the playe" performed by the players of Durham. See J. J. Anderson, ed., *REED: Newcastle upon Tyne* (Toronto: University of Toronto Press, 1982), 53.

106. Roger Fouquet and Peter J. G. Pearson, "Long Run Trends in Energy Services: The Price and Use of Light in the United Kingdon (1500–2000)," Centre for Energy Policy and Technology, Imperial College London, September 2003, from a conference paper no longer available online.

107. Chatsworth, Bolton Abbey MS 62, f 10v. In 1568 the Newcastle Chamberlains spent 12d "for iij laid [loads] of colles for fyer to the playe*rs*": Anderson, *REED: Newcastle upon Tyne,* 53.

108. Richard Cowen, Notes for Geology 115, "Geology, History, and People" at http://www.geology.ucdavis.edu/~cowen/~GEL115/; consequent book, "Exploiting the Earth," reported on the Web site as under contract to Johns Hopkins University Press.

109. Chatsworth, Hardwick MS 10b, f 63.

110. Chatsworth, Bolton Abbey MS 142, f 13.

111. C. M. Woolgar, *The Great Household in Late Medieval England* (New Haven: Yale University Press, 1999), 191–92.

112. Palmer, "Mobility," 279–80, 303–4.

APPENDIX A

COMPARATIVE PAYMENTS TO TRAVELING PROFESSIONAL COMPANIES:
CITY OF YORK 1576–1636
BOROUGH OF DONCASTER 1574–1642
HOUSEHOLDS OF CLIFFORDS, EARLS OF CUMBERLAND 1594–1635
(Skipton Castle and Londesborough)
HOUSEHOLDS OF BESS OF HARDWICK, WILLIAM CAVENDISH 1593–1620
(Chatsworth and Hardwick)

Decade	Total Visits	Played Towns	Played Houses	Average £ Towns	Average £ Houses	# Times "Not to Play"	Average Towns £	Average Houses £
1570s	13	12	0	13s.6d.	—	1 T	5s	—
1580s	22	22	0	27s	—	0	—	—
1590s	69	25	37	30s	10s + keep	7 6T, 1H	25s	3s.4d
1600s	36	16	15	26s	12s + keep	5 3T, 2H	30s	10s
1610s	52	15	30	21s	35s + keep	7 1T, 6H	10s	13s.8d
1620s	34	12	17	15s.6d	62s + keep	5 5H	—	10s
1630s	29	22	6	15s.6d	20s +keep	1 1T	5s	—
1640s	1	1	0	10s	—	0		
TOTAL	**256**	**125**	**105**			**26: T12, H14**		

120   BARBARA D. PALMER

APPENDIX B
EARL OF DERBY'S PLAYERS
**[William Stanley (ca. 1561–September 29, 1642),
succeeded as 15th earl April 16, 1594]**

Troupe Name	Place	Date	Payment	Source
Earl of Derby's players	Norwich	9.15.1594	20s	Norwich 105, Chambers 2:127
Lord Derby's players	Dunwich, Suffolk	1594/95	5s	Malone XI, 156, Chambers 2:127
Earl of Darby's players	Dunwich, Suffolk	1595/96	5s	Malone XI, 156, Chambers 2:127
Earl of Derby's players	Gloucester	1595–96	30s	Gloucester 314
Earl of Derby's players	Canterbury	1595–96	18s	Kent 1:232
Lord Derby's players	Bath	1595–96	14s 6d	Somerset 1:17
Derby's players	Stratford	1595–96		Chambers 2:127
Derby's players	Leicester	Oct–Dec 1596		Chambers 2:127
Earl of Derby's players	Oxford	1596	20s	Oxford 1:240
Earl of Derby's players	Coventry	1596	10s	Coventry 346
Lord of Derby's players played in the Guildhall	Bristol	11–24 July 1596	30s	Bristol 147
Lord Derby and Lord Darcy's players	York	30 Sept 1596	10s	York 1:471
Lord Derby's players	Bath	1596–97	13s 4d	Somerset 1:17
Derby's players	Maldon, Essex	1597		Chambers 2:127
Lord of Derby's players	Bristol	4.24–5.14.1597	10s	Bristol 150
Earl of Derby's players	Coventry	1597	10s	Coventry 349
Derby's players	Leicester	1597–98		Chambers 2:127
Earl of Derby's players	Kendal	1597–98	10s	Westmorland 177
Earl of Derby's players	Leominster	1597–98	10s	Herefordshire 146
Lord of Derby's playres/"for 3 playes"	Londesborough	2.27.1597/98	20s + 3s8d for horsemeat, hay	Unpub MS
another company claiming to be Lord of Darby's players	Londesborough	2.27.1597/98	3s 4d not to play	Unpub MS
Lord of Darby's players	Londesborough	3.2.1597/98	10s	Unpub MS
Lord of Darby's players/11	Londesborough	3.1–2.1598/99	5s + 2 dinners and supper	Unpub MS
Earl of Derby's players	Coventry	1598	10s	Coventry 350
Earl of Derby's players by a mayor's warrant	Coventry	1598	20s	Coventry 351
Derby's players	Leicester	Oct–Dec 1598		Chambers 2:127
Derby's players	Wollaton, Notts: Percival Willoughby's	10.7.1599		Chambers 2:127
Derby's players	Leicester	10.16.1599		Chambers 2:127

PLAYING IN THE PROVINCE: FRONT OR BACK DOOR? 121

Troupe Name	Place	Date	Payment	Source
500s				
Earl of Derby's servants to show their devices & sports	Norwich	27 Feb 1601/2		Norwich 120
Earl of Derby's players	Faversham	10 Mar 1601–2	10s	Kent 2:565
Earl of Derby's players	Coventry	1602	13s 4d	Coventry 360
Earl of Derby's players not to play in Norwich by mayor's command	Norwich	10 June 1602		Norwich 120
Lord darbies players	Coventry	1603	5s	Coventry 362
Earl of Derby's players	Coventry	1604	5s	Coventry 364
Earl of Derby's players	Coventry	1607	10s	Coventry 371
Earl of Derby's players	Barnstaple	1607–8	10s	Devon 48
Earl of Derby's players	Coventry	Dec1608	10s	Coventry 373
Earl of Derby's men	Kendal	3.18.1608–9	5s	Westmorland 181
Lord Derby's players	Coventry	24 May 1609	10s	Coventry 376
Derby's players	Gawthorpe	2 Dec 1609	6s 8d	Lancs 170
510s				
Lord Darby's players /14	Londesborough	6.6.1611	£3: played 2 plays on 5 June (1 after dinner & 1 after supper)	Unpub MS
Earl of Derby's players	Coventry	1612	10s	Coventry 384
Lord Darby's players/13	Londesborough	3.26.1612	£4 for 4 plays: there 2 days & 2 nights	Unpub MS
Derby's players	Gawthorpe	12 Aug 1612	26s 8d	Lancs 173
Derby's players	Gawthorpe	12 Dec 1612	8s 4d	Lancs 174
my Lord of Darbie his . . .	Gawthorpe	4–21 Sept 1613	20s	Lancs 175
Derby's players	Dunkenhalgh	before 14 Jan1613–14	20s	Lancs 185
Lord Darby's players	Skipton	5.31.1615	£5: Skipton summary record 12.21.1613 to 5.31.1615	Unpub MS
Derby's players	Dunkenhalgh	21 July 1615	13s 4d	Lancs 185
Lord of Derby's players	Coventry	14 May 1616	10s	Coventry 397
Derby's players	Gawthorpe	18 March 1616/17	3s 4d	Lancs 176
Derby's men	Dunkenhalgh	22 March1616/17	13s 4d	Lancs 187
Lord Darby's players: Bradshaw & his company	Skipton	7.28.1617	20s "in reward from my Lo: in spit he wold not heare them play"	Unpub MS
Derby's men	Dunkenhalgh	2 Aug 1617	20s	Lancs 188
Earl of Derby's players	Leominster	1616–17	5s	Herefordshire 148

BARBARA D. PALMER

Troupe Name	Place	Date	Payment	Source
Lord Darby's players	Londesborough	2.4.1619/20	£5 for 5 plays: stayed 3 nights	Unpub MS
Derby's men	Dunkenhalgh	12 Feb 1619/20	10s	Lancs 189
Earl of Derby's players	Leominster	1619–20	6s 8d	Herefordshire 149

1620s

Troupe Name	Place	Date	Payment	Source
Earl of Derby's players	Workington	12–13 Dec1628	20s	Cumberland 129
Earl of Derby's players	Kendal	1628–9	5s	Westmorland 204
Derby's players one night [pantry a/c]	Dunkenhalgh	11.25–12.1. 1620		Lancs 190
Lord Darby's players	Londesborough	12.2.1624	10s not to play	Unpub MS
Derby's players [pantry a/c]	Dunkenhalgh	2.4–10.1624–25		Lancs 193

1630s

Troupe Name	Place	Date	Payment	Source
Earl of Derby's players	Kendal	23 Nov 1635	10s	Westmorland 212
Lord Darby's players	Doncaster	2.5.1636/37	6s 8d	Unpub MS

RICHARD BRADSHAW THE PLAYER
(active 1594–1633)

Troupe Name	Date	Place	Payment	Source	Other Info
?Spencer's 'man'	[Bradshaw]end of 1592–93	London		Wentersdorf 65	**Gabriel Spencer with Pembroke's players**
?Spencer's 'man' [Bradshaw]	1597	Feb–July: the Swan; Fall: the Rose:		Wentersdorf 64–66	**Spencer with Pembroke's & then to Admiral's**
Bradshaw, Rich	2.16.1595 or 1598/9	Chester: warrant to play all over country		Murray 2:42 Chester 177–78	**Dudley's servants francis Coffyn and rich bradshaw**
	by 11.11.1602	warrant revoked		Chester 178	**Dudley has appointed others, discharged Coffyn et al. named above**
Bradshawe	5.19.1598	London		Henslowe 83	10s lent to Gabriel Spencer to buy plume of feathers: his mane bradshawe feched of me
Richard Bradhawe	10.10.1598	St Saviour's Southwark		Henslowe 287, Nungezer 55	bond of 50s to Wm Bird to be pd 3.2.1599
Bradshawe	10.16.1598	London		Henslowe 100	30s to Dekker & Drayton for Conan, Prince of Cornwall; 10s more, both sums by Bradshaw's hand
Richard Bradshawe, player	12.15.1600	in London but Bradshaw away		Henslowe 165	sold 1 lb. 2 oz. copper lace for 14s to be pd when he returns again to London*

PLAYING IN THE PROVINCE: FRONT OR BACK DOOR?

Troupe Name	Date	Place	Payment	Source	Other Info
Richard Bradshawe player	4.29.1601	in London but Bradshaw away		Henslowe 165	lent 5s more in mony to be payd at his next Retorne to london
Richard Bradshaa	1.8.1604	St. Saviour's, Southwark		Henslowe 287, Nungezer 55	Bird's 10s debt to Alleyn to be pd by Bradshaw as owing on bond above
Lord Darby's players: Bradshaw & his company	7.28.1617	Skipton, West Riding	20s not to play	Unpub MS	"in reward from my Lo: in spit he wold not heare them play"
mr Bradshaw 2	1.26–2.1. 1621/2	Dunkenhalgh, Lancs		Lancs 191	pantry a/c: 2 nights board
Bradshaw the player & his co.	2.11.1624/5	Dunkenhalgh	20s	Lancs 193	
King's players	6.14.1625	Doncaster	10s	Unpub MS	**"mr Bradshawe & his Company the Kinges players"**
Bradshay the plaier	1.2.1625/6	Dunkenhalgh		Lancs 195	one night: pantry a/c
Bradshaw & his company	8.26.1626	Dunkenhalgh		Lancs 196	plaiers one night: pantry a/c margin
Bradshaw the player	4.4.1628	Dunkenhalgh	10s	Lancs 197	
Bradshaw & his company	10.22.1629	Dunkenhalgh	20s	Lancs 198	
Bradshaw and his company of players	12.9.1630	Dunkenhalgh	13s 4d	Lancs 202	
Bradshaw and his company	11.16–30.1635	Dunkenhalgh	20s	Lancs 209	
Richard Bradshawe and company	11.12.1630	Reading		Murray 2:110, 2:386	**"Richard Bradshawe hath licens and company."**
Bradshaw	May 1633	trouble at Banbury		Murray 2:106–10	see 2:163–67

Nungezer, p. 55, reads this entry as Bradshaw's buying the copper lace and also borrowing 14s in money.

EDWARD, LORD DUDLEY
[Edward Sutton or Dudley (before September 17, 1567–June 23, 1643), succeeded as 5th Lord Dudley by August 12, 1586]

Troupe Name	Place	Date	Payment	Source
Bradshaw as Dudley's players	Chester warrant	"16 Feb 1595" but "41 Eliz" is not 1595		Chester 177–8
Dudley revoked the licence and authorized other players	Chester	by 11 Nov 1602		Chester 178
Earl of Dudley's players with Earl of Darcy's	Leicester	10.3–5–1599	10s total	Unpub MS

BARBARA D. PALMER

Troupe Name	Place	Date	Payment	Source
1600s				
Earl of Lincoln and my Lord Dudleys their players	Newcastle	March 1600	40s	Newcastle 133
Lord Dudley's players	Leominster	1600–1601	6s	Herefordshire 147
Lord Dudley's players	Coventry	1601	6s 8d	Coventry 358
Lord Dudley's players another time	Coventry	1601	3s 4d	Coventry 358
Lord Dudley's players	Leicester	1601–2	10s	Unpub MS
Lord Dudley's players	Coventry	1602	10s	Coventry 360
Lord Dudley's players	Coventry	1603	5s	Coventry 362
Lord Dudley's players	Coventry	1603	5s	Coventry 362
Dudley's players	Leicester	12.24–25.1604	10s	Unpub MS
Lord Dudley's players	Coventry	10 Jan 1604/5	5s	Coventry 364
Lord Dudley's players	York	20 Aug 1605	20s	York 1:517
Lord Dudley's players	Newcastle	March 1606	50s	Newcastle 141
Lord Dudley's players which played not	York	28 Mar 1607	30s	York 1:524
Lord Dudley's players	Coventry	1607	6s 8d	Coventry 371
Lord Dudley's players	Coventry	Mar 1608/9	20s	Coventry 373
Dudley's players	Doncaster	6.19.1608	10s	Unpub MS
Lord Dudley's players	Coventry	Leet Day 1609	20s	Coventry 375
1610s				
Lord Dudley's players	Londesborough	1.12.1610/11	40s	Unpub MS
Lord Dudley's players	Coventry	1612	6s 8d	Coventry 384
Distley and his company my Lord Dudley his players	Gawthorpe	7 Oct 1612	30s	Lancs 173
Lord Dudley's players	Congleton (Cheshire)	1613–14	2s 6d	Unpub MS
Lord Dudley's players	Maidstone	1613–14	3s 4d	Kent 2:724
Lorde Dudlies playors	Leicester	12.16.1614	10s	Unpub MS
Lord Duddleys players	Congleton	Michaelmas 1615/16	3s 4d	Unpub MS
Lo: dudley's players: disley & his company	Londesborough	9.9.1619	20s (for one play)	Unpub MS
Dudley's players	Carlisle	1619–20	10s	Cumberland 93
1620s				
Lord Dudley's men	Dunkenhalgh	7 Nov 1620	13s 4d	Lancs 189
Lord Dudleyes players	Leicester	1620–21	10s	Unpub MS
Lord dudleyes players	Londesborough	2.11.1621/22	10s: "offered to play but were not suffered"	Unpub MS
a Company of Players beinge the Lord Dudleys Servants	Leicester	3.2.1621/22	5s not to play	Unpub MS
lord dudleyes players	Leicester	1623	10s not to play	Unpub MS

PLAYING IN THE PROVINCE: FRONT OR BACK DOOR? 125

Troupe Name	Place	Date	Payment	Source
Dudley's players	Carlisle	18 June 1626	3s 4d	Cumberland 107
Lord Dudley's players	Worcester	1625–26	10s	Worcestershire 455
Lord Dudley his players	Leicester	1627/28	5s	Unpub MS

DISLEY (DISTLE, DISHLEY, DISTLEY) THE PLAYER
(active 1599–1633)

Troupe Name	Date	Place	Payment	Source	Other Info
Earl of Dudley's players with Earl of Darcy's	10.3–5.1599	Leicester	10s total	Unpub MS	
Deshley & co.	4.21.1601	Londesborough	13s 3d	Unpub MS	
Lord Dudley's players	1601–02	Leicester	10s	Unpub MS	
Dudley's players	12.24–25. 1604	Leicester	10s	Unpub MS	
Dudley's players	6.19.1608	Doncaster	10s	Unpub MS	
Dishley the player	12.31.1608	Belvoir	30s	Unpub MS: HMC, p. 464, "Belvoyr.— Rewards given ther."	
Dishley the player	1.2.1608/9	Belvoir	20s	Unpub MS: HMC, p. 464, "Belvoyr.— Rewards given ther."	Mounteagle's players paid 30s on 12.27.1608
Distle & co	3.13.1609/10	Gawthorpe	20s	Lancs 171	[Lent]
Lord Dudley's players	1.12.1610/11	Londesborough	40s	Unpub MS	
Distley & his co. my co: dudley his plaeres	10.7.1612	Gawthorpe	30s	Lancs 173	
Distle & his co.	3.4.1612/13	Gawthorpe	6s 8d	Lancs 175	[Lent]
Lord Dudley's players	1613–14	Congleton, Cheshire	2s 6d	Coman, REEDN 14:1, 7	
Lorde Dudlies players	12.16.1614	Leicester	10s	Unpub MS	
the Lord Duddleys players	Michaelmas 1615/16	Congleton, Cheshire	3s 4d	Coman, REEDN 14:1, 7	
Shrewsbury's men	11.6.1616	Dunkenhalgh	6s 8d	Lancs 186	
Distle & his co.	11.7.1616	Gawthorpe	6s 8d	Lancs 176	
Earl of Shrewsbury's players	11.27.1616	Coventry	5s	Coventry 396	
Earl of Shrewsbury's players	9.10.1617	Newark	10s	Unpub MS	

Troupe Name	Date	Place	Payment	Source	Other Info
Earle of Shrewsburies plaieres	October 1617	Nottingham	10s	Unpub MS	
Earl of Shrewsbury's players	12.20.1617	Coventry	10s	Coventry 405	
Lo: shrewsbury's players: disley & his co.	3.12.1617/18	Londesborough	13s 4d	Unpub MS	not to play [Lent]
Lo: dudley's players: disley & his co.	9.9.1619	Londesborough	20s	Unpub MS	for one play
disley and his company	bwn 7.25–9.22.1620	Dunkenhalgh	5s	Lancs 189	
"my Lord Dudleyes men"	11.7.1620	Dunkenhalgh	13s 4d	Lancs 189	
Lord Dudleyes Players	1620–21	Leicester	10s	Unpub MS	
dishley & his co.	5.4.1621	Londesborough	11s in gold	Unpub MSnot to play	
Lo: dudleyes players	2.11.1621/22	Londesborough	10s	Unpub MS	"offered to play but were not suffered"
a Company of Players beinge the Lord Dudleys Servants	3.2.1621/22	Leicester	5s	Unpub MS	not playing
lord dudleyes players	1623	Leicester	10s	Unpub MS	"for the like": i.e., "that played not"
disley the player & his co.	3.2.1624/25	Dunkenhalgh	8s 4d	Lancs 193	[paid on Ash Wednesday]
disley the plaier	7.27.1625	Dunkenhalgh	6s 8d	Lancs 194	
disley the Plaier	3.21.1625/26	Dunkenhalgh	5s	Lancs 195	[Lent]
Disley the plaier	2.23.1626/27	Dunkenhalgh	3s 4d	Lancs 197	[Shrove Tues 2.21.1626/27]
Lord Dudley his players	1627/28	Leicester	5s	Unpub MS	
Dishley and his ffellowes	1628/29	Leicester	5s	Unpub MS	
disley & his co.	12.10.1629	Dunkenhalgh	6s 8d	Lancs 199	
dishley & co.	2.19.1629/30	Doncaster	10s	Unpub MS	[Lent]
Disley the player	Mar or Apr 1629/30	Dunkenhalgh	10s	Lancs 200	for one play [Lent: 2.10–4.11. 1629/30]
dishley & co.	9.12.1632	Doncaster	5s	Unpub MS	"not play in the towne"
Mr Dishley, a player	1633	York	15s	York 1:593	

Sources Cited

Chambers, E. K., *The Elizabethan Stage.* 4 vols. Oxford: Clarendon, 1923.

Coman, Alan C. "The Congleton Accounts: Further Evidence of Elizabethan and Jacobean Drama in Cheshire." *REED Newsletter* 14, no. 1 (1989): 3–18.

Foakes, R. A., ed. *Henslowe's Diary.* 2nd ed. Cambridge: Cambridge University Press, 2002.

Galloway, David and John Wasson, eds. *Records of Plays and Players in Norfolk and Suffolk, 1330–1642,* Malone Society *Collections.* Vol. 11. Oxford: Oxford University Press, 1980.

Lyte, H. Maxwell and W. H. Stevenson, eds. "Extracts from household accounts." *HMC Report on the Manuscripts of the Duke of Rutland preserved at Belvoir Castle* (1905), 4:270.

Murray, John Tucker. *English Dramatic Companies 1558–1642.* 2 vols. 1910; New York: Russell & Russell, 1963.

Nungezer, Edwin. *A Dictionary of Actors.* New Haven: Yale University Press, 1929.

REED VOLUMES: David Galloway, ed., REED: *Norwich 1540–1642* (1984); Mark C. Pilkinton, REED: *Bristol* (1997); R.W. Ingram, ed., REED: *Coventry* (1981); John M. Wasson, ed., REED: *Devon* (1986); Alexandra F. Johnston and Margaret Rogerson, eds., REED: *York* (1979); David George, REED: *Lancashire* (1991); James M. Gibson, ed., REED: *Kent: Diocese of Canterbury* (2002); Lawrence M. Clopper, REED: *Chester* (1979); J. J. Anderson, REED: *Newcastle upon Tyne* (1982); David N. Klausner, REED *Herefordshire and Worcestershire* (1990); James Stokes, ed., REED: *Somerset, Including Bath,* ed. Robert J. Alexander (1996); Audrey Douglas and Peter Greenfield, eds., REED: *Cumberland, Westmorland, Gloucestershire* (1986); John R. Elliott Jr., Alan H. Nelson, Alexandra F. Johnston, Diana Wyatt, eds., REED: *Oxford* (2004)

Wentersdorf, Karl P. "Origin and Personnel of the Pembroke Company." *Theatre Research International* 5 (1979/80): 45–68.

Dux Moraud: Criminality and Salvation in an East Anglian Play

Clifford Davidson

ONE of the most intriguing among the handful of extant fragments of medieval British drama included in Norman Davis's Early English Text Society edition of *Non-Cycle Plays and Fragments* is *Dux Moraud,* a 265-line item contained in Bodleian Library MS. Eng. Poet. f.2.[1] This manuscript is a parchment roll originally used for accounts in the early fourteenth century and then later reused for a single actor's part which is all that is extant of this play.[2] It represents, however, an important theater document since it is something rare in the history of the medieval theater in Britain—a script prepared for an actual stage performance by an individual player. The location of early performance is not known specifically, but the parchment itself has been identified with William de Ormesby, a prominent judge from East Anglia who owned property at Caister, which is not far from Ormesby, Norfolk, and only a short distance north of Great Yarmouth. Both the author and the scribe were East Anglian, with the latter's handwriting dated in the second quarter of the fifteenth century.[3] The play's subject matter, which is based on the tale of the incestuous daughter found in the Middle English *Gesta Romanorum* and elsewhere,[4] is perhaps the most sensational to be found in British drama of the period, and has been claimed, I think quite plausibly, as originally concluding with a miracle of the Virgin Mary.[5] Its potential for effective staging has been argued by Victor I. Scherb,[6] but as might be expected from a single actor's part without stage directions, a considerable number of questions concerned with presentation before an audience must necessarily be shrouded in ambiguity. A further, and even more serious complication, is that the play clearly did not, as Joseph Quincy Adams thought, end with the final words of the fragment.[7] The role of the speaker for whom the text was written was clearly only a part of a longer play about which we can only surmise the contents from other sources.

The play's opening lines, in three thirteen-line stanzas, contain the male speaker's command for attention from the audience and his assertion of authority as a duke as he makes his appearance with his wife and his retainers at his side. Scherb notes a comparison with Mundus in *The Castle of Perse-*

verance,[8] but more broadly the speech seems quite typical of the arrogance shown, for example, by Cyrus in the Digby *Mary Magdalen* or Herod in the N-town collection.[9] He clearly represents those who, all too familiar in fifteenth-century England, were possessed by pride and the will to power, whether among the aristocracy or even the town elite. His self-praise is directed to his courtesy, his generosity, his toughness "in dede" (presumably in martial encounters), and his comely appearance "on stede" (36, 38) when mounted on his horse. In production he surely would have projected a commanding appearance and one that appropriately reflected his self-love, a form of love that seems to reach out to embrace the audience but actually arches back to enclose only the speaker himself—and hence to make him vulnerable to the temptations that will follow. The point, theologically consistent with the Augustinian analysis of self-love as ultimately self-destructive,[10] seems to require gestures that extend his arms and then bring them back to himself politician-wise. He offers himself as a secular image of adulation, a model of stability, but very soon he is shown to be privately unstable, overcome through his illegitimate desires, which lead him to seduce his daughter.

The lines that must have followed the opening speech are of course missing, but must have introduced the duke's wife and daughter into the play in speaking roles. There would be no need for his retainers, his "mené," also on stage, to have speaking roles. The duchess wishes to go on a journey, perhaps even a pilgrimage to a holy site.[11] Walsingham, England's most popular Marian shrine and located conveniently in Norfolk, is one of a number of possibilities. The duke encourages her to "do now þi wylle / Þi wyage to fulfylle" (40–41), promises to be faithful, and looks forward to her return home again. She speaks once more, and he announces his resolve to avoid temptation: "I xall me kepyn from fondyng / And als from blame and synne / With gras" (48–50). He then calls on Jesus, who is his Maker and who by his wounds has provided salvation, to save him "fro wykyt thowtys" (53)—an ominous sign of what is to follow. One of Freud's achievements was to unveil in his writings the fact that human beings may be afflicted with powerful fantasies of impermissible or transgressive acts, which may involve family members with whom one lives in close proximity. Responding to the prodding of such fantasies, including father-daughter desire, has been shown to be much more common than would be suggested by documentation in medieval court records and other sources. That father-daughter incest in particular was so hidden is due to the fact that it would have been regarded as among the most shameful practices that could be imagined at that time, when incest prohibitions had in fact been expanded to the point where even fairly distantly related persons were prevented from marrying.[12] One would expect that the duke's next speech, following some words, probably brief, by his duchess, was presented by the actor in a manner that would, through deliberate awkwardness perhaps, have suggested the violence of his "wykyt thowtys"

130   CLIFFORD DAVIDSON

as he ironically wished her a happy journey. As his wife exits, the duke is now left with his daughter, who will be revealed to be the object of his temptation. When his "mené" would have left the stage we do not know, but surely they are not present in this scene.

From analogues of the story which is dramatized in the play, we may guess that the daughter was portrayed as recently having arrived at puberty (the Middle English *Gesta Romanorum* has her at fourteen or fifteen years of age)[13] and influenced by the "fend of helle," according to MS. Rawlinson 118.[14] No evidence is, however, forthcoming to indicate that the devil appeared visibly as a character in *Dux Moraud* in this portion of the play. All that can be surmised about the first part of the drama is that two stanzas of thirteen lines each, between which a speech (probably a single stanza of the same length by the daughter) was sandwiched, appear enough to seduce her successfully so that she is willing to go with him for sex to her "chambyr þat is so louely of lythe" (84). It is difficult to know precisely how stylized this interchange would have been. The duke calls her "fayrest to fonde" (81), but I cannot imagine that the kiss that precedes their retreat to the room in which they will have their tryst would have been performed with the realism that might be expected in a contemporary television show. Since the daughter would fairly certainly have been played by a boy whose voice had not yet broken—and this was at a later age than in the present, perhaps as late as eighteen or nineteen[15]—the erotic element inherent in the script would have demanded only a mere hint since a fully realistic depiction would have been found to be shameful for the players or a source of laughter for the audience.

But it is the danger perceived in the possible wider detection of the incest that hangs over the discovery of the tryst by the wife, who returns remarkably soon in the play. Time is severely condensed. At least one speech by her is required, undoubtedly the duchess coming onto the stage and lamenting her misfortune in only a few lines, whereupon she must exit. But during this time she must not be alone, for the duke's next speech makes clear that he and the daughter are both present. His response in this speech is most inappropriate, for the revelation of his transgression to his wife causes him not only, as expected, to fall into a depressed state but also to call for the slaying of "yon traytowr," who is ironically regarded as a "rebel in sawe" (95–96)—that is, in speaking or revealing secrets. A gesture expected here would involve pointing with the index finger extended in accusation.[16] In the duke's view, the duchess is rebelling against his patriarchal status as the head of the household. Her act of discovering their relationship is regarded, according to the husband's twisted moral logic, as a capital crime. The daughter obviously agrees to do the deed, and the duke's next speech acknowledges that his wife now indeed has been "slayne" (98). The daughter has committed the murder, as in the analogues. In MS. Rawlinson 118, for example, she uses a "knyfe" with which she "smote hire modyr to þe herte."[17] In the play an even more

DUX MORAUD: CRIMINALITY AND SALVATION IN AN EAST ANGLIAN PLAY 131

chilling description would seem to have been called for by the daughter in her next speech, and the duke's response is to express his joy that the "schrewed qued" or villainess (103) has been eliminated from their lives.

How the playwright created a bridge between this speech and the discovery of the birth of his daughter's child is unclear. What device was used to indicate the passage of time, here again abruptly telescoped? Has the duke in his gladness left the stage, only to return when the birth has taken place? If the birth occurred in full view of the audience, did midwives appear, or was there other action? How many lines of dialogue might have been required? Many options seem to emerge here, though all of them, like the slipping away into the daughter's "chambyr" earlier, would have been facilitated by the use of a booth stage set up on some sort of scaffold such as we see in illustrations of the Flemish theater by Pieter Bruegel and others.[18] Such an option would have been precisely right too for staging the duke's return onto the scene, whereupon he again expresses his terror, as we would expect, surely in fear of exposure and consequent shame.

In the play the plan to kill the baby, who is "fayr and bryt" (119), must have come from the daughter. The duke commands that the deed is to be done out of his sight and that it should be done immediately on this very day. The "lordys of þis lond" must not know about the child and that he "[h]ad synd" with his daughter (125–27); therefore, he says, "Slo yt with þin hond" so that they might "ben in pes" (134). There are echoes here of Herod's fright in learning of the Christ Child and of the acts of *Kindermord* subsequently ordered by him in the N-town plays or in the East Anglian *Candlemas and the Killing of the Children* in MS. Digby 133. Since it is done offstage, the manner in which the murder is committed is not specified, but in the version of the story in the Rawlinson manuscript the daughter "brake þe childys necke-bone,"[19] while in the Middle English *Gesta Romanorum* she "wrothe in sondre the necke, and went, and beried it in the dunge-hille."[20] In the play the duke thanks his daughter for helping him in her "werkyngys þis [h]oure," since she has thus protected him "fro scham and dolowr" (140, 144). While her speech in response is of course missing, in his next he announces that he is now going to set forth to meet with other lords "in fylde and toun" (150). There is clearly some love banter, for he calls her his "der . . . paramowre, . . . semly in syth" (155, 162) as he prepares to set out. Unfortunately, the text of this speech is very damaged, but whatever her response, he is made very happy indeed as he leaves, most likely stepping down from the booth stage to walk forth "in pride" (172). Acting as if nothing has happened, he has returned to the self-centered love of self that had characterized his pride in his opening speech as he begins his journey.

Though a line is drawn across the page to indicate a new speech, there is no need for dialogue separating this speech from the next one, in which he reports hearing a church bell ringing at a distance "in þe kyrk" (179). His

132   CLIFFORD DAVIDSON

announcement that he will go there, for he is suddenly "in gret care" and in need of "sum god ded to werk" (181–82), marks a transformation, which, if Constance Hieatt is right in the conjecture that she derives from analogues and Continental miracle stories, may be followed by his arrival at the church and a sermon encouraging penitence.[21] The duke's journey to the church is a journey like that of St. Paul on the road to Damascus in the dramatization in the Digby *Conversion of St. Paul*,[22] for it involves a movement in space that signifies a spiritual change of his personal condition from pridefulness to humility and an appropriate sense of guilt at what he has done. Scherb indicates that the journey in which the duke crosses the platea is also consistent with the stage business required in other East Anglian plays, while likewise it is "a clear example of symbolic action" away from the polluted house where incest has been committed and across to the sacred space of the church.[23] Here he has indeed become, as the name Moraud seems to indicate, a voyager, a traveler.

The line designating a new speech at line 183 is again likely to indicate the duke's movement rather than the presence of intervening dialogue. Here, as he crosses to the church, which may well be an actual ecclesiastical building if the booth stage he has left has been set up out of doors,[24] he laments the enormity of his crime, which he says is the worst that anyone has committed "þat euer tok lyf with flesch and bone" (190). Presumably this statement would have been accompanied by gestures such as beating his breast, wringing his hands, or pulling of his own hair.[25] An implicit comparison is herein invited with the most notorious sinners such as Judas Iscariot and Herod the Great, the latter taken away by the devil to his "celle" after the killing of the Innocents in the N-town plays (20.233). In his contrition, the first stage of the sacrament of Penance, the duke recognizes that without transforming grace he will be lost and destined to be taken to hell where he will be punished eternally. Hence he explains the purpose of going to the church: to seek out a priest who can hear his confession and assuage his guilty conscience that so recently has been awakened by the sound of the church bell.

There must be a speech in which the priest introduces himself, followed by the duke's words expressing his relief at the opportunity to confess his "dedly syn" (208). His confession begins on stage openly before the audience. This must, as Scherb has pointed out, be consistent with current practice and depictions of it in East Anglian iconography, of which he chooses to emphasize the Confession scenes in the painted glass of the parish church at North Tuddenham, Norfolk, and in the widespread seven sacrament fonts of East Anglia.[26] The North Tuddenham glass has a priest seated and holding a scourge, while a fashionably dressed man kneels before him with hands joined prayerfully. The priest, seated and wearing a surplice and stole, has his hand on the man's head in the sign of absolution, and the scroll, quoting Matthew 9:2, likewise indicates that the man's sins are being forgiven.[27] The

DUX MORAUD: CRIMINALITY AND SALVATION IN AN EAST ANGLIAN PLAY 133

glass painting shows the moment of absolution, in *Dux Moraud* about to take place immediately after the duke has spoken the words "Grant me my synnus to flee" (229) at the end of his full and free words of confession. At this point, as on several East Anglian fonts, the iconography may present a devil, having been defeated in his effort to snare the soul, fleeing from the scene.[28] While a possibility in the play, there is no evidence for such an elaboration, nor is there any suggestion that the opposing guardian angel, again present on some Seven Sacrament fonts,[29] might have been present. One must allow for the possibility of devils on stage later in the play's concluding segment, as we shall see.

The act of listening to a person's confession is normally represented either by a priest holding the hands of the person, as on the font at Brooke, or perhaps by having the penitent place his hands on the clergyman's knees or on a faldstool.[30] But since the act of confession, or holy shrift, was not then necessarily the private rite that it presently is—instead the penitent was often accompanied by others, either themselves penitents, members of one's kinfolk, or neighbors[31]— the scene here draws the audience at the play into the action in a demonstration of the principle of symbolic engagement that is characteristic of the early religious drama.

Dialogue by the priest is supplied in the version of the story contained in MS. Rawlinson 118, and this may suggest the gist of what was included in his missing speech in *Dux Moraud:*

> Þe prest sayd: "hast þou good wille,
> Of þi dedis þou hast done ille
>   Shrift for to take?
> Þat þou ne shalt with þi douter dele,
> At bed, at bord, at mete ne at mele,
>   Hire þou most forsake.
> If þou wolt penauns fonde,
> Take þi wey into holylond,
>   Þer God was qwicke and dede."[32]

At this point in this telling of the story, he agrees to do as the priest has told him to do.

In the play, the duke requests his penance from the priest and has received absolution. Because of the seriousness of his guilt, his penance, which is reported later in his penultimate speech to his daughter, is quite extreme, for he must surrender all his property—his "tresorys rych and gay"—and then leave on a pilgrimage to an unspecified location to expiate his "wykyt fam" (250–53). Now he must have returned to the scaffold or booth stage that had held the initial action. He has greeted the daughter in humble terms appropriate to one who has been absolved of such serious sins, and undoubtedly

134 CLIFFORD DAVIDSON

his gestures are indicative of his changed condition. She, on the other hand, is in no mood to accept the father's decision to impoverish himself—and, of course, impoverish his daughter as well. A motive is introduced, but the Rawlinson manuscript analogue also introduces another though one for which we have no evidence in the play. This involves the "fendes entysynge," which led her to "anoþer þinge"—that is, to thoughts of murder.[33]

In the night before the day on which the duke was to begin his pilgrimage "ffor his synnes sake," according to the Rawlinson version,[34] the daughter decides on drastic action. She goes to her father in his sleep and cuts his throat. A variant of the same version contained in Cambridge University Library MS. Ff.V.48 has her "karve his hart in-twoo."[35] The Middle English *Gesta Romanorum* makes her into an axe murderer who, with such an instrument, "kylled here fadre."[36] The extant analogues then only indicate that she absconded with her father's treasure. The play fragment, however, gives the duke some final words in which he announces he is dying. A stage direction embedded in his speech suggests the use of an axe or other object by which he has been struck; he is "smetyn in þe fas / With carful strokys and rownde" (255–56). The next words are very significant and must be regarded as indicative of his daughter's fate, for he forgives her and prays that she might be given grace to "blin" (discontinue) her sinful life and what she has "don so fre" (260–62)—that is, done voluntarily. His final words echo Christ's on the cross—"*In manus tuas, domine!*—and ask Jesus to "haue mercy on me / And saue my sowle fro helle" (266–67). In spite of being a victim of violence, therefore, his end represents the good death as described in manuals on death and dying that became so popular in the early years following the invention of printing.[37] The words "In manus tuas," commending his soul to God, are also spoken by the protagonist in *Everyman* when he is at the point of death.[38]

But in the analogues to the play the daughter does anything but discontinue her wicked life, and there seems to be every likelihood that the dramatization of her misdeeds represented a substantial portion of the play. As her father was to go on a pilgrimage to the holy land, so now she goes on another kind of journey in which she wastes the wealth she has pilfered from her father's estate and becomes a common prostitute. One may be tempted to think of the foray into the world of the prodigal son in the parable (Luke 15:11–32), though his story of willful impoverishment and dissipation is really not at all comparable to the criminality displayed by the incestuous daughter.[39] In Cambridge MS. Ff.V.48 she is described as a "faire woman in alle thynge" who "gaf to lechory hir likynge" and in her despair entertained no hope of "heuen to wynne . . . Bute helle with-owt ende."[40] She is reported to have entertained all who came to her asking for sexual favors, not even turning away priests, friars, or clerks.[41] In setting out to dramatize her downward career, we should expect that the playwright would have kept in mind the need to give her the opportunity to change her costume from that of an affluent

DUX MORAUD: CRIMINALITY AND SALVATION IN AN EAST ANGLIAN PLAY 135

young woman to the gown of a prostitute. The latter would perhaps have been tight-fitting, red in color, with the addition of yellow, a color traditionally associated with prostitution, and perhaps striped.[42] A wig would have been required in the first part of the play for the boy actor playing the role, but here presumably would demand hair loosened over the shoulders as in many depictions of Mary Magdalen, who even after her conversion was traditionally given garments associated with her previous profession. After a time in the city to which she had first gone, according to the Middle English *Gesta Romanorum,* she descended to such depths that she had slept with every man available to her, and all of them now "lothed here company." So she chose another city, and continued in her wickedness,[43] though of course such a change of location was unlikely to have been a detail included in the play.

In these accounts her sexual openness may be compared to the early carved figures that have been called the *sheela-nagig,* the Irish term for these images of women holding open their genitals as if welcoming all comers.[44] This iconography would not have influenced either the narrative or the play directly, but in spite of its rarity in England it may be regarded as an analogue of sorts to the story. Attempts to argue that these figures were benign and related to fertility or that, as a recent writer has it, they merely in a neutral and non-moralizing manner "speak to the physiological processes of reproduction"[45] cannot be sustained. They clearly represent lack of control and lust, which under the rubric of Luxuria is one of the Seven Deadly Sins. Parallel male figures published by Anthony Weir and James Jerman show the penis, distended and even on occasion involved in masturbation.[46] One needs to keep in mind that in *Dux Moraud* the father and the daughter are both supremely guilty of lack of self-control. They are mutually guilty for their incest and their deeds of murder. The modern idea of father-daughter incest solely as child-victimization does not apply. Neither does the story subsequently narrated in the analogues support the view of the daughter as simply a benign worker in the sex trade. The point is always to represent her as falling to the lowest condition possible. To her incest, murder, and theft are added the most demeaning levels of sexual depravity.

The depth to which the daughter falls in the analogues to *Dux Moraud* is meant to verify great potential for grace to rescue the soul from despair and to offer salvation, even in the instance of a conversion at the final moments of one's life. The story that is told in the analogues is decidedly not a tragedy but, as the basis for a drama, points to its opposite, the miracle play. R. M. Wilson commented some years ago that *Dux Moraud,* "though frequently cited as the earliest example of secular drama, . . . could equally well have been a miracle play,"[47] but the former option seems well nigh out of the question. I thus would argue too that Marion Jones seems off the mark when she suggests that the daughter's death might have been in the form of "an Awful Warning, carried away by demons amid showers of squibs," or that this sort

136   CLIFFORD DAVIDSON

of ending would have had "at least an aesthetic propriety."[48] Jones cites *The Cradle of Security,* a sixteenth-century morality that concluded with the damnation of the protagonist, and could well have pointed to *Enough Is as Good as a Feast,* an extant Protestant morality by W. Wager that likewise possesses a protagonist who fails to persevere in the faith. "Certainly it would take," she writes, "a most spectacular intervention by the Blessed Virgin to pluck this particular sinner from the burning,"[49] but such an intervention seems theoretically to be very possible in this case. Spectacular effects of various kinds were common enough in other East Anglian plays, including *The Castle of Perseverance,* which dates from roughly the same time period as *Dux Moraud.*

There are sensational details in the daughter's story in the analogues that seem ripe for dramatization. Though only a holy preacher, identified in Lincoln Cathedral MS. 51 as St. Augustine, could see them, she was accompanied by seven "fendys withe burnyng cheynes abowte hyr necke an abowte hyr myddull" that controlled her.[50] The fiends are the Seven Deadly Sins, the same as those who afflicted and controlled Mary Magdalen in the saint play representing her life in the Digby MS. 133. In that drama, also from East Anglia but of a later date, Jesus but speaks the words "Vade in pace" to exorcise the seven devils representing the Seven Deadly Sins, who spectacularly "*xall dewoyde from þe woman,*" while the Bad Angel who has been tempting the Magdalen will "*entyr into hell wyth thondyr.*"[51] The account in Cambridge MS. Ff.V.48 tells how, at the moment when the holy bishop speaks, tears of contrition appear in the eyes of the sinful daughter, and the collar by which the devils had held her broke. Then the fiends who had led her "be þe armus" broke the chains, and "away þei fledde."[52] A theatrical effect of this kind would have been very much within the capabilities of East Anglian players, particularly in a major center such as Norwich or Bury St. Edmunds, though many lesser centers can hardly be ruled out.

The daughter, as the Cambridge manuscript has it, was unhappy on a Good Friday that "noman with hir wold play: / Siluer myȝt she non gete."[53] She has companions, however, who urge her to go with them to the church in the expectation of finding "sum ȝong man" who "is both curtesse and hynde/ þat wille with vs play."[54] The same church site where her father confessed and was absolved could likely have served again for the daughter. This text specifically credits God's grace, which "is mercifulle to euery wyȝt" and "his modur Mary" for acting through the "wordis bothe fayre and gode" of the bishop.[55] Seeing the fiends about her, the clergyman knows her condition and speaks of "goddis mercy . . . lowde and stille."[56] The words of his sermon, because they stress mercy, are through grace able to enter so that her hardened heart is softened, and she weeps profusely. Like her father before her, she is moved to contrition and wishes to confess her sins, which, she tells the bishop, involves "þe grettist synne / þat any woman may be inne /

DUX MORAUD: CRIMINALITY AND SALVATION IN AN EAST ANGLIAN PLAY 137

Agaynes God and his seyntys ychon."[57] Continuing, she tells him that she has "done foly" with her father,[58] with whom she maintained a relationship in this version of the story for a much longer period than in the play. Here, instead of the one child of the drama, she has had three children by him—and all of them she has slain, along with her mother and father. Requesting shrift, she "swonyd and fel downe there / So ful she was of sorow and care."[59] Indeed, for sorrow her heart bursts even before the bishop can properly absolve her sins and establish her penance. Then, specifically including a request that those standing round about should fall to their knees, the bishop asks them to pray for her. In Lincoln Cathedral MS. 51, however, the people at first "blamyd her gretly and seyde sche was not worþi to be beryd in cristen mennyr beryells."[60] In this account, a miracle of four roses springing forth from her mouth with assuring texts written on them will prove that she has entered into bliss.

A voice from heaven is introduced in Cambridge MS. Ff.V.48 and Bodleian Library, MS. Ashmole 61, with the former giving the following words to a heavenly voice, first speaking generally to the audience and then specifically to the bishop:

> "Þe saule of is synfulle wyȝt
> Is wonnen in-to heuon bright,
> To Jhesu lefe and dere
>
> . . . .
> "Asoyle þe body with alle þi myght
> And bery hit in a graue!
> Alle-if it did gret foly,
> With rufulle hert hit cryed mercy;
> God graunt þat hit shuld haue."[61]

There is an oddity here, to be sure, if God is speaking. The final line refers to God in the third person, which hardly would have been the case in the play, assuming that its ending bore a strict resemblance to this analogue at this point. But if the speech were given to the Virgin Mary, the anomaly would immediately be cleared up. Yet we must not place too much credit on such a speculative reading, especially since the Middle English *Gesta Romanorum* version clearly gives the speech to another heavenly figure, who refers to the Virgin also in the third person: "Be the grete mercy of Iesu Criste, and prayere of hys blessyd modre, and the grete sorowe that she had for here synnes, she [i.e., the daughter] is right wele, and sittes full hye in heauyn blisse, and is as white as lille floure, and as bryght as any golde in Goddis sight."[62] However it might have been dramatized, the main point is that forgiveness has been extended to the deceased and repentant sinner, and that heaven has spoken definitively on this point.

In the *Gesta Romanorum* the association of the daughter's conversion and salvation with the Virgin Mary is made explicitly, for the clergyman who has heard her confession sends her to "yonder autere" where she is to "knele downe before oure ladie, and pray here hertly and deuoutely, that she wolde be good meane to here sone; for she is all weye modre of mercy, and remedie for to helpe."[63] It is here before this altar with its image of the Virgin that her heart burst, causing her confessor to make "grete mone" and to ask God's forgiveness since he had given "here no penaunce."[64] In this account, the priest hears a voice from on high which assures him that all is well with her soul: "Be the grete mercy of Iesu Criste, and the prayere of hys blessyd modre, and the grete sorowe that she had for here synnes, she is right wele, and sittes full hye in heuyn blisse, and is as whit as lille floure, and as bryght as any golde in goddis sight."[65] There is no miracle specifically wrought by the Virgin, as in Miracles of the Virgin plays on the Continent or in the famous Cantigas attributed to Alfonso El Sabio in Spain, but bringing Mary fully into the action would surely have seemed a logical embellishment, especially in East Anglia where her veneration was very strong.[66] Hieatt's hypothesis that Mary was indeed present and that *Dux Moraud* should at least tentatively be considered to be a miracle of the Virgin[67] will thus seem quite plausible, even if certainty can never be possible without the discovery of the full text of the drama, as now seems less than likely. But that the play would, like the text in Cambridge MS. Ff.V.48 and Bodleian Library MS. Ashmole 61, have been regarded as an antidote to "wanhope"—that is, despair, regarded as a subspecies of accidia and the final stage of a thoroughly sinful life[68]—is surely most probable. Indeed, upon consideration it is extremely difficult to believe that the ending of the play would have differed significantly in this respect from the analogues that offer salvation even to the most wicked of transgressors and the most despairing.

The final scene as tentatively reconstructed also gives occasion for a number of staging options, but speculation needs to remain focused on the kinds of theatrical effects known to have been used in East Anglia in the fifteenth century. The setting designating the church in part 1 of the play would likely have been used again in the second part, and with such a setting there is no reason that a higher level for God and, very possibly, the Virgin Mary could not have been managed. There may even be precedent in another East Anglian drama, *The Play of the Sacrament,* for using the interior of a church, to which a procession from the previous stage platform could have taken place.[69] Perhaps a small doll— the conventional depiction of the human soul—representing the daughter's spirit was borne up as if from earth to heaven from her body. A cloister roof boss at Norwich Cathedral shows such a scene, with angels holding the soul of a man in a cloth in the process of being raised to paradise.[70] And why not music? Further, could this play have been a substitute for a Coronation of the Virgin play ordinarily played on

DUX MORAUD: CRIMINALITY AND SALVATION IN AN EAST ANGLIAN PLAY 139

August 15, the feast of the Assumption? I am thinking here of the demands of the Assumption play in the N-Town collection (play 41), though of course lacking the bodily rising of the deceased person to heaven.

If the now lost text of *Dux Moraud* culminated in a miracle of the Virgin, the effect of it may be compared with other legends of the Virgin,[71] some of which appear in East Anglian iconography. For example, one might cite the legend of Theophilus, whose story is presented on cloister bosses at Norwich Cathedral,[72] formerly in wall paintings at Bury St. Edmunds,[73] and in relief sculpture in the Lady Chapel at Ely Cathedral.[74] In this legend, Theophilus, though transgressing greatly by attempting to make a pact with the devil, never abandons veneration of the Virgin and hence is rescued by her from certain damnation. *Dux Moraud* is even more sensational and pushes to an extreme the criminality of the daughter while at the same time, in the case of both guilty father and daughter, would seem to have, assuming that the play followed the narrative established in the analogues, promised God's mercy even in such circumstances. If the play offers cheap grace, as Protestants would have argued in the sixteenth century, it nevertheless is consistent with the protagonists' deaths and their fate in *The Castle of Perseverance* and *Everyman.* Both the daughter and the father of *Dux Moraud* probably, as in the analogues, transcend the sin against the Holy Spirit which is the sin of Judas Iscariot, who believed that he had wickedly performed a crime so terrible that he could not be eligible for salvation and who was thus brought to take his own life—a death that would be an emblem of despair for all subsequent ages. The story of the incestuous and murderous daughter and her father proves otherwise—that is, that salvation is available to all, through God's grace, to those who repent, even if their repentance occurs at the final hours or minutes of their lives.[75]

Notes

1. Norman Davis, ed., *Non-Cycle Plays and Fragments,* EETS, s.s. 1 (London: Oxford University Press, 1970), 106–13. Quotations from *Dux Moraud* in the present article are from this edition; line numbers are cited parenthetically in my text.

2. See *Non-Cycle Plays and the Winchester Dialogues: Facsimiles of Plays and Fragments in Various Manuscripts and the Dialogues in Winchester College MS 33,* introd. Norman Davis (Leeds: University of Leeds School of English, 1979), 69–72.

3. Davis, ed., *Non-Cycle Plays and Fragments,* c–ciii.

4. Sidney J. H. Herrtage, ed., *The Early English Versions of the Gesta Romanorum,* EETS, e.s. 33 (London: N. Trübner, 1879), 390–92 (hereafter cited as *Gesta Romanorum*). A portion of this text appears along part of the tale in Bodleian Library MS. Rawlinson 118 and other analogues in W. Heuser, "Dux Moraud, Einzelrolle aus einem verlorenen Drama des 14. Jahrhunderts," *Anglia* 30 (1907): 180–208 (hereafter cited as Heuser); C. Horstmann, *Altenglische Legenden, Neue Folge* (Heilbronn:

Gebr. Henninger, 1881), 335–38 (hereafter cited as *Altenglische Legenden*); and Richard L. Homan, "Two *Exempla:* Analogues to the *Play of the Sacrament* and *Dux Moraud,*" *Comparative Drama* 18 (1984): 245–47, 250–51.

5. Constance B. Hieatt, "A Case for *Duk Moraud* as a Play of the Miracles of the Virgin," *Mediaeval Studies* 32 (1970): 345–51.

6. Victor I. Scherb, *Staging Faith: East Anglian Drama in the Later Middle Ages* (Madison: Fairleigh Dickinson University Press, 2001), 58–63.

7. Joseph Quincy Adams, ed., *Chief Pre-Shakespearean Dramas* (Boston: Houghton Mifflin, 1924), 211.

8. Scherb, *Staging Faith,* 60.

9. *Mary Magdalen,* lines 49ff, in Donald Baker, John L. Murphy, and Louis B. Hall Jr., eds., *The Late Medieval Religious Plays of Bodleian MSS Digby 133 and E Museo 160,* EETS, o.s. 283 (Oxford: Oxford University Press, 1982); Stephen Spector, ed., *The N-Town Play,* EETS, s.s. 11–12 (Oxford: Oxford University Press, 1991), play 20.129ff.

10. See for convenience, *An Augustine Synthesis,* ed. Erich Przywara (New York: Harper: 1958), 341–59.

11. Adams's interpolated stage direction suggested that the wife was planning "*probably to visit relatives or friends*" (*Chief Pre-Shakespearean Dramas,* 207).

12. Elizabeth Archibald, *Incest and the Medieval Imagination* (Oxford: Clarendon, 2001), 49 and passim. Literary accounts were another matter, for, as Archibald says, "[w]hether consummated or merely threatened, father-daughter incest seems to have been the most common literary form of incest in the later Middle Ages, at least in extended narratives" (190).

13. *Gesta Romanorum,* 390.

14. Line 19, in Heuser, 202.

15. Richard Rastall, "Female Roles in All-Male Casts," *Medieval English Theatre* 7 (1985): 28–29.

16. For distinguishing finger gestures, see Clifford Davidson, "Gesture in Medieval English Drama," in *Gesture in Medieval Art and Drama,* ed. Clifford Davidson, Early Drama, Art, and Music Monograph Series 28 (Kalamazoo: Medieval Institute Publications, 2001), 79.

17. Lines 70–71, in Heuser, 203.

18. See W. M. H. Hummelen, "The Boundaries of the Rhetoricians' Stage," *Comparative Drama* 28 (1994): 235–51.

19. Line 41, in Heuser, 202.

20. *Gesta Romanorum,* 390.

21. Hieatt, "A Case for *Duk Moraud,* 350–51.

22. See Scherb, *Staging Faith,* 94–105.

23. Ibid., 62.

24. It should be noted that if the play were initially intended for out-of-doors production, this would not preclude performance in an indoor space such as a hall or even a church.

25. See Davidson, "Gesture in Medieval British Drama," 80–83.

26. Scherb, *Staging Faith,* 60.

27. Christopher Woodforde, *The Norwich School of Glass-Painting in the Fifteenth Century* (London: Oxford University Press, 1950), 60, pl. 20.

DUX MORAUD: CRIMINALITY AND SALVATION IN AN EAST ANGLIAN PLAY 141

28. Ann Eljenholm Nichols, *Seeable Signs: The Iconography of the Seven Sacraments, 1350–1544* (Woodbridge: Boydell Press, 1994), 224–25, esp. pls. 55, 57, 59.

29. Ibid., 231–33.

30. Ibid., 223, pls. 52–53.

31. Ibid., 226.

32. Lines 97–105, in Heuser, 204; see also Cambridge University Library MS. Ff.V.48, which specifically sets forth the prohibition "Þou shalt not be þi douȝtur lye / Nor touche hir with no vilany" (lines 100–101, in *Altenglische Legenden,* 335).

33. Lines 139–40, in Heuser, 205. The Cambridge manuscript indicates that the "anodur thynge" was "Hir fadur for to sloo" (lines 140–41, in *Altenglische Legenden,* 335).

34. Line 138, in Heuser, 205; see also Lincoln Cathedral MS. 51, in Homan, "Two *Exempla,*" 250.

35. Line 144, in *Altenglische Legenden,* 336.

36. *Gesta Romanorum,* 391.

37. These are conveniently described by Nancy B. Beaty, *The Craft of Dying: A Study in the Literary Tradition of the* Ars Moriendi *in England* (New Haven: Yale University Press, 1970). For an example in the visual arts, see the illumination in the *Rohan Hours* (Paris, Bibliothèque Nationale, MS. lat. 9471, fol. 159); reproduced in color in T. S. R. Boase, *Death in the Middle Ages: Mortality, Judgment and Remembrance* (London: Thames and Hudson, 1972), fig. 102.

38. Line 887, in A. C. Cawley, ed., *Everyman* (Manchester: Manchester University Press, 1977), 26.

39. The prodigal son motif in European iconography has recently been discussed by Gerald B. Guest, "The Prodigal's Journey: Ideologies of Self and City in the Gothic Cathedral," *Speculum* 81 (2006): 35–75. The prodigal's descent, which takes place in an urban setting, includes the underworld of prostitution, depicted in brothel scenes.

40. Lines 162–68, in *Altenglische Legenden,* 336.

41. See the complaint by Knowledge in *Everyman* that "some [priests] haunteth womens company / With vnclene lyfe, as lustes of lechery" (lines 761–62).

42. See Ruth Mellinkoff, *Outcasts: Signs of Otherness in Northern European Art of the Late Middle Ages,* 2 vols. (Berkeley: University of California Press, 1993), 1:20–25, 25, 35–36, 44, 220–22, and 2:fig. XI.11, illustrating Mary Magdalen in Roger van der Weyden's Altarpiece of the Seven Sacraments, dated c. 1445. For tight clothing, see Guest, "The Prodigal's Journey," 58.

43. *Gesta Romanorum,* 391.

44. See Anthony Weir and James Jerman, *Images of Lust: Sexual Carvings on Medieval Churches* (London: B. T. Batsford, 1986), 11–22.

45. Marian Bleeke, "Sheelas, Sex, and Significance in Romanesque Sculpture: The Kilpeck Corbel Series," *Studies in Iconography* 26 (2005): 21.

46. Weir and Jerman, *Images of Lust,* figs. 8, 10.

47. R. M. Wilson, *The Lost Literature of Medieval England,* 2nd ed. (London: Methuen, 1970), 232. Cf. Hardin Craig, *English Religious Drama of the Middle Ages* (1955; rpt. Oxford: Clarendon, 1960), 329.

48. Marion Jones, "Early Moral Plays and the Earliest Secular Drama," in *The

142 CLIFFORD DAVIDSON

Revels History of Drama in English, gen. ed. Lois Potter, 1: *Medieval Drama* (London: Methuen, 1983), 290.

49. Ibid.

50. Homan, "Two *Exempla,*" 250.

51. *Mary Magdalen,* l. 691 s.d.

52. Lines 229–30, in *Altenglische Legenden,* 337.

53. Lines 185–86, 215, in ibid., 336–37.

54. Lines 190–92, in ibid., 336. MS. Ashmole 61 has "both god and kynde" (ibid.).

55. Lines 193–97, in ibid.

56. Lines 221–22, in ibid., 337.

57. Lines 241–43, in ibid.

58. Line 244, in ibid.

59. Lines 244, 256–57, in ibid., 337–38.

60. Homan, "Two *Exempla,*" 251.

61. Lines 274–76, 278–82, in *Altenglische Legenden,* 338.

62. *Gesta Romanorum,* 392.

63. Ibid., 391.

64. Ibid., 392.

65. Ibid.

66. See, for example, Gail McMurray Gibson, *The Theater of Devotion: East Anglian Drama and Society in the Late Middle Ages* (Chicago: University of Chicago Press, 1989), 137–77.

67. Hieatt, "A Case for *Duke Moraud,*" 345–51.

68. A metrical Advent sermon describes the way that Satan binds persons in the Seven Deadly Sins one by one until finally "at the last" he enmeshes the soul in his "prisoun," which is wanhope — and from which it is very difficult to escape (John Small, ed., *English Metrical Homilies from Manuscripts of the Fourteenth Century* [1862; rpt. New York: AMS Press, 1973], 58–59). Attention is directed to this passage by Morton Bloomfield, *The Seven Deadly Sins: An Introduction to the History of a Religious Concept, with Special Reference to Medieval English Literature* (1952; rpt. East Lansing: Michigan State University Press, 1967), 161–62.

69. See, for example, Scherb, *Staging Faith,* 82–83.

70. In this case the figure represents Bishop Wakering; see Ann Eljenholm Nichols, *The Early Art of Norfolk,* Early Drama, Art, and Music Reference Series 7 (Kalamazoo: Medieval Institute Publications, 2002), 256.

71. See, for example, Beverly Boyd, *The Middle English Miracles of the Virgin* (San Marino: Huntington Library, 1964).

72. Nichols, *The Early Art of Norfolk,* 116.

73. E. W. Tristram, *English Medieval Wall Painting: The Thirteenth Century,* 2 vols. (London: Oxford University Press, 1950), 1:516.

74. Alfred C. Fryer, "Theophilus, the Penitent, as Represented in Art," *Archaeological Journal* 316–17.

75. Jones mentions the doctrine of *clara visio* introduced by Uthred of Boldon, but does not attempt to apply it to *Dux Moraud.* Uthred held that each "human soul . . .

DUX MORAUD: CRIMINALITY AND SALVATION IN AN EAST ANGLIAN PLAY 143

enjoyed one moment of clear sight just before death, in which it was free to choose or reject God: upon this moment depended irrevocably its portion in eternity" ("Early Moral Plays," 290–91). But there seems no reason to introduce this discredited theological view to explain the idea of a deathbed conversion in the case of the legend dramatized in the analogues to the play.

Alice Layston and the Cross Keys

David Kathman

UNTIL very recently, the four London inns that served as playhouses in the last quarter of the sixteenth century—the Bell Savage on Ludgate Hill, the Bull in Bishopsgate Street, and the Bell and the Cross Keys in Gracechurch Street—have been sadly neglected by theater historians. Despite their importance for Elizabethan theater history, the late Herbert Berry was able to write of these inns as recently as 2000 that "virtually nothing is known for certain about either the ownership of these places or what was done to make them playhouses."[1] Happily, the situation is now improving, as much previously unknown information about all four inn-playhouses is emerging from the archives. Herbert Berry's last publication was a thorough history of the Bell Savage, including a discussion of its owners and leaseholders during its years as a playhouse.[2] My own archival research into these inns, initially undertaken in close consultation with Herb, has uncovered much valuable information about the people who owned and operated the other three inns, as well as the physical characteristics of all four.

One striking tidbit that has emerged from this research is the fact that three of these four inns were owned or leased by women during their time as playhouses. Margaret Craythorne owned the Bell Savage from 1568 until her death in 1591, Alice Layston owned the Cross Keys from 1571 until her death in 1590, and Joan Harrison was the proprietor of the Bull from the death of her husband Matthew in 1584 to her own death in 1589. This, perhaps, should not be too surprising, because it was not uncommon for women (almost always widows) to own or lease inns and similar buildings in London during this period. Two inns that were later converted into full-time playhouses, the Boar's Head and the Red Bull, were owned by women (Jane Poley and Anne Bedingfeild respectively) when those conversions took place, and another woman, Susan Browne Greene Baskerville, was a shareholder in both of those playhouses as the widow of players Robert Browne and Thomas Greene.[3]

Berry's article on the Bell Savage provides much information about Margaret Craythorne, including a portrait of her that still hangs in Cutlers' Hall in London, and I present some key facts about Joan Harrison in two forthcoming articles.[4] However, nothing has yet been written about Alice Layston,

144

who led the best-documented and arguably the most interesting life of the three, and who deserves to be rescued from oblivion after more than 400 years. Her inn, the Cross Keys, is especially interesting for its Shakespearean connections—Strange's Men played there in 1589, when Shakespeare may have been with them, and the Lord Chamberlain's Men asked for permission to play there in 1594, by which time Shakespeare was definitely a sharer. This paper is an initial attempt to remedy this situation by presenting my findings on Alice Layston and the Cross Keys, part of a planned book on inns, taverns, and similar playing places within the walls of sixteenth-century London. While Alice Layston is the central figure here, there will also be biographical sketches of her two husbands and of the four leaseholders of the Cross Keys during its years as a playhouse—Richard Ibbotson, Edward Walker, John Franklin, and James Beare. In that sense, this paper is a (partial) biography of the inn as well as its owner.[5]

The future owner of the Cross Keys was born Alice Poore, daughter of John Poore of Meopham, Kent (five miles south of Gravesend) and his wife Dorothy.[6] She had two sisters, Cicely and Dorothy, and a brother, Thomas. John Poore died in 1548, and around the same time or soon afterward, Alice Poore married her first husband, Richard Westerfield. Westerfield was from Kent also, but he soon left to seek his fortune in London, if he had not already done so at the time of the marriage. On July 24, 1551, he bought a house in Knightrider Street, London, in the parish of St. Benet Paul's Wharf south of St. Paul's, from Richard Hyndeman, citizen and broderer.[7] Fifteen months later, on October 15, 1552, Westerfield paid twenty shillings to become a freeman of the Vintners' Company by redemption, allowing him to trade in London.[8] He most likely imported wine and sold it wholesale, but did not have a retail outlet. I have found no evidence that he ran a tavern, though there was a tavern or brewhouse in Knightrider Street, the White Hart, owned and operated by other people.[9] In fact, the Knightrider Street house appears to have been used primarily as an investment, since by the late 1550s, Westerfield was both living and working in other areas of London. In the 1559 London tax assessment, "Richard Westerfeld" is listed as a resident of St. Vedast Foster Lane parish, at the west end of Cheapside near St. Paul's, where he was assessed on £120 of goods, the fifth most out of the twenty-two householders listed in the parish.[10] St. Vedast was a wealthy parish where many goldsmiths lived, and it was also the location of the Horsehead in Cheap, a popular tavern where plays were being performed a dozen years later.[11] Also in 1559, Westerfield was leasing a "great cellar" underneath Scales Inn, a large building in Maiden Lane in St. Michael Paternoster parish.[12] This was a quarter mile east of Knightrider Street near Vintners' Hall and St. Martin Vintry church, in the area where vintners unloaded their wares from the Thames and did much of their business. Westerfield served as a warden of the Vintners' Company in 1558–59 and bound one apprentice, Edward

146 DAVID KATHMAN

Browne, in 1561. He also freed two other apprentices (Rowland Chatterton and Rauf Rydlay) who had originally been bound to other vintners.[13]

By 1551 or soon afterward, Richard and Alice Westerfield had two sons, John and Henry.[14] The elder son, John, was an "idiot," meaning, in modern parlance, that he was mentally handicapped in some way and unable to care for himself. We may tend to assume that the Elizabethans tossed such people aside or shut them away in asylums such as the notorious Bedlam, but this did not happen to John Westerfield; he was well provided for in his father's will, lived into his forties, and eventually married. In fact, Richard Westerfield's provisions for his son John would eventually, through a circuitous route, end up having a significant effect on the history of the Cross Keys inn during its time as a playhouse.

Richard Westerfield made his will on December 4, 1565, when his sons were still teenagers.[15] His estate consisted mainly of the house in St. Benet Paul's Wharf, then in the tenure of Francis Segar, citizen and scrivener, plus two houses and eighty acres of land in Boxley and Bearsted, Kent, two villages near Maidstone about five miles apart, which he had recently purchased from William and Lettice Collins and John Godden. Ordinarily, at least some of this property would have gone to the eldest son, John, but the boy, as his mother would later write, "was so symple that he was not fytt nor able by hymself to dispose give or order eyther lands or goods."[16] So Richard gave these properties to Alice for use during her natural life, while also specifying that she should "stande charged and burdoned withe the kepinge fyndinge and meynteyninge of my sonne John Westerfeld duringe her saide Naturall lief withe meate drincke lodginge dyett Apparell and all other necessary provision meete and conveniente for him." After the death of "the saide Alice his Mother my wief," the rents from the properties were to be used for "the kepinge fyndinge lyvinge and Meyneteyning of the saide John my sonne," though John would have no control over them. Control would go first to John's brother Henry, then in trust to the will's overseers as long as John was still alive. After John's death, the properties were to go to any heirs of John, then to Henry and his heirs, then to William Bromfeld, the son of Richard's sister Isabell.

Apart from some minor bequests to servants, including his former apprentice Rauf Rydlay, the rest of Richard Westerfield's goods were equally divided between Alice and Henry, who were also the will's executors. Henry would receive his portion once he turned 21, until which time it was to be "discretely pollitiquelie frendly and Motherly putt Owte by the said Alice his Mother and my Overseers hereafter named." The will specified that "the saide Henrie my sonne shall be broughte vppe in lerninge and other vertuous exercises," and also gave Henry "Advertisement hereby that he be not to hastie hereafter to occupie before he can bothe governe his yonge age and well decerne of the thinges he myndethe to trade and Medell withe." It is hard not to think that Richard, having provided for the lifetime care of his mentally handicapped son, invested considerable hopes in his other son. Henry apparently did receive a decent education, since in 1575 he signed a deposition "*per* me Henricum Westerfild*um*" in an italic hand, demonstrating some knowledge of Latin; however, he failed to live up to his father's high expectations in other ways, as we will see later.[17] Alice and Henry proved Richard Westerfield's will on August 26, 1566.

The overseers of the will were "my lovinge ffrendes William Abraham Citizen and Vinetener of london and Henrie fissher of Boxley in the saide Countie of Kente Gent." The fact that William Abraham was Richard Westerfield's "lovinge ffrend" is potentially significant for our purposes, for Abraham had numerous connections, albeit indirect ones, to early London theatrical activity. Since 1553, he had been leasing the Cardinal's Hat tavern in Lombard Street, one of three taverns in St. Mary Woolnoth parish, where he may have been a customer of Richard Westerfield's wholesale wine business. The other two taverns in the parish, the Bishop's Head and the White Horse, were hosting plays a few doors away in 1543.[18] Admittedly this was a decade before Abraham took over the Cardinal's Hat, but Abraham was also a friend of Robert Fryer, another resident of the parish who was hosting plays in 1566, when Abraham lived there. When Fryer made his will a decade later, Abraham was one of his overseers.[19]

Two years after Richard Westerfield's death, Alice Westerfield married John Layston, a fellow Kent native who had become a citizen and girdler of London, and was himself a recent widower. Layston was about forty-three years old at the time of the marriage and quite wealthy, having improved his lot eight years before by marrying Joan Crowley, the widow of his fellow girdler Robert Crowley. That marriage had taken place in Allhallows Lombard Street on October 16, 1560, less than five months after Robert Crowley's death on 1 June of the same year.[20] Joan had brought to the marriage two buildings in Allhallows Lombard Street that she had inherited from Crowley for use during her lifetime, along with unspecified goods, chattels, and other resources.[21] Circumstantial evidence suggests that these resources were considerable, for John Layston, who is not known to have owned any property before this first wedding, made several major real estate purchases during the five years he was married to Joan Crowley. One of these purchases was of the Cross Keys inn and related buildings in Allhallows Lombard Street, which Layston only accidentally ended up owning after a rather complicated series of events. Understanding how this happened will require us to back up in our narrative a bit and consider the history of the Cross Keys.

The Cross Keys was located on the west side of Gracechurch Street in the parish of Allhallows Lombard Street, immediately north of the parish church and immediately south of the Bell Inn, where plays were also performed regularly in the late sixteenth century. It was about 140 feet long extending west

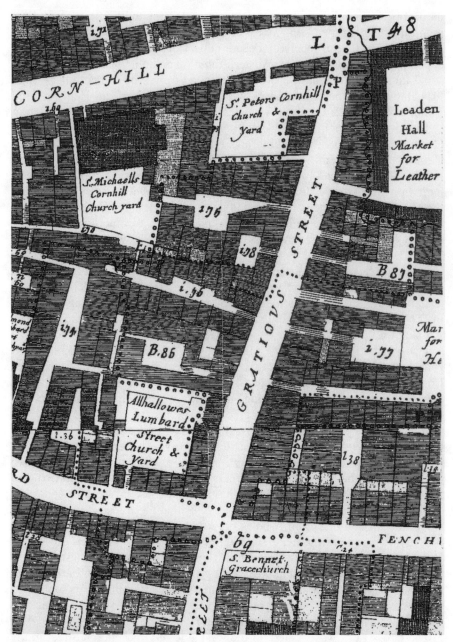

Allhallows Lombard Street in the 1676 Ogilby and Morgan map of London. The Cross Keys is B.86, and the Bell is i.76, directly to the north. Courtesy of City of London Archives and Libraries.

from the street, and was 80 feet wide at the back end but narrower on the Gracechurch Street end, with 32 feet of street frontage. There was a single yard in the middle, roughly 48 feet long (east-west) by 32 feet wide (north-south).[22] The Cross Keys had been owned since 1407 by the College of Pontefract, Yorkshire, but in 1548 it was seized by Edward VI following the second Chantries Act, which dissolved all collegiate churches.[23] On April 18, 1549, the king granted all of the College's London-area properties, along with much other property in London and elsewhere, to William Warde, gentleman; this included "the Crossekeyes" in Gracechurch Street, then said to be in the tenure of Richard Walton.[24] Warde sold the Cross Keys almost immediately to William Johnson alias Fawne, citizen and innholder, and his wife Alice, who definitely owned and occupied the inn a few years later. In fact, William Johnson alias Fawne had apparently been living in the parish since at least 1541, possibly subletting the Cross Keys from Richard Walton, who disappears from our story after 1549.[25] On December 18, 1550, the Johnsons purchased from the Merchant Tailors' Company an adjacent group of buildings formerly called the Scutt on the Hoop, now called the Lion on the Hoop or Lion Alley. The entire complex was 53 feet long (east-west) by 30 feet wide (north-south), wedged between the Cross Keys to the south and west and the Bell inn to the north, fronting on Gracechurch Street and with a small yard behind, about 16 by 30 feet.[26]

Within a few years, the Johnsons appear to have needed cash, possibly due to financial troubles. On November 14, 1552, they mortgaged the Cross Keys to Richard Spryngham, citizen and mercer, and a year later, on November 17, 1553, they sold the Lion on the Hoop to Christopher Clifford, citizen and saddler, who had been leasing it along with three other tenants.[27] They may have used the proceeds from the Lion on the Hoop sale to help pay off the Cross Keys mortgage, in order not to lose the inn. In any case, the mortgage was definitely paid off by June 30, 1556. On that date, the Johnsons once again mortgaged the Cross Keys, this time for £418 to Richard Clifton, citizen and skinner, who then leased it back to the Johnsons; as long as they repaid the £418 by Christmas 1561, they would regain ownership of the inn then. Not quite six months later, on December 14, 1556, Christopher Clifford similarly mortgaged the Lion on the Hoop for £50 to John Wetherell, goldsmith, with the same end date of Christmas 1561.[28] As that dual deadline approached, Johnson apparently decided to retire rather than pay off the mortgage, so he reached a deal with Clifford, who had aspirations to be an innkeeper. The core of the deal provided that Johnson would sell the Cross Keys to Clifford for £500, of which £418 would go to Richard Clifton to repay the mortgage; Johnson, his wife, and a maid would then be guaranteed rooms in the Cross Keys for the rest of their natural lives.[29]

Now Clifford had to find a way to borrow £500, since he did not have that kind of money lying around. Banks in the modern sense did not exist in

150   DAVID KATHMAN

Elizabethan London, so Clifford had to resort to private lenders. He "travelled a long tyme *with* dyuers and sundrie *persons*" before finally, "*with* muche ado," he was able reach an agreement with his wealthy neighbor John Layston, whom he had known since the mid-1540s.[30] The agreement involved a complicated four-way transaction. First, Clifford paid off his mortgage to John Wetherell, probably with financial help from Johnson, after which he transferred part of the Lion on the Hoop to Johnson while keeping part of it for himself. Layston then purchased the Lion on the Hoop in two parts, buying Johnson's part on November 12, 1561, and Clifford's part two days later. It was probably at least partly with the proceeds of this transaction that Clifford then paid Johnson £200 for the furniture and other household stuff of the Cross Keys.[31] On Christmas Eve, the day before the end of the mortgage to Richard Clifton, Layston summoned Clifford to his house in Lombard Street and lent him £500 in "Angels ffrenche Crownes Spanysshe money and money of thys Realme." Of this amount, £418 was set aside to repay the mortgage, with the other £82 going to Johnson as the remainder of the £500 that Clifford was paying him for the Cross Keys. Layston paid £400 to Clifton, but deliberately withheld the other £18 so that the mortgage would default the following day and Johnson would no longer have any rights to the property. The day after that, on December 26, Clifton signed a deed transferring ownership of the Cross Keys to Layston in exchange for the £418. In turn, Layston and Clifford signed an agreement whereby Clifford would would repay the £500 to Layston over the next ten years, in quarterly installments of £12 10s plus interest, apparently 10 percent annually. If Clifford made all the payments, then at the end of the ten years he would own the Cross Keys outright, and Layston would relinquish any rights to it.[32] In effect, Layston was acting like a modern bank issuing a ten-year mortgage to Clifford with the right to foreclose on the property if Clifford failed to make his payments. Just to be safe, Layston filed two quit-claims on March 19, 1562, in which Johnson and Richard Spryngham (of the 1552 mortgage) surrendered any claim to the Cross Keys or the Lion on the Hoop.[33]

Within less than a year, this mortgage agreement between Layston and Clifford had unraveled. The dispute centered around the two houses in the Lion on the Hoop which Clifford had sold directly to Layston, rather than indirectly through Johnson. Clifford had been under the impression that these two houses were part of the mortgage deal, so that if he paid Layston an extra £100 at the end of the ten years, he would own them again along with the Cross Keys; presumably this was why he had separated them from the rest of the Lion on the Hoop at the time of the sale. However, Layston denied that these houses were part of the deal. After making his first three quarterly payments to Layston, Clifford refused to make any more until he received assurances that he would eventually get the two houses back, but Layston would not agree. For whatever reason, this became a huge sticking point, and Clifford never did make any further payments after the first three as he pursued various options, including a petition to the recorder of London. But Layston held most of the cards, since he now had legal title to the Cross Keys as well as the two disputed houses, and by the end of 1563 he was able to foreclose and evict Clifford under the terms of their agreement. He apparently began leasing the Cross Keys to Richard Ibbotson, citizen and brewer, who had children baptized in Allhallows Lombard Street starting in 1564, and who was definitely the leaseholder several years later. In 1566, the crown brought suit against Layston for usury over the Cross Keys sale, but nothing came of this, and thenceforth Layston was the undisputed owner of the Cross Keys.[34] By this time he was also the owner of various cottages in Mason's Alley, St. Katherine Cree parish, which he had bought on December 20, 1563, from William Browne, citizen and haberdasher.[35]

John Layston became a widower in August 1565 when Joan Crowley Layston died less than five years into their marriage.[36] Almost exactly one year later, Alice Westerfield became a widow when Richard Westerfield died, as we saw earlier. Soon afterward, the widower John Layston got together with the widow Alice Westerfield, and by early 1568 the couple was preparing to marry. As part of these preparations, Layston had a deed made up on February 11, 1568, in which he granted the Cross Keys, the Lion on the Hoop (including the two disputed houses), and the cottages in St. Katherine Cree to two trustees (William Abraham and John Fisher, the overseers of Richard Westerfield's will) for the use of himself and Alice during their lives.[37] This was done to settle these properties on Alice as her jointure, which would provide for her if she should outlive her husband. The effect of this common legal maneuver was that John and Alice would jointly own the properties while they were married, and after one of them died, the other would retain control for his or her natural life, after which they would revert to John's right heirs. Since John Layston had no children, his nearest heir was his brother Robert, who lived in Gravesend, Kent, with his wife and children. Robert Layston does not appear to have liked his new sister-in-law, and over the next two decades, Robert and his heirs would be perpetual thorns in Alice Layston's side.

John Layston and Alice Westerfield must have married soon after this, though they did not do so in Allhallows Lombard Street, and no record of the exact date has been found. Not long into the marriage, the Laystons found themselves the target of a lawsuit brought by the relatives of Robert Crowley, the first husband of John Layston's first wife Joan. In his will, Robert Crowley had left to Joan two buildings in Lombard Street which he had purchased in 1548, a tavern called the Three Crowns and a house called the Blue Bell.[38] The will specified that Joan would only have these properties during her natural life; they were thus her jointure, similar to the Cross Keys and other properties which John Layston had settled on Alice to provide for her after his

152   DAVID KATHMAN

death. After Joan's death, the properties were to be sold, with the proceeds
being divided up among Robert Crowley's relatives; alternatively, if one of
those relatives wanted to buy the properties, they could do so. The ambiguity
here would seem to be inviting disputes among Crowley's relatives, but when
a dispute came, it centered around John Layston, who had taken control of
the properties while married to Joan Crowley. Upon Joan's death in 1565,
Layston showed no sign of giving up the properties, so after a few years,
some of Robert Crowley's relatives began taking steps to get them.

On May 24, 1569, nine years after Robert Crowley's death, an inquisition
post mortem was finally taken of his goods, probably at the instigation of his
relatives. It found that Joan Crowley had enjoyed the profits of the two Lombard Street houses (now in the tenure of John Layston and John Laycocke)
during her life, and that Robert Crowley's next heir was John Ferror, son of
his sister Isabella.[39] Then in early 1570, Alexander Banks, on behalf of more
than forty other named relatives of Robert Crowley, filed suit against Layston, Laycocke, and Layston's servant William Andrews, claiming the right
to the two houses according to Crowley's will.[40] John Layston, in his answer,
claimed to be subletting one of the houses (the Blue Bell) on a year-to-year
basis from John Cooke, who had leased it from Robert and Joan Crowley
during their lifetimes. Andrews, who occupied the shop, backed up this story.
Laycocke said that he occupied his house (the Three Crowns tavern) on a
twenty-one-year lease, originally granted by the Crowleys to Baldwin Smith
on March 1, 1554. However, neither of these answers addressed the question
of who was now collecting the rents on these leases after Joan Crowley's
death. Layston and Andrews did address this question in their rejoinder,
where they claimed that John Ferrer (named as Robert Crowley's heir in the
inquisition post mortem) and his cousin Agnes Jackson had sold the properties to Thomas Fanshawe of London, esquire. The implication was that Layston was a mere tenant who had never owned the properties, and that Banks
and the other complainants had no right to them, since the proper heir had
already sold them. However, later evidence suggests that John Layston was
almost certainly lying about these key points.

This evidence emerged after Layston died on April 1, 1571 with the dispute still unresolved.[41] The Crowley relatives continued to pursue their legal
claims, and one of these relatives, Margaret Spencer, filed suit in Chancery
on June 18 against Alice Layston, her son Henry Westerfield (now about
twenty years old), and Mary Langley, after they did not show up to answer
her suit in the Mayor's Court.[42] Spencer claimed her right to the Blue Bell,
and also asked that Alice be forced to "pay all rents that is dewe since the
wife of Robt Crowley died." The court ordered the defendants either to give
the house to Spencer or to appear personally within ten days, whereupon
Alice Layston told a somewhat different story than her late husband had. She
said in her answer that John Layston had indeed owned the Blue Bell, and

ALICE LAYSTON AND THE CROSS KEYS 153

that it was he who had sold it to Thomas Fanshawe. However, Fanshawe then "privily" let it back to the Laystons for the term of their lives at no rent, as part of a secret agreement; he then sold the reversion of the property to one Oldshawe, who agreed to respect Alice's interests as long as she was alive.[43] It is difficult to avoid the conclusion that John Layston was trying to hide his ownership of the Blue Bell (and presumably the Three Crowns as well) to protect himself and Alice from legal claims by Robert Crowley's relatives, but Alice was unable to keep up the charade and lost the houses. The Blue Bell ended up in the hands of four of the Crowley relatives, who on March 25, 1572, sold it for £160 to Anthony Higgins, scrivener, and Thomas Peerson, merchant. The indenture by which they did so includes legal language to cover every contingency, and was originally accompanied by a long list of supporting docments, including a deed of feoffment from John Layston to Thomas Fanshawe and other documents supporting Alice Layston's version of the story.[44]

In the middle of all this, Alice Layston had to deal with the more direct consequences of her husband's death, including yet another legal challenge. Almost immediately after John Layston's death on April 1, his brother and heir Robert Layston began aggressively challenging the deed of jointure by which Alice Layston was poised to inherit the Cross Keys and the other properties. Undoubtedly weary from the Crowley litigation, eager to avoid another lengthy and expensive court case, and sensing the law on her side, Alice agreed to arbitration. A four-person arbitration panel was quickly convened, and on April 7, Alice and Robert Layston signed a £1000 bond under which they agreed to abide by the panel's decision. On April 13, the arbitrators issued their ruling. The jointure deed of February 11, 1568, was to be enforced "without the lawful lett impediment or deniall of the said Robarte Laystone his heires or assignes," meaning that Alice was to "have houlde and enioye All that messuage called the crosse keys . . . then in the tenure of Richarde Ibbottson of London brewer sett and beinge in gracious streete in London," along with the various other properties included in the jointure, and the properties, leases, goods, and chattels she had inherited from her first husband Richard Westerfield and from John Layston. Apparently at the request of Robert Layston, the arbitrators also ruled that Alice "sholde have the ward shipp custodie rule and gouernement of John Westerfelde the Ideott and all the estates terms comodeties and profitte which may arise come or growe by reason theirof." The arbitrators further ruled that Alice must administer the goods of John Layston within fifty days, and that during her natural life she should not "doe nor comitt, nor prove to be done or comitted any manner of waste for in and uppon the premises or any part or parcell theirof." This last provision was undoubtedly requested by Robert Layston to make sure that the properties were in good shape when he or his heirs took possession after Alice's death, though it would later be used for hostile purposes.[45]

154 DAVID KATHMAN

With this resounding victory behind her, and the litigation over the two disputed Lombard Street houses apparently also resolved, Alice Layston settled in as the landlord of the Cross Keys and the other properties she had inherited from John Layston. She lived in Allhallows Lombard Street while caring for her now-adult son John Westerfield; that parish would be her London base for the remaining nineteen years of her life, though she also spent time back home in Kent, where she was still collecting rents on the lands left to her by Richard Westerfield for the care of John. At some point before 1579, she also gained land in Newport, Shropshire, and sometimes described herself as being from there; presumably this was through inheritance, though it is not clear from whom she got this land. All this income allowed her to live quite comfortably, and to lend out money on occasion; the only legal issue she faced between 1571 and 1584 was a suit over a £100 debt owed to her by Robert Marshall alias Marchant of Maidstone, Kent.[46] During that same period, in contrast to the turmoil of the previous decade, the Cross Keys had a single owner (Alice Layston) and a single leaseholder (Richard Ibbotson).

It was during this period of relative calm, probably by 1576 and certainly by 1579, that the Cross Keys began regularly hosting plays. On 11 February 1579, a player named John Gibbes testified to the Court of Governors of Bridewell Hospital that a woman named Amy Mason alias Foster, "beinge at the crosse keyes wher he plaied wth his fellowes then she desired one Thomas Rowe his fellowe to bring her acquainted wth him," and that "Thomas did soe at anothe metinge on sondaie after at ther plaie."[47] On June 23 of the same year, James Burbage, owner of the Theater and father of Richard Burbage, was arrested at two o'clock in the afternoon "as he came down Graces street towardes the Crosse Keys there to a Playe," as part of a dispute with former business associate John Hind.[48]

The most pertinent question for our purposes is how much Alice Layston had to do with this playing. It is reasonable to think that she at least tolerated it and possibly encouraged it, especially since she lived in the parish at least some of the time. Her first husband's good friend William Abraham, with his various connections to London playing, was a trustee for the Cross Keys and lived less than a five-minute walk to the west on Lombard Street.[49] Abraham's friend and neighbor Robert Fryer had been hosting plays in Lombard Street in 1566 and possibly later, as we saw above, and a few years later there was playing at the Horsehead tavern in Alice's former home parish of St. Vedast Foster Lane. On the other hand, it was the leaseholder who actually operated the inn on a daily basis, and who presumably made the ultimate decision to start renting to players. From 1564 to 1584, that leaseholder was Richard Ibbotson, and it was Ibbotson who was perceived as the host by players. When one of James Burbage's lawyers asked John Hind about Burbage's arrest in 1579, he asked whether Hind had sent a sheriff's deputy "vnto the

Croskeys in gratious street being then the dwelling howse of Richard Ibotson Cittizen and Bruer of London" to find and arrest Burbage.[50]

Richard Ibbotson was born about 1527 in Kettlewell in Craven, Yorkshire.[51] He came to London to be apprenticed to a brewer and was eventually "abled" as a member of the Brewers' Company in 1559–60, at the somewhat advanced age of thirty-two or thirty-three. Soon after this, on June 30, 1560, he married Emma Neal at St. Andrew Hubbard, a little southeast of Lombard Street.[52] When the Cross Keys became available a few years later after John Layston evicted Christopher Clifford, Ibbotson seized the opportunity and began leasing it from Layston. He was named as the leaseholder when Layston included the Cross Keys in the deed of jointure in 1568, as we saw above, and also at the time of Layston's inquisition post mortem in 1576. Ibbotson and his wife Emma had seven children baptized in Allhallows Lombard between 1564 and 1573, and buried three children there, the last one in 1577. Their third daughter, baptized September 28, 1567, was named Alice, and it is tempting to wonder whether Alice Layston may have been that child's godmother.[53] On October 16, 1567, Richard Ibbotson became a "brother" of the Brewers' Company, a higher level of membership that required paying quarterage dues but allowed him to register apprentices with the company, among other privileges. Over the next eleven years, he registered seven apprentices, of whom six were from Yorkshire, and two were from his own hometown of Kettlewell in Craven.[54] Presumably these apprentices helped out at the Cross Keys in some capacity, perhaps even helping with plays when they were performed there.

By the time the Cross Keys started hosting plays, Ibbotson had become wealthy enough to start buying real estate as an investment. On May 24, 1576, he bought from Thomas Challoner of Lynfield, Sussex, and Anna his wife, several properties in the north part of the city inside Bishopsgate.[55] On October 4, 1580, on behalf of his son John (then not quite twelve years old), he bought from Sir Thomas Heneage, treasurer of the queen's chamber and a future privy councillor, meadow lands in the manor of Bretts in West Ham, Essex, and probably around the same time, he bought other lands in Essex from Anthony Cooke and John Stepneth.[56] It was Heneage who paid players for court performances between 1570 and 1595, and it is tempting to think that Ibbotson may have met him through some of these players.[57] Ibbotson's London property included two buildings in White Horse Yard, mostly in the parish of St. Peter le Poer but partly in Allhallows London Wall to the north, plus another building to the north, entirely in Allhallows London Wall parish.[58] It is interesting to note that White Horse Yard was connected to the yard of the Bull inn in Bishopsgate Street, one of the other three inns that became playhouses around the same time as the Cross Keys. One entered White Horse Yard off Broad Street, and at the south end of the long, L-shaped yard was a passage into the westernmost of the Bull's three yards, from which

156   DAVID KATHMAN

one could go east and eventually come out on Bishopsgate Street.[59] Further solidifying the connection between Ibbotson and the Bull is the fact that in 1582, Ibbotson testified that he had personally known William Mease, the former owner of the Bull who had died in 1573, and whose son George owned the Bull during the time it hosted plays.[60]

Richard Ibbotson made his will on October 27, 1584, and was buried in Allhallows Lombard Street on November 26.[61] By that time, he had only two surviving children, John (baptized November 3, 1568) and Mary (baptized July 26, 1573), plus Elizabeth Ibbotson, "my mayde whome I have broughte vpp and kepte from her childhoode." To John he gave his lands and tenements in Essex; to Mary he gave his London properties, including his "greate Messuage" in Allhallows London Wall, then in the occupation of Peter Foy. If both John and Mary died without issue, the "greate Messuage" would go to his maid Elizabeth, and the other properties would go to his widow Emma, but only as long as she remained a widow. If she remarried, then the properties would go to Ibbotson's executors, with the revenue going to pay various annual charitable bequests. Those executors were Ibbotson's neighbors Simon Horspoole, citizen and draper, and Roger Preston, citizen and scrivener.[62]

As for the Cross Keys, the lease initially went to Ibbotson's widow Emma, so that, for a few months at least, the owner and the leaseholder of the Cross Keys were both women. However, a little more than three months later, on March 8, 1585, Emma Ibbotson married Henry Smith in Allhallows Lombard Street.[63] Smith brought to the marriage two leases for various properties in Lambeth and Southwark which he was subletting to others, and another lease for a building on Thames Street in St. Lawrence Pountney parish, which he now occupied. Four days before the wedding, on March 4, Smith transferred these leases in trust to Simon Horspoole and Roger Preston, Richard Ibbotson's executors, in a standard jointure agreement intended to provide for Emma should he predecease her.[64] On the other hand, Emma's lease of the Cross Keys apparently became invalid upon her remarriage, with Horsepoole and Preston temporarily holding the inn's contents in their roles as executors until a new leaseholder could be found. That did not take long, for control of the inn passed smoothly to Edward Walker, citizen and saddler, a fellow innkeeper who (by his own testimony) had known Richard Ibbotson personally. The day after the wedding, on March 9, Walker bought the inn's "goodes ymplyments and houshold stuff" from Horspoole and Preston for £160, of which half was to go to each of Ibbotson's two children when they married or turned twenty-one. Then Alice Layston granted Walker a new lease of the Cross Keys for a term of forty years at a rent of £24 a year, starting on Lady Day (March 25) 1585.[65]

For the previous ten years, Walker had occupied the Green Dragon inn on Bishopsgate Street, immediately north of the Bull, first leasing it and eventually buying it outright. Walker later testified that he "came to dwell in Ibottsons hows called the Cross keys in Graces street" after Ibbotson's death, and he was definitely living there between July 5, 1585, and January 19, 1586, when a fishmonger named Walter Woodward claimed that "Edward Walker of Gracioustrete Inholder" had sold "fleshe victualls" on Fridays and Saturdays at his "common Inne or victualinge howse wherunto dyvers persons resorte for lodging and victualls."[66] However, Walker continued to run the Green Dragon at the same time, and would later go back to it full-time.[67] Walker was undoubtedly familiar with the playing at the neighboring Bull, which he would also eventually buy years later; thus, in 1585 he must have known what he was getting into at the Cross Keys, and the playing there may even have been an attraction.[68] He also would have been familiar with playing at the Bell, directly north of the Cross Keys, through his fellow saddler Henry Haughton. Haughton held the lease on the Bell from about 1575 until his death in 1601, including the entire period when it hosted plays. He and Walker were active in the Saddlers' Company over the same period of time, serving as auditors and wardens of the Saddlers multiple times in the 1580s and 1590s, and serving together as wardens in 1594–95.[69]

Around the same time that Edward Walker was settling in at the Cross Keys, Alice Layston faced renewed trouble from her late husband's family. Her husband's brother Robert Layston, who had challenged the deed of jointure back in 1571, had died in 1580. In his will (made on February 5, 1580, and proved on January 10, 1581), he had left all of his London properties to his son William, paying particular attention to the Cross Keys, which Robert's heirs were scheduled to inherit after Alice Layston's death. If William died without issue, the properties were to go to another son, John, on condition that within one year he pay £200 to a third son, Thomas; if John did not do so, then Thomas could "enter into all that my messuage or Tenement Comonlie called the Crosse Keyes Scituate lyinge and beinge in Gracyous streete wth in the saide cittie of London."[70] All that was to be moot for our purposes, though, since William Layston survived through the rest of the sixteenth century. On September 4, 1581, Robert Layston's widow Cicely remarried, to Thomas Tuttesham in West Peckham, Kent.[71]

In early 1585, William Layston, along with his mother and stepfather the Tutteshams, launched a legal attack against Alice Layston in an effort to get the Cross Keys while Alice was still alive. The dispute centered around the two houses in the Lion on the Hoop that had once belonged to Christopher Clifford, and which had caused the rift between Clifford and John Layston in 1562. At some point before 1585, Alice, perceiving that the houses were "in greate decaye," had them pulled down, "and newlie builded and erected in the same place wheare the other stood one new tenemente vearie substanciall stronge fayrer and far excellinge the former at any tyme in goodnes strongnes and comodetie," at a cost of £100.[72] The Tutteshams and William Layston filed suit against Alice Layston in Queen's Bench, claiming that by tearing down the two houses, she had commited "waste" in violation of the 1571 arbitration award. Since she had signed a £1000 bond promising to uphold that award, the plaintiffs claimed that the bond should be forfeit, and that Alice should pay them the £1000 and surrender the properties, including the Cross Keys.

On June 30, 1585, Alice countersued them in the Court of Requests, asking the crown to issue a writ ordering the Tutteshams and William Layston to surcease and no longer pursue the suit. She claimed that whereas the old buildings "weare before of smale value, the said tenement is greatly bettered and not impairyied," and that the rent from the new building was at least as much as that from the two old ones. The Tutteshams and William Layston claimed that Alice had built the new tenement using the timbers and tiles from the old ones, adding a claim that she had "suffered the grete messuage or tenement called the cross keis to run greatlye to ruiyn and decay, and divers other lesser tenements, for want of necessarye and sufficient repara-cions, to the greate scandale and impechment of the inheritance belonging to this defendant William Layston."[73] Other evidence we will see below supports the claim that the Cross Keys had become run-down and in need of repairs by the late 1580s. The partial surviving records of the Court of Requests do not reveal the results of this case, but Alice Layston must have won, since she continued to own the Cross Keys and collect the rent until her death.[74]

With this challenge from her late husband's relatives taken care of, Alice Layston still had to deal with her own offspring. Her mentally handicapped eldest son John Westerfield was still living with her, being cared for with the rents and profits from the properties his father had left—the house in Knight-rider Street and the eighty acres of land in Kent. Her other son Henry, despite his father's high hopes, had turned out to be something of a wastrel, "geven to some unthryftines & prodigall in expenses" as his mother put it. Around 1583 Henry Westerfield, "beinge in some wante & distres for moneye," sought to make some fast cash from his future rights in the land in Kent now being used to support his brother, which he stood to inherit once both Alice and John were dead. He went to Thomas Wrothe of the Inner Temple, who was from Bexley, a village in Kent about twenty miles from Boxley and Bearsted, where the lands were located.[75] For a fine of £5 paid up front, Henry granted Wrothe a one hundred-year lease on the Kent lands, to begin after Alice Layston's death. This fine seems suspiciously low, but Henry Westerfield was financially unsophisticated and prone to being taken advantage of, to judge by the evidence and his mother's later testimony. Wrothe got him to sign a £200 performance bond promising to make good on the lease when the time came.[76]

By this time, both John and Henry Westerfield were unmarried and thus

ALICE LAYSTON AND THE CROSS KEYS

lacked heirs, raising the question of what would happen to Richard Westerfield's legacy once they were gone. In the first half of 1586, both brothers married, most likely at the instigation of their mother. On March 14, John married Agnes Ryley at St. Leonard Shoreditch in London, and the couple came to live with Alice Layston.[77] On June 29, Henry married Lydia Skinner in Bury St. Edmunds, Suffolk. She was the only daughter of Andrew Skinner, a minor householder of Bury St. Edmunds.[78] Neither marriage was a step up the social scale, but the brothers' options were undoubtedly limited. If this was a plan to continue the Westerfield family line, it failed, for both brothers would eventually die without issue anyway. John Westerfield died only eighteen months after his wedding, and was buried in Allhallows Lombard Street on July 25, 1587.[79] His death set off a chain of events that would cause an irreparable rift between Alice Layston and Edward Walker, and which thus had a significant effect on the history of the Cross Keys.

Soon after John's death, Alice Layston learned for the first time about the lease on the Kent lands that Henry had granted to Thomas Wrothe. She was not amused, and became determined to get the lease back on Henry's behalf, "for the motherlye love & affeccion which she dyd & dothe beare to her sayde sonne." She knew that her tenant Edward Walker had a friend named John Persehouse who was a member of the Inner Temple with Wrothe, so she asked Walker and Persehouse to go there and try to buy the lease and the related performance bond from Wrothe on her behalf, saying she would reimburse them for whatever they paid and give them some extra for their troubles. Persehouse's maternal grandfather Myles Wymbish had owned Walker's other inn, the Green Dragon, from 1545 to 1552, and his parents had later been involved in a legal dispute over the ownership of the inn, which is undoubtedly how he met Walker.[80] Some time in August 1587, Walker and Persehouse went to Wrothe's chamber in the Temple and persuaded him to sell them the lease and the bond.[81] They had to pay him a fine of £10, rather than the original £5, because John Westerfield's death had made the lease more valuable.[82]

Instead of going to Alice Layston with the documents, however, the pair went to Henry Westerfield and persuaded him to sell them the Kent lands outright, bypassing Alice altogether. They did this by exploiting an ambiguity in Richard Westerfield's will combined with a somewhat obscure corner of property law. Recall that the will had granted the Kent lands to Alice for her lifetime, so that she might provide for her son John with the profits; after her death, Henry was to continue providing for his brother with the profits, and once John died, the lands were to go to any heirs he might have, or, in the absence of such heirs, to Henry and his heirs. However, the will did not provide for the possibility that John might die before Alice and Henry, which is in fact what happened. Alice already had possession of the lands, and had a strong claim to keep them, since they had been granted to her for her life.

160   DAVID KATHMAN

But the will also said explicitly that Henry would inherit the lands if John died without heirs, providing him with a plausible claim as well; only if this claim was valid would the sale to Walker and Persehouse be valid. Alice demanded that Walker and Persehouse sell her the lease and the bond according to their agreement, but they refused, and instead demanded of her the ownership documents for the lands, which they now claimed for themselves.

After several months in which neither side budged, the tension between Alice Layston and her tenant must have become unbearable. On January 6, 1588, Edward Walker sold his lease of the Cross Keys to John Franklin, citizen and clothworker, and went back to the Green Dragon full time while continuing to battle his former landlady.[83] On February 13, Persehouse and Walker filed suit against Alice in Chancery, accusing her of "misconveyance suppressing or imbeselling" the ownership documents for the Kent lands. They asserted that Henry's claim to the lands trumped hers because of the custom of gavelkind, an ancient form of land tenure that still survived mainly in Kent. Under this custom, property descended to all of a man's sons equally at his death; thus, they claimed, Henry had actually owned half of the lands at his father's death, and after his brother's death he owned them all, giving him the right to sell them.[84] Alice responded by countersuing them on May 13, asking the court to issue a subpoena so that Walker and Persehouse would have to come to court and answer under oath concerning their promise to convey the lease and bond to her. In an obvious bid for sympathy, she called herself "a verye aged woman & *with*out anye ayde or frends to assyst her in her sut*es* & troubles." She also claimed that Persehouse and Walker "subtillye & craftelye by deceite & covine have allured & entyced" Henry Westerfield, "beinge a simple yonge man," to sell them all his lands, tenements, and hereditaments for one-tenth their value, bringing him to financial ruin.[85]

These cases dragged on for more than two years and were only ended by Alice Layston's death, so that Persehouse and Walker eventually triumphed by default.[86] When Walker made his will fourteen years later on April 20, 1602, among the bequests were lands and tenements in Bearsted and Weavering, Kent, which he left to his son John.[87] Given that Bearsted was (and is) a fairly small village, and no other evidence links Walker to it, or to Kent in general, it seems very likely that this is part of the land that was the subject of the dispute. Persehouse's 1636 will mentions various lands in Staffordshire but none in Kent, but this was nearly fifty years after the dispute. Persehouse, along with his father and various other relatives, had been actively buying and selling land in Staffordshire between 1585 and 1601, and he most likely sold any Kent lands during that time.[88]

Meanwhile, as noted above, John Franklin, citizen and clothworker, was now in charge of the Cross Keys after having purchased the lease from Edward Walker. Franklin had become a freeman of the Clothworkers' Company on July 16, 1582, by redemption, meaning he bought his freedom and must have had some connections.[89] By his own later testimony, Franklin found the Cross Keys in great need of repairs, so he spent considerable money on wainscot, glass, settles (high-backed wooden benches), and ironwork, among other things, to get the inn into presentable shape.[90] He may have done this at least partly to make it more attractive as a playing space, for we know that Strange's Men, at least, were playing there during Franklin's tenure. On November 6, 1589, Lord Mayor Sir John Harte wrote to the Privy Council complaining about his attempt to enforce a recent order of theirs suspending playing within the city. The Lord Admiral's players "very dutifullie obeyed," but the Lord Strange's players "in very Contemptuous manner departing from me, went to the Crosse keys and played that afternoon, to the great offence of the better sorte that knewe they were prohibited by order of your L."[91]

Eight months later, on Thursday, July 9, 1590, Alice Layston's former daughter-in-law Anne Westerfield, widow of her son John, was buried in Allhallows Lombard Street.[92] At six o'clock that same evening, perhaps right after the funeral, Alice sent for Thomas Stallard, Doctor of Divinity, William Horne, and "divers others" (apparently several female servants), and made her nuncupative (oral) will. Describing herself as "Alice Layston widowe . . . of the parishe of All Hallowes Lambardstreete London beinge sicke in bodie yet of good and perfect memorye," she took William Horne by the hand, bequeathed to him "all her Landes Leases and goods whatsoeuer," and named him her executor. She must have died almost immediately, for this nuncupative will was written down and proved the following day.[93] For whatever reason, she was not buried in Allhallows Lombard Street, despite apparently dying there; she may have been buried with her first husband Richard Westerfield, perhaps in St. Benet Paul's Wharf, whose registers do not survive from this period.

Who were Thomas Stallard and William Horne, the two friends who were with Alice Layston at her death? Stallard had studied at Corpus Christi College, Cambridge, where he received a BA in 1565–66, an MA in 1569, and a Doctor of Divinity in 1585. He was a fellow of Corpus Christi in 1567–70, and served as domestic chaplain to Archbishop Matthew Parker, who had earlier been Master of Corpus. Stallard had been rector of Allhallows Lombard Street in 1573, which is undoubtedly how he met Alice Layston, but since 1574 he had been rector of St. Mary at Hill near Billingsgate, where he was to remain until 1606.[94]

William Horne was a longtime resident of Allhallows Lombard Street who had been freed as a Grocer on October 6, 1551, after serving an apprenticeship with John Gresham.[95] At the time of Alice Layston's death, he was living in the parish with his second wife Isabel and his daughter Alice. His sons Thomas and Nicholas also lived in the parish, as did his daughter Margaret and her husband William Albert, citizen and draper, who lived in Lombard

162 DAVID KATHMAN

Street in a house owned by Horne.[96] The lands and leases that Alice Layston bequeathed to William Horne did not include the Cross Keys or any of the other properties in her jointure, which were automatically going to William Layston no matter what she did. They also did not include the house in Knightrider Street, which was automatically going to her son Henry Westerfield according to the terms of Richard Westerfield's will. However, that house, which was now subdivided into four messuages, ended up with William Horne in any case; Henry sold three of the messuages to Horne shortly after Alice's death, while keeping one for himself, perhaps to live in.[97] It may seem strange that Alice did not mention Henry in her will, but he was already being provided for, and nuncupative wills such as this one do not include much extraneous information. In any case, Henry Westerfield was dead by July 1, 1591, when William Horne's will mentions the messuages in Knightrider Street "which I late had and purchased to me & my heires and Assignes for ever of Henry Westerfeilde late citizen and vintenar of London deceased."[98] Within six months after that, Henry's wife Lydia had remarried, for when Horne bought the remaining messuage of the Knightrider Street house on January 29, 1592, the seller was John Cadiolde of Cockfield, Suffolk, and his wife "Lidea," the widow of Henry Westerfield, late citizen and vintner of London.[99]

William Horne died on May 4, 1592, and was buried in Allhallows Lombard Street on May 9, and his will was proved on June 19.[100] The will shows that he owned or leased numerous London properties besides the Knightrider Street house and the Lombard Street house occupied by his daughter.[101] Most significantly for our purposes, he was leasing the former Lion on the Hoop complex on Gracechurch Street from William Layston, who had inherited it from Alice Layston along with the rest of the jointure properties.[102] Horne was subletting one of the houses to John Winge, citizen and saddler, and the other to Elizabeth Fisher, widow; the will specified that Elizabeth Fisher should be allowed to stay in her house for the next two years, and that his sons Thomas and Nicholas should live together in the other house during the same period, with Thomas taking over the lease. On February 9, 1593, William Layston sold the Lion on the Hoop buildings to Thomas Horne, who was occupying them along with his brother Nicholas, Isabell Horne, widow (their stepmother), and Elizabeth Fisher.[103]

The transfer of the Cross Keys did not go nearly so smoothly. After Alice Layston's death, John Franklin's lease of the Cross Keys had automatically expired, but Franklin assumed that he would be able to get a new lease from William Layston, so he sent his brother George to negotiate. They eventually agreed to a lease for twenty-one years from Michaelmas 1590 at a rent of £40 a year, otherwise under the same terms as in Richard Ibbotson's lease from Alice Layston. Franklin was to pay a fine of £200 at the start of the lease, with £100 due on Michaelmas and £100 due on Christmas. However, when

ALICE LAYSTON AND THE CROSS KEYS 163

Franklin brought £100 to the Cross Keys on September 28, the day before Michaelmas, William Layston was nowhere to be found. It turns out that the day before, Layston had asked George Franklin to come to Gravesend, Kent, to confer about the articles of the lease, and he subsequently refused to grant a lease without such consultation.

On October 22, 1590, accompanied by an alderman's deputy and the constable, Layston tried to evict Franklin from the Cross Keys, but Franklin denied them entry. Layston complained to the recorder of London, then filed suit in Chancery to evict Franklin, whereupon Franklin countersued in Chancery on October 25 to stop the eviction. He said in his complaint that he had spent much money on repairs to the Cross Keys, had bought "greate store of Haye strawe and other fodder" in preparation for the upcoming winter, and had nowhere else to live with his pregnant wife, five children, and other family members if he was evicted. He also claimed that Layston had been posting slanderous bills on the doors of the Cross Keys, thus "troublinge and disturbinge" the guests, and that Layston got all of Franklin's creditors to dun him for money he owed. In his answer, dated November 4, Layston admitted that he had made a verbal agreement with George Franklin about a lease, but said that he was unwilling to grant a lease without consulting about the terms in person. Among other things, he said that the Cross Keys had recently sustained fire damage, and that he and the Franklins had not been able to agree on who was to pay for the repairs.[104] On November 18, Franklin suggested a compromise: he would be allowed to occupy the inn until the following Lady Day (March 25) at a prorated annual rent of £40, same as in the proposed lease, so that he could use up the hay he had bought and find a new place to live, but after that he would relinquish the inn. The court agreed and issued an order to that effect on November 24, with Aldermen Sir George Barnes and Sir George Bond appointed to make sure the order was carried out. In late January 1591 some of Layston's followers were accused of violating the order, so the sheriffs of London arrested Layston on a writ of corpus cum causa and hauled him into court on February 3 to be interrogated about the violation. After several more appearances by Layston over the following week, the court was satisfied, and the rest of Franklin's tenure passed without incident.

After John Franklin finally left the Cross Keys, William Layston began leasing it to a somewhat unlikely tenant—James Beare, who until recently had been a sailor and privateer by profession. He was apparently active in Chester in 1586, when mayor Edmund Gamell wrote to Sir Francis Walsingham complaining about "two pirates named Wyse and Beare in Pulhelly Road, who intended to lie off Holyhead to intercept all ships trading from those parts into Ireland."[105] Three years later, Beare was master of the *Swiftsure,* a privateering ship owned by George Ryman and based out of Chichester with letters of reprisal permitting it to capture any ships belonging to the

164   DAVID KATHMAN

queen's enemies. The *Swiftsure* had been built three years earlier by Ryman and George Somers, later Sir George, the future New World adventurer.[106] In late 1589, the *Swiftsure* teamed up with three other ships—the *Julian,* its pinnace the *Delight* (both owned by Somers and Amyas Preston), and the *Unicorn* (owned by William Morecombe)—in an attempt to capture Spanish ships, agreeing to split among them any prize they captured.[107] In October 1589, the four hit the jackpot when they captured two Spanish ships called the *St. John Baptist* and the *Gallego,* and later brought them into port at Dartmouth, Devonshire, with a staggering £30,000 worth of silks, hides, cochineal (a type of red dye), plate, and bullion. James Beare was appointed to observe the unloading of this prize and make an account so that it would be divided fairly, and so that the necessary customs and tenths could be paid to the authorities.

Beare had owned a £10 share in the *Swiftsure,* and later sold his share of the £30,000 prize to a Mr. Tompson, a London merchant. With this money, which must have been considerable, he apparently decided to retire from privateering. Beare presumably knew William Layston from Gravesend, where he lived before moving to London, and where he was still leasing land at his death.[108] On May 27, 1590, Beare was still describing himself as "James Beare of Gravesende marin*er*," but he probably began leasing the Cross Keys from Layston ten months later on March 25, 1591, as soon as John Franklin's court-ordered tenure ended.[109] He was certainly living in Allhallows Lombard Street by February 20, 1592, when his son Robert was baptized in the parish.[110] He had five more children baptized in the parish over the next decade: John (April 7, 1594), Simon (August 14, 1597), Katherine (November 26, 1598), Mary (January 9, 1600), and William (December 28, 1600), and his will shows that he also had three older children, a son James and daughters Anne and Ellen, both before he moved to the parish.[111]

Playing appears to have continued at the Cross Keys during James Beare's tenure, at least in the early years, to judge by one well-known piece of evidence. On October 8, 1594, Lord Chamberlain Henry Carey wrote to Lord Mayor Richard Martin that "where my now company of players have been accustomed for the better exercise of their quality, and for the service of her majesty if need so require, to play this winter time within the City at the Cross Keys in Gracious Street; these are to require and pray your lordship (the time being such as, thanks be to God, there is now no danger of the sickness) to permit and suffer them so to do."[112] Carey promised Martin that the players would start their plays at two and be done between four and five, that they would not use drums or trumpets to call people to the plays, and that they would contribute to the poor of the parish where they play, in this case Allhallows Lombard Street. Whether or not Martin granted Carey's request, the clear implication is that the Lord Chamberlain's Men were used to playing at the Cross Keys. That company had only been formed the previous spring, but the core was former members of Strange's Men, the same company that had played at the Cross Keys in 1589, while John Franklin was running it.

After he had been running the Cross Keys for more than a decade, James Beare was dragged into a complex, long-simmering legal dispute over the goods taken from the captured Spanish ships in December 1589. George Ryman, the owner of Beare's former ship the *Swiftsure,* had made his will on March 29, 1591, twelve days before he set sail with three ships on an ill-fated expedition to the East Indies, the first ever attempted from England.[113] In this will Ryman granted all his goods and chattels in trust to his brothers William and John, whom he also named executors. While George was at sea William Ryman, acting as his brother's factor, began settling the remaining customs and other taxes due from the *Swiftsure* for the captured Spanish prize. In that capacity, on August 2, 1591, he went with William Morecombe, the owner of the *Unicorn,* to St. Christopher's parish in London and paid £200 in plate to royal official Edward Moore. Ryman later claimed that he had paid this money to Moore at Morecombe's request and on his behalf, and that Morecombe had verbally promised to repay the money to the Rymans. Morecombe, in contrast, later claimed that this £200 was paid because Moore had been an investor in the Unicorne; he further claimed that William Ryman owed *him* £111, which he (Morecombe) had allegedly paid as custom for George Ryman's portion of the captured goods immediately after the ships were unloaded.[114]

Meanwhile, on September 14, 1591, George Ryman's expedition ran into a storm off the Cape of Good Hope as they were rounding the southern tip of Africa. Ryman's ship, the *Penelope,* was lost, though the party's other remaining ship, the *Edward Bonaventure,* continued on to India. When word of this tragedy eventually reached England, William and John Ryman were left in a sort of legal limbo as George Ryman's executors. Because their brother had been lost at sea more than five thousand miles from England, he could not be legally presumed to be dead until some time had passed, and his will could not be proved (and thus his debts fully settled) until he was legally dead. This left the dispute between Morecombe and the Rymans unresolved, much to Morecombe's frustration. At one point he sued the Rymans in the Court of Arches, claiming that by not proving George Ryman's will they were preventing him from collecting on the debts that Ryman owed him, but this suit went nowhere. James Beare drew up several new versions of the account he had made when the Spanish ship were unloaded, including one on May 4, 1597. These mainly supported the Rymans' version of events, but Morecombe still claimed that George Ryman's estate owed him money.[115]

Nine years after George Ryman's disappearance at sea, he was finally considered legally dead, and his brothers proved his will on October 15, 1600.[116] Soon afterward, William Morecombe sued William Ryman first in Queen's

166   DAVID KATHMAN

Bench, then in the Court of Common Pleas, for the £111 that Ryman supposedly owed him.[117] After much legal maneuvering, Morecombe convinced a
jury in his home county of Devonshire that he was entitled to £171 in damages from the Rymans. The Rymans responded on October 30, 1602, by
bringing an action against Morecombe in the London Sheriff's Court for the
£200 that they claimed he owed them, and soon afterward they sued Morecombe in Chancery over the same debt plus other issues stemming from the
division of the Spanish prize. Morecombe retaliated in late 1602 and early
1603 with a flurry of lawsuits in Queen's Bench and Common Pleas that the
Rymans claimed were meant to "terrefy" and extract money from them.[118]
The Rymans were not deterred, and their Sheriff's Court case came to trial
on June 4, 1603, before sheriff John Swynnerton and a jury at the Guildhall.
There James Beare and John Ryman both testified that Morecombe had
promised to repay the £200 to William Ryman, and on the basis of their testimony the jury awarded to Ryman damages of £300 plus court costs. On June
30, Beare gave a deposition in the Rymans' Chancery suit against Morecombe, describing himself as "James Beare of the parishe of Allhallowes
Lumberd street london inholder aged 52 yeares or therabouts."[119] Responding
to interrogatories from Morecombe's lawyer, he told the same story as in his
Guildhall testimony, saying that everyone had agreed at the time that the
£200 was to be repaid by Morecombe to William Ryman, and that his account
had reflected this debt.

   None of this settled anything, for in the spring of 1604 the Rymans and
Morecombe filed dueling suits in the Court of Star Chamber, accusing each
other of perjury. The Rymans claimed that Morecombe had only won his
Common Pleas suit against them by soliciting false testimony from witnesses, and that he had lied in his answer to their Chancery suit. Morecombe,
in turn, claimed that John Ryman and James Beare had committed perjury in
their Sheriff's Court testimony against him the previous June.[120] Beare finally
filed an answer in the latter suit after a delay of nine months, and he was
deposed on February 25, 1605, describing himself as "James Beare of Graci-
ostreete London Marriner." He refused to answer most of the questions posed
by Morecombe's lawyer, saying they were irrelevant to the issue at hand, and
merely reiterated that his testimony to the Sheriff's Court had been truthful.
On June 13, John and William Ryman both gave depositions saying essentially the same thing. Unfortunately, the outcomes of these cases are not recorded, and nothing more is heard of the disputes after 1605.

   James Beare's entire family survived the terrible plague epidemic of 1603,
but on August 8, 1607, his son John was buried in Allhallows Lombard
Street. Almost exactly a year after that, with the plague again raging, tragedy
struck the family. On August 13, 1608, James Beare's wife ("Mistris Beare")
and his two youngest daughters, Katherine and Mary, were buried in the parish, and on the same day Beare made his will.[121] In that will, he called himself

ALICE LAYSTON AND THE CROSS KEYS

"citizen and innholder" and left money to the Innholders' Company for a feast. He also gave forty shillings to be distributed "amongest my tenants in the Yarde of my house the Crossekeyes where I now dwell," and bequeathed to his sons "all suche leases and severall Interests for yeares which I haue aswell of the Mesuage or Inne called the Cross keys in Gracechurch Streete in London as of my landes or tenements in Gravesend in the countie of Kent." Two-thirds of the value of the leases was to go to his son James to pay for the education of James's brother Robert (the child baptized in 1592), who was now a student at Eton College and planning to go to Cambridge, with the other one-third to go to the youngest son, William. His wife's apparel was to go to his surviving daughters, Anne and Ellen, and there is also mention of Anne's daughter Mirrable. Beare also owned a one-fifth interest in a ship, the Anne Awdley, which he left to be divided equally among his children. Two days after making his will, James Beare was buried in Allhallows Lombard Street on August 15, 1608.[122] On March 7, 1609, his eldest son James exhibited an inventory showing that Beare had a net worth of £843 19s 0d at his death, including a lease in the Minories (not mentioned in the will) worth £21, and the leases of the Cross Keys and the lands in Kent, worth a combined £75 a year.[123]

By the time Beare died, regular playing had long ceased at all four London inns, including the Cross Keys. The exact date is not known; the mid-1590s are the most common estimate, but some inn playing may have continued into the early seventeenth century.[124] On April 5, 1600, William Layston sold to Richard Cheney of London, goldsmith, the cottages in St. Katherine Cree that he had inherited from Alice Layston, leaving the Cross Keys as the only part remaining from her jointure.[125] He never sold it, passing it down to his descendants, who continued to own it until it was destroyed in the Great Fire of 1666.[126] The Cross Keys was still being remembered as a playhouse then; in 1664, Richard Flecknoe wrote that players in Queen Elizabeth's reign had "set up theaters, first in the City (as in the inn-yards of the Cross Keys and Bull in Grace and Bishopsgate Street at this day is to be seen), till that fanatique spirit which then began with the stage and after ended with the throne banished them thence into the suburbs."[127] However, Alice Layston and the other figures we have seen had already been forgotten, and would remain almost entirely forgotten for another three centuries and more.[128] In rescuing Alice and her associates from obscurity, I hope to restore her to a position of interest as one of the most interesting and important women in the Elizabethan theater.

Notes

1. Herbert Berry, "Playhouses, 1560–1660," in Glynne Wickham, Herbert Berry, and William Ingram, eds., *English Professional Theatre, 1530–1660* (Cambridge: Cambridge University Press, 2000), 295.

168 DAVID KATHMAN

2. Herbert Berry, "The Bell Savage Inn and Playhouse in London," *Medieval and Renaissance Drama in England* 19 (2006): 121–43.

3. For Jane Poley, see Herbert Berry, *The Boar's Head Playhouse* (Washingtond, D.C.: Folger Books, 1986), 23–26; for Anne Bedingfeild, see Eva Griffith, "New material for a Jacobean playhouse: the Red Bull Theatre on the Seckford estate," *Theatre Notebook* 55 (2001): 5–23; for Susan Baskerville, see Eva Griffith, "Baskervile, Susan (bap. 1573, d. 1649)," *Oxford Dictionary of National Biography,* Oxford University Press, 2004. http://www.oxforddnb.com/view/article/74435.

4. David Kathman, "Innyard Playhouses," in Richard Dutton, ed., *Oxford Handbook of Early Modern Theatre* (Oxford: Oxford University Press, 2009); David Kathman, "London Inns as Playing Venues for the Queen's Men," in Helen Ostovich, ed., *Locating the Queen's Men, 1583–1603: Material Practices and Conditions of Playing* (Aldershot: Ashgate, 2009).

5. Although I found most of the material here, several key documents were brought to my attention by Oscar Lee Brownstein based on his unpublished research, and the late Herbert Berry provided much invaluable help in the early stages. An earlier version of this paper was presented at the 2007 meeting of the Shakespeare Association of America in San Diego.

6. Alice's parentage is mentioned in the answer of a 1569 lawsuit, Harper vs. Layston (National Archives C3/97/47), where John Poore, late of Meopham, Kent, yeoman, deceased, is described as the father of Alice (by then Alice Layston) and of Cicely and Dorothy Poore. The lawsuit involved a building in Meopham called Northwood that John Poore, at his death in 1548, had left to his wife Dorothy for a term of twenty-one years, after which it was to go to his son Thomas, or, if Thomas had no heirs, to his (John's) three daughters. Thomas died with no heirs, after having sold the reversion of the property to John Harper of Cobham, Kent; when Harper tried to claim it after the twenty-one-year term ended in 1569, he sued the three sisters, who had taken possession according to their father's will. Also included as defendants in the suit were John Layston, then married to Alice (the other two sisters were still unmarried), and Thomas Garrett, the second husband and widower of Dorothy Poore (and thus Alice Layston's stepfather).

7. London Metropolitan Archives (henceforth LMA) CLA/023/DW/01/245, Hustings Roll 246, #44.

8. Guildhall Library MS 15211/1, f. 79 (91).

9. John Schofield, ed., *The London Surveys of Ralph Treswell* (London: London Topographical Society, 1987), 126–28, includes a ground plan of the White Hart and a history of the property going back to 1553.

10. Guildhall Library MS 2859, f. 17.

11. The evidence for playing comes from a 1572 complaint by Thomas Giles, a haberdasher from nearby Allhallows Honey Lane, who complained that the Revels Office had been lending out their costumes to players, including yellow cloth-of-gold gowns lent to "the horshed tavern In chepsyde" on January 21, 1572. The complaint, British Library MS Lansdowne 13, no. 3, is transcribed by Albert Feuillerat, ed., *Documents Relating to the Office of the Revels in the Time of Queen Elizabeth* (London: David Nutt, 1908), 409–10, and is discussed by William Ingram, *The Business of Playing* (Ithaca: Cornell University Press, 1992), 69–70, and E. K. Chambers, *The*

Elizabethan Stage, 4 vols. (Oxford: Clarendon, 1923), 1:79–80. My book will have much more on the Horsehead, its owner John Langley (uncle and guardian of Francis Langley of the Swan and Boar's Head playhouses), and its leaseholder Christopher Edwards.

12. Westerfield leased the cellar from Sir Thomas White, alderman of Cornhill Ward and Lord Mayor in 1553–54. He was leasing the cellar by December 24, 1558, when he was named as the tenant in one of White's wills, and was still there at his death in 1566. White's final will, dated November 8, 1566, and his inquisition post mortem the following year both name Westerfield as the tenant of the cellar, though he had actually died a few months before. See H. E. Salter, "Particulars of Properties in the City of London Belonging to St. John's College, Oxford," *London Topographical Record* 15 (1931): 99 (where the name is transcribed as "Ric. Westersoulde, vintner," in context an obvious mistranscription), and Sidney Madge, ed., *Abstracts of Inquisitiones Post Mortem for the City of London Part II, 1561–1577* (London: British Record Society, 1901), 106 and 109.

13. Guildhall Library MS 15211/1, ff. 103r, 107v (Browne's binding, April 16, 1561), 108v (Chatterton's freedom, December 23, 1561), 118r (Rydlay's freedom, April 29, 1566).

14. Henry Westerfield, the younger of the two, claimed his freedom in the Vintners' Company on April 6, 1573 (Guildhall Library MS 15211/1, f. 133), which he had to be at least twenty-one years old to do, In a Star Chamber deposition on January 26, 1575, he gave his age as twenty-four years "and above" (National Archives STAC 5/M21/29), and in a Chancery deposition on May 3, 1589, he gave his age as thirty-seven "or therabouts" (National Archives C24/208/12), all of which implies that he was born about 1551.

15. National Archives PROB 11/48/411v-413.

16. The quote is from Alice Layston's bill of complaint in *Layston vs. Persehowse* (National Archives C3/226/84), dated May 15, 1588.

17. The signature is at the end of his deposition in National Archives STAC 5/M21/29.

18. The Bishop's Head and White Horse were being leased by Thomas Hancock and George Tadlowe respectively in 1543, when Hancock and Tadlowe had to sign bonds promising not to allow plays to be performed in their establishments. I presented much evidence concerning these men and their taverns in "St. Mary Woolnoth: A Forgotten Performance District in 1543 London," a paper written for the 2006 Shakespeare Association of America meeting, and this evidence will be incorporated into my forthcoming book. Abraham leased the Cardinal's Hat from the parish, and the rent is recorded in the Churchwardens' Accounts (Guildhall Library MS 1002/1A).

19. On April 30, 1566, London's Court of Aldermen made Fryer sign a bond restricting the times when he could host plays through the end of August; see E. K. Chambers, "Dramatic Records of the City of London: The Repertories, Journals, and Letter Books," in Malone Society *Collections,* vol. 2, part 3 (Malone Society, 1931), 301. Fryer's will, dated March 5, 1575, and proved October 10, 1576, is National Archives PROB 11/58/193v.

20. John Layston gave his age as forty in a deposition taken on May 4, 1565 (Na-

170 DAVID KATHMAN

tional Archives C24/68/21). The marriage of John Layston and Joan Crowley is in the Allhallows Lombard Street parish register (Guildhall Library MS 17613). The date of Robert Crowley's death is from his inquisition post mortem in Madge, *Inquisitiones Post Mortems, Part II,* 123–24.

21. Robert Crowley's will, dated June 12, 1555, with a codicil dated February 20, 1559, is National Archives PROB 11/42B/94v-95v. Interestingly, the original overseer of Crowley's will was Richard Berde, citizen and girdler, who had earlier held the lease on the Bull in Bishopsgate Street, one of the other three inn-playhouses besides the Cross Keys. Berde's death led to the codicil, in which Crowley named a new overseer.

22. These dimensions are based on the reconstructed post-Fire version depicted in the 1676 Ogilvy and Morgan map, as reproduced in Ralph Hyde, John Fisher, and Roger Cline, *The A to Z of Restoration London* (London: Guildhall Library, 1992), 55, 57. However, dimensions given in several pre-Fire sources, including Sir Robert Knolles's will, cited below, show that the reconstruction did not change the inn's dimensions or footprint.

23. The Cross Keys had been bequeathed to the College at its founding in 1407 by Sir Robert Knolles, who had become rich as one of the military heroes of the Hundred Years' War. His will, which will be discussed more fully in my book, is LMA CLA/023/DW/01/135, Hustings Roll 135, #88, and his biography can be found in Michael Jones, "Knolles, Sir Robert (d 1407)," *Oxford Dictionary of National Biography,* Oxford University Press, September 2004; online ed., May 2006, http://www.oxforddnb-.com/view/article/15758. During the period we are concerned with, both the Cross Keys and the Lion on the Hoop were technically owned by the crown, but controlled by a crown tenant who paid a nominal rent. Such "tenants" (including Alice Layston) were owners for all intents and purposes, since they could hold the properties indefinitely and sell or bequeath them, and I will refer to them as owners in this paper.

24. National Archives C66/818, m.18; an English abstract of the grant is in *Calendar of the Patent Rolls Preserved in the Public Record Office, Edward VI, vol II. A.D. 1548–1549* (London: His Majesty's Stationery Office, 1924), 324–29, esp. 325.

25. A William Johnson, probably but not certainly the same man, was assessed for £66 13s 4d of goods in 1541 in Allhallows Lombard Street; see R. G. Lang, ed., *Two Tudor Subsidy Assessment Rolls for the City of London: 1541 and 1582* (London: London Record Society, 1993), 21. Richard Walton does not appear at all in the 1541 London assessment, and I have been unable to find other useful information about him.

26. The date of the purchase is from John Layston's inquisition post mortem, National Archives C142/174/11 (an English abstract is in Madge, *Inquisitiones Post Mortems, Part II,* 206–7, though it mistakenly gives the year as 1551 rather than 1550). The Scutt on the Hoop had been a brewhouse in 1422 when it was bequeathed to the Tailors and Linen Armourers (the predecessors of the Merchant Taylors) by John Buke. See Reginald R. Sharpe, ed., *Calendar of Wills Proved and Enrolled in the Court of Husting* (London: John C. Francis, 1890), 2:445, and Charles Pendrill, *Wanderings in Medieval London* (London: George Allen & Unwin, 1928), 103. As with the Cross Keys, the dimensions of the Lion on the Hoop are based on the 1676 Ogilvy and Morgan map but confirmed by pre-Fire sources, in this case by the deed of Christopher Clifford's 1556 mortgage to John Wetherell, cited below.

ALICE LAYSTON AND THE CROSS KEYS

171

27. The 1552 mortgage deed is LMA CLA/023/DW/01/245, Hustings Roll 246, #108, and the 1553 sale is described in LMA CLA/023/DW/01/247, Hustings Roll 248, #100.

28. The two mortgage deeds are in LMA CLA/023/DW/01/247, Hustings Roll 248, #101 (Clifford's mortgage to Wetherell), and LMA CLA/023/DW/01/250, Hustings Roll 251, #45–46 (Johnson's mortgage to Clifton).

29. The deal for the Cross Keys is described in the second interrogatory asked of William Johnson alias Fawne on June 16, 1566, as part of a set of Baron's Court depositions (National Archives E133/1/70).

30. These quotations are from William Johnson's answer to the third interrogatory in National Archives E133/1/70. Clifford's deposition, taken on 2 April 1566, stated that he had known Layston for more than twenty years.

31. These two sales to Layston are described in his inquisition post mortem, cited above; I have inferred the other transactions from the fact that Layston bought part of the Lion on the Hoop from Johnson rather than Clifford, even though Clifford had bought the whole complex in 1553. Clifford's purchase of the furniture and household stuff is described in his deposition in National Archives E133/1/70.

32. I have reconstructed most of the details of this complicated deal from the depositions of Clifford, Johnson, and Clifton in National Archives E133/1/70, no single one of which tells the entire story. The deed of December 26, 1561, by which Richard Clifton sold the Cross Keys to John Layston is LMA CLA/023/DW/01/250, Hustings Roll 251, #113.

33. LMA CLA/023/DW/01/250, Hustings Roll 251, #121–22.

34. The depositions from this 1566 usury suit, National Archives E133/1/70, are the source of most of the preceding details about the Cross Keys sale. Clifford's deposition describes the unraveling of the agreement with Layston.

35. LMA CLA/023/DW/01/251, Hustings Roll 252, #70. This transaction is also described in John Layston's inquisition post mortem, cited above.

36. She was buried in Allhallows Lombard Street on August 18 (Guildhall Library MS 17613). Both of Joan's marriages, to Robert Crowley and John Layston, are described in two related lawsuits, National Archives C3/8/119 and C3/9/1, which are discussed below.

37. The deed of jointure is described in John Layston's inquisition post mortem, National Archives C142/174/11. An English abstract of the inquisition post mortem is in Madge, *Inquisitiones Post Mortem Part II,* 206–7.

38. As noted above, Robert Crowley's will, dated June 12, 1555, with a codicil dated February 20, 1559, is National Archives PROB 11/42B/94v–95v. The 1548 purchase date is from Crowley's inquisition post mortem, cited below. Neither building is named in the will, the later inquisition post mortem, or the 1570 Chancery suit described below, but they are named in the 1571 Chancery suit and 1572 Hustings Roll deed.

39. Madge, *Inquisitiones Post Mortems, Part II,* 123–24.

40. National Archives C3/8/119 ad C3/9/1.

41. Layston's date of death is given in his inquisition post mortem, cited above. He was buried on April 3 in Allhallows Lombard Street (Guildhall Library MS 17613).

42. The suit is National Archives REQ2/166/169. Margaret Spencer had not been

172 DAVID KATHMAN

one of the forty-plus Crowley relatives named in Alexander Banks's suit, but there were several Spencers listed there, and I assume she was related to them. It is not clear who Mary Langley was, but she may have been a servant, given that John Layston's servant William Andrews had been his codefendant in the earlier lawsuit.

43. According to Alice, John Layston transferred the property to Fanshawe through enfeoffment, a very public form of sale that required witnesses.

44. These relatives were John Goldesburgh of Cambridge, butcher; his son Thomas; William Giblet of St. Olave Southwark; and William Grange of West Wratlinge, Cambridgeshire, clothworker. The indenture is Hustings Roll 257, #32 (London Metropolitan Archive CLA/023/DW/01/256).

45. These quotations are from Alice Layston's bill of complaint in a later lawsuit, REQ 2/148/48.

46. National Archives C3/213/57. In her bill of complaint for this suit, dated May 13, 1579, Alice described herself as Alice Layston, widow, of Newport, Salop.

47. Guildhall Library MS 33011/3, f. 367.

48. Charles William Wallace, "The First London Theatre: Materials for a History," *University of Nebraska Studies* 13 (1913): 90. The dispute between Burbage and Hind is discussed in detail in David Mateer, "New Light on the Early History of the Theatre in Shoreditch," *English Literary Renaissance* 36 (2006): 335–75.

49. Abraham was Master of the Vintners' Company in 1576–78, and was still alive in 1585, when he had two servants buried at St. Mary Woolnoth. Kenneth Rogers, *Old London: Cornhill, Threadneedle Street and Lombard Street, Old Houses and Signs* (London: Whitefriars Press, 1935), 12; J. M. S. Brooke and A. W. C. Hallen, eds., *The Transcript of the Registers of the United Parishes of S. Mary Woolnoth and S. Mary Woolchurch Haw, in the City of London, from their Commencement 1538 to 1760* (London: Bowles & Sons, 1886), 196–97.

50. Wallace, "The First London Theatre," 82.

51. Ibbotson gave his age as fifty-five in a deposition in mid-1582 (National Archives REQ2/40/3), and his will, cited below, named Kettlewell in Craven as his hometown.

52. Brewers' Wardens' Accounts 1547–62 (Guildhall Library MS 5442/3); St. Andrew Hubbard parish register (Guildhall Library MS 1278/1).

53. Allhallows Lombard Street parish register, (Guildhall Library MS 17613). I listed all of the Ibbotsons' children in David Kathman, "Citizens, Innholders, Playhouse Builders 1543–1622," *Research Opportunities in Medieval and Renaissance Drama* 44 (2005): 43.

54. I also listed these seven apprentices, the dates of their registration, and their hometowns in Kathman, "Citizens, Innholders, Playhouse Builders," 43–44, citing the Brewers' Wardens' Accounts and Court Minutes.

55. LMA CLA/023/DW/01/262, Hustings Roll 263, #49.

56. The purchase from Heneage is recorded in National Archives C66/1241, with an English abstract in Simon R. Neal, ed., *Calendar of Patent Rolls 26 Elizabeth I (1583–1584) C66/1237–1253* (List and Index Society, 2001), 39. The purchases from Cooke and Stepneth are mentioned in Ibbotson's will, cited below.

57. Chambers, *Elizabethan Stage,* 4.134.

58. One of the White Horse Yard properties had formerly been in the tenure of

ALICE LAYSTON AND THE CROSS KEYS

173

Richard Peter and was now occupied by John Williams, citizen and weaver; the other was divided into two tenements occupied by John Hinde and Nicholas Cooke. The Allhallows London Wall property had formerly been in the tenture of Richard Ap Thomas, deceased, and was now occupied by Bonaventure Creake, citizen and grocer. Ibbotson's tenant John Hinde was not the same man who had a dispute with Richard Burbage; the latter lived in Pudding Lane in the parish of St. George, Botolph Lane, and the name was common.

59. Hyde, Fisher, and Cline, *A to Z of Restoration London,* 56, depicts White Horse Yard and the Bull. Since this area of London survived the 1666 fire, the Ogilby and Morgan map is probably a fairly accurate depiction of what the buildings were like a century earlier.

60. Ibbotson's deposition in National Archives REQ2/40/3.

61. National Archives PROB 11/68/405v; Guildhall Library MS 17613.

62. Simon Horspoole lived in Allhallows Lombard Street, in a large house on Gracechurch Street called the Falcon, and was the brother-in-law of Thomas Smythe, who owned the Bell inn, which also hosted plays just north of the Cross Keys. I discuss Thomas Smythe and the Bell in the forthcoming "London Inns as Playing Venues for the Queen's Men."

63. Guildhall Library MS 17613. In Kathman, "Citizens, Innholders, and Playhouse Builders," 44, I mistakenly wrote that the wedding was on March 20, but the eighth is the correct date.

64. The structure of this agreement was the same as the jointure agreement by which Alice Layston took control of the Cross Keys for her lifetime after John Layston's death. Henry Smith's three leases, and the trust agreement with Horspoole and Preston, are described in detail in Henry and Emma Smith's bill of complaint in National Archives REQ2/71/80, in which they accused Horspoole and Preston of appropriating the leases for their own purposes. This Henry Smith may have been the son of the Bell's owner, Thomas Smythe, who definitely did have a son named Henry, but I have so far been unable to find any good evidence for the identification.

65. The quotation is from Walker's deposition in National Archives C24/230/36. Another deponent, John Harris, said that Mary Ibbotson received her portion on May 13, 1589, after she had married William Havard, and that John Ibbotson received his portion on March 5, 1590, after he had turned twenty-one. Walker's lease of the Cross Keys following Ibbotson is described in National Archives C2/Eliz F8/52, to be described further below.

66. The first quotation is from Walker's deposition in National Archives C24/230/36, and the second is from National Archives E133/10/1592, the interrogatories from an otherwise lost Barons' Court lawsuit against Walker.

67. Walker's 1582 lease of a moiety (i.e. half interest) of the Green Dragon from John White of Edmonton and his wife Joan is in Hustings Roll 266, #8 (LMA CLA/023/DW/01/265). The dates of his occupation of the Green Dragon can be deduced from the St. Ethelburga churchwardens' accounts (Guildhall Library MS 4241/1), which list all the householders in that parish in a consistent order along with their quarterly payments toward the parish clerk's wages. I discuss these accounts in Kathman, "Innyard Playhouses."

68. Walker definitely owned both the Bull and the Green Dragon when he made

174 DAVID KATHMAN

his will on April 20, 1602 (National Archives PROB 11/99/269). He said in the will that he had "lately" purchased the Bull from George Mease, but I have not been able to find a record of the exact date.

69. Saddlers' Audit Book 1555–1822 (Guildhall Library MS 5384).

70. National Archives PROB 11/63/17.

71. Centre for Kentish Studies P285/1/1, which records that Tuttesham "was marryed to one Leastons widdowe of grauesend." I am grateful to Debbie Hogan of the Centre for Kentish Studies in Maidstone for finding and photographing the record for me.

72. These quotations are from Alice Layston's bill of complaint in National Archives REQ 2/148/48.

73. All the quotations in this paragraph are from National Archives REQ 2/148/48.

74. The decree book covering the relevant period, National Archives REQ 1/14, has suffered extensive water damage. I searched the legible parts, but found no mention of this case.

75. In Wrothe's will (National Archives PROB 11/117/118–119v), dated August 14, 1610, he left to his sister Anne Shirley a house in Bexley called Blunden Hall, which he was leasing to her for a term of sixty years.

76. The lease and the bond are described in Alice Layston's bill of complaint in National Archives C3/226/84, which is also the source of the quotations in this paragraph.

77. John Westerfield's marriage is recorded in Guildhall Library MS 7493, a transcript of which is on Alan Nelson's Web site at http://socrates.berkeley.edu/~ahnelson/PARISH/Leonard.html. A license for the marriage had been obtained on February 8, as recorded in Joseph Foster, ed., *London Marriage Licenses, 1521–1869* (London: Bernard Quaritch, 1887), 1440, where John Westerfield is described as a "vintner." Though the records of the Vintners' Company do not contain any record of John claiming his freedom in the company by patrimony, as Henry certainly did, it was not uncommon for adult sons of freemen to describe themselves as being of their father's livery company, whether or not they had formally registered with the company.

78. Henry Westerfield's marriage is recorded in the parish register of St. Mary, Bury St. Edmunds, in the Bury St. Edmunds branch of the Suffolk Record Office. I am grateful to Jean Deathridge of that branch for finding the exact date of the marriage for me. Andrew Skinner's will, dated November 25, 1592 and proved February 7, 1593, is National Archives PROB 11/82/360–360v. In it he bequeaths £5 and his best carpet to "my daughter Cadiolde," Lydia's married name with her second husband John Cadiolde.

79. Allhallows Lombard Street parish register (Guildhall Library MS 17613).

80. The Green Dragon will be discussed more in my book, but Myles Wymbish's ownership of it and the later dispute are described in National Archives C3/89/5. Myles Wymbish's 1552 will, including bequests to his daughter Alice (John Persehouse's mother), is National Archives PROB 11/35/236–236v.

81. A record of the Inner Temple parliament held on November 26, 1587, shows that Thomas Wrothe was sharing a chamber with "Mr. Otley" in an upper chamber in "Mr. Bradshaw's Buildings"; see F. A. Inderwick, ed., *A Calendar of the Inner Temple Records* (London: Henry Sotheran, 1896), 1:347–48.

ALICE LAYSTON AND THE CROSS KEYS 175

82. This paragraph is based on Alice Layston's bill of complaint in National Archives C3/226/84, which is also the source of the quotation.

83. The sale of the lease is described in Franklin's bill of complaint in National Archives C2/Eliz F8/52. Both Franklin's bill of complaint and William Layston's answer have suffered considerable damage, obscuring some details.

84. National Archives C2/Eliz/P11/31. For more on gavelkind, see A. W. B. Simpson, *An Introduction to the History of the Land Law* (Oxford: Oxford University Press, 1961), 21, and Michael Zell, "Landholding and the Land Market in Early Modern Kent," in *Early Modern Kent 1540–1640* (Woodbridge, Kent: Boydell Press, 2000), 39–74, esp. 40–49.

85. National Archives C3/226/84. Alice Layston's quotation about herself is from her bill of complaint, and her quotation about Henry Westerfield is from her replication.

86. On July 2, 1590, one week before Alice Layston's death, the Court of Chancery issued a decree in the case of *Alice Layston v. John Persehowse* and others, saying that if the defendants could show no cause for stay of publication, then publication would be granted. This decree is recorded in National Archives C33/79, f. 793v and C33/80, f. 789v.

87. National Archives PROB 11/99/269–270v. Weavering is the village directly west of Bearsted.

88. The will is National Archives PROB 11/171/229v-303. For the buying and selling of land in Staffordshire by Persehouses, including John the younger (our man), see *Collections for a History of Staffordshire* (London: Harrison and Sons), vol. 15 (1894), 165, 188, 191, 193–94, 197; vol. 16 (1895), 102, 111, 113, 132, 139–40, 174, 178, 191, 197, 198. 200, 201, 206, 210.

89. Clothworkers' Hall, Clothworkers' Orders of Courts 1581–1605, f. 15. Franklin may have been related to William Franckland, a prominent Clothworker and benefactor of the company who had died in 1577, but I have found no specific connection between them.

90. This testimony is in Franklin's bill of complaint in National Archives C2/Eliz F8/52, described more fully below.

91. Transcribed in Chambers, *The Elizabethan Stage,* 4:305.

92. Allhallows Lombard Street parish register (Guildhall Library MS 17613). She had been called Agnes in the record of her marriage to John Westerfield, but Anne and Agnes were interchangeable names in early modern England.

93. National Archives PROB 11/76/26v.

94. John Venn and J. A. Venn, *Alumni Cantabrigienses* (Cambridge: Cambridge University Press, 1922–54), 1405. Christopher Marlowe and John Fletcher both studied at Corpus Christi College, though not until after Stallard's primary time there. Marlowe was a student when Stallard got his DD in 1585, but there is no evidence that the two men knew each other.

95. Grocers' Wardens' Accounts 1534–55 (Guildhall Library MS 11571/5).

96. Thomas and Nicholas Horne were baptized in Allhallows Lombard Street on September 14, 1558, and March 2, 1561, respectively, and were both made free of the Grocers by patrimony on October 9, 1587 (Guildhall Library MS 11571/7). William Horne's other daughter Mary lived with her husband Daniel Dickinson, citizen and

176 DAVID KATHMAN

draper, in St. Antholin parish, about five hundred yards to the west. After Alice Horne married Roger Spratt, citizen and draper, in Allhallows Lombard Street on February 2, 1591, they also lived in St. Antholin.

97. Henry Westerfield's sale of the house is noted in William Horne's will, cited below.

98. National Archives PROB 11/80/28. I have not found a record of Henry Westerfield's burial; this may be because he was living in the Knightrider Street house in the parish of St. Benet Paul's Wharf, whose burial records do not survive from this period.

99. LMA CLA/023/DW/01/271, Hustings Roll 272, #8.

100. Allhallows Lombard Street parish register (Guildhall Library MS 17613). The date of Horne's death is from his inquisition post mortem, an English abstract of which is in Edward Alexander Fry, ed., *Abstracts of Inquisitiones Post Mortem for the City of London Part III, 1577–1603* (London: British Record Society, 1908), 193–95.

101. Horne owned several messuages in St. Botolph Bishopsgate, some of which had been owned by his wife Isabel's first husband, and some of which he had bought from William Abraham, the trustee of the Cross Keys and friend of Alice Layston's first husband. He also owned a complex of buildings called the Wrestlers on Bishopsgate Street, St. Ethelburga parish, purchased of Matthew Piggott, and was leasing a messuage called the Jackanapes in St. John Zachary from the Dean and Chapter of St. Paul's.

102. The will does not name the Lion on the Hoop, which seems to have lost its sign by this time, but it is clear from the description and the later deed of sale that this is the same property.

103. LMA CLA/023/DW/01/272, Hustings Roll 273, #9. According to the deed of sale, the property stood between a messuage of William Layston (the Cross Keys) on the west, Gracechurch Street to the east, a messuage of John Bendy to the north, and a messuage of Thomas Sherman, citizen and grocer, to the south. Bendy occupied a shop just south of the gate to the Bell inn, and Sherman occupied a shop north of the Cross Keys gate. In "London Inns as Playing Venues for the Queen's Men," I discuss a 1597 lawsuit by John Bendy against Henry Haughton, the leaseholder of the Bell, from whom Bendy was subleasing his shop.

104. Franklin's bill of complaint and Layston's answer, from which most of the details in this paragraph come, are part of National Archives C2/Eliz F8/52. All the later developments, plus a few from between Franklin's bill and Layston's answer, are recorded in National Archives C33/82, ff. 87v, 93v, 116, 169–169v, 184v, 194, 201–201v, 315, 342v, 352, 366, 373v, and 379.

105. Robert Lemon, ed., *Calendar of State Papers, Domestic Series, of the reign of Elizabeth, 1581–1590* (London: Her Majesty's Stationery Office, 1865), 351.

106. Kenneth R. Andrew, *Elizabethan Privateering: English Privateering During the Spanish War, 1585–1603* (Cambridge: Cambridge University Press, 1964), 93. Ryman's surname is given as "Raymond" by Andrew and most other modern sources, but he called himself "Ryman" in his will, and was so called in most of the lawsuits cited below. In 1610 Somers was admiral of the Sea Venture, whose wreck in Bermuda on its way to the Jamestown colony probably inspired Shakespeare's *The Tempest.* See William Sears Zuill sen., "Somers, Sir George (1554–1610)," *Oxford*

ALICE LAYSTON AND THE CROSS KEYS

Dictionary of National Biography, Oxford University Press, 2004, http://www.ox forddnb.com/view/article/26001.

107. The four ships and their activities in 1589 are described in Andrew, *Elizabethan Privateering,* 93, 249, 253, 258; in a set of depositions taken in the High Court of Admiralty on May 27, 1590 (National Archives HCA 13/28, ff. 409–414v); in a 1592 lawsuit, Christmas vs. Morcombe (National Archives REQ 2/186/39); and in the later lawsuits cited below. Beare described the capture in some detail in his 1590 deposition (National Archives HCA 13/28, ff. 413–414), though he could not remember the exact date when it occurred, and he described how he sold his share of the prize in his deposition in National Archives C24/301/61.

108. Beare's leases in Gravesend are mentioned in his will (National Archives PROB 11/112/187v-188v) and the inventory of his goods (London Metropolitan Archive CLA/002/01/1, f.275v-276), both described below. He also owned a house and twenty-one acres of land in "Bastall," Kent (probably Borstal).

109. National Archives HCA 13/28, f. 409.

110. Guildhall Library MS 17613 (parish register).

111. Guildhall Library MS 17613. Only Mary and William are specifically recorded as children of James Beare, since the parish clerk only started naming fathers in 1599, but James, Robert, William, Anne, and Ellen are named in James Beare's will, cited below, by which time the other children were dead.

112. Berry, "Playhouses," 304.

113. Ryman's will is National Archives PROB 11/96/553, and his expedition to the East Indies is described in Andrew, *Elizabethan Privateering,* 93, and in Robert Kemp Philp, *The History of Progress in Great Britain* (London: Houlston and Wright, 1859), 327. It became famous through its inclusion in the second edition (1598–1600) of Richard Hakluyt's *Voyages and Discoveries;* see, for example, the modern edition edited by Jack Beeching (London: Penguin, 1972), 360–69.

114. William Ryman's and William Morecombe's versions of these events are given in their very detailed bills of complaint in *Ryman v. Morecombe* (National Archives STAC 8/248/5) and *Morecombe v. Ryman and Beare* (National Archives STAC 8/210/ 32), each of which quotes various earlier lawsuits.

115. The loss of George Ryman's ship is described in the account in Hakluyt's *Voyages and Discoveries,* cited above. The Court of Arches suit is described in the Ryman's bill of complaint in National Archives STAC 8/248/5; the original, along with nearly all early Court of Arches proceedings, perished in the Great Fire of London in 1666. The 1597 account is described in Morecombe's bill of complaint in National Archives STAC 8/210/32.

116. The period after which a missing person is presumed dead is now seven years in English common law, but this presumption did not become codified until the Bigamy Act of 1604; see James Bradley Thayer, *A Preliminary Treatise of Evidence at the Common Law* (Boston: Little, Brown, 1898), 319–21.

117. This suit, technically an action of trespass upon the case, is described in detail in the Rymans' bill of complaint in STAC 8/248/5.

118. These suits alleged, among other things, that shortly after the unloading of the Spanish ships, William Ryman had appropriated for his own use goods belonging to Morecombe, including two silver bars worth £300 and ten chests of "Quythenall" worth £700. All the suits are described by the Rymans in STAC 8/248/5.

178 DAVID KATHMAN

119. National Archives C24/301/61. George Somers had given his deposition in the case almost four months earlier on March 4.

120. *Ryman v. Morecombe* (National Archives STAC 8/248/5) and *Morecombe v. Ryman and Beare* (National Archives STAC 8/210/32). Neither bill of complaint is dated, but Morecombe's answer in the first suit is dated May 7, 1604, and the demurrer of the Rymans and Beare in the second suit is dated May 9, 1604. Beare did not file an answer until February 12, 1605.

121. Guildhall Library MS 17613 (parish register); National Archives PROB 11/112/187v–188v (James Beare's will). The will was proved on September 29, 1608. Beare's son Simon, baptized in 1597, is not mentioned in the will and had presumably died, though his burial is not recorded in the parish register.

122. Guildhall Library 17613.

123. The inventory is in Common Serjeants Book I, 1586–1614 (London Metropolitan Archive CLA/002/01/1), f.275v-276. It reveals that Beare's daughter Anne was married during his lifetime, and that since his death his daughter Ellen had married Thomas Joyce of Gravesend, baker.

124. Berry, "Playhouses," 304–5, presents the evidence for the traditional estimate, and Menzer, "The Tragedians of the City?" argues for a later date.

125. National Archives C54/1657.

126. The history of the Cross Keys in the decades before the fire is recounted in a case in the ad hoc Fire Court, abstracted in Philip E. Jones, ed., *The Fire Court,* vol. I (London: William Clowes & Sons, 1966), 39–40. I will go into this history in my book.

127. Berry, "Playhouses," 305.

128. An English abstract of John Layston's inquisition post mortem, which mentions the Cross Keys, was printed in 1901, as cited above, but as far as I can tell it has never been noted by theater historians before. The reference to the Cross Keys as being Richard Ibbotson's house in 1579 was printed by Charles William Wallace in 1913, also as cited above, but it was included as part of a massive transcription of lawsuits involving the Theater, and has only been mentioned in passing by theatre historians since then.

Puritanism and the Closing
of the Theaters in 1642

N. W. Bawcutt

UNTIL comparatively recently, the stock assumption of literary historians was that in the later sixteenth and early seventeenth centuries there was an intense mutual antipathy and hostility between Puritanism and the stage. Puritans regarded theaters as abominable haunts of vice and corruption which a well-regulated state would completely suppress. Dramatists regarded Puritans as hypocrites, who pretended to be holier than other people but were in fact motivated by various kinds of greed, for food, sex, and money. The standard view can be seen in three American studies from the first half of the twentieth century: E. N. S. Thompson, *The Controversy between the Puritans and the Stage* (1903), A. M. Myers, *Representation and Misrepresentation of the Puritans in Elizabethan Drama* (1931), and W. P. Holden, *Anti-Puritan Satire 1572–1642* (1954). They provide useful surveys of attitudes on both sides, and also have considerable value as repositories of raw material: they combed through the various dramatists and brought to light the comments made on Puritans.

In 1980 appeared Margot Heinemann's *Puritanism and Theatre: Thomas Middleton and Opposition Drama under the Early Stuarts.* Her main argument was that there existed a Parliamentary Puritan opposition to King James, notably in the second half of his reign, and that Middleton was writing on behalf of this opposition, particularly in his notorious play *A Game at Chess* (1624), which she saw as a scathing satire on royal policy. She used various arguments to show Middleton as working for Puritan patrons, but I will not spell them out as I have already expressed my reservations about them elsewhere.[1] Her book aroused considerable enthusiasm among literary scholars, though it has to be said that historians reviewed it much less favorably.[2] She established "opposition drama"—plays attacking King James's policies, especially his foreign policies—as a kind of literary genre, and subsequent critics extended her approach to other dramatists, as did Julia Gasper in her book on Dekker, *The Dragon and the Dove: The Plays of Thomas Dekker,* which appeared in 1990.

Heinemann was rather dismissive of Caroline drama, the drama of the

1630s, seeing it as enfeebled by harsh censorship and lacking the radical and populist elements of the best Jacobean drama. Martin Butler, however, in his *Theatre and Crisis 1632–1642,* published in 1984, argued that Caroline drama was not simply royalist and sycophantic, as used to be commonly thought, but independent and intelligently alert to the social and political crises of the time, and was often hostile to the policies of king Charles. In the same year, 1984, Jonathan Dollimore published his *Radical Tragedy,* which argued that Jacobean tragedy was skeptical toward, and subversive of, current political and religious orthodoxies. The books by Heinemann, Butler, and Dollimore differed in various ways, but shared a basic assumption that early seventeenth-century drama was critical of James I and Charles I. Not surprisingly, this could lead to the suggestion that drama played a part in the shift of attitudes which provoked the civil war. Butler put the idea fairly cautiously:

> It has become fashionable among historians to see the Civil War as the product as much of miscalculation, accident and circumstance as of design, but if we wish to see the readiness of those who *were* prepared to go to war as part of something much more deeply-rooted, then we may conclude that the drama too, by calling the old certainties into question and educating attitudes to them over a period of years, was in part responsible for creating the conditions in which men would have the capacity, and the will, to take such a step.[3]

An Italian critic, Franco Moretti, made a much more sweeping claim: "Elizabethan and Jacobean tragedy contributed, more radically than any other cultural phenomenon of the same period, to discrediting the values of absolute monarchy, thereby paving the way, with wholly destructive means, for the English revolution of the seventeenth century . . . Tragedy disentitled the absolute monarch to all ethical and rational legitimation. Having deconsecrated the king, tragedy made it possible to decapitate him."[4] Radical tragedy, as defined by Dollimore, led directly to the execution of Charles I, and indeed made it possible. More recently, David Scott Kastan has offered a subtle variant on this kind of idea, based mainly on plays deriving from English history: "In setting English kings before an audience of commoners, the theater nourished the cultural conditions that eventually permitted the nation to bring its king to trial, not because the theater approvingly represented subversive acts but rather because representation itself became subversive."[5] To show kings in action was implicitly to question them.

Sooner or later, however, this approach comes up against the awkward and inconvenient fact that the suppression of the theaters in 1642 came from parliament, not from the king. If drama had been so radical, so obviously questioning of royal authority, we might have expected parliament to pass a vote of thanks to the players and to give them every encouragement to continue. Martin Butler confronts this problem by arguing that the closure of the the-

PURITANISM AND THE CLOSING OF THE THEATERS IN 1642

aters was "an act of public safety rather than of puritan reform."[6] As he rightly points out, the civil war had broken out shortly before, and it was a period of major national crisis. Parliament's attempts to suppress drama in the 1640s and '50s should be seen, says Butler, as "typically precautionary measures such as had often been taken before at times of crisis or instability when governments wished to disperse the people and maintain a tight rein on law and order."[7] We should not interpret what happened as "an act of puritan aggression against an institution irretrievably riddled with 'royalism.'"[8] As we shall see later, Kastan takes the same approach and pushes it to an extreme.

This complex of ideas—that Puritans were sympathetic to drama and actively patronized it, that early seventeenth-century drama was frequently hostile to royal policy, that the closure of the theaters in 1642 was intended chiefly to preserve public order—could be regarded as the revisionist attitude to Puritanism and the theater, and has become the current orthodoxy on the question. To challenge the whole of it would be a very large undertaking—I do not believe, for example, that the drama was quite as subversive and radical as some recent critics have made it out to be, but to argue the case effectively would involve detailed analysis of numerous plays. I therefore propose to look at three interlinked issues. The first concerns attitudes to drama in the 1630s, the decade preceding the closure; the second is the interpretation of parliamentary regulation of the theater from 1642 onward; and the third is the nature of royalist and parliamentary attitudes to drama in the years following the closure, with material taken mainly from the huge collection of civil war pamphlets assembled by George Thomason.

In his discussion of the first of these issues, Butler wishes to demolish what he calls "the assumption that the theatres were swept aside in 1642 by a tidal wave of puritan protest which had gradually been gathering head throughout the 1630s."[9] William Prynne's notorious attack on the stage, *Histriomastix,* published in 1633, was, he says, "the last of its kind," and did not "initiate a new wholesale onslaught on the stage."[10] Kastan puts forward an identical argument: "Prynne's vituperative *Histrio-mastix* was . . . an anachronism at the time of its publication in 1633, and it had no immediate successors."[11] This may be so, but a simple and plausible explanation would be that the barbaric punishments inflicted on Prynne made it clear that discretion was the better part of valor, and that it would be wise for objectors to the stage to keep silent for the time being.

Even so, some hostility surfaced. King Charles visited Oxford in 1636, and saw three plays including Strode's *The Floating Island,* which ridiculed both Prynne and Puritanism. Henry Burton, who was to be put on trial with Prynne and Bastwick in 1637, objected to the performance only because, according to Butler, "it had caricatured Prynne and had been organised by the bishops."[12] This calm summary, which seems to suggest that in different cir-

182   N. W. BAWCUTT

cumstances Burton would not have objected to the play, fails to do justice to Burton's tone of outraged indignation and heavy sarcasm: "Nor are they content, to abuse our pious Princes eares in the Pulpit, but also on the Stage, O pyous, holy, reverend, grave, gracious Prelates, whose Academicall Entertainment of pious and religious Kings and Princes (in stead of learned and Scholasticall disputations or exercises suitable to the condition of a learned Academy) is a scurrilous Enterlude, and this in disgrace of that, which is the greatest beauty of our religion, to wit, true piety and vertue!"[13] Furthermore, it was a time of plague in London, not an appropriate time for "Entertaining the Court and poysoning their eares with Enterludes." Burton, it seems clear to me, felt that Oxford should have provided academic disputations and sermons, rather than plays of any kind.

Butler goes on to argue that what he calls "the decline of puritan militancy against the stage" can be easily explained. The two main grounds of hostility were, he says, "the social dangers the theatres posed and the fact that they did not observe the Sabbath."[14] By the 1630s, we are told, both complaints had been answered: theatergoing had become more orderly and respectable, and Sunday performances had been forbidden. I do not want to do Butler an injustice by simplifying his arguments, but they could surely be taken to imply that theological hostility to the theater came to an end in the 1630s, and ceased to exist as a historical phenomenon. If that is indeed what Butler means, it is staggering, for nothing could be further from the truth. The hostility went underground in the later 1630s, but it burst out again as soon as conditions were favorable, as we shall see later. It survived for at least two centuries more: pamphlets with such titles as *Balls and Theatres: or the duty of reproving the works of darkness,* and *The theatre: fourteen reasons why we should not go to it,* and *The play-house: its hurtful influence on society and morals* were published in, respectively, 1846, 1856, and 1865.[15]

A further token that mutual hostility had not ended in the 1630s is that dramatists continued to attack Puritans in the years immediately preceding the civil war. There were numerous incidental jeers, and also more extended portrayal of mocked Puritan characters, and the plays containing these figures often had some link to the king. Strode's *The Floating Island* was performed at the king's visit to Oxford in 1636, and Jasper Mayne's *The City Match* was written for that visit but not actually performed, though it was later put on in London. Davenant's masque *Britannia Triumphans* was mounted at court in January 1638. Cowley's *The Guardian* was presented before the king at Trinity College, Cambridge, in March 1642. The play was set in London, and in his prologue Cowley expressed a fear that Puritan sympathizers would try to disrupt the play if they knew about it:

> But our Scean's *London* now, and by the Rout
> We perish, if the *Round-heads* be about.

PURITANISM AND THE CLOSING OF THE THEATERS IN 1642

> For now no Ornament, the head must wear,
> No Bayes, no Myter, scarse so much as hair.
> How can a Play passe safely?[16]

Cowley's prologue and epilogue were printed separately as a little pamphlet in London in 1642, perhaps a slightly provocative gesture.

Puritans were fully aware of this kind of mockery and bitterly resented it. John Bastwick argued that Puritans were the holiest and most contented of people, "yet are they made but the off-scouring of the world, and of all things, and brought upon every Stage, and into the Pulpit, as fittest for ludibry by the Players, Priests, and Prelates."[17] Henry Parker claimed in *A Discourse concerning Puritans* (1641) that they were hated because they were transparently virtuous and their enemies were not; it was because of their "Truth, Holinesse, and Goodnesse . . . that Stage-poets, Minstrels, and the jesting Buffoones of the age, make them the principall subject of derision."[18] Lucy Hutchinson made the same point: in an extended passage obviously written with deep feeling, she protested against the way in which all those who showed any trace of godliness or public spirit or resistance to royal tyranny were branded as Puritans:

> and if Puritanes, then enemies to the king and his government, seditious factious hipocrites, ambitious disturbers of the publicke peace, and finally, the pest of the Kingdome, enemies of God and good men, according to the Court account. Such false logick did the children of darknesse use to argue with against the hated children of light, whom they branded besides as an illiterate, morose, melancholly, discontented, craz'd sort of men, not fitt for human conversation; and as such they made them not only the sport of the pulpit, which was become but a more solemne stage, but every stage, and every table and every puppett-play belcht forth prophane scoffes upon them.[19]

All the quotations in this paragraph relate to the period in which Butler claims that Puritan animus against the stage had died out.

Butler's sarcastic reference to a nonexistent "tidal wave of Puritan protest against the theatre" may be accurate, but it could certainly be argued that there was a rise in Puritanism during the 1630s. The ecclesiastical policies of King Charles and Archbishop Laud deeply alarmed many Protestants, and were often seen as the opening stages of a sinister plot to return England to Catholicism. (This was quite untrue; neither Charles nor Laud had the slightest intention of doing so.) This helped to promote a fundamentalist type of extreme Protestantism, and was indeed one of the numerous factors which gave rise to the civil war. Puritanism seems to have had one effect on drama in the 1630s, relating to the traveling companies of players that toured the provinces. The local authorities in towns and cities could not give an outright refusal to companies which had a license from the king, together with what

184   N. W. BAWCUTT

was termed a "confirmation," renewed annually, from the Master of the Revels, but they increasingly resorted to a practice by which they paid the visiting company a "gratuity" on the explicit understanding that it was to go away without playing, so that actual performances steadily declined. This was a complex business, and the authorities were not motivated solely by hostility to drama, but the end result, according to Peter Greenfield, was that provincial touring had "almost disappeared" by 1642.[20]

I would like now to look more closely at the parliamentary closure of the theaters in 1642, and the various ordinances relating to drama which were passed later in the 1640s. One preliminary point must be made. Parliament passed no laws concerning the theater before 1642 because it had no authority to do so. Acting companies received the licenses authorizing them to perform from the king, and the major companies were assigned to the patronage of various members of the royal family (the King's company, the Prince's company, and so on) and were in effect part of the royal household, though at a fairly low level. Without this patronage they would not have been able to survive the hostility of Puritan preachers and the civic authorities in London. Control of them was vested in the King, the Lord Chamberlain, and the Master of the Revels, though some other bodies—the Privy Council, the Bishop of London, and the Archbishop of Canterbury—could occasionally intervene in theatrical matters. But prior to the breakdown of royal authority after 1640, if parliament wanted restrictions placed on theatrical activity it could only address a petition to the Lord Chamberlain, to which he could respond as he pleased.

Some of those connected with the stage seem to have suspected, before the actual closure, that its days were numbered. In 1641 appeared *The Stage-Players Complaint,* an imaginary dialogue between two well-known comic actors of the time, Andrew Cane and Timothy Reade. Cane gave a list of practices and institutions which were linked with the monarchy and had recently been put down by parliament, and gloomily forecast that the theater would have the same fate: "For Monopolers are downe, Projectors are downe, the High Commission Court is downe, the Starre-chamber is downe, & (some think) Bishops will downe, and why should we then that are farre inferior to any of those not justly fear least we should be downe too?"[21] The law courts of High Commission and Star Chamber were what was known as prerogative courts, set up (perfectly legally) in earlier times by royal authority, but they were not part of Common Law, and in the 1630s came to be seen as increasingly authoritarian and royalist. Parliament abolished them both in 1641.

The earliest parliamentary attempts at closure were unsuccessful. On February 26, 1641, the London parish of Blackfriars, together with two other parishes, presented a petition for the suppression of the Blackfriars theater, the chief venue of the King's company. The House of Commons *Journal* for that day notes that "The Petition of the Inhabitants of the *Black Friars, St.*

PURITANISM AND THE CLOSING OF THE THEATERS IN 1642

Martin's, Ludgate, and *St. Bride*'s, *London* was read; and is ordered to be referred to the Committee for Secretary *Windebank*'s Business."[22] A brief account of the proceedings was recorded by Sir Simonds D'Ewes, who spoke for the petition: "Then a petition preferred by the inhabitants of Blacke Friers and others against the Play howse ther etc. hinderance of trade, by Alderman Pennington. Hee spake to further it. I etc. A good petition. Gods howse not soe neare Divils. This a particular greivance this and the other a generall. All the objection men without them could not tell how to imploy themselves etc. Others spake against this playhowse and others."[23] It is striking how what may be termed the practical objections to the theatre and the theological objections were mingled together, as D'Ewes himself recognized, if we can assume that "hinderance of trade" was the "particular greivance," and "Gods howse not soe neare Divils"[24] was the "generall." It is clear from the last sentence that some M.P.s wanted playhouses other than Blackfriars to be taken into account. Pressure of business, however, meant that in the end nothing was done.

More attempts at closure were made less than a year later. One was recorded in the parliamentary diary for January 26, 1642, of John Moore: "Ordered, that the lord chamberlain be desired to move his majesty that in these times of calamity in Ireland and the distractions in this kingdom, that all interludes and plays be suppressed for a season. This was Sir Edward Partridge's motion, but laid aside by Mr. Pym his seconding of Mr. Waller in alleging that it was their trade."[25] The argument that "it was their trade" (in other words, closure would destroy the players' livelihood) echoes the objection made in 1641 ("men without them could not tell how to imploy themselves"). But the hostility of many M.P.s was undiminished, and only a few days later, on February 4, a fresh attempt was made, if we may believe a contemporary report: "This day also there was a great complaint made against the Play-houses, and a motion for the suppressing of them."[26] Neither of these motions was recorded in the *Journals of the House of Commons,* presumably because they were not carried.

In the spring of 1642 parliament still felt that motions affecting the stage had to take the form of petitions to the Lord Chamberlain, and unemployment among the players was an important factor, but by late August, shortly after the civil war had broken out, neither of these considerations carried any weight, and on August 31 parliament carried an order closing down the theaters: "*Ordered,* That a Message be sent to the Lords, To-morrow Morning, to desire them to join with this House in an Order that all Stage Plays may be put down, during this Time of Distractions, and of Fasting: And Mr. *Rowse* is appointed to bring in an Order to this Purpose."[27] Two days later, on September 2, an order was passed dealing with naval affairs, and "Sir Ro. Harley carried up to the Lords this Order, and the Order for putting down Stage Plays."[28]

186 N. W. BAWCUTT

The order concerning plays was subsequently published, rather tagged on at the end of a totally different order.[29] Interpretation of the closure has proved to be controversial, and it is helpful to have the text of the ordinance available:

> Whereas the distressed Estate of Ireland, steeped in her own Blood, and the distracted Estate of England, threatned with a Cloud of Blood, by a Civill Warre, call for all possible meanes to appease and avert the Wrath of God appearing in these Judgements; amongst which, Fasting and Prayer having bin often tryed to be very effectuall, have bin lately, and are still enjoyned; and whereas publike Sports doe not well agree with publike Calamities, nor publike Stage-playes with the Seasons of Humiliation, this being an Exercise of sad and pious solemnity, and the other being Spectacles of pleasure, too commonly expressing laciuious [sic] Mirth and Levitie: It is therefore thought fit, and Ordeined by the Lords and Commons in this Parliament Assembled, that while these sad Causes and set times of Humiliation doe continue, publike Stage-playes shall cease, and bee forborne. Instead of which, are recommended to the people of this Land, the profitable and seasonable Considerations of Repentance, Reconciliation, and peace with God, which probably may produce outward peace and prosperity, and bring againe Times of Joy and Gladnesse to these Nations.

As Susan Wiseman sternly remarks, "much depends on how we decide to interpret this document."[30] Perhaps Wiseman's "decide to interpret" is not intended to suggest that we are free to make of it what we like; at any rate it seems to me that the surface meaning is explicit enough and is clearly constructed in theological language. The recent crises and calamities are interpreted in providential terms as tokens of God's wrath against Britain, which needs to be appeased by religious practices such as fasting and prayer. Stage-plays, which are frivolous and often obscene, are quite inappropriate in the circumstances, and the people (which must include theater audiences) are recommended to repent of their sins and to attempt to reconcile themselves to God.

There is not a word in the whole document relating to a parliamentary fear of unruly behavior and disorder, but Butler's assertion that this is really what it is all about has become an accepted orthodoxy. Kastan, for example, confidently declares that "parliament in its considerations was motivated by practical concerns for security more than by religious zeal."[31] Wiseman sees the document as addressed to "the London 'public' in the very guise the authorities found most unruly—the theatre-going crowd."[32] Theater audiences varied: playgoers at the Red Bull theater might well be unruly, but those at Blackfriars or the Phoenix were not likely to give much trouble. Certainly London could produce violent mobs—one such forced the king to sign Strafford's death-warrant in May 1641—but the tone of the closure document does not suggest for a moment that parliament had them in mind. Those

PURITANISM AND THE CLOSING OF THE THEATERS IN 1642

members of "the people of this land" who might want to go to the theater are calmly and politely "recommended" to repent and become more devout, and it seems to be assumed that a mere recommendation might reasonably be expected to produce the desired effect.

Kastan strongly supports the interpretation of the closure as a wish to prevent disorder, but he pushes the argument a degree further than Butler. Repeatedly stressing that all drama, regardless of its overt ideology, is inherently unsettling and subversive, Kastan sees parliament as frightened of the threat posed to itself by the theater: "Indeed, the order to close the theaters in September 1642 may best be understood less as part of a parliamentary offensive against the monarch than as a defensive tactic, demanded by parliament's awareness of its own increasing vulnerability to the unruliness that the theater allowed, both on stage and in the audience."[33] The most extreme statement of this approach comes at the end of his book: "For Parliament in the late summer of 1642 the threat of the unauthorized and unruly voices—the threat of a public, however diverse in social identity and interest, increasingly independent of the control of government authority—was too great to bear."[34] With all respect to Kastan, an extremely able and intelligent critic, I have to say that this strikes me as sheer fantasy. According to the closure document, the theater provides "Spectacles of Pleasure, too commonly expressing laciuious Mirth and Levitie"; in other words, entertainment, fun and games, laughter and dirty jokes. There is nothing remotely suggesting that parliament regarded the theater as a powerful and threatening political agency, needing to be suppressed at all cost. I do not see why parliament's clear and explicit statement has to be pushed aside and something totally different substituted for it.

The closure order contrasted fasting and play-going, and this was not accidental; on August 24, 1642, parliament had passed an ordinance for the compulsory observance of monthly fasting days.[35] One extreme Presbyterian, John Vicars, in a pamphlet published a year later, argued that God had been so pleased with the order for fasting that he had inspired what Vicars called "our most renowned and religious Parliamentary Worthies" to close down the theaters, described in colorful terms as "those most dirty and stinking sinks or lestalls of all kinde of abominations, those odious Hell-houses of the land."[36] Puritans were clearly delighted by the closure, whether or not it was inspired by puritanical motives. The contrast persisted into later writers, and could take on a clear political significance; Lois Potter quotes from a fast-sermon of 1644 in which the author Edmund Staunton reminds Members of Parliament that "when perhaps some elsewhere Nobles may be solemnizing these approaching Idolized Festivals, with Playes and Interludes . . . Your Honours, I hope, will be fasting, praying, hearing, and receiving the word with all readines of mind."[37] Potter very plausibly suggests that "elsewhere"

188   N. W. BAWCUTT

refers to the royalist court at Oxford, which was repeatedly accused by parliamentary pamphleteers of frivolous or indecent behavior.

The closure was to operate "while these sad Causes and set times of Humiliation doe continue," and it could reasonably be inferred that if the civil war came to an end playing would be allowed to resume. But the anonymous actor or actors who wrote *The Actors Remonstrance,* which appeared a few months later in January 1643, prophetically feared that the stage would undergo "a perpetuall, at least a very long temporary silence."[38] This shrewd pessimism was justified by my next piece of evidence. Late in 1644 there was an attempt at what might now be called a "peace process"; if the king agreed to a series of acts and bills drawn up by parliament the fighting would cease. Presented to the king on November 24, 1644, the propositions were discussed by the two sides at Uxbridge, and are hence sometimes termed the Propositions of Uxbridge or the Treaty of Uxbridge. The terms represented such a total and humiliating capitulation by the king that it is not surprising that he eventually rejected them and the war continued. Among the acts to which the king was required to give his assent was one "to be agreed upon for the suppression of Interludes and Stage plays, this Act to be perpetuall."[39] The 1642 closure might have appeared to be temporary, but only two years later it was to be permanent.

About a year later, in December 1645, another set of proposals to be submitted to the king included an act "for the putting downe of stage-playes."[40] For a while there seems to have been no more parliamentary consideration of the theater, but between the summer of 1647 and the summer of 1649 there was a flurry of activity, with a succession of motions, ordinances, and orders to the sheriffs of London and Middlesex. On at least seventeen separate occasions the Lords or Commons turned their attention to the stage, but it would be tedious to go through all the material in detail. Butler argues that this activity should be related to contemporary social and economic crises; I would prefer to suggest that the ending of what historians call the First Civil War in 1646, when fighting stopped, led the players to assume, on a literal interpretation of the ordinance of 1642, that acting could legitimately recommence. This was a grave misunderstanding. The suppression order of July 1647 was restricted to six months on the suggestion of the House of Lords, which was always slightly more sympathetic to players than the Commons, though six peers, including the Earl of Pembroke, protested bitterly at the limitation.[41] But when this expired at the beginning of 1648, parliament passed "An Ordinance for the utter suppression and abolishing of all Stage-Plays and Interludes."[42]

The preamble to this ordinance, as Butler rather reluctantly concedes, is distinctly "puritanical." Stage plays are "condemned by ancient Heathens, and much less to be tolerated amongst Professors of the Christian Religion" and they are "the occasion of many and sundry great vices and disorders,

PURITANISM AND THE CLOSING OF THE THEATERS IN 1642   189

tending to the high provocation of Gods wrath and displeasure." Six months later, in a letter to the General Assembly of the Church of Scotland, parliament included among its achievements this ordinance suppressing stageplays, which were described as "the Nurseries of Vice and Prophaneness."[43] The provisions of the ordinance were severe. Players were to be punished as rogues, and licenses issued by the king or anyone else were to be ignored. The interiors of theaters were to be demolished in order to make them unusable. Members of the audience were to be fined five shillings for attending a play, in those days by no means a trivial sum. But the players stubbornly continued to act, and in September 1648 parliament instituted a Provost Marshall, together with a deputy and twenty men, whose combined wages came to over thirteen pounds a week.[44] Their job was to act as a police corps enforcing the provisions of the ordinance. I find it difficult to see all this as indicating anything other than a deep-seated and persistent hostility to drama and a determination to suppress it completely.

The coming of the civil wars, and the temporary breakdown of official censorship, led to an outpouring of pamphlets, books, and newspapers discussing issues of the day. The largest surviving collection of these, now in the British Library, was assembled by a contemporary bookseller named George Thomason, and comprises approximately twenty-two thousand printed items published between 1640 and 1661. They contain a strikingly large number of allusions to plays and dramatists, and to attempts made at the time, many of them unsuccessful, to revive the drama after 1642 by means of surreptitious performances. They also make frequent use, in a variety of ways, of theatrical language to describe current events. A few of these allusions were noted in 1888 by Sir Charles Firth,[45] but the fullest surveys were made in the 1920s, first by Hyder Rollins and then by Leslie Hotson.[46] (However, more have been brought to light since then, and it can be taken as certain that still more remain to be discovered.) They usually take the form of crude and extremely biased propaganda, but even so they reveal patterns of thought and feeling which are relevant to this inquiry.[47]

Puritan denunciation of the theater continued unabated, several choice specimens of which were noted by Hotson. In 1647 one writer complained bitterly at attempts to revive playing: "The Common Inns of sin, and Blasphemy, the *Play-houses* began to be custom'd again, and to act filthinesse and villanny to the life."[48] He went on to gloat over the fact that one recent performance at Salisbury Court had been interrupted and suppressed by the city authorities. Another author, identified only by his initials "J.P.," made in 1654 a hysterically lurid and violent attack on the pre-war court, even though the king had been dead for over five years, and his court was only a memory. He gave examples of notorious adulterers in history:

> Are not these the very characters of many of our late wanton Courtiers, men and women of debaucht consciences and conversations, impudent, impenitent, jearing,

190   N. W. BAWCUTT

> mocking and scoffing at all means of recovery, wasting their precious times in
> Plays, Pastimes, Masks, and such fooleries, spending their wits and parts in Com-
> plements and Courtships, rising up in the morning wreaking from their beds of
> lusts, no sooner up but their lustful drinks are tempered for them, then to their pow-
> dering, trimming and tiring, then to their devotion to their bellies, I mean their glut-
> tonous dinners; then to Black-fryers, or other places, to see Plays, to offer up their
> evening sacrifices to the Devil; then to their junkets and jollities, and then again to
> their beds of lusts; and thus they wheel'd about their time *de die in diem*.[49]

For this writer the link between royalism and drama could hardly be more
clear and explicit.

If the theater was associated with courtiers, it was emphatically not somewhere Puritans would visit, and often formed part of an unholy trinity of dis-
reputable places to be avoided, along with ale-houses or taverns and brothels.
This conjunction was established well before the civil war: in *The Gallants
Burden,* a Paul's Cross sermon of Lent 1612, Thomas Adams saw the epicure
as moving from one to the next: "First, they visit the Tauerne, then the Ordi-
narie, then the Theater, and end in the Stewes, from Wine to Ryot, from that
to the Playes and from them to Harlots."[50] In 1616 Daniel Dyke saw "the
Alehouse, the Stewes, and the Stage" as snares of the devil intended to lure
men from going to church.[51] Henry Parker, in his *Discourse concerning Puritans* (1641), complained of the crudity of attacks on Puritans by the Laudian
clergy, which encouraged the common people ("the vulgar") to spread about
monstrous calumnies concerning the Puritans: "Neither could this audacity
be so prevalent amongst the vulgar, but that Scholars, and the greatest of the
Clergie are now become the most injurious detesters and depravers of Puritans, having taken up in Pulpits and Presses, almost as vile and scurrilous a
licence of fiction and detraction, as is usuall in Play-houses, Taverns, and
Bordelloes."[52] Perhaps the most striking illustration comes from the *Description of a Puritan,* written in verse and appended to *A Dialogue wherin is
Plainly layd Open The Tyrannicall Dealing of Lord Bishops against Gods
Children* (1640), by "Martin Mar-Prelat." One stanza reads:

> A Puritan, is he, that for no meed,
>   will serve the time, and great mens humors feed,
> That doth the selfe-accusing Oath refuse:
>   That hates the Ale-house, and a Stage, and Stews.[53]

It should be emphasized that this portrait is a celebration of the Puritan, not
an attack, and it might make us wary of recent attempts to play down Puritan
hostility to the stage.

As we might expect, royalist pamphleteers made extensive use of theatrical
allusions and metaphors. One usage could be said to follow from Henry Parker's complaints against the Laudian clergy, and links together bishops and

PURITANISM AND THE CLOSING OF THE THEATERS IN 1642 191

players as fellow-sufferers from parliamentary persecution. Sometimes the idea was expressed very briefly:

> *Bishops* and *Plays* were in a day put down . . .[54]
> In one day they cry'd down *Prelates* and *Players* . . .[55]

The fullest use occurs in a complimentary poem by Alexander Brome written for a collection of plays by Richard Brome, *Five New Plays,* published in 1653:

> *Tis worth our note,*
> Bishops, *and* Players *both suffer'd in one* Vote.
> *And reason good, for they had cause to feare 'em,*
> *One did* suppresse *their* Schismes, *and tother jeere 'em.*[56]

This explains clearly why the connection was made. Bishops and players were both seen as hostile to puritanism; the bishops had administrative powers which enabled them to suppress Puritan preachers, and the players waged a propaganda campaign of mockery against them.

A very common device among royalists was to assert that parliament had closed the theaters because it wanted to monopolize drama itself: "But now farewell Playes for ever, for the Rebels are resoloved to bee the onely Tragedians, none shall act *Cataline* but themselves."[57] The choice of Jonson's *Catiline* is not accidental; the play is about an attempt to usurp imperial power. John Cleveland said tersely that "since the Stages were voted downe, the onely Play-house is at *Westminster.*"[58] (This provoked a snarling reply which referred to "dirty ragges, raked out of the dunghill of ruined stages."[59]) There were sarcastic congratulations that parliamentary drama was much more powerful than that provided by the actors because the deaths in it were not merely pretended:

> Your Tragedies more real are exprest,
> You murther men in earnest, we in jeast.[60]

This was evidently felt to be a telling point, and was used several times. According to one writer, the players were hoping that "they shall returne to their old harmelesse profession of killing Men in Tragedies without Man-slaughter."[61] Samuel Butler expressed himself with characteristic pungency: "We perceive at last, why Plays went down; to-wit, that Murders might be acted in earnest. Stages must submit to Scaffolds, and personated tragedies to real ones."[62] This seems to have been written after the execution of Charles I in 1649, which obviously gave an added resonance to the idea.

Some Presbyterian ministers gave electrifying performances as preachers, and their royalist opponents jokingly asserted that their behavior was so

192   N. W. BAWCUTT

richly comic that there was no need to regret the closing of the theaters; the preachers were as entertaining as any of the great comedians of the time: "indeed we need not any more *Stage-playes,* we thanke them for suppressing them, they save us money; for Ile undertake we can laugh as heartily at *Fox-ley, Peters,* and others of their godly Ministers, as ever we did at *Cane* at the *Red Bull, Tom: Pollard* in the humorous Lieutenant, *Robins* the Changeling, or any humorist of them all."[63] On other occasions, attacks on the suppression of the stage were more serious in tone. Some used the Shakespearean notion of drama as holding the mirror up to nature (*Hamlet,* 3.2.22), and argued that parliament was embarrassed to see its tricks and devices exposed on the stage: "There you may read the Parliament in print, there you may see Treason courting *Tyranny,* and Faction prostituted to *Rebellion,* there you may see (as in a mirrour) all State-judglings, clenly conveyances, and underhand dealings pourtray'd to the life; therefore Players and Pamphleters, they must, they shall come down."[64] A more restrained version occurs in Christopher Wase's dedication to his highly politicized translation of Sophocles' *Electra* published in 1649: "Playes are the Mirrours wherein Mens actions are reflected to their own view. Which, perhaps, is the true cause, that some, privy to the Uglinesse of their own guilt, have issued out Warrants, for the breaking all those Looking-glasses; lest their deformities recoyl, and become an eye-sore unto themselves."[65] Martin Butler argues that Caroline drama exposed the iniquities of Charles I; these royalist writers unhesitatingly assumed that it was parliament whose iniquities were being exposed.

Opponents of royalism also used allusions to plays and theatrical language, but as Lois Potter observes, the use of such language is not always complimentary,[66] and the parliamentarians repeatedly and consistently sneered at drama. One who wrote for the newsletter *Mercurius Britanicus* claimed that a writer for the royalist newsletter *Mercurius Aulicus* had lost his wits, and no form of stimulant, alcoholic or literary, would rouse him from this state of dullness: "not to be recovered by the Protestant or *Catholique liquour,* either *Ale* or strong beer, or Sack, or Claret, or Hippocras, or Muscadine, or Rosasolis, which hath been reputed formerly by his Grand-father *Ben Iohnson,* and his Uncle *Shakespeare,* and his Couzen Germains, *Fletcher,* and *Beamont,* [*sic*] and nose-lesse *Davenant,* and Frier *Sherley* the Poets, the onely blossoms for the brain, the restoratives for the wit."[67] The writer knew the leading dramatists of the time, but his references to "nose-lesse *Davenant*" and "Frier *Sherley*" (apparently Shirley converted to Catholicism in the 1620s) were clearly contemptuous. The royalist general William Cavendish, made Duke of Newcastle in 1665, wrote two plays, *The Variety* and *The Country Captain,* not long before the closing of the theaters. Butler presents him as satirizing the decadent culture of the Caroline court,[68] but this did not redeem him in the eyes of his political enemies, who consistently ridiculed him both as a dramatist and as a military leader.[69] Revisionist critics

PURITANISM AND THE CLOSING OF THE THEATERS IN 1642   193

have argued that drama was helping to "educate" audiences into accepting the idea that kings could be put on trial and even executed, but there is not the slightest hint in the parliamentarian writings of the period that any one was aware of this.

It is certainly true that some of the satirical pamphlets of the day were cast into a kind of dramatic form, a sketch or brief play. This device was used in the early 1640s by supporters of parliament, as a means of attacking hate-figures such as Strafford and Laud. A few years later, after both men had been executed, it was taken over, mainly by royalists, in order to ridicule Cromwell and parliament. But I cannot believe that the parliamentarians who originated the genre did so out of a deep and genuine respect for drama. The playlets had only one function, to express loathing and contempt, and their dramatic technique was clumsy in the extreme, with none of the qualities traditionally associated with great drama, except perhaps an occasional pungency of language. Indeed, it could be suggested that their writers despised conventional drama, so that to force a hitherto dignified and powerful public figure into a playlet of this kind, the mere fact of staging him, was a means of making him absurd and ludicrous.

This applies to the attacks on Archbishop Laud, which offer nothing more than a brutally simplified and repulsive caricature.[70] A very different approach was taken by Peter Heylyn in his pamphlet on the death of Laud which included the text of his last speech on the scaffold: "It is a preposterous kinde of writing to beginne the story of a great mans life, at the houre of his death; a most strange way of setting forth a solemne *Tragedie,* to keep the *principall Actor* in the *tyring-house,* till the *Play* be done, and then to bring him on the *Stage* onely to speake the *Epilogue,* and receive the Plaudites. Yet this must bee the scope and method of these following papers."[71] We might juxtapose what a distinguished recent historian has said about Laud's execution: "The 71-year-old prelate was beheaded on Tower Hill, as Strafford had been, and he died as bravely. The Hothams, father and son, had suffered the same fate there a few days earlier, for trying to betray Hull. Unlike them, Laud had never broken faith and had long ceased to pose a threat to the parliament. The malignity with which it pursued him to death is a stain on its cause."[72] The royalist was able to see Laud's death as tragic; the play-pamphlets exhibit the "malignity" which brought about his death.

On the whole parliamentarians used terms like "tragedy" and "tragical" in a special and limited sense. It was possible for the words to be given a dignified and powerful meaning; one striking example occurs in the famous letter written by Sir William Waller to his old friend Sir Ralph Hopton in 1643, when they had taken opposite sides in the civil war: "wee are both upon the stage and must act those parts that are assigned to us in this Tragedy."[73] But it was much more common, especially among Puritan clergymen, for the words to be used to jeer and gloat over the misfortunes of their ene-

194   N. W. BAWCUTT

mies, who thought all was going well for them until disaster struck. The usage is especially appropriate in a theatrical context, and was employed when attempts at surreptitious performances during the interregnum went wrong. On October 2, 1643, soldiers occupied the Fortune playhouse, ending the play and confiscating the players' costumes; as the unsympathetic narrator of this event put it, "it turned their Comedy into a Tragedy."[74] September 14, 1655, was a day which "proved Tragical to the *Players* at the *Red Bull*"; soldiers occupied the theater, seizing the costumes and fining the spectators five shillings each. The narrator mockingly comments that "the Tragedy of the Actors, and the Spectators, was the Comedy of the soldiers."[75]

The most elaborate account of a theatrical disaster occurs in John Rowe's *Tragi-Comaedia,* published at Oxford in 1653. On February 3 of that year a group of amateur actors performed the old Elizabethan comedy *Mucedorus* in the large upper chamber of the White Hart Inn at Witney. Rowe clearly had access to a copy of the play, from which he made a number of quotations. Probably most modern readers would find the play inoffensive, but for Rowe "The matter of the *Play* is scurrilous, impious, blasphemous in severall passages,"[76] and he was particularly offended by a jeer at Puritans and their love of fasting. About two-thirds of the way through the play "it pleased God to put a stop to their mirth" (*2ᵛ). The floor of the chamber slowly collapsed into the room below, causing the death of five people and many injuries. "The Comedy being turned into a Tragedy, it had a sad *Catastrophe,* ending with the deaths of some, and hurts of many" (¶¶1ᵛ). Rowe brushed aside attempts at naturalistic explanation ("too many apt to say it was but a chance, a misfortune, the beame was weake, there were so many load of people there, and the like," ibid.), and he ignored the fact that there had been several earlier performances with no ill effect. He stressed the suffering of many members of the audience, but showed no sympathy: "So by the just hand of God came it to passe" (¶¶2). In this context tragedy is no more than God's ruthless punishment of those who have offended him.[77]

Plays published between 1642 and 1660 frequently contain prefaces and complimentary poems which are useful evidence concerning contemporary attitudes to drama. (Some lines have already been quoted from one of these, a poem by Alexander Brome included in the 1653 edition of Richard Brome's *Five New Plays.*[78]) Overwhelmingly the writers of this material were royalists; indeed Kastan, in a discussion of the printing of plays in this period, writes of "the manifest royalism of much of what was published," and describes the 1647 Folio edition of Beaumont and Fletcher's plays as "unmistakably Royalist in sympathy."[79] The poets lamented the destructive effects parliament had had on literature; Thomas Stanley referred to "*They* that silenc'd Wit,"[80] and a few years later Jasper Mayne complained of living in "Times which make it Treason to be witty."[81] There were some attempts at

PURITANISM AND THE CLOSING OF THE THEATERS IN 1642   195

consolation; Sir Aston Cokayne was pleased that plays were available in print:

> Then we shall still have *Playes!* And though we may
> Not them in their full Glories yet display;
> Yet we may please our selves by reading them . . .[82]

but he clearly felt that reading was an inferior substitute, and eagerly looked forward to a time when the stage would revive and the great dramatists of the early seventeenth century would once again be performed.

Very occasionally the royalism became explicit. James Shirley, writing in the Beaumont and Fletcher folio of 1647, still found it possible to hope that the king would return to London and presumably revive the drama:

> A Balme unto the wounded Age I sing,
> And nothing now is wanting but the King.[83]

Two years later the king was dead, and it must have been painfully clear that the theaters would remain closed for the foreseeable future. There was an extraordinary outburst in the dedication "To the Honour'd Few, Lovers of *Drammatick Poesie*" of Fletcher's *The Wild-Goose Chase,* 1652, signed by John Lowin and Joseph Taylor, the senior members of the now-defunct King's company: "And now Farewell our *Glory!* Farewell your *Choice Delight,* most noble Gentlemen! Farewell th' *Grand Wheel* that set *Vs* smaller Motions in Action! Farewell the Pride And Life o' th' Stage! Nor can we (though in our Ruin) much repine that we are so little, since *He* that gave us being is no more."[84] Bentley terms this "a valediction to the Caroline theatre,"[85] but it seems odd to refer to a theater as "He," and I feel that the passage laments the death of the king, the company's patron, and the "*Grand Wheel* that set *Vs* smaller Motions in Action."

Butler's treatment of this kind of evidence is extremely unsatisfactory. He merely labels the poems as "conscious acts of propaganda,"[86] as though this is enough to dismiss them as insignificant and negligible. His attitude is very biased and one-sided. Many of the writings on behalf of parliament that Butler considers are "conscious acts of propaganda," but he treats them sympathetically and in detail, whereas royalist propaganda is brushed aside. Perhaps more importantly, by defining them as royalist he makes a significant though unacknowledged concession which damages the whole approach of his book. If play publication during the interregnum is regularly and consistently accompanied with royalist propaganda, this would surely suggest that the drama was indeed (to turn Butler's own phrase against him) "an institution irretrievably riddled with royalism." The evidence assembled in this paper indicates that the old-fashioned view of puritanism and drama, while

196   N. W. BAWCUTT

perhaps needing a certain amount of refinement and modification, was basically right.

Notes

1. "Was Thomas Middleton a Puritan Dramatist?" *Modern Language Review* 94 (1999): 925–39. This article pointed out, among other things, that Middleton repeatedly and consistently jeered at Puritans and Puritanism in his writings.

2. See reviews by Robert Ashton, *History* 66 (1981): 489; Kevin Sharpe, *The Historical Journal* 25 (1982): 737–38; and Christopher Haigh, *English Historical Review* 98 (1983): 194–95.

3. Martin Butler, *Theatre and Crisis 1632–1642* (Cambridge: Cambridge University Press, 1984), 24 (henceforward abbreviated to "Butler").

4. Franco Moretti, *Signs Taken for Wonders: Essays in the Sociology of Literary Forms* (London: Verso, 1983) 27 and 42. King Charles's status had undoubtedly declined by 1649, but it is an oversimplification to say that the monarchy had been "deconsecrated"; for evidence to the contrary see Andrew Lacey, *The Cult of King Charles the Martyr,* Studies in Modern British Religious History, 7 (Woodbridge: The Boydell Press, 2003).

5. David Scott Kastan, *Shakespeare After Theory* (New York: Routledge, 1999), 111 (henceforward abbreviated to "Kastan").

6. Butler, 138.

7. Ibid., 136.

8. Ibid., 140.

9. Ibid., 95

10. Ibid., 96.

11. Kastan, 203.

12. Butler, 94.

13. Henry Burton, *For God and the King* (1636), 49–50.

14. Butler, 97. This is surely a very inadequate summary of Puritan objections to the stage.

15. For full details of these and other pamphlets see J. F. Arnott and J. W. Robinson, *English Theatrical Literature 1559–1900* (London: Society for Theatre Research, 1970), 65–70. The theater's increasing respectability in the nineteenth century is discussed by Richard Foulkes, *Church and Stage in Victorian England* (Cambridge: Cambridge University Press, 1977).

16. Reprinted in *Rare Prologues and Epilogues 1642–1700,* ed. Autrey Nell Wiley (London: Allen and Unwin, 1940), 6. The pamphlet of 1642 is BL Thomason Tracts E144.9. Cowley also wrote two pungent anti-Puritan verse satires, *The Puritan Lecture,* first published as *A Satire against Separatists* in 1642, and *The Puritan and the Papist,* published in 1643. Both are reprinted in *The Collected Works of Abraham Cowley, Volume 1,* ed. Thomas O. Calhoun, Laurence Heyworth, and Allan Pritchard (Newark: University of Delaware Press, 1989).

17. John Bastwick, *The Confession of the Faithfull Witnesse of Christ* (1641), A2^v (BL E175.3).

PURITANISM AND THE CLOSING OF THE THEATERS IN 1642 197

18. Henry Parker, *A Discourse concerning Puritans* (1641), 53–54 (BL E204.3).

19. Lucy Hutchinson, *Memoirs of the Life of Colonel Hutchinson,* ed. James Sutherland (London: Oxford University Press, 1973), 44. This resembles Sir Benjamin Rudyerd's complaint, in a parliamentary speech of November 7, 1640, against defenders of royal ecclesiastical policies such as Peter Heylyn that "They have so brought it to passe, that under the Name of Puritans, all our Religion is branded . . . Whosoever squares his actions by any rule, either Divine or Humane, hee is a Puritan. Whosoever would bee govern'd by the Kings Laws, hee is a Puritan. He that will not doe whatsoever other men will have him doe, he is a Puritan. Their Great worke, their Master piece now is, To make all those of the Religion, to bee the suspected partie of the Kingdome." *The Speeches of Sir Benjamin Rudyer in the High Court of Parliament* (1641), 3 (BL E196.2).

20. "Touring," in *A New History of Early English Drama,* ed. John D. Cox and David Scott Kastan (New York: Columbia University Press, 1997), 265.

21. *The Stage-Players Complaint In A Pleasant Dialogue between Cane of the Fortune and Reed of the Friars* (1641), 4 (BL E172.23).

22. *Journals of the House of Commons,* 2:94.

23. *The Journals of Sir Simonds D'Ewes,* ed. Wallace Notestein (New Haven: Yale University Press, 1923), 412. Elizabeth Sauer, *"Paper Contestations" and Textual Communities in England, 1640–1675* (Toronto: University of Toronto Press, 2005), 24–25, shows that depriving a man of his trade or livelihood was regarded as a very serious offense, and opponents of projectors and monopolists used this argument to attack them.

24. The Blackfriars Theatre was very close to St Paul's Cathedral.

25. *The Private Journals of the Long Parliament 3 January to 5 March 1642,* ed. W. H. Coates, A. S. Young, and V. F. Snow (New Haven: Yale University Press, 1982), 182.

26. *The True Diurnal Occurances, or The heads of the Proceedings of Both Houses in Parliament 31 Jan to 7 Feb 1642,* A4ᵛ (BL E201.13).

27. *Journals of the House of Commons,* 2:747.

28. Ibid., 2:749.

29. *A Declaration Of The Lords and Commons Assembled in Parliament For the appeasing and quietting of all unlawfull Tumults and Insurrections in the severall Counties of England, and Dominion of Wales . . . Also an Ordinance of both Houses, for the suppressing of Stage-Playes,* A4–4ᵛ (BL E115.15). The first of these orders instructs unruly people who have broken into and plundered the houses of suspected recusants and "malignants" (the current term for supporters of the king) without authority from parliament not to do so, and to restore any money and goods which have been seized. The order was probably inspired by incidents of the kind which occurred near Colchester on August 20, when a Puritan mob from the town besieged and sacked the house of Sir John Lucas, who was about to set off to join the king's army. See Austin Woolrych, *Britain in Revolution 1625–1660* (Oxford: Oxford University Press, 2002), 230. Woolrych comments that "outbreaks like this were exceptional, and even now the fear that the rule of law was collapsing was exaggerated." This order suggests that where issues of public behavior were concerned parliament was fully prepared to say so explicitly.

198   N. W. BAWCUTT

30. Susan Wiseman, *Drama and Politics in the English Civil War* (Cambridge: Cambridge University Press, 1998), 1.

31. Kastan, 204. Compare similar remarks on 215.

32. Wiseman, *Drama and Politics,* 2. It is hard to reconcile this with Butler's claim that Puritan hostility to the stage had declined in the 1630s because theatergoing had become more orderly and respectable (Butler, 97).

33. Kastan, 160. An almost identical formulation is on p. 210.

34. Kastan, 219.

35. There already existed a royal proclamation enjoining the observance of a day of fasting each month, but the results had been disappointing to Puritans, who strongly believed in the practice, and the new ordinance tried to enforce stricter regulations—all trades and businesses were to close on the day, and clergymen who failed to officiate in fast-day services were to be reported and punished. See *Acts and Ordinances of the Interregnum 1642–1660,* ed. C. H. Firth and R. S. Rait, 3 vols. (London: H. M. Stationery Office, 1911), 1:22–24.

36. [John Vicars], *God on the Mount, or a Continuation of Englands Parliamentary Chronicles* (1643), 152 (BL E73.4). "Lestall" is a form of "laystall," defined by *OED* as "a place where refuse and dung is laid."

37. Lois Potter, *Secret rites and secret writing: Royalist literature 1641–1660* (Cambridge: Cambridge University Press, 1989), 140. The sermon in question was *Phinehas's Zeal in Execvtion of Ivdgement* (1645), A2, preached to the House of Lords on October 30, 1644. It is a repulsive and bloodthirsty piece of work in which Staunton assures his audience that God will be delighted if parliament destroys as many of its opponents as possible.

38. *The Actors Remonstrance, Or Complaint: For the silencing of their profession, and banishment from their seuerall Play-houses* (1643), 4 (BL E86.8).

39. *The Humble Desires and Propositions For a safe and well-grounded Peace. . . . of the Parliaments of Both Kingdoms . . . Presented unto His Majesty at Oxford the 24. of Novemb. last* (1644), 6 (BL E21.18).

40. *Mercurius Civicus No. 132 27 November–4 December 1645* (1645), 1158 (BL E311.6). The writer comments on the proposals that "the particulars of them are much to the effect of those at Uxbridge."

41. *Journals of the House of Lords,* 9:334 (July 16, 1647).

42. All quotations from the reprint in *Acts and Ordinances of the Interregnum 1642–1660,* ed. Firth and Rait. 2:1070–72. The published version is entitled *An Ordinance of the Lords and Commons Assembled in Parliament, for, the utter suppression and abolishing of all Stage-Playes and Interludes. With the Penalties to be inflicted upon the Actors and Spectators, herein exprest,* February 11, 1647/48 (BL E426.22).

43. *A Letter from the House of Commons to the General Assembly of the Church of Scotland* (1648), 8 (BL E457.13).

44. See Leslie Hotson, *The Commonwealth and Restoration Stage* (Cambridge: Harvard University Press, 1928), 38–39.

45. C. H. Firth, "The Suppression of the Drama during the Protectorate and Commonwealth," *Notes and Queries,* 7th series, 6 (August 18, 1888): 122–23.

46. Hyder E. Rollins, "A Contribution to the History of the English Commonwealth Drama," *Studies in Philology* 18 (1921): 267–333, and Leslie Hotson, chapter 1 of *The Commonwealth and Restoration Stage.*

PURITANISM AND THE CLOSING OF THE THEATERS IN 1642   199

47. I shall also occasionally bring in material which is not taken from the Thomason Tracts. These pamphlets have been increasingly discussed by scholars; two recent books, published while this essay was in preparation, are Jason Peacey, *Politicians and Pamphleteers: Propaganda During the English Civil War and Interregnum* (Aldershot: Ashgate, 2004), and Elizabeth Sauer, *"Paper Contestations" and Textual Communities in England, 1640–1675* (see above, note 23). Sauer stresses the transference of dramatic conventions and proceedures into other contexts, but there is little overlap between her book and the final section of my essay.

48. *Mercurius Melancholicus: Or, Newes From Westminster Octob. 2–9 1647,* 32 (BL E410.12).

49. "J. P." [? = John Price], *Tyrants and Protectors, Set Forth To their Colours* (1654), 16 (BL E738.18).

50. Thomas Adams, *The Gallants Burden* (1612), E4ᵛ·

51. Daniel Dyke, *Two Treatises, the one, of repentance, the other, of Christs temptations* (1616), 216. He comments that "the Spirit of God carries us to no such places." No doubt there were also numbers of respectable people, not necessarily "Puritanical," who would have avoided them.

52. Parker, *A Discourse,* 2. Compare the passage quoted above from Parker, n. 18.

53. "Martin Mar-Prelat," *A Dialogue,* D2ᵛ (BL 698 g 9.4).

54. *A Bartholomew Fairing* (1649), 14 (BL E572.7).

55. Thomas Jordan, *Tricks of Youth, or The Walks of Islington and Hogsdon, with The Humours of Woodstreet-Compter* (1663), A2 (BL 644 b 60). This is a reissue of a play first published in 1657. The line comes from a newly written dedication celebrating the revival of drama.

56. Richard Brome, *Five New Plays* (1653), A3ᵛ (BL E1423.1).

57. *Mercurius Bellicus,* February 14–20, 1647/48, 7 (BL E428.4).

58. John Cleveland, *The Character of a London Diurnall* (Oxford, 1644), 2 (BL E268.6).

59. *A Character of the New Oxford Libeller* (1645), 3 (BL E269.7).

60. Thomas Jordan, "The Players Petition to the Long Parliament," in *A Royal Arbor of Loyal Poesie* (1664), 80. The poem was written in 1642. Rather surprisingly Rollins, who was superbly well-read, did not recognize the authorship and quoted it as anonymous from Bodleian MS Ashmole 47, f. 133 (Rollins, "A Contribution," 275–76).

61. *Mercurius Anti-Britannicus* (Oxford, 1645), 20 (BL E296.9). Royalist pamphleteers repeatedly used the word "harmless" to describe play-performances; see the quotations in Hotson on pages 28, 38, 44, and 49–50.

62. Samuel Butler, *Mercurius Menippeus,* 1682, in Butler, *Satires and Miscellaneous Poetry and Prose,* ed. R. Lamar (Cambridge: Cambridge University Press, 1928), 363. This was probably written in late 1649 or 1650.

63. *A Key to the Cabinet of the Parliament* (1648), 8 (BL E449.2).

64. *Mercurius Melancholicus,* January 22–29, 1648, 130 (BL E423.30).

65. "C.W.," *Electra of Sophocles: presented to her Highnesse the Lady Elizabeth At the Hague* (1649), ¶2ᵛ–3 (BL E1216.2). For discussion of this play see Potter, *Secret Rites,* 53–54, and Dale Randall, *Winter Fruit: English Drama 1642–1660* (Lexington: University Press of Kentucky, 1995), 216–19.

200 N. W. BAWCUTT

66. Potter, *Secret Rites,* 116.

67. *Mercurius Britanicus,* no. 20, January 4–11, 1643/44, 152 (BL E81.20).

68. Butler, 195–98.

69. See the quotations assembled in G. E. Bentley, *The Jacobean and Caroline Stage,* 7 vols. (Oxford: Oxford University Press, 1941–68), 3:144–45. Another jeer, from *The Kingdomes Weekly Intelligencer,* No. 198, February 23–March 2, 1647, 438 (E378.18), is quoted by Nigel Smith, *Literature and Revolution in England, 1640–1660* (New Haven: Yale University Press, 1994), 75.

70. See Butler, 236–46. I cannot accept Butler's suggestion (246–47) that violently abusive playlets were performed on the London stages in 1641 and 1642.

71. *A Briefe Relation of the Death and Sufferings of the Most Reverend and Renowned Prelate the L. Archbishop of Canterbury* (Oxford, 1644), A2 (BL E269.20). Royalist pamphleteers repeatedly portrayed the death of King Charles as a tragedy, but to discuss this adequately would require a disproportionate amount of space. See Nancy Klein Maguire, "The Theatrical Mask/Masque of Politics: The Case of Charles I," *Journal of British Studies* 28 (1989): 1–22.

72. Woolrych, *Britain in Revolution 1625–1660,* 295.

73. Mary Coate, *Cornwall in the Great Civil War and Interregnum 1642–1660* (Oxford: Clarendon Press, 1933), 77.

74. *The Weekly Account,* September 27–October 4, 1643, 6 (BL E250.17).

75. *The Weekly Intelligencer,* September 11–18, 1655, 38 (BL E853.16).

76. John Rowe, *Tragi-Comaedia, Being a Brief Relation of the Strange, and Wonderfull hand of God discovered at Witney . . .* (Oxford, 1653), *1[v.] Rowe's "Brief Narration" of events is reprinted in Thornton S. Graves, "Notes on Puritanism and the Stage," *Studies in Philology* 18 (1921): 150–57. According to Muriel Bradbrook, "a debased version of *Mucedorus* was still being played in Shropshire villages in the early nineteenth century," *The Growth and Structure of Elizabethan Comedy* (London: Chatto and Windus, 1955), 24.

77. There is a perceptive discussion of Puritan attitudes to tragedy in "Puritanism and the Dramatic Attitude," chapter 5 of Patrick Cruttwell's *The Shakespearean Moment and its Place in the Poetry of the 17th Century* (London: Chatto and Windus, 1954), 138–61.

78. See above, note 56.

79. "Performances and playbooks: the closing of the theatres and the politics of drama," in *Reading, Society and Politics in Early Modern England,* ed. Kevin Sharpe and Stephen N. Zwicker (Cambridge: Cambridge University Press, 2003), 176 and 180.

80. "On the Edition," in *Comedies and Tragedies Written by Francis Beaumont and John Fletcher Gentlemen* (1647), b4[v.]

81. "To the deceased Author of these poems," in *Comedies, Tragi-Comedies, with other Poems,* by William Cartwright (1651), b6.

82. "A Praeludium to Mr Richard Bromes Playes," in Richard Brome, *Five New Plays* (1653), A2.

83. "Upon the Printing of Mr. Iohn Fletchers workes," in *Comedies and Tragedies* (1647), g1[v.]

84. John Fletcher, *The Wild-Goose Chase. A Comedie* (1652), A2.

85. G. E. Bentley, *The Jacobean and Caroline Stage,* 3:247.

86. Butler, 9–10.

My Magic Can Lick Your Magic

Richard Levin

THIS is an inquiry into a certain kind of episode found in earlier literature that I call the "magic contest" because it centers on a confrontation between two people (or sometimes between one person and a group) in which each side makes use of or calls upon some supernatural power in order to defeat the opposing side. It would obviously be impossible to survey all these contests in the literary archive, and so I have limited the inquiry by beginning with the oldest examples of the contest that have come down to us, then proceeding to a few treatments of it in early modern English drama, and concluding with an examination of its transformation and decline in Shakespeare. The best known of the ancient contests is recorded in Exodus 7:9–12, where the Lord tells Moses that he must order Pharaoh to release the children of Israel, and that

> When Pharaoh shall speak unto you, saying, Shew a miracle for you: then thou shalt say unto Aaron, Take thy rod, and cast it before Pharaoh and it shall become a serpent. And Moses and Aaron went in unto Pharaoh, and they did so as the LORD had commanded: and Aaron cast down his rod before Pharaoh . . . and it became a serpent. Then Pharaoh also called the wise men and the sorcerers: now the magicians of Egypt, they also did in like manner with their enchantments. For they cast down every man his rod, and they became serpents: but Aaron's rod swallowed up their rods.[1]

This contest continues into the plagues that Moses, following the directions of the Lord, brings down on Egypt. After the first plague, when he makes the rivers run with blood, we are told that "the magicians of Egypt did so with their enchantments" (7:22), which is the same locution used for the serpents and apparently means that they were able to duplicate his feat. And after the second, when he covers the land with frogs, this is made explicit: "the magicians did so with their enchantments, and brought up frogs upon the land of Egypt" (8:7). But after the third, when he turns dust into lice, we find that "the magicians did so with their enchantments to bring forth lice, but they could not," and therefore "the magicians said unto Pharaoh, This is the finger of God" (8:18–19). And after the sixth plague, when he turns ashes into boils

201

202 RICHARD LEVIN

breaking forth with blains, "the magicians could not stand before Moses because of the boils; for the boil was upon the magicians, and upon all the Egyptians" (9:11). This marks the end of the contest and their complete defeat, for we hear no more of them.

There is another contest of this kind in Genesis 41:1–39 that is initiated by an earlier pharaoh. He had a dream that troubled him, so "he sent and called for all the magicians of Egypt, and all the wise men thereof" to interpret it (8), but not one of them could do it. Then he sends for Joseph, who is able to explain its true meaning. Moreover, Joseph repeatedly attributes both Pharaoh's dream and his own correct interpretation of it to the God he worships (16, 25, 28, 32), and at the end this pharaoh agrees with him (38, 39) and makes him the chief officer of the government of Egypt.

The theological stakes are even clearer in a later contest arranged by Elijah between him and the 450 prophets of Baal that is played out on Mount Carmel before King Ahab and the assembled people of Israel in 1 Kings 18:19–40. The Baalim sacrifice a bullock on their altar and pray to Baal to respond, but nothing happens; and then Elijah sacrifices another bullock on his own altar and prays to the Lord for a response, whereupon fire descends from heaven and consumes the sacrifice. Thus Elijah wins the contest and orders the people to slay the 450 prophets of Baal, and "let not one of them escape" (40).

There are three of these contests in the book of Daniel, each of which pits Daniel against opponents who are variously called the "magicians," "astrologers," "Chaldeans," "soothsayers," "sorcerers," and "wise men" of Babylon. The first two (2:1–49 and 4:4–37) are very similar to Joseph's contest in Genesis: in both of them King Nebuchadnezzar has a dream that troubles him and sends for his magicians and the like, who cannot interpret it, and then sends for Daniel, who can. In both episodes Daniel, like Joseph before him, repeatedly attributes the king's dream and his own interpretation of it to God (2:18, 23, 28–29, 44–45, 4:24–25), and the king finally agrees with him and accepts his God as the "God of gods" whose "dominion is an everlasting dominion" (2:47, 4:34). The third contest (5:5–31) is initiated by King Belshazzar, the son and successor of Nebuchadnezzar, who is holding a great feast in his palace when a hand appears and writes some words on the wall. Like his father, Belshazzar first calls on his magicians and others to interpret the words, but again they fail. Then he calls on Daniel, who explains that the words mean that God will punish Belshazzar and destroy his kingdom. And this is confirmed on the same night when Babylon is invaded by Darius and Belshazzar is killed.

All these biblical magic contests follow the same basic pattern. They are always staged before the ruler of the country, who is always a pagan (this includes Ahab, who became an apostate). On one side is a Hebrew hero, who is usually alone, the only exception being Moses, since he is accompanied by

MY MAGIC CAN LICK YOUR MAGIC 203

his brother Aaron, and on the other side are a number of nameless men who claim to have some special magical ability. They always lose, of course, and the Hebrew hero always wins; but what he does to attain his victory is never called magic—indeed, this victory is never attributed to any special ability of his, because he functions as a conduit through which is conveyed the power of the one true God, who is the real victor in these contests. We are even told that the purpose of each contest is to demonstrate that God has this power and is indeed the one true God. That is why the identity of the opposing magicians does not matter. They are not regarded as individuals and, except for the Baalim in 1 Kings, their religious beliefs are not specified, although we can assume that they are all pagans, like their king, and worship false plural gods, who are the real losers in these contests.[2]

None of this is true, however, of another magic contest that has come down to us in several versions that may be as old as some of the biblical stories, and that are recorded by Strabo. One of the contestants is Calchas, who was the chief prophet accompanying the Greek forces attacking Troy—he is credited by Homer with discerning the cause of the plague in their camp and with foretelling the length of the war, among other things. In his post-Homeric travels after the war, he came to Italy where, according to Strabo,

> having met near Clarus a prophet superior to himself, Mopsus, the son of Manto, the daughter of Teiresias, he died of grief. Now Hesiod revises the myth as follows, making Calchas propound to Mopsus this question: "I am amazed . . . at all these figs on this wild fig tree; . . . can you tell me the number?" And he makes Mopsus reply: "They are ten thousand in number, and their measure is a medimnus [bushel]; but there is one over, which you cannot put in the measure." "Thus he spake," Hesiod adds, "and the number the measure could hold proved true. And then the eyes of Calchas were closed by the sleep of death." But Pherecydes says that the question propounded by Calchas was in regard to a pregnant sow, how many pigs she carried, and that Mopsus said, "three, one of which is a female," and that when Mopsus proved to have spoken the truth, Calchas died of grief . . . in accordance with a certain oracle. Sophocles tells the oracle in his *Reclaiming of Helen,* that Calchas was destined to die when he met a prophet superior to himself, but he transfers the scene of the rivalry and of the death of Calchas to Cilicia. Such are the ancient stories.[3]

The differences between this magic contest and those recounted in the Bible are very striking. There is no monarch present to initiate or preside over or judge the contest, which is managed entirely by the two contestants. Nor is there any theological dimension to their contest. Homer tells us elsewhere that Calchas received his prophetic ability as a gift from Apollo,[4] and we can assume that Mopsus inherited his ability from his grandfather Teiresias, who received his ability from Zeus or Athena (depending on which version one believes); but that is wholly irrelevant here, because, unlike the biblical contests, no deity speaks through either man, and neither of them represents any religious beliefs or anything else beyond himself. This means that they are regarded just as two individuals, each of whom possesses his own personal magical skills, and that Mopsus wins because his personal magical skill in divination is superior to that of Calchas. Consequently there is no lesson to be derived from the defeat of Calchas, unless it is that the predictions of an oracle are always fulfilled. And perhaps we are also supposed to infer from Calchas's extreme overreaction to this defeat that his earlier Homeric achievements had infected him with *hubris,* which we know always goeth before a fall.

From this contrast between the two kinds of magic contests—or, more precisely, between the two ways of treating these contests—we could proceed up the ladder of abstraction to two opposing *Weltanschauungen* inhabiting an ethereal realm already explored by Matthew Arnold in "Hebraism and Hellenism" and by Erich Auerbach in the opening chapter of *Mimesis,* but that is not where I want to go. Instead I would like to leap forward over two thousand years to look at a few of the magic contests in early modern English drama, before focusing on the treatment of the concept in Shakespeare. The one that is probably most familiar to students of this body of drama occurs in scene 9 of Robert Greene's *Friar Bacon and Friar Bungay* (ca. 1590) during the visit of King Henry III and his guest, Emperor Frederick of Germany, to Oxford, and I will examine it in some detail because it is the most extended and elaborate account of a magic contest that I have been able to find in this period.

The emperor has brought with him Jacques Vandermast, the most renowned magician of Germany, who initiates the contest by implying that the doctors of Oxford are not very "learned" (11–12). This leads Friar Bungay, with King Henry's encouragement (18–19), to challenge him, first to a dispute about the nature of "magic," which is inconclusive (24–71), and then to a demonstration of their "art," which he begins by "conjuring up" the golden-leaved tree in the Garden of Hesperides and the dragon who guarded it (79–85). But Vandermast counters this by "raising up" Hercules and ordering him to unseat the dragon and to break off the branches of the tree (88–97). He then calls on Bungay to stop Hercules, and when Bungay says, "I cannot" (102), Vandermast proclaims victory and boasts about his "art," listing all the cities of Europe where he has "given nonplus" and been crowned "with laurel" (107–15). Friar Bacon then enters to join the contest, and the two monarchs cheer on their respective champions (125–27). Bacon has Vandermast order Hercules to continue disbranching the tree, but Hercules replies, "I dare not. Seest thou not great Bacon here, / Whose frown doth act more than thy magic can?" (136–37), and so Vandermast must admit defeat, because "Bacon doth more than art" (147). Bacon then has Hercules transport Vandermast back to Germany (156–61), and King Henry sums up the outcome: "Bacon, thou hast honored England with thy skill, / And made fair Oxford famous by thine art" (165–66).[5]

It is obvious that this episode is much closer to the contest between Calchas and Mopsus than it is to the biblical contests, although there are some very significant differences. It is presented before a monarch, as in the Bible, but here there are two monarchs, each supporting the contestant from his own country, and, unlike the biblical pharaohs and kings, they have no personal stake in the contest itself—in fact, they view it as an entertaining "game" or "sport" (76–77), and at the end they join amicably in the festivity that Bacon provides. Nor do their two countries have any stake in it, beyond national pride, since there is no conflict between England and Germany. But the reason that the monarchs take sides introduces a new sense of nationalism, which does not figure in the Hebraic contests or the Hellenic one. Some critics have suggested that its role in this play may be related to the defeat of the Spanish Armada in 1588, which is possible, although a more general cause would be the rise and consolidation of early modern nation-states in western Europe.

Nationalism itself, however, does not explain the outcome of this contest. We know that Bacon must win since he is English and Vandermast is not; but that cannot be the actual cause of his victory, since Bungay is just as English and yet he loses. This means that, unlike the biblical heroes, Bacon is not regarded as a conduit through which an external energy (here, Englishness) is conveyed to produce the magic that wins the contest. Instead he is to be seen, like Calchas and Mopsus, as an individual whose magic is a personal possession, and he wins because it is more powerful than the magic personally possessed by Vandermast, which in turn is more powerful than the magic personally possessed by Bungay. This is made very clear in the dialogue, since the magic of these three men is regularly called a "skill" or "art" throughout the contest (7, 74, 85, 109, 147, 149, 160), and again at the end, as we saw, in King Henry's summation (165–66). Moreover, they themselves are regularly called "scholars" or "doctors" (6, 11, 17, 21, 86), and the adjective most frequently applied to them is "learned" (7, 11, 101, 106, 122, 129). We are also told that they acquired this "learning" by arduous reading and study (14, 159), which is why they own it. In contrast to the Hebrew heroes and Calchas and Mopsus, who received their magical power as a gift from God or a god, these three men earned this power by their own hard labor, and therefore should be considered self-made magicians, so that their appearance at this time in history may be related to the rise of capitalism and the "work ethic," with its ideals of rugged individualism and the self-made man. Moreover, their labors are what make them superior to those people whom Vandermast dismisses as mere "jugglers, witches, and vild sorcerers" (69), who are not "learned." Thus we find in this contest not only a new sense of nationalism but also a new sense of professionalism.

206   RICHARD LEVIN

I believe that these new concepts of nationalism, earned individual merit, and professionalism are also involved in our feeling that another reason that Vandermast must lose the second contest is his overweening pride. We could only infer this pride in the case of Calchas, but here it is forcefully called to our attention by Vandermast's very un-English and very unprofessional boasting about all the cities where he has won similar magic contests (107–15). Indeed, the main dramatic purpose of his victory over Bungay seems to be to give him this opportunity to display his pride and therefore to set him (and us) up for his well-deserved downfall when he encounters Bacon.

This contest also seems to resemble the one between Calchas and Mopsus in the apparent absence of a theological dimension. We realize, if we think about it, that the two monarchs and the three magicians all share the same Christian faith—in fact, two of the magicians are friars. But we probably do not think about it, because religion does not play any part in the nationalist rivalry of the monarchs or the professional rivalry of the magicians. Moreover, the magic contest itself centers on a pagan myth about Hercules that has no religious significance to the contestants or to their audience, both on the stage and off it. There is, however, a suggestion that a theological problem may be involved in the entities that the magicians conjure up in this scene, for while they are usually called "spirits," they are also referred to as "demones," "devils," and "fiends" (39, 45, 53, 64, 99, 146), which at least raises the suspicion that this magical enterprise is not appropriate for Christians, especially for Christian friars. And this suspicion is confirmed in scene 13, where Bacon realizes that the use of his magic glass has resulted in the violent deaths of two young men, and reacts to this by breaking the glass, renouncing his "magic" and his "art" (79), with its "Conjuring and adjuring devils and fiends" (90), and telling Bungay, "I'll spend the remnant of my life / In pure devotion, praying to my God / That he would save what Bacon vainly lost" (106–8). And at the end of the play, in scene 16, he is so conspicuously detached from the general mood of celebration that King Henry finally asks "But why stands Friar Bacon here so mute?" and he replies, "Repentant for the follies of my youth, / That magic's secret mysteries misled" (35–37).

This religious rejection of magic is even more emphatic in *The Famous History of Friar Bacon,* an anonymous prose romance that served as the principal source of Greene's play. In addition to the magic contest adapted by Greene, which it narrates in chapter 7, it also includes in chapter 14 a second and much more disturbing contest between Bungay and Vandermast,[6] where they conjure up two armies (Greek and Trojan, of course) to fight each other, and give the Devil some of their blood in order to secure victory, which places them in his power, so that after the battle he raises a great tempest and "then tooke them in the height of their wickednesse, and bereft them of their lives" (145). And Bacon's repentance in the final chapter goes much further

MY MAGIC CAN LICK YOUR MAGIC 207

than it does in Greene. He not only renounces all his magic and burns all his books in a large bonfire, but also locks himself in a cell, where he spends the rest of his life "in prayer, meditation, and such divine exercises, and did seeke by all means to perswade men from the study of magicke," and where he "dyed a true Penitent Sinner, and an Anchorite" (150).[7]

It would seem, then, that Greene's play has deliberately toned down these theological problems raised by magic contests, although I have tried to show that some suggestions of the problems are still present. Even these suggestions, however, point to an entirely new role of religion in the contests. In all the biblical encounters God is a partisan who supports and enables the good, victorious side while opposing and condemning the evil, defeated side. But here God, in effect, opposes both sides by condemning magic itself. I believe we can now see, aided by hindsight, that this change is related to the concerted efforts of the church during this period to claim for itself a monopoly on all licit forms of magic (which it did not call magic), and therefore to relegate all other forms of magic which were not under its control (which it did call magic) to the Devil and to hell.[8]

Both nationalism and religion have a much more obvious and important role in *The Birth of Merlin, or The Child Hath Found His Father* (c. 1608), which was attributed to William Rowley and Shakespeare on the title page of the first quarto (1662), and thus earned a place in the Apocrypha, but is now generally believed to be the work of Rowley and perhaps some other collaborator. Here these national and religious dimensions define the central conflict of the play, which pits the Britons, who are Christian, against the Saxons, who are pagan, and each side has its own champion in the realm of the supernatural—Anselm the Hermit, a British Christian, and Proximus, a Saxon pagan. They confront each other in 2.3 in a competition that exhibits a number of superficial similarities to the magic contest in *Friar Bacon and Friar Bungay* and may even have been influenced by it. It is staged before two monarchs, Aurelius, king of Britain, and Ostorius, the Saxon king, each of whom supports the contestant on his side. And the specific actions of the two contestants resemble those of Vandermast and Bacon. Proximus begins by boasting of his prowess in magic (63–65, 73–77), and then conjures up two "spirits" in the likeness of Hector and Achilles and orders them to fight; but, according to the stage direction, *"the Hermit steps between them, at which seeming amaz'd the spirits tremble,"* and then they have to admit to Proximus that "We dare not" obey his command because "Our charms are all dissolv'd" (95–97), so that he loses the contest and Anselm wins it.[9]

Although this episode may look at first glance like an abbreviated version of the magic contest in Greene's play, there are some very important differences that bring it much closer to the contests in the Bible, and these differences all turn on the role of religion here, which we saw did not figure in the competition between Vandermast and Bacon. Indeed, because of the role of

208   RICHARD LEVIN

religion, this cannot really be considered a contest in magic where the outcome is determined, as it was in Greene, by the relative skill of the contestants. Both the Christian Britons and the pagan Saxons recognize that Proximus is a bona fide practitioner of magic (he is defined as "a Saxon Magician" in the list of "*Drammatis Personae*" in the 1662 quarto) and a "cunning" and "learned" master of his "art" (60, 66, 68, 79, 115). But only the Saxons call Anselm a "Sorcerer" (49) and claim that he deals in "magick spells" and "charms" (32, 35, 37), while Aurelius recognizes that he is a "Most reverent" holy man (10, 66) and attributes his success, not to his expertise in magic, but to "the hand of heaven" and "That heavenly power" (41, 116); and Anselm himself explains both the cause and the significance of his victory when he says to Proximus: "Know, mis-believing Pagan, even that Power / That overthrew your Forces, still lets you see, / He onely can controul both hell and thee" (108–10). Thus Anselm, like the Hebrew heroes, is presented not as an individual who wins the contest because of his own personal skill, but as another conduit through which divine power flows to defeat the opposition.

That opposition, however, is defined very differently here than it is in the biblical contests. Unlike the unnamed and undifferentiated collection of magicians, astrologers, and the like, who take on this role in the Bible, it is now a single individual, as in the confrontations between Calchas and Mopsus and between Vandermast and Bacon, and this individual, like them, is reputed to be a "learned" master of the "art" of magic, as we just noted. But the nature of this magic has undergone a crucial change. Anselm connects Proximus's art with "hell" in the passage just quoted (108–10), and Proximus himself invokes "hell" and "all the Infernal powers" (94, 102), calls his spirits "Hellhounds" (100), and threatens to "enforce new charms, / New spells, and spirits rais'd from the low Abyss / Of hells unbottom'd depths" (111–13). It would seem, then, that magic itself is now associated with the Christian hell. We found suggestions of this connection in Greene's play, and even stronger ones in the prose romance that was its source, but here it is made very explicit, and is limited to only one of the contestants—the one who actually does claim to practice magic. Therefore, along with nationalism, individualism, and professionalism, Christianity must be added to the new influences that affected the ancient magic contests, because it has transformed this particular contest into a victory of the forces of God over the forces of the Devil.

The Devil himself appears in this play since he is Merlin's father, which gives the play its title but complicates the position of Merlin in what I identified as the central national/religious conflict here. He is clearly not of the Devil's party—in fact, he defeats the Devil in a brief magic contest in 5.1 and imprisons him within a rock. And he always sides with the Britons against the Saxons; but because of his father he cannot be a Christian, although he is not a pagan and does not seem to have any religious beliefs. His specialty is prophecy (he is called "the Prophet" in the "*Drammatis Personae*"), and he engages in a prophetic contest in 4.1 that resembles those in the Bible. It is initiated by Vortiger, king of the Welsh Britons, who has encountered some supernatural interference in building his castle and, like the biblical kings and pharaohs, seeks help by summoning the experts in "the secrets of futurity," including all "The Bards, the Druids, Wizards, Conjurers," as well as every "Auraspex," "Capnomanster," "Witch," and "Juggler" (59–62). The most expert of them all is Proximus, who begins by boasting of what he calls "My Art infalable" (215), which we recognize as the kind of *hubris* typically displayed by the contestant who is going to lose. On the basis of this "Art" he prophesies that the castle will not stand unless Merlin's blood is sprinkled on the foundation; but Merlin counters with his own prophecy that Proximus is about to be killed by an object hanging over his head, and he then states the terms of this contest:

> here before the King
> Make good thine Augury, as I shall mine.
> If thy fate fall not, thou hast spoke all truth,
> And let my blood satisfie the Kings desires.
>
> (225–28)

Merlin's "Augury" immediately comes to pass when, according to the stage direction, "*A stone falls and kills Proximus,*" so that he, like the 450 prophets of Baal and Calchas before him, suffers the ultimate defeat.

Thus Proximus, the evil magician, loses in two contests with two quite different good magicians. We know that the ability of Anselm the Hermit derives from the Christian God, but that cannot be the source of the ability of Merlin the Prophet, who is not a Christian. (This may explain why these two men never meet, since their relationship would pose a problem for the playwright.) Nor could he have acquired it by study or "learning," like Bacon, because he possessed it at his birth. According to Lucina's statement just before this birth, his gift of "all-admiring Prophecy, to fore-see / The event of times to come" (3.3.27–28) is apparently bestowed by the Devil and the spirits he calls upon then, although that would not explain why Merlin opposes and defeats Proximus, who himself calls on the demonic spirits. But it may be pointless to look for theological coherence in what is, after all, a mediocre and confused play, which I have discussed in such detail only because it shows the complexities involved in some of the different kinds of magic contests that were presented in the drama of this period.

If we turn now to Shakespeare, we will not find any actual contests that are staged between two competing magicians. Indeed, we will find very few pro-

210   RICHARD LEVIN

fessed magicians, and none of them—except for Prospero, of course—has a major part in the action. Calchas appears very briefly in *Troilus and Cressida*, 3.3, but his only function is to arrange for the transfer of his daughter Cressida from Troy to the Greek camp, and thereby to precipitate the crisis in the titular love story. In his successful attempt to persuade the Greek leaders to approve of this transfer, he refers to "the service I have done . . . through the sight I bear in things to come" (1, 4, 11, 29),[10] in order to remind them (and presumably the audience) that in the past he has employed his prophetic powers to aid the Greeks in their attack on Troy, as I noted above. However, he does not engage in any prophesying in this play (that "service" is restricted to Cassandra), and his divination contest with Mopsus, which is still far off in the post-Homeric future, may not even have been known to Shakespeare.

Prophetic magic does play a role in *2 Henry VI,* although it is a minor one. In 1.2 Eleanor Cobham, the ambitious Duchess of Gloucester, has the priest John Hume arrange a meeting with Margery Jordan, a "cunning witch," and Roger Bolingbrook, a "conjurer," so that she can consult them about the future. (Hume tells us that he was paid to do this by the enemies of her husband, the "good Duke Humphrey," in order to trap her and thus discredit him, but that is not relevant here.) They come to her in 1.4 with John Southwell, another priest, and, after some elaborate "ceremonies," they conjure up a "Spirit" who answers her questions about the fates of King Henry, the Duke of Suffolk, and the Duke of Somerset with some enigmatic predictions, which will, of course, come true later in the play, when interpreted correctly. But then they are arrested, and in 2.3 the king sentences all of them to death except for Eleanor, who is banished to the Isle of Man after undergoing open penance.

Although this encounter between King Henry VI and the magicians is obviously not a contest, it can be related to the contests we have examined. Monarchs are present in all of them, except for those between Mopsus and Calchas and between Merlin and the Devil. And these monarchs are present either as interested parties who are concerned about the problem that has become the subject of the contest, and who therefore have what we now call "the need to know" its outcome (this appplies to all the biblical pharaohs and kings and to Vortiger), or else as spectators who are there to enjoy the show, cheer for their countryman, and determine the winner (King Henry III and Emperor Frederick, Aurelius and Ostorius). Here, however, the monarch is present, not as an observer of the magicians, but as their adversary in a completely one-sided confrontation in which they do not even speak and his own activity is limited to confirming the judgment against them and meting out their punishments.

Several factors are involved in this change. One of them is the new conception of nationalism—or, more precisely, of the early modern nation-state under the "rule of law," which is supposed to govern and be enforced by the will of the monarch. Thus in 2.3 King Henry specifically invokes "the law" (3) when he sentences the magicians and Eleanor, and her husband, Duke Humphrey, reluctantly agrees that they must accept the judgment of "the law" (15–16). But equally important is the influence of Christianity, since the King, in the same speech (2–4), asserts that "in sight of God" the culprits are guilty of "sins," and that their punishment is "adjudg'd" by the Bible, which he calls "God's book."[11] We have already observed this Christian condemnation of magic itself in *Friar Bacon and Friar Bungay* and *The Birth of Merlin,* but in those two plays it is limited to Bacon's final repentance and to Anselm's explanation of his victory over Proximus, while the Christian monarchs witnessing the magic (Henry III, Frederick, and Aurelius) apparently are not troubled by it; but here the religious prohibition is joined with and expressed through the secular power of the king and the state and the state's law, which is what we actually see in operation.

In fact, this encounter with the law was to become the standard ending in plays like *The Witch of Edmonton* (1621), by Thomas Dekker, John Ford, and William Rowley, and *The Late Lancashire Witches* (1634), by Thomas Heywood and Richard Brome, where the witches are ultimately defeated and punished by the judicial system. And in the final act of *The Late Lancashire Witches* we are even told that "Witches apprehended under / Hands of lawfull authority, doe loose their power, / And all their spels are instantly dissolv'd" (5.2631–33),[12] so that the state's "lawfull authority" seems to have acquired a kind of superior magical power that nullifies the inferior magical power of witches, in much the same way that the superior magic of Bacon and Anselm nullifies the inferior magic of Vandermast and Proximus. But this question of the relationship of magic to the state will arise again, in a very different form, when we move on to *The Tempest.*

Prospero is Shakespeare's most important magician, and he also has the most impressive repertoire of magical skills that we have yet encountered, as demonstrated by the many feats that he is able to perform, either directly through his own actions or indirectly through those of Ariel and the other spirits whom he commands to do his "strong bidding." He can see events in the past and the future, make himself invisible, create a tempest to sink a ship and then rescue its passengers and crew, put people to sleep or in a trance and then wake them, produce and then dissolve a banquet and a masque, make men dance through a "filthy-mantled pool . . . up to th' chins" (4.1.182–83),[13] and do anything else that he pleases. The sole limitation on these powers, apparently, is distance, since we learn from his expository opening speeches to Miranda that he was only able to gain control over his enemies when "By accident most strange, bountiful Fortune" brought their ship close to the island (1.2.178–80), which means that his magical sphere of influence does not extend very far beyond it, although we know that he can send Ariel on errands to the ends of the earth, and even to the "veins" beneath it (252–56).

With the possible exception of Bacon, he is also the most learned magician we have seen so far, which would explain that remarkable magical repertoire. His powers were not given to him by a divine gift, like the biblical heroes and Calchas, Mopsus, and Anselm, or by the Devil, like Merlin, but are entirely the result of his own extensive reading, which is stressed in those opening speeches where he tells Miranda that while he was the Duke of Milan he spent all his time in his library and was so "transported / And rapt in secret studies" (76–77) that his brother Antonio was able to take over governmental affairs and then form an alliance with Alonso, King of Naples, to depose him and to cast him and the infant Miranda adrift in a small boat. He also tells her that the books from "mine own library" that "I prize above my dukedom" (167–68) were placed in the boat by his friend Gonzalo and taken to the island, so we can infer that he continued to study them there to expand his magical powers (in fact, Caliban believes that without those books he would be powerless—3.2.89–95). Thus he is in the tradition of professional magicians that we saw in Bacon, Bungay, and Vandermast, who acquired their skills by their own hard work and hold them as their own personal possession. Unlike these three, however, he is not a self-made man in the new capitalist mode, since he inherited his position in society in the old feudal mode, but like them he is a self-made magician.

Because of his inherited position, Prospero is also the highest ranking magician we have encountered. Almost all the others serve monarchs (this would include Calchas in his role during the Trojan War), but Prospero was himself a monarch who, as the duke of an independent Milan, was not subject to any higher authority. And on the island his rule is even more absolute. Like Louis XIV, he is the state here, and whatever he wills becomes the law, which he enforces by punishing anyone (mainly Caliban) who disobeys it and him. This is an important factor in our inquiry, since it means that there is no one in the play who can sit in judgment over him, and therefore that we will not find here any simple, direct opposition between Prospero's magic and the state, such as we just saw in 2 *Henry VI* and the two witch plays. Indeed, he does not face any significant opposition at all, because his two enemies, Antonio and Alonso, are completely in his power, and the comic rebellion of Caliban, Stephano, and Trinculo is easily put down by his magical intervention, delegated to Ariel, which forces them to take that detour through the filthy-mantled pool.

The perspective of this inquiry, however, points to the tantalizing possibility that there could have been a real opposition here, and even some kind of magic contest, if Sycorax were still alive. Almost all that we know about her is confined to a single stretch of very clumsy exposition in 1.2.257–93 where Prospero, after putting Miranda to sleep with his lengthy account of the events that brought them to their island cell, has to remind the conveniently forgetful Ariel of the "foul witch Sycorax" from Algiers who "with age and envy / Was grown into a hoop," and who, because of her "mischiefs manifold, and sorceries terrible," was banished to this island, where she gave birth to Caliban, and imprisoned Ariel in a cloven pine, and then died some years before the boat carrying Prospero and Miranda landed there. I do not think that we are supposed to ask how Prospero acquired all this information, although we probably assume that he could have posited Sycorax's osteoporosis from the popular stereotype of witches,[14] and that the other facts about her could have been derived earlier from Ariel (when his memory was in better condition) or from his own magical ability to see into the dark backward and abysm of time. A much more interesting question raised by our inquiry is why Shakespeare killed off Sycorax before the arrival of Prospero, and so lost the opportunity to dramatize a contest between them in which his magic would defeat her magic. One possible reason is that the presentation of such a contest would have forced him to violate the "unity of time" that he has preserved in *The Tempest;*[15] but I believe that a more relevant explanation, since it is specific to the dramatic effect of this particular plot, is that this contest would have distracted attention from his primary concern here, which focuses on Prospero's successful resolution of all the problems created by his deposition and exile, which in turn requires that he be placed in complete control of the island and of the play from the outset.

Actually we do have a suggestion of such a contest (or perhaps we should say a substitute for it) at the end of this same exposition when Prospero reminds Ariel that Sycorax had confined him to the cloven pine by means of a spell that she "Could not again undo. It was mine art, / When I arriv'd and heard thee, that made gape / The pine, and let thee out" (291–93). Thus he had, in effect, won a magic contest with her by demonstrating that his "art" could accomplish what hers could not, so that she suffered a posthumous defeat. (We also learn in this exposition that she suffered an earlier defeat in Algiers in her confrontation with the state that led to her banishment, which is similar to the judicial defeat of magic in *2 Henry VI* but here is only a narrative device to bring her to the island.) It is noteworthy that Prospero's victory over her was the exact opposite of the victories in three other magic contests we have examined. Merlin defeats the Devil by imprisoning him in a rock,[16] and Bacon and Anselm defeat Vandermast and Proximus by immobilizing the spirits (Hercules, and Hector and Achilles) raised by them, which is also a kind of imprisonment; but Prospero defeats Sycorax by freeing Ariel, who is the spirit she imprisoned. Thus this victory prepares us for the final scene where he releases both Ariel and Caliban from his service, which takes on a special significance because he inherited both of them from Sycorax, so that their final liberation constitutes another kind of victory over her magic, and contributes to our general feeling of satisfaction and of clo-

214   RICHARD LEVIN

sure that he is able to produce through his unchallenged control over the resolution.

What I have called the new sense of nationalism has very little effect on
the treatment of magic in this play. Sycorax is a foreigner, but that does not
matter because she is defined here as a witch rather than as an Algerian. All
the other human characters except Caliban are Italian, but that does not matter either, because Italy was not yet a unified country. In fact, Prospero makes
it very clear in his expository speeches to Miranda that under his rule Milan
was an independent dukedom (1.2.70–73), and he condemns his brother Antonio, not only for deposing him, but also for accomplishing this by an ar-
rangement with Alonso that subjugated Milan to Naples and even required
Milan to pay homage and an annual tribute (111–16, 121–24). That is corrected at the end when, as a result of Prospero's master plan, Alonso submits
to him ("The dukedom I resign"—5.1.118), but this resolution is complicated by the forthcoming marriage of Alonso's son Ferdinand to Miranda,
which is also part of Prospero's plan but presents some problems. One of
them is that Miranda is marrying the man chosen by her father, although a
basic dramatic law (violated by Portia in *The Merchant of Venice*) dictates
that any suitor favored by a young woman's parents will never suit her; but
Shakespeare gets around this by having Miranda propose to Ferdinand in
3.1.83, while she is still under the mistaken impression that Prospero disap-
proves of him. A second problem is the role of Prospero's "art" in this marriage, since another basic law (violated by Demetrius in *A Midsumnmer
Night's Dream*) dictates that real love cannot be generated by supernatural
means, which would be another form of external coercion like parental pressure; but Shakespeare gets around this, too, by showing us that, even though
Prospero uses his magic to bring Ferdinand and Miranda together, he never
attempts to use it to make them fall in love, which they obligingly do "at the
first sight" in response to their own internal chemistries.

The political problem created by their marriage is not so easily avoided,
however, because after the deaths of Prospero and Alonso the young couple
will reign in their stead, which means that Milan will once again be under
the sway of the king of Naples. Good old Gonzalo tries his best to put a positive spin on this prospect by rejoicing that Prospero's issue will now "become kings of Naples" (5.1.205–6), but he fails to add that Alonso's issue
will now become dukes of Milan. Apparently we are supposed to approve of
this consequence of Prospero's plan because it will bring about a voluntary
union of two equal states, whereas Antonio's treachery had resulted in the
subjugation of one state by the other; but perhaps by pursuing this inquiry
into the problem of nationalism here we would be thinking too precisely on
the event by considering it too curiously, as Hamlet and Horatio warn us.[17]

The relationship of religion to the presentation of magic in this play is even
more problematic. It has a role in the definition of Sycorax, since we are told,

MY MAGIC CAN LICK YOUR MAGIC

after the expository passage in which Prospero has to remind Ariel about her, that Caliban was engendered by her copulation with "the devil himself" and that she worshipped a false god named Setebos (1.2.319–20, 373), so she is condemned on theological as well as moral grounds. All the other human characters are Italian, as we noted, and therefore must be Christian, but we find no indication of this in their dialogue. They regularly swear by or refer to Jove, Neptune, Phoebus, "you gods," "some god," "any god of power," or a nondenominational "heaven," "the heavens," "some heavenly power," or "the wills above," and regularly locate the cause of events in a nontheistic "Fate," "Destiny," or "Fortune," and never use any locution that is specifi-cally Christian.[18] I do not think we can attach any special significance to this, however, because an Act of Parliament in 1606 prohibited "the greate Abuse of the Holy Name of God in Stageplayes,"[19] and references to pagan or un-named "gods" on the stage and off were a convention that certainly did not imply a belief in them—even today, at least according to American movies, upper-class Englishmen still say "ye gods" and swear "by Jove." Much more to the point is the fact that no character voices any religious objection to the magic employed by Prospero, except for Caliban, who accuses him of being a "sorcerer" (3.2.43, 52), but we discount this just as we discounted the at-tempts by the Saxons in *The Birth of Merlin* to pin this same label on Anselm the Hermit. It is even more important that Prospero himself does not seem to be aware of any conflict between his religion and his magical practices, and that he sharply distinguishes these practices, which he thinks of as "mine art" (1.2.291), from those of Sycorax, which he thinks really were "sorceries terrible" (1.2.264). That is why his final decision to renounce magic is so surprising and so difficult to account for.

This renunciation is presented at the end of a soliloquy in the last scene, where Prospero announces that "this rough magic / I here abjure," and that he will break his magical staff and bury it deep in the earth and "drown my book" deep in the sea (5.1.50–57). He does not give us any reason for this, and I said that the play does not prepare us for it, but our inquiry may have provided a kind of preparation in the actions of Friar Bacon, since we saw that he too renounces his magic and breaks his magical glass near the end of Greene's *Friar Bacon and Friar Bungay,* and also burns all his books near the end of the prose romance that is Greene's principal source. Bacon does supply the reason for his behavior, which is the religious condemnation of magic that leads to his remorse and repentance, and to his promise to spend the rest of his life "In pure devotion, praying to my God / That he would save what Bacon vainly lost" (we saw that in the prose romance he goes even further by locking himself in a cell, where he dies "a true Penitent Sinner, and an Anchorite"). This in fact seems similar to Prospero's statement, at the very end of *The Tempest,* that he will "retire me to my Milan, where / Every third thought shall be my grave" (5.1.311–12), which could mean that he,

216   RICHARD LEVIN

like Bacon, will retire from the world to repent and to prepare for God's judgment after his death.

There are, however, some very important differences between Prospero's
renunciation of magic and Bacon's. Unlike Bacon, Prospero never invokes
any religious sanctions against magic (indeed, he does not even touch on religion), and he never expresses any remorse or repentance for his magical practices—he merely "abjures" the future use of them. This in turn is the result
of a crucial difference in the preceding actions in these two plays. Bacon
renounces all magic and repents because he sees that his magical glass has
caused the deaths of two young men, which he had not intended (and in the
prose romance he also learns about the horrible, and again unintended, catastrophe that terminated the second magic contest between Bungay and Vandermast). But Prospero's magic does not have any bad consequences, intended
or unintended. On the contrary, it brings about the successful completion of
his benign master plan, which leads to the restoration of his dukedom, the
marriage of his daughter, the defeat of and (partial) reconciliation with the
men who had wronged him, and the final liberation of Ariel and Caliban, so
he has nothing to repent for.

Another problem with this account of why Prospero renounces his magic
is that in the same soliloquy, leading up to this renunciation, he dwells at
some length on the remarkable achievements of what he terms "my so potent
art": "I have bedimm'd / The noontide sun, call'd forth the mutinous
winds . . ." (5.1.41–50). We have already come upon this kind of speech in
Friar Bacon and Friar Bungay and *The Birth of Merlin,* but there it was confined to the boasting of Vandermast and Proximus just before they lost their
magic contests to Bacon, Anselm, and Merlin. Prospero cannot be boasting
in this manner, of course, since no one else is present for him to boast to and
he is not engaged in a contest, but he does seem to be reminding himself—
and therefore the audience—of how much he will be giving up, just before
he does this, and it is very clear that he is immensely proud of his magical
"potent art" and its accomplishments, and certainly does not feel any remorse about them or any need to repent.[20] It would seem, then, that there are
serious difficulties with trying to explain Prospero's renunciation of magic
by applying what might be called the Bacon paradigm.

A second possible way to explain this renunciation is by the application of
what I will call the Lear paradigm. When Prospero says, at the end of his
play, that he will "retire" to Milan, where he will think continually about his
"grave," he could simply mean that he plans to pass the task of governing
Milan on to the next generation because he sees himself as a very old man
whose life is almost over, much like Lear who plans, at the beginning of his
play, to "shake all cares and business from our age, / Conferring them on
younger strengths, while we / Unburthen'd crawl toward death" (1.1.39–41).
Lear obviously does not feel remorseful or repentant; he is just renouncing

his political power because he feels that he is too old and weak to be troubled with it any longer, and Prospero might be making the same decision for the same reason, although his power has a magical as well as a political dimension and thus requires two renunciations, so that he gives up his magical power at the beginning of this scene and his political power at the end, and both of these actions could be attributed to his advanced age.

The problem here is that we are not sure of Prospero's age. Modern productions of *The Tempest* often stage him as a very old man with a long white beard, which is the popular image of the Merlin-figure or "wizzard,"[21] but the textual evidence for this is conflicted. Our only specific information about his age is that he is the father (or so her mother assured him) of a fifteen-year-old daughter (1.2.41, 53), and that he regards her as "a third of mine own life, / Or that for which I live" (4.1.3–4), which would make him about forty-five.[22] During most of the play he seems to be a vigorous man in the prime of life, since he is robustly proactive in micromanaging the tempest and shipwreck, the defeat of the plot to kill Alonso, the banquet and betrothal masque, and so on, and is in complete control of all his faculties and of the entire situation, which certainly could not be said of Lear, whose utter helplessness and physical and mental debility are continually emphasized ("Here I stand your slave, / A poor, infirm, weak, and despis'd old man"—3.1.19–20). The only lapse in Prospero's control over himself and over events occurs during the masque, when he suddenly realizes that he forgot the rebellion of Caliban, Stephano, and Trinculo and is very angry (4.1.143–45), although we cannot be sure if he is angry at Caliban's ingratitude, which is implied when he condemns him as a "devil" a few speeches later (188–93), or at his own forgetfulness, which is implied when he asks Ferdinand to excuse him because "my old brain is troubled" (159). This is our first intimation that he is an old man, and it seems to be ignored in the final scene when he reveals himself to Alonso, Antonio, and the others, since they never remark on his age. Indeed, in this scene we learn that he told Ariel about "the good old Lord Gonzago" (5.1.15), whom he later greets by saying, "Let me embrace thine age" (121), which is not how one old person would speak of or to another. But then at the end we found that he speaks of himself as a very old man who is close to death. I do not know how to explain away this discrepancy, which confronts any attempt to apply the Lear paradigm to resolve the problems raised by the conclusion of this play.

Another way to approach these problems, which does not necessarily contradict either of the two paradigms we have been testing, would be to ask, not why Prospero might want to abjure magic and feel very old at the end of his play, but why Shakespeare might want to end *his* play by having Prospero abjure magic and feel very old. The answer to this question must lie in the feeling of closure that the playwright is aiming for in the final scene, and it is significant, therefore, that this scene begins with Prospero telling Ariel,

218   RICHARD LEVIN

"Now does my project gather to a head" (5.1.1). He means that the principal
goals of his master plan, which we saw are the restoration of his dukedom
and the marriage of his daughter, have almost been attained, since all that is
now needed is the assent of Alonso and Antonio, the two enemies who
wronged him, and their assent is assured because they are now completely in
his power. His only remaining problem, then, is what to do with these two
men, which is resolved in his ensuing dialogue with Ariel when he decides to
forgive them. Since this decision is immediately followed by his renunciation
speech, Shakespeare creates the impression that Prospero abjures magic because he has successfully completed his "project" and so there is nothing
more for his magic to do.

Shakespeare may also have felt that it would not be appropriate for Prospero to practice magic when he returns as the restored Duke of Milan, which
brings up the question of the new relationship of magic to the state that we
examined in *2 Henry VI*. I said earlier that on the island Prospero is the state
and his wishes are its laws, which therefore cannot be in conflict with his
magical activities. But Milan is presented here as an early modern nation-
state, and while Prospero will again be its ruler, it has its own laws (like the
England of King Henry) that he is supposed to enforce. It is noteworthy that
when he told Miranda at the outset about his "secret studies" of magic in
Milan, he never suggested that he actually practiced magic there, which establishes another contrast with Sycorax, who did engage in "sorceries" in
Algiers and therefore was banished by the state. Thus he is now acting in
advance for the state by banishing his own magic from it, so this would be
another reason why Shakespeare has him abjure magic in the final scene before he leaves the island to reenter the early modern world.

I would argue that Shakespeare's need to enhance our feeling of closure
can also account for his sudden reinvention of Prospero at the very end of the
play as an old man preoccupied with his own death, since we are given the
impression that this too is a result of the successful completion of his "project," which leaves him with nothing more to accomplish or to live for. He
clearly cannot resume the study of his abjured magic, which consumed all
his time in Milan previously, and when he says that he will "retire" there he
seems to be passing on the task of governing (which he never did much of)
to the next generation, as we noted. I think it is significant, therefore, that his
statement about retiring and thinking of death comes immediately after his
announcement that he will attend the marriage of Miranda and Ferdinand in
Naples, and that in this same announcement he also tells us that immediately
after their marriage he will retire to Milan, so we feel that his old age and
approaching death are intimately related to the life of the young couple who
represent the hope of the future, as other young couples do at the end of
Pericles and *The Winter's Tale:*

MY MAGIC CAN LICK YOUR MAGIC

And in the morn
I'll bring you to your ship, and so to Naples,
Where I have hope to see the nuptial
Of these our dear-belov'd solemnized,
And thence retire me to my Milan, where
Every third thought shall be my grave.

(5.1.307–12)

Finally, Shakespeare may have felt that closure here requires that Prospero's magical activities lead to his impending death. In the play these activities and their consequences have come full circle: his study of magic in Milan is responsible for the loss of his ducal crown and his exile to the island, and then his practice of magic on the island is responsible for the restoration of the crown and his return to Milan. But these magical activities apparently carry some kind of taint, since he has to renounce magic before he leaves the island, and has to die soon after he arrives in Milan. (This taint does not extend to Miranda and Ferdinand, however, for we saw that, while their meeting is produced by Prospero's magic, their love is not, which is why they can be the hope of the future.) I found it difficult to determine just what Prospero's taint is supposed to be, but perhaps it has at last come to light in our own day with the recent discovery that he used his magic on the island to promote sexism, racism, and—even worse—colonialism.[23]

In *Romeo and Juliet* there is also an opposition, although not an actual contest, between a benign and a malign form of "magic," if that term is defined more loosely than it was in the discussion of Prospero and Sycorax. One form is embodied in Friar Lawrence, who is introduced to us in 2.3, where he identifies himself in a long soliloquy as an expert on the properties of herbs and flowers, and the other form is embodied in the unnamed apothecary of Mantua, who is only seen in 5.1, where Romeo visits him to buy poison. There is a sharp contrast between the two settings (indeed, no other purpose is served by dramatizing Romeo's visit, which could easily have been narrated).[24] The friar is in an open garden lit by the morning sun and is surrounded by living plants, while the apothecary is in a confined, dark shop, surrounded by ugly, dead animals ("a tortoise hung, / An alligator stuff'd, and other skins / Of ill-shap'd fishes"). The contrast also extends to their appearance, since the apothecary is dour and gaunt ("meagre were his looks, / Sharp misery had worn him to the bones"; "Famine is in thy cheeks, / Need and oppression starveth in thy eyes"), but the friar is cheerful and presumably chubby, if he conforms to a well-established mendicant tradition that goes back at least as far as Robin Hood's rotund Friar Tuck and Chaucer's Friar Hubert, who wore a double worsted "semycope, / That rounded as a belle, out of the presse" (262–63).[25]

Neither of these men engages in real magic. Lawrence, unlike Bacon and

220   RICHARD LEVIN

Bungay, is a functioning friar who performs marriages, hears confessions, and serves as a spiritual adviser, and he is recognized throughout Verona as "a holy man" (4.2.31, 4.3.29, 5.3.270), so he would not traffic in the suspect realm of the supernatural—in fact, he insists that the herbal properties he deals with in what he later calls "my art" (5.3.243) are entirely natural, since the plants all come from the "earth that's nature's mother" and are found "sucking on her natural bosom" (2.3.9–12); and while the apothecary is certainly not holy, his art is also limited, as far as we can tell, to natural ingredients. Yet each of them uses his art to concoct a potion that has extraordinary and almost magical powers. The friar distills a "liquor" whose effects he describes to Juliet at some length and in great detail: it will send a "cold and drowsy humor" through all her veins that will stop her pulse and breath and drain all color from her face, so that every part of her body "Shall, stiff and stark and cold, appear like death" for forty-two hours (4.1.93–106). And the apothecary's description to Romeo of the effects of his powder, although much shorter and lacking any physiological details, is just as impressive: "Put this in any liquid thing you will / And drink it off, and if you had the strength / Of twenty men, it would dispatch you straight" (5.1.77–79).[26] (Another aspect of the contrast between them is that the friar's art only produces a feigned death, while the death produced by the apothecary's art is very real.)

These two men never meet but their two potions do in a lethal sequence. To escape marriage to Paris, Juliet drinks the friar's potion and is interred in the family vault, but Romeo does not receive the friar's message explaining the ruse and so, thinking that she is really dead, he goes to the vault where he drinks the apothecary's potion and dies, and then Juliet awakes, drinks the potion from Romeo's lips, and stabs herself. But no guilt for this attaches to the friar or the apothecary. In rendering his judgment at the end, the Prince insists that the blame falls on Montague and Capulet and their feud, since that is what led Juliet to resort to the friar's benign art, which miscarried, and this led Romeo and then Juliet to resort to the apothecary's malign art, which succeeded. That is the tragedy.

Although it is not related to this opposition between the friar and the apothecary, we should note that there is a marked discrepancy in Lady Capulet's age that is similar to the one we found in the age of Prospero. In her first scene she tells Juliet, "I was your mother much upon these years / That you are now a maid" (1.3.72–73), which would make her about twenty-eight, and nothing more is said of her age until the last scene, when she laments that the sight of Juliet's corpse "is as a bell / That warns my old age to a sepulchre" (5.3.206–7). Thus in both plays Shakespeare has a character suddenly become very old at the very end, but the effects of this are strikingly different. In *The Tempest* he wants Prospero to be an old man thinking of his grave in order to set up a valedictory final contrast between his age and the youth of

MY MAGIC CAN LICK YOUR MAGIC 221

the couple who will carry on after his death. But here he wants Lady Capulet to be as old as the other onlookers, whose age is also emphasized (Montague asks, "What further woe conspires against mine age?" and Friar Lawrence speaks of "my old life" being "sacrific'd some hour before his time"), in order to set up a poignant final contrast between these people, whose lives are nearing their natural ends (hastened by grief), and the dead couple they stand over, whose lives were unnaturally cut off before they had really begun. That, too, is the tragedy.

The last play to be considered is *The Two Noble Kinsmen,* a joint effort by Shakespeare and Fletcher that brings this inquiry back to the world of Greek mythology that gave us the magic contest between Calchas and Mopsus, although here the nature of the contest and of the magic are much closer to the biblical stories with which we began. It will be more useful to look first at the playwrights' principal source, Chaucer's "The Knight's Tale," where the relationship to the biblical contests is clearer.[27] The two heroes of this tale are the Theban nobles Palamon and Arcite, who are cousins and very close friends. They are captured in battle by Theseus, Duke of Athens, and brought back to prison in Athens, where they both fall in love with Emilia, Theseus's sister-in-law, and fight a duel over her. But Theseus intervenes and orders each of them to collect one hundred knights and meet in a formal tournament, with the winner gaining Emilia's hand.

This initiates the magic contest, since the three parties involved offer prayers and sacrifices to different gods for help. First Palamon prays to the statue of Venus (2221–60), telling her that he only wants Emilia and is not interested in gaining "renoun" or "veyne glorie" by winning the tournament, and does not care if he has "victorie of hem or they of me, / So that I have my lady in myne armes," and even asserts that if he cannot have her he would rather be killed; and the statue gives a sign that "his preyere accepted was," although it "shewed a delay." Then Emilia prays to the statue of Diana (2297–2328), saying that she would prefer to remain a maiden, but if this is impossible she asks Diana to "sende me hym that moost desireth me"; and Diana answers that she must be married to Palamon or Arcite. The last is Arcite's prayer to the statue of Mars (2373–2420), which is the simplest since he only asks "that I tomorwe have victorie" in order to win Emilia; and the statue murmurs "Victorie!" This creates a quarrel between Venus and Mars that is settled by Saturn, who promises Venus that "Palamon, that is thyn owene knyght, / Shal have his lady . . . / Though Mars shal helpe his knyght" (2471–73). In the tournament Palamon is forced to the barrier and therefore loses to Arcite, but when Arcite rides in triumph across the arena Saturn causes his horse to rear and he falls off, mortally injured, and after a tender farewell to Emilia he dies, so Theseus gives Emilia to Palamon.

There is an obvious similarity between this magic contest and the contests we examined in the Bible, especially the one between Elijah and the prophets

222   RICHARD LEVIN

of Baal. In both situations the contestants do not claim to have any magical or supernatural power in themselves; rather, they attribute this power to the deity they worship, and they petition their deity, through prayers and a sacrifice, to project this supernatural power through them into the natural world. But there are some very important differences. In all the biblical stories, the contestants and their deities represent two competing religions, and a major purpose of the contest is to validate and valorize the Hebrew religion by demonstrating the superiority of its one true God and the inferiority (or nonexistence?) of the false gods of the gentile religion. In Chaucer's contest, however, the three deities involved all belong to the same Greco-Roman pantheon, and while they compete among themselves, there is no competition with any other religion or its deities. Moreover, the authors and implied narrators of the biblical contests are always fervent partisans who really believe in the God of the Hebrews and therefore side with the contestant who invokes him, while Chaucer and his Knight do not take sides in this contest. Indeed, since they are both Christians, they do not even believe in the pagan gods engaged in the contest, and present it to us simply as an interesting and emotionally satisfying fiction or "tale."[28] In their hands, therefore, the basic pattern of the biblical magic contests has been emptied of any religious significance and has become aestheticized.

Another striking difference between this magic contest and all the others we have considered so far, both ancient and early modern, is that there is no winner—or, more precisely, the three contestants and the three gods they appeal to are all winners. Venus gives Palamon the woman he prays for, although this "shewed a delay"; Diana gives Emilia the man she prays for, who is the one "that moost desireth" her, as we will see; and Mars gives Arcite the "victorie" in the tournament that he prays for. But while my summary is literally correct, I think we are supposed to feel that Palamon actually wins the contest, and that he deserves to win it. The explanation can be found in the comparison of his prayer with Arcite's, since for Arcite the most important goal is to win the tournament, while for Palamon the most important goal is to win Emilia, and he does not care if he must lose the tournament in order to have her. Thus with this prayer he takes the moral high ground, or at least the romantic high ground, and so proves that his love for Emilia is greater than Arcite's,[29] which is why he deserves her and why the outcome answers her prayer to Diana as well as his prayer to Venus. (He also scores some extra points because he is the first one to pray, rising two hours before dawn, while Arcite gets up an hour after dawn and is the last.) What we have here, then, is a new kind of magic contest where the victor is determined, not by the authenticity or omnipotence of the deity he worships (since Venus is no more "real" or powerful than Mars), nor by his acquired magical skills (since neither contestant possesses any), but by his own inner character or worthiness. That is why Palamon is more deserving than Arcite and, therefore, why his victory is so satisfying to us, which is just another way of saying that the contest has been aestheticized. May the best man win![30]

In *The Two Noble Kinsmen* Shakespeare and Fletcher make many changes in Chaucer's tale that do not significantly affect the nature of the magic contest or its outcome—among other things, they reduce the number of knights supporting Palamon and Arcite from one hundred to three, and omit Arcite's elaborate funeral, and add a comic subplot about the love of the Jailer's Daughter for Palamon. But other changes are more relevant to our inquiry. The playwrights add a decree by Theseus that the loser of the tournament and his knights shall be beheaded (3.6.296–97), [31] and reorient the dying Arcite's farewell to Palamon and Emilia (5.4.86–95). Much more important is the fact that they never show us the gods or even report their actions, so there is no quarrel between Venus and Mars and no role for Saturn, either in settling this quarrel or in causing Arcite's fatal fall from his horse, which is described by Pirithous as a lamentable accident with an entirely natural explanation (5.4.58–82).[32] Even more significant for our purposes, however, is a change in one of the prayers preceding the tournament. The playwrights follow Chaucer by having Emilia pray to Diana (5.1.137–73) to give her "He of the two pretenders that best loves me / And has the truest title in't," and by having Arcite pray to Mars (34–68) to make him the victor in the tournament ("the lord o' th' day") so that he can obtain his "prize," which is Emilia, but there is a major alteration in Palamon's prayer to Venus (69–136). He begins by saying that his goal "is love, / Which if the goddess of it grant, she gives / Victory too" in the tournament. Unlike his Chaucerian namesake, however, he never insists that he does not care if he wins or loses the tournament as long as he has Emilia. Instead, he devotes the rest of his prayer to a witty demonstration that he has always been loyal to Venus because he did not boast of his amorous conquests or approve of men who did, and even believed a "lass of fourteen" when she swore that the father of her child was her decrepit husband "of eighty winters."

As a result of this change, the only way that the playwrights can distinguish Palamon's prayer from Arcite's is by his simple reversal of the rhetorical sequence: Arcite proceeds from victory to Emilia, while Palamon proceeds from Emilia to victory, which is supposed to explain why one man prays to Mars and the other to Venus. But it is a distinction without a difference, since both men are in fact praying for victory in the tournament in order to obtain Emilia. This is crucial, because we saw that in Chaucer's tale the assertion by Palamon that he would rather lose the tournament than lose Emilia proves that he loves her more that Arcite does, which makes him the answer to her prayer to Diana. Moreover it proves that he is superior to Arcite in terms of his inner worth or character, so that he seems more deserving to us. Here, however, the two men stand on exactly the same moral and romantic ground,

224 RICHARD LEVIN

and consequently we are left without any grounds for choosing between them.

The playwrights make a feeble attempt before this to differentiate these men on the basis of an opposition between love and war, and therefore to prepare us for their prayers to Venus and Mars, by having Palamon say that if Emilia refuses him he will die "And lovers yet unborn shall bless my ashes," and having Arcite respond that he, too, will die "And soldiers [will] sing my epitaph" (3.6.282–85), but it will not work. On their first appearance, when we would ordinarily expect them to define themselves, Palamon shows much more concern for soldiers and war than Arcite does, and Arcite even criticizes him for this (1.2.12–31); and in their other scenes together, including the one I just quoted from, Palamon speaks of armies, battles, weapons, and the martial virtues about as often as Arcite speaks of love.[33] Judged by their own words, both of these men are from both Mars and Venus.

It would seem, then, that these playwrights, unlike Chaucer, are not really interested in distinguishing Palamon from Arcite; or, putting this in positive terms, that they want to make their titular heroes indistinguishable.[34] And the reason for this can be found in what they really are interested in, which is the presentation of a sort of contest in the exercise of an extraordinarily elevated conception of honor or nobility that is shared equally by two friends who fall in love with the same woman. This conception of honor is displayed in all their scenes together, especially in 3.3 and 3.6, where Arcite brings Palamon food and then helps him to put on his armor so they can fight their duel over Emilia, and again in 5.4 where Palamon bravely faces the executioner—indeed this episode, and the last-minute reprieve that immediately follows it, are the only reasons for Theseus's earlier decree, which is not in Chaucer, that the loser of the tournament must be beheaded.[35] This conception also accounts for the change in Arcite's death speech, which in Chaucer is directed at Emilia (2765–97) but here is directed at Palamon (5.4.90–95) in order to focus on the special friendship between the two men and on Arcite's concern for honor ("I was false, / Yet never treacherous") and his generosity ("Take Emilia, / And with her all the world's joy"). But in these episodes the two men are interchangeable, since Palamon would have been just as willing as Arcite to feed and arm his rival before the duel, and Arcite would have been just as brave as Palamon if he were on the scaffold, and Palamon would have been just as honorable and generous as Arcite if it had been his death speech.[36]

As we might expect, this change in purpose or focus has a devastating effect on the magic contest that is supposed to be initiated by the prayers to Venus, Mars, and Diana. Theseus, in his summary of the action at the end of the play, says that Mars answered Arcite's prayer by giving him victory, and Venus answered Palamon's prayer by giving him Emilia (5.4.105–9), which is true enough, but it would be just as true if the outcome had been reversed, since we saw that both men prayed for both victory and Emilia. And in Theseus's summary Diana is conspicuous by her absence, which is understandable because Emilia prayed to the goddess for the man who loved her best, and we saw that the two men are not differentiated in this respect, so her prayer cannot be answered. Moroever, we also saw that in this play, unlike Chaucer's tale, Mars and Venus do not enter into a contest with each other and do not have any effect on the outcome. Thus when Theseus later attributes the outcome to "the gods" or "you heavenly charmers" (115, 120, 131), who are not identified, he is in effect passing over Venus and Mars and their magic contest. The explanation for this has already been given: the contest in Chaucer's tale involving the magical powers of Venus and Mars has been transformed by the play into a very different kind of contest involving what Emilia calls the "nobleness peculiar" to the two equally noble and interchangeable kinsmen (5.3.87), which is another way of saying that the contest itself and the prayers initiating it have now become irrelevant. Thus while Chaucer's tale emptied the biblical magic contest of any religious significance, this play empties it of all signifance, so it is reduced to a vestigial remnant of Chaucer that survives only as an ornamental spectacle and therefore leaves us with a very anticlimactic conclusion to our inquiry.

Notes

1. All biblical quotations follow the King James Version. In Cecil B. DeMille's 1956 remake of *The Ten Commandments,* Moses (Charlton Heston) casts down his rod before Pharaoh (Yul Brynner) and it becomes a serpent, then Pharaoh has his magicians cast down three rods that also become serpents, and then Moses's serpent eats their serpents.

2. The same pattern reappears in various stories of magic contests held in fifth-century Ireland, usually before a king, in which St. Patrick defeats the Druid priests.

3. Strabo, *Geography,* tr. Horace Leonard Jones, Loeb Classical Library (Cambridge: Harvard University Press, 1989), 14.1.27. He repeats some of this in 14.5.16.

4. Homer, *The Iliad,* tr. E. V. Rieu (Harmondsworth: Penguin, 1950), 25 (1.69–72).

5. I quote from the edition of Daniel Seltzer, Regents Renaissance Drama (Lincoln: University of Nebraska Press, 1963), which indicates scenes but not acts.

6. I argued that this contest may have been adapted in one of the lost closing scenes of the sequel to Greene's play, which survives in an anonymous, untitled, and incomplete manuscript written about 1592 that is now called *John of Bordeaux, or The Second Part of Friar Bacon.* See *"Friar Bacon and Friar Bungay, John of Bordeaux,* and the 1683 Edition of *The History of Friar Bacon," Research Opportunities in Renaissance Drama* 40 (2001): 54–66.

7. I quote from *The Famous Historie of Fryer Bacon,* Early English Prose Romances, 3 (Edinburgh: Otto Schulze, n.d.) and number the chapters. The earliest ex-

226 RICHARD LEVIN

tant edition is dated c. 1625 (*STC* 1182.7), but there must have been a text available when Greene wrote his play.

8. The classic study of this development is Keith Thomas, *Religion and the Decline of Magic* (New York: Charles Scribner's Sons, 1971). He does not deal with magic contests.

9. I quote from *The Shakespeare Apocrypha,* ed. C. F. Tucker Brooke (Oxford: Clarendon, 1918).

10. All Shakespeare quotations follow *The Riverside Shakespeare,* ed. G. Blakemore Evans et al. (Boston: Houghton Mifflin, 1974).

11. Even the magicians seem to be at least nominal Christians: Hume and Southwell are priests; Bolingbrook invokes "God's name" before the conjuration (1.4.9); Jordan commands the Spirit to answer their questions "By the eternal God, whose name and power / Thou tremblest at" (25–26); and at the end Bolingbrook calls him "False fiend" and orders him to "Descend to darkness and the burning lake" (39–40).

12. I quote from the edition of Laird Barber (New York: Garland, 1979).

13. This was a favorite magic trick: Bacon's servant Miles does it to three thieves in *The Famous History of Friar Bacon,* ch. 9 (see note 7), and Mother Sawyer's familiar Tom to Cuddy Banks in Dekker, Ford, and Rowley's *The Witch of Edmonton* (1621), 3.1.90 (ed. Fredson Bowers, *The Dramatic Works of Thomas Dekker,* 3 [Cambridge: Cambridge University Press, 1958]), and there are referencs to it in Jonson's *The Entertainment at Althorp* (1603), 69–70 (ed. C. H. Herford and Percy and Evelyn Simpson, *Ben Jonson,* 7 [Oxford: Clarendon, 1941]), and Scot's *The Discovery of Witchcraft* (1584), 13.30 (ed. Montague Summers [New York: Dover, 1972]).

14. In *The Witch of Edmonton* Mother Sawyer complains that she is taken for a witch because she is "deform'd" and "like a Bow buckl'd and bent together" (2.1.3–4; see note 13). Henry Goodcole, in his examination of the real Mother Sawyer, says that "Her body was crooked and deformed, even bending together," and blames this on "the Devill" (*The Wonderful Discovery of Elizabeth Sawyer a Witch, Late of Edmonton* [1621], A4ᵛ), just as Prospero blames Sycorax's deformity, in part, on her "envy."

15. The only other play where he does this is *The Comedy of Errors,* and there he must also begin with a series of long and awkward expository speeches.

16. Prospero also confined Caliban to a rock, not for losing a contest but for trying to rape Miranda (1.2.342–43, 361), and at the end he is freed from the rock as well as from any further service when Prospero leaves the island.

17. There is a good example of such overcuriosity in Stephen Orgel's argument that the marriage is Prospero's plan (never mentioned, of course) "to prevent the succession of his brother" Antonio to the ducal throne after his own death ("Prospero's Wife," *Representing the English Renaissance,* ed. Stephen Greenblatt [Berkeley: University of California Press, 1988], 217–29, esp. 228). But when Prospero dies his throne will be inherited by Miranda, whether she is married or not, because we are told that in the Italian world of this play a monarch's title descends to his daughter before his younger brother (2.1.245, 255–56).

18. The one exception I noted is Gonzalo's "By'r lakin" (3.3.1), which refers to the Virgin Mary. We saw that Prospero thanks "bountiful Fortune" for bringing his enemies' ship to the island (1.2.178), but a few lines earlier he says that his own ship

MY MAGIC CAN LICK YOUR MAGIC 227

was brought there "By Providence divine" (159). And in 4.1.16–17 he warns Ferdinand not to touch Miranda before "All sanctimonious ceremonies may / With full and holy rite be minister'd," which can only be a church wedding (see also 5.1.309–10).

19. For the full text see E. K. Chambers, *The Elizabethan Stage,* 4 vols. (Oxford: Clarendon, 1923), 4:338–39. It only applied to words spoken in performance, but that presumably would have affected the manuscript on which the Folio text was based.

20. Later in this scene he tells the assembled nobles of the remarkable magical achievements of Sycorax (she "could control the moon," etc.—5.1.269–71), which is a kind of retroactive boasting for her, but also indirectly for him, since it makes his victory over her in their magic contest even more impressive (1.2.290–93).

21. In *The Birth of Merlin* a special point is made of the fact that Merlin is born with a beard, but we are not told its color (3.4.50, 53, 68, 124; see note 9).

22. See Wallace A. Bacon, "A Note on *The Tempest,* IV.i," *Notes and Queries* 192 (1947): 343–44; but other interpretations of these lines—less convincing, I think—are recorded in the New Variorum edition of Horace Howard Furness (Philadelphia: J. B. Lippincott, 1897), 187–89.

23. For an early discoverer see Lorie Jerrell Leininger, "The Miranda Trap: Sexism and Racism in Shakespeare's *Tempest," The Woman's Part: Feminist Criticism of Shakespeare,* ed. Carolyn Ruth Swift Lenz, Gayle Greene, and Carol Thomas Neely (Urbana: University of Illinois Press, 1980), 285–94, and "Cracking the Code of *The Tempest," Shakespeare: Contemporary Critical Approaches,* ed. Harry Garvin and Michael Payne, *Bucknell Review* 25 (1980): 121–31.

24. Almost all the details are added by Shakespeare. His source, Arthur Brooke's *Romeus and Juliet,* only says that the apothecary has a "heavy countenance" and that his shop displays very few "wares," which are not described (*The Sources of Ten Shakespeare Plays,* ed. Alice Griffin [New York: Thomas Y. Crowell, 1966], 37).

25. I quote from Geoffrey Chaucer, *Canterbury Tales,* ed. John Matthews Manly (New York: Henry Holt, 1928). Manly says that "presse" is a large cupboard (690), but it is more likely that the word refers to the mould used in casting a bell.

26. Shakespeare makes the poison even more powerful than in the source, where the apothecary says that it will "kill the strongest man alive" (37; see note 24).

27. I give Chaucer's characters the names they bear in the play, and pass over events that are not relevant to the magic contest. Quotations are from Manly's edition (see note 25).

28. There are a number of references to "God" by the Knight and some of the characters (see, for example, lines 886, 1084, 1282, 1317, 1599, 1665, 1800, 2558, 2563, 2782, 3064, 3099, 3108), and the Knight says that Arcite sacrifices to Mars "With alle the rytes of his payen wyse" (2370), which further distances the narrator from the religion practiced in his narrative.

29. This may be distantly related to the judgment of Solomon who, when confronted by two women claiming to be the mother of a baby, orders that the baby be cut in two and divided between them, but one woman protests that she would rather give up the baby than have it killed, so Solomon says she is the real mother. The story reappears in a Seinfeld episode where Kramer and Elaine claim ownership of a bike, and Newman offers to settle the dispute by a bisection.

30. This was the referee's ritual invocation after his instructions to the boxers pre-

228 RICHARD LEVIN

ceding their contest, but why did he not say, "Let the best boxer win"? Perhaps he, too, wanted victory to go to the one with the better character, or perhaps he simply assumed a high correlation between manliness and pugilistic skills.

31. They also omit the passage in Chaucer (2537–60) where Theseus modifies the rules of combat to make it less lethal, so as a result of these two changes, their Theseus seems more bloody minded than Chaucer's, although I do not think that was their purpose.

32. A vestige of the Chaucerian account survives in Pirithous' statement that the horse reared when its hooves struck the street's "flinty pavement" and an "envious flint, / Cold as old Saturn, and like him possess'd / With fire malevolent, darted a spark" that frightened it (5.4.59–63), but he never suggests that Saturn caused this, or had any connection to Venus or to Palamon's prayer to her. This change also explains why the playwrights have Arcite riding in triumph on the streets of Athens, rather than across the tournament arena as in Chaucer (2676–79).

33. See, for example, 2.2.6–25, 28–32, 51–55, 174–82, 209, 248–52; 3.6.4, 13, 99, 161–70, 269, and especially 92–93, which is the reverse of the passage quoted above from 282–85.

34. This is confirmed by the fact that Emilia is given two long soliloquies (4.2.1–54, 5.3.41–66) in which she tries to find a significant difference between her two suitors and cannot do it—in fact, she concludes in the first one that they are so "equal" that she "Cannot distinguish" them.

35. Last-minute improbable reversals and especially conflicts based on a refined and exalted sense of honor are Fletcherian specialties (witness Amintor in *The Maid's Tragedy,* Leucippus in *Cupid's Revenge,* Thierry in *Thierry and Theodoret,* and Virolet in *The Double Marriage*). Some of the scenes that present them in this play are usually attributed to Shakespeare on stylistic grounds, but we do not know how he interacted with Fletcher in the planning, which is why I have been referring to "the playwrights" as if they were a single entity.

36. Their interchangeability is emphasized in Theseus's final speech when he points out that "But one hour since" he felt "sorry" for Palamon and "glad" for Arcite, and now these feelings are completely reversed (5.4.129–31). It does not seem to make much difference to him, and I do not think it is supposed to make much difference to us.

New Books on Theater History

Cosmetics in Shakespearean and Renaissance Drama, by Farah Karim-Cooper. Edinburgh: Edinburgh University Press, 2006. Pp. x + 221, 17 ill. Hardback £ 50.00.

Reviewer: FRANCES TEAGUE

From Farah Karim-Cooper's study of cosmetics in the early modern period, one learns a vast amount about the material world of makeup. Karim-Cooper includes inventories of ingredients, with discussion of what those ingredients suggest; recipes for particular effects; and a sampling of passages from letters and pamphlets, which extol or excoriate the practice of maquillage. From such information Karim-Cooper moves to a discussion of how cosmetics served the early modern dramatist, both as tools to alter an actor's appearance and as a topos within a playtext. Her thesis in this study seems clear-cut, yet she moves beyond that thesis fairly consistently, following the traces of cosmetics into interesting cultural moments. Let me begin with her thesis. Midway through the book, she remarks, "What I have been arguing throughout this book is that Shakespearean and Renaissance drama elevates cosmetics by reinvigorating their metaphorical uses as well as by dynamically reasserting their materiality on the stage" (135). That statement echoes what she says on page 2: "early modern dramatists attempt to *revalue* the cosmetic, first by transporting it out of the feminine domestic interior and into a theatrical and poetic context, and secondly, by reasserting its materiality rather than merely endorsing its hypothetical usage in contemporary debates." Such declarations seem straightforward enough, perhaps even formulaic given the amount of work that has been done on the material culture of the early modern stage. More interesting, I think, is the sentence that ends her first chapter: "Appropriated by dramatists and popularized by the stage, the cosmetic materials, language and face painting scenes enraptured audiences, while plunging them into the thick of a cultural phenomenon that would gesture towards monarchy, death, art, poetry, race, and gender" (32). When I reached that sentence, after working my way through a chapter entitled "Defining Beauty in Renaissance Culture," I was cheered. While she commendably examines the commonplaces about beauty and painting, with attention to the emblem books as well as to samples of lyric poetry, here was a sentence that showed a writer passionate about a subject and that promised some lively analysis ahead.

The following chapter, "Early Modern Cosmetic Culture," surveys those writing against makeup, and those explaining how to make up the face. Unsurprisingly, such accounts about cosmetic practice are often misogynistic, as Karim-Cooper details. A substantial portion of the chapter concerns Elizabeth I, and Karim-Cooper makes the argument that "The Queen's painted face haunts many dramatic representations of face painting" (63), a more startling observation than what she says of misogyny. I looked forward to

232   NEW BOOKS ON THEATER HISTORY

learning more about cosmetics and monarchy onstage, as well as those other gestures listed on page 32. To demonstrate her claim about Elizabeth Tudor, she proceeds to the next chapter, "Cosmetic Restoration in Jacobean Tragedy," in which she considers *The Revenger's Tragedy* and *The Second Maiden's Tragedy*. The skull of Gloriana is our destination in *The Revenger's Tragedy*, while in *The Second Maiden's Tragedy*, it is the Lady's corpse, painted with poison. For myself, I admire the wide-ranging sources that Karim-Cooper has consulted, but remain less convinced that the Jacobean audience would have regarded *The Second Maiden's Tragedy* as a meditation on Queen Elizabeth's use of cosmetics. However, *The Revenger's Tragedy* refuses straightforward meaning, as critics acknowledge. By the conclusion, the vengeance of Vindice has passed from the mode of tragedy into melodrama, even burlesque. The play comments on women's beauty and the use of face-painting, and it recalls another Gloriana, yet how is one to understand that web of references? In her analysis, Karim-Cooper turns to the idea of death and eros quite effectively. Whether one accepts her belief that Elizabeth is a presence in *The Second Maiden's Tragedy*, it is clear that in that play, as in *The Revenger's Tragedy*, the painted dead flesh is powerfully erotic as well as poisonous.

Subsequent chapters concern John Webster (especially *The Duchess of Malfi* and *The White Devil*) and Ben Jonson (*Epicoene* and *The Devil Is an Ass*); in the case of Jonson, one could wish for a fuller analysis of the makeup scene in *Sejanus* and some discussion of the masques, especially *The Masque of Beauty* and *The Masque of Blackness*. The book concludes with three chapters on Shakespeare. These cover the early comedies, particularly *A Midsummer Night's Dream*, the Venetian plays, and *Hamlet*. Shakespeareans will find the discussions of the plays offer new information about the material context within which the works are embedded, although that information will not, of course, necessarily alter the way that later production and critical traditions understand the texts. Knowing that an early modern audience might have recognized a casket as the container for cosmetics cannot help us as we struggle to discuss *The Merchant of Venice* after the Holocaust.

I sometimes found what Karim-Cooper had to say compelling, sometimes not, but the book did engage me. One of its strengths is the amount of disparate material that it covers, although the broad coverage at times results in the author's offering a reading that seems less nuanced than one might expect. An instance is the book's analysis of *The Duchess of Malfi* 3.2. Farim-Cooper argues that the scene shows the Duchess applying makeup and beautifying herself (94), yet one may read it equally well as a scene in which the Duchess prepares for bed by removing her makeup and brushing her hair. In the latter case, it becomes an interesting parallel to *Othello* 4.3. Yet the possibility is never even mentioned, which seems a pity given what she later says about cosmetic use in *Othello*. Again, when discussing a sonnet by Bartholomew

NEW BOOKS ON THEATRE HISTORY

Griffin (22), Karim-Cooper considers the couplet that ends the blazon—"But ah the wors and last is yet behind, / For of a Gryphon she doth beare the mind"—as an instance of "the poet's disdain for the mistress." While she discusses the images in the sonnet that refer to cosmetics or standards of beauty, Karim-Cooper never even mentions that tantalizing pun on the poet's name in the last line. Similarly, while she has much to say about Elizabeth I's cosmetic practice, she quotes accounts without taking into account the bias of the reporter: one cannot read a negative description of Elizabeth's appearance, especially one that comments on the queen's health, without considering whether the person offering that description is hostile to the monarch. I am delighted to have such accounts but would like to have more consideration about what they suggest about both the queen and the person who speaks of her.

Let me offer another instance in which discussion of Queen Elizabeth I and cosmetics shows the book's strength and weakness. In her final chapter, Karim-Cooper quotes an anecdote from the 1650s about two scholars who had "their Faces meal'd" to play the roles of ghosts or apparitions. She goes on to link that anecdote to the way in which Shakespeare's company presented the ghost of Hamlet's father, suggesting that the pale makeup created by mealing the face might recall the heavily made–up monarch Queen Elizabeth I:

> In a stunning example of meta-drama, the Ghost (played by an actor whose face would have been adorned with cosmetics), represents a monarch who is no longer of this world, but whose transition is yet to be made into the next; it is this figure that triggers the events of a play that mediates upon the forms of paintedness and its potentially destabilising effect upon bodies—physical and political. . . . It can be argued that the image of the cosmeticised ghost walking the Globe stage in armour, with the beaver up so that the actor's face can be seen, and who emerges out of trapdoors to stalk the imaginary battlements, is a startling allusion to the declining political authority and physicality of Queen Elizabeth I.
>
> (176–77)

This reading, which is, as Karim-Cooper remarks, "startling," asks that we believe the original audience would make the same connection between the queen's painted face and the actor's makeup as Karim-Cooper does. While such an argument works more effectively to explain a scene with a painted skull named Gloriana, I find myself resisting the equation of Elizabeth I and old Hamlet because of skepticism about whether this identification would apply to every stage ghost in Elizabethan drama. (I must also admit that the reference to "Faces meal'd" makes me think the ludicrous trick of Jasper in *Knight of the Burning Pestle,* not an association that lends itself to serious contemplation of mortality.) Later in the discussion, Karim-Cooper returns to Elizabeth in her consideration of the arras in Gertrude's closet. Here she

234 NEW BOOKS ON THEATER HISTORY

mentions two events from Elizabeth's life when an arras is important, commenting that the play's moment operates "perhaps to gesture toward Queen Elizabeth I" (189). Five sentences later, the qualifier has gone: "No doubt, Elizabeth's own chamber or closet is present in the play's subtext" (189). Now the second claim makes good sense from the point of view of a dramaturg, because a play's theatrical subtext does not depend on scholarly claims, but instead implies the sort of emotional meanings that operate beneath the play's text. Yet from the point of view of literary analysis, I would prefer the qualified version: the moment is *perhaps* a gesture toward Elizabeth I.

The book has a great deal of information, some of which was completely new to me. Its sensitivity to matters of performance will make it particularly valuable to those readers who are concerned with how cosmetics elements will work on the stage. That approach, seen relatively rarely in materialist criticism, is a welcome one, although some of the author's analysis will provoke disagreement.

Voice in Motion: Staging Gender, Shaping Sound in Early Modern England, by Gina Bloom. Philadelphia: University of Pennsylvania Press, 2007. Pp. 277. Cloth: $59.95.

Reviewer: GENEVIEVE LOVE

Gina Bloom's *Voice in Motion* takes the movement of the voice—"from the speaker's body, through the air, and to the listener's body" (17)—as its principle of organization; this trajectory is both satisfyingly clear and unpredictably illuminating. As she develops the book's fundamental argument, that "it is the voice's distance from, rather than presence in, the body that constitutes the conditions of agency" (17), this guiding structure allows Bloom to decenter her readings of early modern plays. That is, the book is not patterned around sustained readings of particular plays; rather, each chapter integrates a range of readings—some brief, some extended—of literary texts with analysis of sixteenth- and seventeenth-century nondramatic texts. Bloom's introduction emphasizes that her readings of these nondramatic texts, which include writings on vocal training and performance, scientific writings on acoustics, and Protestant sermons, are not treated as "simply an historical 'context' to facilitate the contemporary critic's reading of drama" (36). As Bloom elegantly marshals a wide range of dramatic and nondramatic texts into her cogent "voice-in-motion" structure, engaging materialist, performance studies, and feminist methodologies and incorporating appealing close readings, the book's method is as intriguing as its matter.

Following an introduction that establishes the methodological stakes of the book's "effort to theorize the relation between voice and agency" (5), chapter 1, "Squeaky Voices: Marston, Mulcaster, and the Boy Actor," examines

NEW BOOKS ON THEATRE HISTORY

the challenges to early modern gender hierarchies posed by instances of the unstable male voice. Unlike the book's other chapters, which address both male and female figures, this chapter focuses exclusively on the male voice as Bloom explores a range of "texts in which the volatile voice is a function of the unmanageable body of its speaker" (17). While the chapter's argument that patriarchal structures are compromised by the "unchoreographable, squeaking voice" (40) takes shape through readings of multiple plays, Bloom engages in extended readings of Richard Mulcaster's *Positions Concerning the Training Up of Children,* a pedagogical treatise that presents "a view of human vocal organs as fragile and vulnerable to malfunction" (36), and John Marston's *Antonio and Mellida,* which "links failing patriarchal power structures . . . with unstable male voices" (50). The chapter's exacting etymological treatment of vocal terminology like "squeake" and "cracke" is characteristic of Bloom's invigorating combination of *OED*-inspired (and *OED*-expanding) close reading and theoretical sophistication.

In chapter 2, "Words Made of Breath: Shakespeare, Bacon, and Particulate Matter," Bloom's analysis of both male and female characters in Shakespearean plays tackles head-on the book's thesis that "the *disarticulation* of voice from body generates vocal power" (68, emphasis in original). Turning to early modern theorists of acoustics enables Bloom to expand chapter 1's analysis of the problematics of men's control over voice, as she examines "how the particular material processes of vocal transmission destabilize a speaker's control over an utterance" (67). Most incisively, Bloom uses the early modern experimental scientist Walter Charleton's theories of sound as particulate matter to establish a "redefinition of voice" (101)—breath as voice—that provides "silenced" female characters with a "more capacious model of agency" (68). While the chapter focuses most on *King John* and especially on Eleanor and Constance, the examples of Desdemona and Lavinia are among the book's most powerful. When Othello pauses over Desdemona's "balmy breath" (5.2.16) and when Marcus describes the "rise and fall" of the "crimson river. . . . coming and going with [Lavinia's] honey breath" (2.4.22–25), Bloom argues for a "tension between the absence of speech and the presence of breath—between the lack of verbal language and the persistence of vocal matter" to come to the persuasive conclusion that "breath [can] be read as virtually sufficient for voice" (101).

Having moved from the speaker's unmanageable body, and through the volatile air, Bloom arrives at the unpredictable ear of the listener in Chapter 3, "Fortress of the Ear: Shakespeare's Late Plays, Protestant Sermons, and Audience." Bloom's analysis of early modern Protestant sermons, which intriguingly depict "hearing as a multistage process" (121), makes clear the "challenging nature of the work of hearing" (120). While the chapter explores the "transformative power of hearing" (122) in Shakespeare's late plays, its central concern is the relationship of "aural obstruction" to "audi-

236   NEW BOOKS ON THEATER HISTORY

tory agency" in those plays (116–17)—a relationship that, importantly for Bloom, is very different for male and female characters. Bloom suggests that previous studies of the relationship between sound and subjectivity in the early modern theater have not sufficiently distinguished male and female audition; her readings of Pericles, Leontes, Marina, Innogen, and Miranda illustrate how "auditory practice becomes . . . a site of gender differentiation" (116). Bloom establishes two categories of aural closure, "constructive defensiveness" and "disruptive deafness" (116), to show how "efforts to shore up female chastity—and female difference—paradoxically imbue female characters who shut their ears with a method of resisting authority" (18). One of the book's characteristic moves is the move from representations of vocality in plays and nondramatic texts to actual speaking and listening in live performance; that move—from the thematic to the theatrical—is most convincing in this chapter, as Bloom offers the possibility that "an audience's aural resistance can be constructive of an ideal theatrical economy" (157).

Chapter 4, "Echoic Sound: Sandys's Englished Ovid and Feminist Criticism," stands apart from the others in its focus on a nondramatic literary text, George Sandys's 1632 English translation of and commentary on Ovid's *Metamorphoses,* and above the others in its analysis of how, in the figure of Echo, "the auditory agency identified in Chapter 3 can become the vocal agency elucidated in Chapter 2" (18). Although the Sandys text might seem a problematic fit in a book so concerned with performance, Bloom argues that Sandys's treatment of Echo is useful in that it "makes explicit representational strategies that are at work more subtly in performance spaces like the theater" (162). Bloom's careful close reading of Sandys's and Ovid's versions of Echo shows how Sandys "normaliz[es] [Echo's] eerie vocality" (168), to ultimately claim that "the sober scientific and historical reality about Echo related in Sandys's commentary, like the personification of Echo in his translation, curbs the potential power of the disembodied voice" (180). Echo—and echoes of Echo, like Sandys's translation—drives home Bloom's assertion of the "potential power of disembodied voice" especially for women, and leads her to a trenchant critique of "feminist treatments of voice," which she believes have been limited by their "tendency to concentrate on the speaker's body" (183). "Alternate readings of female agency become available," Bloom finally maintains, "when we interrogate, rather than assume, that vocal power derives from the speaker's body" (183).

Bloom's epilogue, "Performing the Voice of Queen Elizabeth," crowns the book's concern with the "volatility of the voice in performance" (19). Bloom examines George Gascoigne's dialogue between the Savage Man and Echo in the entertainments at Kenilworth Castle on the occasion of Queen Elizabeth's 1575 visit, a performance that was both transcribed by Gascoigne and reported in a joke document (a purported eyewitness account) known as *Laneham's Letter.* The *Letter* reports Gascoigne's dialogue as a theatrical fail-

NEW BOOKS ON THEATRE HISTORY 237

ure, in which an onstage accident prompted Elizabeth to cry out, which cry the *Letter*'s author calls "the best part of the play." This praise for Elizabeth's unscripted, spontaneous utterance brings Bloom to her conclusion that "early modern performance conditions, because they were so volatile, left room for alternative forms of female vocal agency to be described and expressed" (194). The epilogue encapsulates the book's contribution to performance studies—Bloom's description of the "strange materiality of the voice: durable, substantial, and potent, yet . . . transient, disembodied, and ephemeral" (2) could describe performance itself—and this contribution, bolstered by the book's lucid, compelling organization and elegant writing, rewards readers with methodological insights to accompany *Voice in Motion*'s important analytical contributions.

Drama at the Courts of Queen Henrietta Maria, by Karen Britland. Cambridge: Cambridge University Press, 2006. Pp. ix + 292. Cloth $96.00.

Reviewer: SUZANNE GOSSETT

Karen Britland's *Drama at the Courts of Queen Henrietta Maria* is an admirable work, revisionist and yet respectful of previous scholarship, theoretically current while based on a significant amount of primary research. Britland presents a positive reading of Henrietta Maria's intelligence, selfawareness, and political and religious development, in contrast to the usual descriptions of the queen consort, which denigrate her as French, foolish, female, and insidiously Catholic. The queen's development is traced through the entertainments associated with her, first in her French girlhood, then during her years in England, and finally in the royalist court in exile.

In the tradition of Stephen Orgel, Leah Marcus, and James Knowles, Britland analyzes Henrietta Maria's masques, pastorals, and incidental performances for their political and cultural resonances at specific historical moments. Britland's work is especially valuable because she brings a European dimension to her analysis, moving fluently between the French and English material. Familiarity with French scholarship and sources like the *Gazette de France* allows her to show how the imagery of the wedding masques reappeared in the entertainments the queen later sponsored, to identify the author of *Florimène,* and to explicate the continental significance of many details.

Britland is part of a generation of younger scholars, largely women, who have reexamined the ways in which women operated in and on the early modern court, stage, and political world. See, for examples, Clare McManus, *Women on the Renaissance Stage: Anna of Denmark and Female Masquing in the Stuart Court, 1590–1619* (2002) and Sophie Tomlinson, *Women on Stage in Stuart Drama* (2005); Britland also cites papers from the 1998 con-

238 NEW BOOKS ON THEATER HISTORY

ference entitled "The Queen's Court: Elite Female Cultural Production and the Cultures of the Early Stuarts (1603–42)." Yet Britland avoids imposing a modern feminist reading on the past. For example, she finds Henrietta Maria's iconography "femino-centric . . . less because she was fighting the good fight for her sisters than because she was actively promoting her role as an exemplary Catholic princess in an apostate land" and interprets her influence on female cultural production "not as a proto-feminist struggle for the rights of female public speech, but as an aspect of the queen consort's religious and social project" (7–8; 14). Nevertheless, Britland's desire to understand Henrietta Maria as more than a "gay butterfly passing lightly from flower to flower," in Samuel R. Gardiner's description (1), offers a feminist rehabilitation of this daughter of Henri IV and Marie de Médicis. Indeed, a major thread of Britland's study is its revelation of how tightly bound Henrietta was to her mother, siding with her in various plots and ultimately bringing Marie to England when Louis XIII exiled her from France. Persuasively, Britland argues that the appearance of common cultural images at the European courts was "aided by the marital exchange of royal women and by those women's continued patronage of the men and motifs familiar to them" (3).

Britland's analyses of individual masques are supported with historical details and frequently based on new research. For example, she identifies an entertainment by Henrietta's attendants earlier than *Artenice,* previously assumed to the queen's first production. When there are alternative possibilities Britland always acknowledges them. For example, she does not deny Erica Veevers's interpretation of *Chloridia* as representing complementary male and female opposites now reconciled, as Henrietta and Charles were by 1631, but goes on to reread the masque politically: in *Chloridia,* staged after France and England had signed a peace treaty, the "image of two large powers (earth and heaven) coming to an harmonious agreement is more compatible with the Anglo-French peace accord than with the resolution of marital conflict" (80). Inevitably in such allegorical interpretations there are debatable details: contending that elements of *Chloridia* reflect the ongoing dispute between Marie de Médicis and Cardinal Richelieu, she identifies Cupid with the cardinal ("Marie de Médicis' former servant, a position of dependence that can be equated with the masque's emphasis on Cupid as a child" [83]), which seems dubious. Nevertheless, the concluding section of this chapter, arguing that attempts were made to keep the news of Marie's exile from Henrietta not simply to avoid upsetting her because it would "destabilise the masque's agenda" (86–87), is a fascinating insight to the role entertainments could play at court.

Henrietta's masques and pastorals reflect her relation to international politics against the background of the Thirty Years' War and the incipient English Civil War. Britland situates *The Shepherds' Paradise* within the "specific context of the early 1630s . . . in the aftermath of Marie de Médicis's exile and in the context of Gaston d'Orleans military mobilization against Louis

NEW BOOKS ON THEATRE HISTORY 239

XIII" (121). At this point Henrietta Maria was involved in the anti-Richelieu Chateauneuf plot; the pastoral was anti-Spanish and commented "obliquely upon the restoration of the Palatinate." *Florimène,* whose author Britland identifies as Francois le Metel, sieur de Boisrobert, a court poet who had written verses for the *Ballet de la Reyne d'Angleterre* at Henrietta's wedding, instead participates in Henrietta Maria's return to a pro-French policy. Britland acknowledges that the play does not appear in lists of Boisrobert's plays, but hypothesizes that it was specially commissioned by Richelieu as part of his cultural program just as he was creating the *Academie Francaise.* Furthermore, information from the *Gazette* that *Florimène* ended with a ballet supports Stephen Orgel's proposal that the Townshend antimasque fragments in the Huntington Library were written for the conclusion of *Florimène.*

Feminist readings are not forgotten as Britland analyzes Henrietta Maria's goals in using cross-dressed women as actresses in *The Shepherds' Paradise*—the event that brought down Prynne's wrath—and *Florimène.* These productions pushed at the boundaries not only of "female theatrical performance" (113) but also of "permitted female behaviour at the Caroline court" (116). *Florimène* may conclude "by locking its meanings down to conservative formulations," but the presiding figure of Diana retains a strong spiritual significance tied to the queen's religion and to suggestions of the symbolic relation between Henrietta Maria and the virgin.

The chapters on *Luminalia* and *Salmacida Spolia* focus on the relation between Henrietta Maria's masques and her religion. Britland ties these productions partly to Henrietta's Salesian Catholicism and particularly to the arrival in England of Marie de Médicis. She also makes a strong case for their "common European iconography," once again showing how the English entertainments of the queen never forgot those of her ancestors, the Médici in Florence and the Bourbons in Paris.

With good reason Britland complains that "after 1644, when Henrietta Maria escaped to France, her presence in historical accounts becomes nearly indiscernible" (192). In a final chapter she counters by tracing the queen's life and entertainments during her quarter century of exile. In the 1650s Henrietta Maria founded a convent to which she frequently retreated, but even there "she pursued a policy of piety, politics and pleasure" (224). Britland's study thus offers a picture of the full trajectory of Henrietta Maria's life in its French and English connections, as well as close readings of some of the most fascinating, if often neglected, performances on the Caroline stage.

Women on Stage in Stuart Drama, by Sophie Tomlinson. Cambridge: Cambridge University Press: 2005. Pp. xii + 308. Cloth $96.00.

Reviewer: KAREN RABER

For so many years, scholars of English Renaissance drama accepted the proposition that no women performed on stage until the Restoration and

240 NEW BOOKS ON THEATER HISTORY

when they did appear on English stages, it was assumed their advent was the direct result of English exposure to female actresses in Europe during the Interregnum. Sophie Tomlinson's *Women on Stage in Stuart Drama* provides a significant and well-argued addition to feminist qualifications to such a narrow view of women's participation in, and influence on, pre-Restoration theater. As Tomlinson rightly points out, Restoration actresses were not a break with tradition, but the logical completion of a process started in the early Stuart courts: as she notes, "women's increasing cultural visibility" led to concern "with issues of liberty and civility that derive from a sympathetic interest in female selfhood" (3); the "sexual realism" and fascination with women's wit and ingenuity on the Restoration stage can trace its origins to Jacobean and Caroline developments in court masques and stage plays. In other words, rather than investing in historical rupture, this study emphasizes continuity, and draws the reader's attention to overlooked aspects of seventeenth-century performance in order to prove its case.

Tomlinson begins with the court masque as it was transformed by the early Stuart queens, Anna of Denmark and Henrietta Maria. The ability of masques to create performance out of non-speaking gesture, costume, symbol, and even silence itself made it a flexible instrument adaptable in promoting "radical sexual and political alternatives" (45). From the start, then, Tomlinson invites us to think more broadly about "acting" that is not limited to the standard devices and performance styles of the public theaters: dance, facial expression, physical postures, approval of scripts, movement and lack of movement, singing, the use of props and scenery—there are myriad ways that "acting" happens in Stuart dramatic environments. In a second chapter, Aurelian Townshend's *Tempe Restored* (which featured a female singer/actress), Walter Montagu's *The Shepherd's Paradise* (performed by Henrietta Maria and her court ladies), and Milton's *Comus* provide evidence of an emergent "female voice" in the pastoral; as divas, diplomats, sirens, and sage virgins, women are accorded a range of roles that promote an important "debate about female performance" (52) that ultimately makes the appearance of professional actresses inevitable.

In subsequent chapters, Tomlinson questions the definition of a term like "actress" by insisting that female characters in Stuart theatrical comedies and tragedies should be read as such: rather than obsessing about the male body within the costume, Tomlinson asks what effect the characters themselves had on cultural beliefs about women as actors. Analyzing Jonson's *The New Inn,* Shirley's *Hyde Park,* and William Cartwright's *The Lady-Errant,* Tomlinson finds that women's "shifting"—"moving from one state to another" (85)—casts them powerfully as theatrical catalysts, often in the interests of arguments about liberty, marital civility, and even intellectual or sexual fulfillment. Caroline tragedies like Ford's *Love's Sacrifice* and *The Broken Heart* explore women's subjectivity, especially as it is riven by conflicts over appearance and actual feeling; the same requirement—to put on a show for others—that makes women chameleon actresses in the comedies, leads to madness and destruction in the tragedies. In either case, however, women as actresses is a consuming theatrical obsession.

To account for performance during the Civil War and Interregnum before she turns to the women writers who benefited from "new opportunities for women" that were generated by the "rupture" and discontinuities in public theaters during that period (156), Tomlinson includes an "interchapter" on the siren appeal of song. Women's singing is a sub-theme throughout the volume, but here it steps center stage in Davenant's *Siege of Rhodes,* which draws on the musical culture of the Royalist elites. Concluding chapters on Margaret Cavendish and Katherine Philips emphasize continuities both with an earlier court performance environment and conventions, and with the emerging place for women on public theatrical stages during the postwar years. Tomlinson returns to the much-cited account in Cavendish's work of her encounter with a woman actor on the Continent during her exile to begin her analysis of Cavendish's theater of the imagination, in which women *can* act, wittily, agilely, and to the good of all. Contra Catherine Gallagher, Tomlinson argues that Cavendish's theater of the mind is all about self-projection, not merely "self-withdrawal" (176), and so is enabling to female performances of all kinds. Her treatment of Katherine Philips also works slightly against the grain in dealing more with the character of Cleopatra than with that of Cornelia in Philips's translation of Corneille's *Pompey.* As elsewhere, Tomlinson insists that we link the creation of a literary persona like Philips's "Orinda" (through which she was able to "exercise her literary gifts with impunity" [202]) to other kinds of performance, like that of a commanding, heroic character within a closet drama.

Tomlinson's work, despite its importance to feminists and critics of the drama, does suffer from some drawbacks. It is at once too narrow and too broad in different aspects of its research and argument: too narrow, because it does not offer an overarching, fully theorized account of all forms of performance (including nonelite) in which women engaged, and too broad because so much of its argument is created through lateral accretions. Because Tomlinson includes a much-neglected form of performance like music, she begs the question how other forms of "performance art" that cropped up shortly before the war and during the Interregnum would also have contributed to the acceptance of women as actors—in other words, why isolate singing from other dramatic skills like public declamation, street performance, political demonstrations, nontheatrical cross-dressing, and the like? Without blaming Tomlinson for these gaps, it is still possible to say that her work points out the need for another kind of project, one that more completely and complexly deconstructs the apparent boundaries between types, locations, and expressions of dramatic performance, in order to give us a better vocabu-

242 NEW BOOKS ON THEATER HISTORY

lary for talking about "performance" in all its registers during the seventeenth century. Tomlinson's is a step toward such a project rather than the final result. And because the occasional female artist noted in Tomlinson's study is decidedly non-elite, the volume sometimes seems to invite further attention to class and social status in determining these various expressions of performance arts (hence, perhaps, the choice of singers who bridge class divides rather than highlight them), while it consistently steers away from such issues. This again suggests a more complete account is possible. At the same time, Tomlinson often argues via addition and analogy: many moments in her readings are compared to moments in a huge variety of other plays (with language like "this may remind us of . . ." or "we can see echoes between . . ." and so on), sometimes without enough clarification of the differences between them. This tends to work against her view of historical continuity, since all the evidence begins to look like all the other evidence; nor do these analogical readings often add much to the final analysis. The project does succeed, however, in its main purpose of making connections between pre-and post-war Stuart culture, convincing us that for women, at least, a slowly growing set of images, practices, and ideas were inexorably opening the way to their full representation, in the flesh and in spirit, on the theatrical stage.

Children of the Queen's Revels: A Jacobean Theatre Repertory, by Lucy Munro. Cambridge: Cambridge University Press, 2005. Pp. 267 + xiii. Cloth $96.00.

Reviewer: MARY BLY

I just finished re-reading every bit of scholarship about boy theater companies that my graduate assistant could rootle out of the stacks, due diligence for a book chapter surveying our critical past. My conclusion after this reading orgy is that many a scholarly snit has arisen from attempts to distinguish between boy and adult companies. One can even see these theories as trying to justify the distinction as a scholarly topic.

For example, Harold Hillebrand's idea that boy actors turned their plays into "bombast," later elaborated by R. A. Foakes (who envisioned boys "consciously ranting in oversize parts"), offered a clear justification for the division between boy and adult plays: boy plays are different because they were acted for laughs.[1] Ejner J. Jensen thoroughly deflated Hillebrand's theory with an intelligent article back in 1968, but scholars still reflexively re-establish the boys' acting credentials. It's as if engaging in that old battle justifes the importance of distinguishing between boy and adult companies. Alfred Harbage's 1952 theory of the rival traditions similarly has had a shelf life far beyond what its flawed, albeit thoughtful, ideas warranted. His distinc-

NEW BOOKS ON THEATRE HISTORY

243

tion between private and public theater audiences offered an organizing principle that substantiated the label "boy company plays"—their elite audiences demanded different fare.

Yet now that boy actors and their audiences are accepted to have been more similar than not to their adult counterparts, how do we define the significance of boy companies? Why should their plays be considered as a group—or how should that grouping be justified? In another article, this one from 1975, Jensen astutely asks whether boy company plays should even be considered together. The plays, he says, "seem like the products of an anti-academic conspiracy intent on frustrating our tendencies to discover order and coherence and unity in the literary works of a single period."[2] What should we be teaching our students about the relevance of the distinction?

One of the biggest shifts in early modern theatrical scholarship as a whole in the last thirty years has been toward examining theater repertories as separate units, whose important referents are management, location, actors, and collaborative playwrights, a move away from considering a single playwright as key to understanding a given text. Roslyn Knutson's 1991 *The Repertory of Shakespeare's Company* takes the bull by the horns: "To approach the success of Shakespeare's company by way of its entire repertory . . . requires a shift in perspective that would have been anathema to most theater historians as recently as a generation ago."[3] Organizing by repertory, she suggests, involves accepting that commercial strategies spring from company management, and that we have to explain the King's Men's success not only by reference to Shakespeare, but by looking at hacks whose plays were "valuable items in the company repertory—if only because their number, conventionality, and appeal to a spectrum of tastes" (13).

Unburdened by a need to foreground Shakespeare, boy company scholars long ago viewed the repertory as a justifiable organizing principle: witness Michael Shapiro's *Children of the Revels: The Boy Companies of Shakespeare's Time and Their Plays* (1979), and Reavley Gair's *The Children of Paul's: The Story of a Theatre Company, 1553–1608* (1984). But Knutson brought a new direction to such studies when she emphasized the economic milieu of the period. In her own words, Knutson moves away from authorship —toward ownership. Looking at who owned a repertory, she argues, allows us to examine the implications of company choices regarding subject matter and kinds of plays.

Work like Knutson's freed scholars to move further away from consideration of the author, an unmooring whose theoretical tenets were authorized by Derrida, though many scholars of theater history may not appreciate that. The sea-change that allowed Knutson's shift in perspective was prompted by deconstruction, hard though it may be to view the work of a detailed archivist and an airy theorist pointing in the same direction.

Yet this unlikely coalition of archivist and anti-author theorist also drives

244   NEW BOOKS ON THEATER HISTORY

Lucy Munro's recent book, *Children of the Queen's Revels: A Jacobean Theatre Repertory* (2006). Munro moves swiftly past the idea of the author, arguing that "Queen's Revels plays were created not only by the dramatists, but also through the ideas and desires of the company's shareholders, licenser, patrons, actors, and audience" (165). Like Knutson, she is an archivist, including five useful appendices detailing everything from Queen's Revels touring performances to actor lists. At the same time, she talks nimbly of Derrida's *Of Grammatology* and uses Foucault's concept of the post-eighteenth-century author as the "regulator of the fictive" to bestow the role of regulator to the playing company, not the author (4).

No matter how you look at it, Munro took on a formidable task. From a theatrical history point of view, the Queen's Revels, which played in the Blackfriars theater and possibly continued to the Whitefriars theater, presents a snarly mess of factual contradictions. Most of what we know of its history springs from a nest of lawsuits. Irwin Smith has pointed out that the Blackfriars management spawned nine intra-partnership litigations and six others involving outsiders.[4] For various reasons only partially understood, the company changed names the way courtiers changed suits: it was known variously as the Children of the Queen's Chapel Royal, then as the Children of the Queen's Revels, the Children of the Revels, and finally, the Children of the Whitefriars.

One problem is that such facts as are known about the company are still vigorously disputed by theater historians. For example, although many historians believe that the Queen's Revels took on their final name when they moved to the Whitefriars, Richard Dutton has suggested that the move wasn't so simple, and that in fact the Children of the Whitefriars was a brand new, amalgamated theater company, engineered as such by the Revels Office.[5] The new company would have had some relation to the Queen's Revels, but would have used the defunct King's Revels patent, and had a new, less politically controversial, artistic policy. In short, Munro took on a company about which there is a welter of conflicting opinions.

And perhaps even worse, the company put on *good* plays. When I wrote a full-length monograph on the King's Revels company, *Queer Virgins and Virgin Queens,* I was comfortably aware of the impoverished nature of their plays. I only had seven core texts to deal with and their literary quality ensured that very few scholars were conversant with *Ram Alley,* for example. My project's scope was correspondingly trimmed. But as Munro notes, the Queen's Revels' plays are "ambitious and innovative, even avant-garde" (1). Not only did the company put on good plays, but those plays often put the actors and authors in peril: "the Queen's Revels were the most prominent, politically contentious and dramatically experimental of the early seventeenth-century children's companies" (ix). Rosencrantz may well be speaking of the Queen's Revels when he says that boys make men "afraid of

NEW BOOKS ON THEATRE HISTORY

245

Goose-quils"; Chapman's *The Conspiracy and Tragedy of Charles, Duke of Biron,* for example, infuriated the French ambassador due to its depiction of the French queen slapping the king's mistress.[6]

The problems facing a theater historian planning to write a monograph on this company are huge. The problems facing someone with ambitions to bring a seasoning of theory to the mix are almost insurmountable. I would say that Munro did an admirable job of bringing together all the available facts about the Queen's Revels. Oddly, for a book focusing on an entire repertory, she is strongest when discussing individual plays. For example, she engages in a fascinating analysis of Quicksilver's ironic use of "master" in *Eastward Ho,* examining the way that Touchstone constructs his social identity (76). A few pages later, she parses mockery of prodigal stories in Gertrude's submission to her father (81). Munro's conclusion that the play exaggerates its own generic conventions is deftly argued and utterly convincing. Yet these thoughtful, learned comments do not prove that the Queen's Revels repertory is the best lens through which to examine *Eastward Ho.* Though its collaboratively authored status makes the tag "Queen's Revels play" an attractive substitute for listing all three authors, I was not convinced that the company was responsible for—or even truly implicated in—exaggeration of generic conventions such as she identifies.

Yet substitution of authorship is a fundamental parameter in Munro's argument. The author, she notes, "is a useful organizing principle, but it is not the only one available" (4). She then argues that the early modern "regulator of the fictive," in Foucault's phrase, was the playing company, not the author (4). This concept allows her to suggest that company repertories need the same attention as do canons of playwrights. In essence, the company replaces the author: regulator of the fiction becomes creator of the fictive. The plays become artifacts of a "collaborative dynamic" (137). Munro wisely avoids the temptation to posit a controlling influence behind the repertory, instead focusing on a series of smaller, overlapping narratives. Yet stripping the "author" from over forty plays without positing a controlling influence would, in a perfect world, require support from a kind of archival material simply not available (along the lines of e-mails among authors and management). Another way to prove the argument might be by bringing a formidable knowledge of other repertories to bear. Likely hoping to publish this book within her lifetime, Munro sticks to the Queen's Revels repertory, organizing her analysis around the genres of comedy, tragicomedy, and tragedy. She hopes thereby to provide the reader with "a historically grounded perspective on the collaborative production of plays and an interpretative link between their production and reception" (5). But without much reference to other repertories as ballast to her argument about the Queen's Revels, the question of whether the company had a relevant, creative influence on its plays is stated, not proved.

246   NEW BOOKS ON THEATER HISTORY

The first chapter is a thoughtful, able recounting of all available information about the company. Munro offers a measured intervention into various vexed questions, such as the ages and acting styles of the boys. Her best comments come from her thorough knowledge of the repertory, as when she maintains that "many of the later Queen's Revels plays are predicated on the interstitial character of the company, which included not only prepubescent children, but also performers who would have been categorized as 'youth'" (45). Her command of the repertory allows her to note fascinating nuances: "During the first decade of James's reign, the Queen's Revels' actors gradually stopped being objects—boy actors controlled by a managing syndicate or the passive cause of lust in an audience—and became subjects, taking a progressively more active role in the company and gaining their own sexual and social reputations and identities" (52). This is perhaps a more complicated idea than she acknowledges (I feel some uneasiness at the idea that boy-as-object includes both an audience relation and a boy-manager relation), but it's very interesting, and all the more so for her knowledge of the plays.

Chapters 2, 3, and 4 address the three genres in question. For example, the chapter on comedy focuses on "the way in which jokes unravel social identity" (56). Munro suggests that we can look for social stress-points by focusing on jokes, puns, and jibes about social status, and that "standard comic structures are manipulated in order to confirm or confound audience expectation, with laughter playing a crucial role in the production or withholding of satisfaction" (57). Looking at plays by Chapman, Jonson, Marston, and Middleton to examine audience composition, Munro argues that Queen's Revels plays "actively interrogate the social identities associated with the spectators, and the performance of social class by actors highlights its mutability outside the theatre" (66). I wouldn't quarrel with that—but I can't see that the practice is limited to the Queen's Revels. I enjoyed reading her thoughtful discussion of joke books, in particular, and her discussion of the use of language as a marker of social class, but Munro's elision of the author is problematic. She uses blanket phrases such as "Many of the Queen's Revels plays are concerned with the question of gentle speech," and follows that up with a medley of quotations from *Eastward Ho* and Beaumont and Fletcher's *The Coxcomb*. The fact that the two plays deal with language and social status in a different manner is indisputable: but why is it important that both were performed by the Queen's Revels? Again, when Munro states "comedy can have conflicting aims and can be interpreted by its audience in different ways," her analytical abilities give away to generalizations. She concludes that "jokes could be an important means of channeling an audience's response" (72). The Queen's Revels surely did try to "make a disparate audience laugh"—but then so did other companies, as Knutson's study of the King's Men proves. What is lost here is a link between company and play that is necessary if one is going to justify a focus on the Queen's Revels as collaborative creators. Similarly, in the tragedy chapter, Munro argues that the Queen's Revels tragedies are "marked by an increasing anxiety about the nature of tragedy" (147). While she engages in an interesting discussion of tragicomedic elements in plays such as *A Christian Turned Turk,* the fact is that many plays of the period showed unease with certain aspects of tragedy (notably, *Hamlet*).

The chapter on tragicomedy is the most compelling, in that Munro makes an argument that the development of tragicomedy was "propelled by the collaborative practices of the playing companies, and one group in particular: the Children of the Queen's Revels" (96). Without an author regulator, she argues, the various source texts behind many tragicomedies (Guarini and Ovid, for example), are "assimilated into a complex cultural network" that fuels the new genre (97). The Queen's Revels company does seem to have broken ground with this genre. Munro's study of the "disjunctive tones" combined within their tragicomedies tends to revert at some times to a more traditional study of Fletcher's work—but it is the stronger for allowing this wildly creative author some space on the page. The question of "queasily comic effects" (155) is brilliantly delineated.

To go back to Ejner's question—why is this body of texts significant?— Munro offers a spirited, learned answer to his question. One closes the book with a sense that the Queen's Revels had a remarkably inventive and creative repertory, particularly when it comes to tragicomedy. It may be that had Munro world enough and time, this study would have examined other repertories and proved her point that the Queen's Revels' plays are best viewed together, and that their similarities to each other grow from production and performance, not from wider theatrical influences. As it is, the book offers a solid, intelligent addition to our understanding of this boy company, as well as a lively entry in the long-standing discussion of the importance of the boy company as a lens for discussion of early modern drama.

Notes

1. Harold Newcomb Hillebrand, *The Child Actors: A Chapter in Elizabethan Stage History* (1926; rpt. New York: Russell and Russell, 1964), 254; R. A. Foakes, "Tragedy at the Children's Theatres after 1600: A Challenge to the Adult Stage," *The Elizabethan Theatre II,* ed. David Galloway (New York: Archon Books, 1970), 45.

2. E. J. Jensen, "The Boy Actors: Plays and Playing," *Research Opportunities in Renaissance Drama* 18 (1975): 5.

3. Roslyn Knutson, *The Repertory of Shakespeare's Company, 1594–1613* (Place: University of Arkansas Press, 1991), 4.

4. Irwin Smith, *Shakespeare's Blackfriars Playhouse* (New York: New York University Press, 1964), 189.

248 NEW BOOKS ON THEATER HISTORY

5. Richard Dutton, "The Revels Office and the Boy Companies, 1600–1613: New Perspectives," *ELR* (2002): 339.

6. William Shakespeare, *Hamlet.* The entire passage, II.ii.354–60, appears in different versions in Q1, Q2, and F, where it is much expanded.

The Early Stuart Masque: Dance, Costume, and Music, by Barbara Ravelhofer. Oxford: Oxford University Press, 2006. Pp. xvi + 318 + 3 plates + 23 figures. Cloth $125.00.

Reviewer: Timothy Raylor

The early Stuart masque was a multimedia spectacle: a rich and complex blend of poetry, music, scenery, lighting, costume, and dance. Students of the form have long recognized this, but our approach to it remains, as Barbara Ravelhofer contends in her new book, primarily text-based. There are good reasons why this should be so: most of our information about masques comes from accounts published retrospectively by librettists, working from a textual angle and (usually) keen to underline the centrality of their own contributions. But such evidence skews our view of the form, privileging abstract invention and its verbal expression over physical incarnation. How far removed are those printed descriptions from the participant's experience or the spectator's view of a masque! Barbara Ravelhofer aims to redress this imbalance by exploring the work of the choreographers and costumiers, the composers and musicians, the scene and lighting designers, who produced the sights and sounds, the textures and movements of the masque in performance, and by folding the resulting insights and discoveries into an enlarged account of the form.

Ravelhofer is not, of course, the first to seek to understand the masque as an artistic construct; she is working in the tradition of Allardyce Nicoll, Enid Welsford, and Lily Campbell (268). While part of her intent is the laudable one of trying to recover the wonder, beauty, and pleasure of these ephemeral spectacles, Ravelhofer is no pure aesthetician. A Cambridge PhD, she is an expert practitioner of the nuanced contextual reading pioneered by the political historians of her alma mater. Nor is Ravelhofer the only scholar in recent years to attempt an understanding of the masque through its extratextual elements: she follows important studies of music, design, and dance—by Peter Walls, John Peacock, Skiles Howard, and others. Where Ravelhofer departs from her predecessors and charts new territory is in her assiduous attention to questions of practice and performance, in her wide European perspective (which both broadens our understanding and fills many gaps in the English record), and in her exemplary demonstration of the kind of integrated reading she advocates: a reading sensitive to the impact of the several arts involved in a masque, both individually and in combination, for particular audiences on discrete occasions. Her book is a contribution of the first importance to

NEW BOOKS ON THEATRE HISTORY

masque scholarship and a work of great interest to students of theater, dance, and performance history.

The Early Stuart Masque falls into three sections: the first two offer explorations of (respectively) dance and costume; the third brings their findings to bear on a small but diverse group of masques, both canonical and lesser-known, in a series of case studies.

The book's most substantial contribution lies in its investigation of dancing. Ravelhofer starts from the dispiriting observation that not a single choreography from a Stuart court masque has survived, and she sets about providing fresh foundations for the study of dancing in the masque. She does so by casting a critical eye over the untested assumptions on which most modern dance scholarship rests: assumptions about the existence of a pan-European tradition of choreography, for instance, or about the canonicity of works like the *Orchésographie* of Thoinot Arbeau. Having cleared the ground, she draws upon a wide range of evidence, archival and performance-based, to build a case for the sources and character of English masque dancing. Through research into the texts and lives of the continental dancing masters who visited England, Ravelhofer makes a good case for the influence of Italian but more notably French styles on English courtly dancing. Her recovery of the colorful plagiary Barthélemy de Montagut, who won entry to the Buckingham circle through his "Louange de la danse"—a work largely lifted from an early draft of François de Lauze's *Apologie*—is particularly satisfying; other important figures (Confesse, the Lapierres, and Bocan) remain tantalizingly in the shadows. Through a careful examination of surviving sources and contemporary accounts, shaped both by a historian's sense of context and a practitioner's sensibility, Ravelhofer offers conjectural reconstructions of the impact of dance in performance. Idealized oppositions between authoritarian masque and transgressive antimasque, between absolutist royal gaze and subservient courtiers, between active male and passive female dancers are broken down and complicated. By recalculating the height of the *chopines* worn by women dancers (these were *not,* as is widely assumed, the towering platforms favored by Venetian courtesans) and registering the difficulty of performing complex steps without looking at one's partner (i.e., while adopting the "female gaze" of post-Lacanian film scholarship), Ravelhofer demonstrates the existence of spaces for female agency within masque dancing. Axioms about the extreme absolutism of the masque—illegible to all but gazing monarchs—are critiqued by reference both to the actual disposition of dancers in front of the stage—clearly visible to spectators on three sides—and to the existence in choreographical manuals of dance formations designed to be seen from several angles. The rigidly hierarchical, antagonistic reading of the relationship between monarch and courtly dancer is refigured in terms of winking ironies and gestures of "sly submission." And the sheer pleasures of dancing—mastering complex, regulated movements and improvising freely around them—are properly stressed:

250   NEW BOOKS ON THEATER HISTORY

a timely counterweight to the obsession with discipline and coercion which marks much recent dance scholarship.

In her second section, Ravelhofer offers a parallel rethinking of the practical and theoretical implications of costuming in the masque—though the evidentiary base here is even less ample; not a single English masque costume survives. Drawing on extensive research in the libraries, art galleries, and museum collections of Europe she builds up responsible conjectures about the several processes of creation and dissemination of masque costumes, from production and payment—either privately or by way of government departments—through to storage and recycling. Such costumes were sometimes but not always paid for by their wearers, were probably not quite as expensive as contemporaries (for various reasons) wished to imply, and were almost certainly not—as we might suspect from the work of Peter Stallybrass and Rosalind Jones on clothing and the early modern theater—recycled in the public playhouses; rather, Ravelhofer suggests, many were reused, either as formal attire, or in other entertainments (including, perhaps, in *Comus* the costumes first worn by the Egerton boys in *Coelum Britannicum*). The last possibility raises tantalizing opportunities for visual echo and irony. With regard to the iconic effect of costume, Ravelhofer helps us to see how high shoes and high-cut tailoring constructed an idealized, elongated profile for the masquers, and she instructs us in the complex language of color symbolism. Ravelhofer follows recent gender studies in distinguishing carefully between male and female garb and registering restrictions on the latter, but she persuasively establishes the power—the "guarded brilliance"—of Henrietta Maria's costumes and performances. Her most important contribution, I think, derives from her taking more seriously than perhaps any previous student of the form the latter part of Inigo Jones's claim that a masque is "nothing but pictures with light and motion." A superb illustration of a rare survival—a French bodice and *tonnelet* of the seventeenth century (plate 3)—clinches the claim that masque costumes, spangled with mirrors, stones, pearls, and gilt and silver wire, were designed to function as "lighting machines," catching and reflecting the artificial lights of the hall as, glittering and shimmering, the masquers moved.

In the final part of her study, Ravelhofer offers a series of aptly chosen case studies. Her readings of *The Masque of Queenes* and *Oberon* argue for a Jonson more collaborative, more open to the opportunities of multimedia spectacle than the anti-theatrical curmudgeon with whom we are familiar. Her account of *Coelum Britannicum* shows how historical costume and dance style provided the sartorial and kinetic expression of an archaeology of Britishness to buttress the Stuart quest for unification of the kingdoms. Moving further afield, Ravelhofer painstakingly reconstructs the occasion and the complex cross-cultural significances of a little-known (and, as it turned out, unperformed) masque prepared by the Levant merchant Robert Bargrave for an ex-patriot nuptial at Constantinople in 1650.

NEW BOOKS ON THEATRE HISTORY

With its sharp illumination of costuming and choreography in the masque, its practitioner's sense of the workings and interactions of such media in performance, and its deft situating of such insights within a broad contextual framework, Ravelhofer's book represents an essential contribution to our understanding of the early Stuart masque. We can expect future work to register its impact through a new alertness to ways of inferring choreographical and costuming details from fragments of textual evidence, and a fresh sensitivity to their complementary interactions. And yet I nevertheless think it unlikely that Ravelhofer's book will effect a fundamental shift in scholarly approaches to the masque. Quite apart from the daunting range of skills required of anyone who would work in this vein, it seems doubtful whether there is enough evidence to support a sustained rereading of the canon in such terms. Unless hitherto unknown sketches, costumes, or choreographies come to light, it is hard to see how we might build significantly on the foundations laid in this assured and groundbreaking study.

Shakespeare in Parts, by Simon Palfrey and Tiffany Stern. Oxford: Oxford University Press, 2007. Pp. 545. Hardback $45.00.

Reviewer: MELISSA AARON

Shakespeare in Parts, which is focused on the "part" or separate written text for the individual actor, sets itself a very ambitious task: part theater history, part interpretation, part performance studies, and part "'how-to' guide" (12). It is slightly less monumental than the authors say they originally intended—"looking into the whole of early modern theatre" (10)—but even this modified goal may have been beyond the limits of one book.

There is much to admire here. While the authors do not say so, it is a logical extension of Dr. Stern's excellent *Rehearsal from Shakespeare to Sheridan* (2000). In particular, it assumes the thesis of the earlier book that most early modern plays had only one group rehearsal.

No theater historian could fail to be pleased at the suggestion that there is more than one early modern written part, and I certainly was hoping that there would be much as-yet-undiscovered material. It is slightly disappointing to find that in fact, while university parts, Restoration parts, and Continental parts may not have been adequately considered in previous work, there is still only one "part" from the professional early modern English stage, that of Orlando from *Orlando Furioso*. The "Shakespeare parts" under discussion, therefore, are reverse-engineered from existing Shakespeare texts. The reader must accept the premise that it is possible to use these "imaginatively reconstructed parts" to discover new information about the plays and how they were, and can be, performed.

Is this a worthwhile endeavor? I believe it is. Theater historians make this

252 NEW BOOKS ON THEATER HISTORY

sort of postulation all the time. The most obvious example, Henslowe's *Diary*, is used to argue issues of casting, economics, props, repertory, and scheduling in Shakespeare's company. It has been argued that the Lord Chamberlain's Men was run similarly to the Lord Admiral's Men; it has been argued that it was not. We simply do not have corresponding records from the Chamberlain's Men, but we begin from Henslowe's *Diary* because, bluntly, without it, there is little to say. The same is true of the "imaginatively reconstructed parts" here: Palfrey and Stern do not claim that they are more than very good educated guesses, and they often provide two or three alternative possibilities.

The book is divided into four sections: History, Interpreting Cues, Repeated Cues, and The Actor With His Part. The first and last sections are best: these are the ones placing the actor's "part" in its historical context and providing "case studies" of the actor's part in action. A few passages in particular are excellent for both the theater and the classroom. Pages 158–62 provide a set of interpretations of the Nurse's long speech in 1.3 of *R & J.* Palfrey and Stern suggest that "& say I," repeated three times by the Nurse, is the cue for both Lady Capulet and Juliet, provoking a babble of unsuccessful interruption from both. Page 318 begins a section on "pointing" (punctuation) and the actor's responsibility for providing it himself. Acting students encountering Shakespeare really must know this as a necessary rejoinder to studying the First Folio as a source for every breath and pause. The discussion on learning "passionate" parts and becoming "perfect" in gesture and cue as well as spoken lines is likewise good.

Much of the material on repeated cues (157–307), ironically, seems to be repetitive. In fact, there are times when the book seems long, especially when it rests on a speculation to begin with. The case studies that conclude the book are good, but is it truly necessary to have eight of them? Would not three or four examples have done just as well? Isn't one of the aims of the book to put these concepts into the hands of actors and scholars so they can use them?

The assumption of learning one's part in solitude and having only one rehearsal does not touch on the issue of dance, fighting, and stage violence. This is most obvious in the discussion on the staging of Gloucester's blinding (244–47). The book seems to presuppose an actor hearing the cuing for this scene for the first time, and yet not to have practiced the blinding scene as a group seems extremely dangerous, nor would it be possible to practice it separated from its lines, as the lines in each of the parts provide a cue for action. While the focus of the book is the individual actor's part, this does not seem to be adequately integrated with the other workings of the playhouse: cuing and being cued by music, costumes, large ensemble pieces, fighting, dancing, and props.

Still, these concerns do not diminish the overall excellence of the book.

NEW BOOKS ON THEATRE HISTORY 253

It provides a much-needed corrective to the habit of "reading" a Shakespeare text on paper in its totality all at once, possibly the way in which it is least authentically experienced.

Teaching with the Records of Early English Drama, edited by Elza C. Tiner. Toronto, Buffalo and London: University of Toronto Press, 2006. Pp. xxvii + 238. Cloth $75.00.

Reviewer: ROSLYN L. KNUTSON

At the University of Arkansas at Little Rock library, the REED volumes stand on their shelves in an unbroken phalanx of big red books. Some years ago, I xeroxed sample documents, all from York: the 1433 inventory of the "Judgment" from the Mercers' pageant documents, payments to professional players in 1593 and 1607, an entry from the town memorandum book in 1417 assigning sites around town for the wagons and scaffolds, and an entry in translation from the memorandum book in 1431–32 ratifying the transfer of the "Herod" play from the Goldsmiths to the Masons. I passed these out in my undergraduate class, English Renaissance Drama 4321, along with Sally-Beth MacLean's map of touring routes,[1] and talked for awhile about the REED project and its impact on theater history. I ran out of time, of course; and my comments had no appreciable effect on my students' understanding of medieval drama and the scholarly revolution precipitated by REED data. More recently, I have cut the handouts to the map and inventory, which I now accompany with a quasi-"translation," that is, an excerpt from the middle of the document in modern type with bracketed glosses for the most unfamiliar words. This reduction takes less time in class but yields no better results. Since I've been presenting this REED material, I know of only one student who has gone to the library on his own initiative to consult one of the volumes. But all this is about to change. Fortuitously, I will be teaching the everybody-but-Shakespeare course again at University of Arkansas at Little Rock in the spring of 2008, and I will redesign the opening two weeks to incorporate what I have learned from essays in *Teaching with the Records of Early English Drama,* edited by Elza C. Tiner. The only problem I have now is choosing among the wealth of superb ideas offered therein.

Teaching with the Records of Early English Drama contains thirteen essays that provide pedagogical advice for assignments in theater history, performance, dramatic and nondramatic literature, social history, and linguistics. The contributors address a variety of academic settings in departments in the humanities, including large sophomore-level lecture sections, enrollment-limited senior seminars, and graduate courses; the contributions also embrace the diversity of students in the spectrum of institutions represented by my own satellite campus in a land-grant university system to premier private uni-

254   NEW BOOKS ON THEATER HISTORY

versities in the United States, Canada, Australia, and the United Kingdom. There are appendixes to each essay with specific assignments. In addition, there is a reference section by Rosalind Conklin Hays meant to allay the anxiety of working with nonliterary records for those only vaguely familiar with civic, guild, ecclesiastical, and legal documents. Editor Tiner provides an introduction, bibliography, and index.

In section 1, "Vital Evidence: Theatre History," Alexandra F. Johnston offers an exercise on provincial audience members, and David Mills focuses on the city of Chester and its Whitsun plays. For her exercise, Johnston creates three people who represent Tudor provincial life in class, gender, and vocation. One portrait is based on the real-life John Bachiler, a mercer of York who actually was a pageant master for his guild in 1536 and 1537. She invents additional details such as his membership in the city council and connections in trade with the Low Countries. A second portrait is the wholly fictitious Robert Millington, a gentleman to whom Johnston gives a provenance of Eton in 1550 (when Nicholas Udall was headmaster), King's College Cambridge in 1554, and connections with various noble households and Elizabeth's court. The third is the also fictitious Jane White, to whom Johnston assigns an early life in Reading but a later move to Shrewsbury with her husband in 1538. This portrait enables Johnston to acquaint students with records of provincial dramatic activity other than the cycle plays including "biblical plays, Robin Hood activities, a king play, morris dancers, and a . . . complex Good Friday ritual" (7). By moving the Whites from Reading to Shropshire, Johnston enables students to notice the effect of the Reformation in the wake of the dissolution of the Benedictine Abbey, and the influence of noble patronage by way of the office of Lord President of the Marches. In contrast to this exploration across records from various counties and towns, Mills immerses students in the documents of Chester and its cycle of plays. He designs three complementary workshops: one on the town and government, another on the play texts and performance, and a third on issues of finance. In the process of describing the workshops, Mills refers to a publication by the Chester City Archives, the *Mystery Plays Study Pack,* which is apparently available for purchase by anyone. This reference illustrates an additional benefit of the REED lessons in that the contributors often mention pedagogical materials supplemental to the REED data.

In section 2, "Documents in Action: Performance Preparation," there are essays by Mary A. Blackstone, Margaret Rogerson and Betsy Taylor, and Stephen F. Page. Blackstone offers different assignments designed to accommodate a large undergraduate introductory course in theater as well as courses for upperclassmen in the theater major. One example is a set of lessons focusing on the Marian period. The project includes study of the 1556 Norwich Major's Pageant, the play of *Respublica,* and details of martyrs such as John Careles, "who was temporarily released from jall [in Coventry] so that he

NEW BOOKS ON THEATRE HISTORY

could play in the city's pageant" (43). Rogerson and Taylor assume the task of "teaching without texts," focusing instead on source material. For two-hour guest appearances in a large survey course in the department of Performance Studies (with a one-hour break-out tutorial), they created an anthology of documents from various REED volumes organized into the following categories: "acting styles," "civic involvement," "costume design and materials," "financing of plays and other performance events," "lighting," "liturgical performance," "music," "performance spaces," "professional and amateur players," "scenery," and "secular dramatic activities." In the third year of their guest appearance with REED material, Rogerson and Taylor assessed their project and decided to devote the first of their two hours to "a performance in tandem of reading, explaining, and contextualizing" selections from their anthology in order to prepare students more successfully for the subsequent small-group tutorials (63). This decision reflects a common denominator in the REED assignments, which is a recognition that students benefit from being led into the REED materials by exercises that model an application of the data. Stephen Page describes an assignment for M.A. students that shares with other contributors a candid assessment of a classroom experiment, with plans for revision. Page assigned each of his eight students one of the REED volumes for a report to the class, saving the *Chester* volume to coincide with the class performance of the Chester "Coming of Antichrist." He found that the students relied too heavily on the introductory material in their volumes, weren't quick to make comparisons with each others' volumes, and generally "did not come to 'own' their assigned volumes" as he had wished (73). So, next time around, Page intends to study the *Chester* volume with the class first, as preparation for students' tackling a volume on their own. In this way, he can provide the three key pedagogical ingredients of successful REED assignments: demonstration, demonstration, demonstration.

In sections 3 and 4, "Critical Illumination: English Literature" and "Dramatic Activity: Social History," the contributors apply the REED records to literary and cultural issues. Anne Brannen uses records from her forthcoming *Cambridgeshire* volume to interrogate the proposition, "what is dramatic activity?" One of her examples is of a man being punished for having taken his penance in jest; another concerns villagers who cart a man "around on a pole, to the accompaniment of music and the throwing of grain" (88); the third recounts a story of some drunks who terrorize a recent widower by howling like ghosts outside his house. Following up this analytical exercise at exam time, Brannen uses a record of a clergyman who invited his congregation to the church to see a play, which turned out to be the priest himself, prancing about buck naked in order to disprove the rumor that he had the French pox. Gloria Betcher applies the *Devon* volume to Robert Herrick's *Hesperides* to interrogate the interplay of autobiography and poetic invention in the poems inspired by Dean Prior. Rosalind Conklin Hays applies REED records to his-

256   NEW BOOKS ON THEATER HISTORY

torical issues such as the effect of England's break with Rome on dramatic activity at one Devon church; she uses incidents of disorderly conduct such as a man who paraded around a dog he had gotten drunk and dressed in a priest's black coat (with a tobacco pipe stuck in its jaws). Barbara D. Palmer tackles the issue of gender studies. She suggests assignments that address categories such as "wife," "widow," "performer," "patron," "adultery," and "bequest" as they pertain to women. In addition, she offers examples of individual women—Bess of Hardwick and Elizabeth, Lady Lowther—for whom "household and pantry accounts, letters, memoranda, receipts, [and] journals" provide a "documentation of domestic matters" (142). Thinking of the Shakespeare class, Palmer recommends the REED records as deep background on topics such as country festivals (*The Winter's Tale*) and household stewards (*Twelfth Night*). James Stokes teaches students to read secretary hand. In perhaps the most challenging and time-consuming yet rewarding use of REED records in the classroom, he offers exercises in paleography that he modestly designates "guided collective tutorials" (155). The students work with a combination of photocopies of documents, resources on local history and handwriting, and the professor's expertise. Stokes takes them through a document with escalating difficulties in letter recognition and the eccentricities of abbreviations. He points out that, in the process, students "re-[enter] the mysterious landscape of what it is to learn to read" (156). Because his illustrative document is a court case that orders the punishment of a couple who conceived a child in an intimate moment on their walk home from a local dance, Stokes extends the lesson in reading to one of context and application: he has students investigate the bias of the judges as well as consider Shakespearean justice in (for example) *Measure for Measure*.

In section 5, "Entertaining Records: Language History," Abigail Ann Young and Elza C. Tiner address the nine-hundred-pound gorilla of using REED documents: language. Young's suggestions are most applicable for those who want data for Anglo-Latin; Tiner's focus is primarily on REED records as examples of early modern English for courses in History of the English Language. Both contributors provide ideas for linguistics generally. As Young points out, the REED records provide instances of Latin from the "international, consciously classical (or at least patristic) literary language of the Middle Ages" to documents in "barely Latinized English" (170). Tiner cites instances of now non-standard forms such as singular verbs for plural subjects ("men . . . selles" [176]), the "be" of continuous or habitual action ("they be" [177]), and instances of regional dialect. She makes a compelling point about language usage in the REED volumes that speaks to the issue of primary texts, namely, that the civic documents—unlike literary manuscripts—are "less likely to have been contaminated by . . . editing or corrections to the original language to fit the scribe's linguistic preferences" (180).

My feeble attempt to bring REED material into the classroom and thereby to impress on students the tectonic shift in the study of drama and early modern life effected by the publication of these records looks even more inadequate to me now that I have reviewed the lessons offered in *Teaching with the Records of Early English Drama.* With the exception of those contributors who have access to unpublished repositories (i.e., Johnston with the Berkshire collection; Brannen with Cambridgeshire; Palmer with Derbyshire and West Riding), I can duplicate any of these exercises. Each essay in this anthology gives advice that will keep me from repeating my mistakes. My new assignment will go something like this:

- I will divide the class into groups and set aside sufficient class time—at least three class periods—to enable the students to concentrate on their assignments (my students have to do all group work in class; no one has any time outside to get together)
- Each group will have the text of the York "Judgment" play as its central focus
- Each group will have the same set of REED documents, including the York Mercers' Inventory; the *Coventry* Drapers' Accounts for 1565 for scenery; the *Coventry* Drapers Accounts of 1567 and 1572 for fabrics; records of pageant wagons (*York,* Mercers' Chartulary, 1501; *Chester,* Cordwainers and Shoemakers' records, 1549); some items pertaining to expenses; and a map of York and/or Chester
- But each group will focus on different combinations of these
- I will ask for in-class presentations that have some visual component
- As follow-up, I will ask the students to choose another cycle play such as the Chester "Noah's Flood," one of the "Herod" plays, and the York "Crucifixion" and to explain how the reading of that text is enhanced by the study of the REED data
- Or, maybe I'll have them put on the "Judgment" play

I have learned from the contributors in this anthology to model the activity of reading REED with my students before I set the groups in action, to provide modern-spelling versions of the documents along with the "original" in the REED volumes, and to gloss the unusual words (as well as to encourage use of the *OED* and *MED*). Though I cannot, as David Mills at the University of Liverpool can, ask the class members to walk the procession route of the medieval pageant wagons in Chester, I am much better prepared now to break that phalanx of dust-covered volumes in the University of Arkansas at Little Rock library into user-friendly resources and thus acquaint my students with the pleasures of archival research.

Note

1. Sally-Beth MacLean, "Players on Tour: New Evidence from Records of Early English Drama," in *Elizabethan Theatre X,* ed. C. E. McGee (P. D. Meany, 1988), 66.

Reviews

Reading the Jewish Woman on the Elizabethan Stage, by Michelle Ephraim. Aldershot: Ashgate Press, 2008. Pp. xi + 179. Cloth, $99.95.

Reviewer: MATTHEW BIBERMAN

In 1996, James Shapiro wrote that literary critics of the English Renaissance had "rediscovered virtually every marginalized Other that passed through early modern England—including witches, hermaphrodites, Moors, cross dressers, Turks, sodomites, criminals, prophets, Eskimos, and vagabonds" while continuing to "have steered carefully around the Other of Others in the Renaissance, the Jews."[1] Shapiro made the observation in his own effort to address this void—the groundbreaking study, *Shakespeare and the Jews.* Since then, scholars in increasing numbers have responded to Shapiro's challenge. The resulting body of work now includes Douglas Brooks's essay collection *Milton and the Jews* (2008), Lisa Lampert's *Gender and Jewish Difference from Paul to Shakespeare* (2004) as well as my own monograph, *Anti-Semitism, Masculinity and Early Modern English Literature* (2004). Now I am happy to welcome a voice new to me—that of Michelle Ephraim.

In *Reading the Jewish Woman on the Elizabethan Stage,* Ephraim examines a range of literary texts with the aim of proving two broad claims. First, Ephraim asserts that for the English, the figure of the Jewish or Hebrew woman functioned as "not only a racial but a textual problem of assimilation" (9). Here it helps to quote her at some length: "it is the Jewish woman-as-scripture who, through her various bodily identities as mother, virgin, and erotic object of desire, symbolically promises and eludes comprehension, barring the reader desired contents. Drawing upon the inherent theatricality and artifice of stagecraft, Renaissance dramatists emphasize the slippage between text and meaning, generating interpretive 'play' that encourages us to read their work as a type of *midrash* that demonstrates the heteroglossia of language rather than its coherence" (17–18). This claim reflects Ephraim's sensitivity to the so-called linguistic turn in the profession. All the requisite language is present (play, heteroglossia), as well as the use of antithetical verbs (promises and eludes). The style, in short, signals Ephraim's mastery of current critical practice, and that approach will, no doubt, help to make her argument persuasive among other active scholars. Indeed, if anything, this claim could be said to suffer from being too obviously correct. In the wake of Derrida, DeMan, and Bakhtin, what textual figure cannot be isolated and pronounced a contested site of "interpretative instability" (9)? Perhaps it is because of this potential weakness that Ephraim offers her second claim. "It is my contention," she writes, "that the archetype of the sacrificed daughter in Marlowe and Shakespeare, for a late sixteenth-century audience, would have been imagistically associated with [Queen] Elizabeth, the perennial daughter" (19). The introduction of this second topical claim effectively limits and so grounds Ephraim's first mode of argument in a provocative way

262 REVIEWS

that resists the book's drift toward repeating what are by now long accepted critical truisms regarding the plasticity of systems of representation.

After introducing her two lines of thought, Ephraim proceeds to test out her ideas in the book's six chapters and epilogue. The choice of texts in itself represents novel scholarship. The first four chapters tackle in succession *The Godly Queene Hester,* the academic interlude *Jacob and Esau,* Thomas Garter's *Susanna,* George Peele's *David and Fair Bethsabe,* and George Buchanan's *Jepthes Sive Votum Tragoedia.* Only in her final two chapters does Ephraim turn her attention to the far more familiar ground of Marlowe and Shakespeare. This progression makes for rewarding reading for both the scholar and general reader.

Indeed, I found Ephraim most interesting when she strayed beyond her stated goals, a development that happens early. The initial chapter on *The Godly Queene Hester* provides all the ground Ephraim really needs to prove the validity of her two main claims. I came away fully convinced that Hester and Elizabeth are bound up in meaning and that "the queen's body, by way of the Jewish woman's, enacts the Protestants' claim to interpretative mastery" (29). With that need dispatched, Ephraim is now free to roam across texts, and this she does, tossing off a string of striking insights. In chapter 2, she observes that "Rebecca" and other Hebrew matriarchs are imaginative renderings of Jewish mothers who are not presented as "unnatural." These figures are not lactating men who also bleed but instead are "the most 'natural' and pure origin of the English self" (53). The larger critical conversation now going on in the profession would benefit from dwelling further on such positive representations. The subsequent chapter's discussion of Bethsabe centers on the equally innovative recognition that as the visual object of desire, the Jewish woman's body disrupts "Christian typology" (88). Ephraim's exploration of her subject is at its richest in her discussion of Jepthes's daughter (chapter 4). She is certainly right that critics of Shakespeare's Jessica and Marlowe's Abigail need to rehearse typological readings that link these Jewish women to that biblical figure with far more care.

The book's final two chapters tie up Ephraim's study artfully by staking out readings of *The Merchant of Venice* and *The Jew of Malta.* Here she persuasively argues that both Jewish daughters "represent the Jewish father's fantasy of concealment and the Christian suitor's wish for penetration" (120). Though by the book's end Queen Elizabeth has retreated somewhat from view, Ephraim's dual claims have been amply demonstrated. Such success made it easy for me to envision how subsequent work might proceed. First, I would contend that greater differentiation ought to be made between the figure of the Hebrew woman and the Jewish woman. (The pagan woman, most especially the sacred prostitute, also deserves real attention as well.) Such an expanded model would enable us to understand better how the economy of desire functions both in early modern England and in our own world

REVIEWS

today. Also, I think the broader discussion would benefit from a re-examination of the general tenets of abjection theory. For what is overdetermined in Ephraim's reading (and seldom if ever remarked upon) is the assumed linkage between abjection and the feminine. In *Empire Burlesque: The Fate of Critical Culture in Global America* (2003), Daniel T. O'Hara writes of male abjection, and I believe that this concept might be of some use to those of us who enjoy talking about Shakespeare and his contemporaries. What I am certain of, however, is that any scholar of early modern English drama would benefit from reading Michelle Ephraim's richly informative study.

Notes

1. James Shapiro, *Shakespeare and the Jews* (New York: Columbia University Press, 1996), 86.

Textual Patronage in English Drama, 1570–1640, by David M. Bergeron. Aldershot, England and Burlington, Vermont: Ashgate Press, 2006. Pp. vii + 247. Cloth $110.00.

Reviewer: ALISON V. SCOT

David M. Bergeron's book provides Renaissance scholars with a long awaited and valuable assessment of prefatory materials to Renaissance dramatic texts, and a unique account of their role in the processes of defining the early modern author and his craft. Comprised of a series of essays which map out the varied ways in which prefaces to printed drama might be appropriated and directed, and punctuated by reproductions of some of the key dedicatory epistles and addresses to readers which it discusses, this book makes a significant contribution to the understanding of Renaissance print culture. Furthermore, in its contextualizing of contemporary "struggles about authorship" in terms of the texts' interchange with both aristocratic patrons and an emerging market of readers (18), it provides an important reassessment of the influences at work in the development of the "author" in Renaissance literary culture. Drawing on recent scholarship (most notably that of Douglas Brooks and Joseph Loewenstein) that has suggested the coexistence of patronage and market economies and their mutual and even interactive influence on playwrights and the production of printed drama in this period, Bergeron persuasively argues that prefatory materials transmitted the discourses and values of aristocratic patronage into an emerging marketplace of print in which the reader now functioned as *another* patron.[1]

Contesting what he calls a "seductive narrative of linear development in which readers replace aristocratic patrons," Bergeron thus "offer[s] a com-

264   REVIEWS

peting, displacing narrative with a more complicated plot," one in which emerging commerce and existing aristocratic patronage "intertwine, mix, and mingle" (14). Adopting Gérard Genette's term "paratexts," the book advances its "displacing narrative" via an analysis of paratextual materials which, Bergeron claims, function variously as "frames" and/or "portals" for the dramatic text and yet—somewhat paradoxically—also as "containers" of the authorial voice. It is unsurprising then to find that Ben Jonson occupies a central position in this book. Drawing on several studies that have presented Jonson as a self-conscious "author" (Helgerson, Brooks, Loewenstein) Bergeron explains that he "explored and exploited the system of textual patronage probably better than any other dramatist of the Tudor-Stuart period" (119).[2] In fact, the chapter on Jonson is a highlight, offering a dense and entertaining discussion, expertly situated in terms of recent Jonson scholarship, of Jonson's construction of an idealized reader. Though its conclusions—like several other chapters here—finally fail to offer anything startlingly new, the chapter nevertheless adeptly enhances our understanding of Jonson's self-presentation and political use of genre. In dedicating *The New Inn* to a patron-reader, Jonson is seen to enact a radical shift toward embracing "the full measure of textual patronage, which includes book-buyers and readers." The move obviously has implications for "the interpretative definition of the text" which, as W. H. Herendeen notes, is begun by a text's prefatory material, and it expands on Loewenstein's theory of possessive authorship to suggest another way in which Jonson's idealized reader and his self-constructed literary persona interact with and depend upon one another.[3]

Jonson is often mobilized by scholars contesting J. W. Saunders's influential thesis of a "stigma of print," but Bergeron's attention to a rich array of dramatic paratexts and the ways in which such material functioned to define authors at once in relation to patron, audience, and reader also enables an important reassessment of writers previously considered marginal to the construction of the modern author. There is a chapter here on Thomas Heywood's textual patronage which examines Heywood's "struggle to position himself as a writer associated with the theatre" (159), and another which considers Marston's "disingenuous stance of lack of agency" in relation to publication in his address to readers which prefaces *The Fawn*. In a further chapter on printed masques and pageants, moreover, Bergeron explores the role of paratexts in constructing a gap between fixed text and ephemeral performance which allowed the dramatist to remake the drama and to redirect its appeal for support.

To my mind, this book is most rewarding when it is focused on the writer's appeal for textual patronage, because when it turns to consider the other agencies involved in the process, certain problems and indeterminacies of Bergeron's definition of textual patronage come into focus. The discussion of prefatory addresses penned by printers in the first chapter, for instance,

REVIEWS   265

suggests that "textual patronage"—apparently constituted and articulated by the prefatory materials which contain the authorial voice—is ultimately shaped and directed by printers and publishers. Likewise, in the discussion of Shakespeare's first Folio, we learn that Heminges and Condell utilize the Folio's bifurcated paratexts (addressed to both patrons and readers) in order to seek the literary canonization of "Shakespeare" through textual patronage. While both chapters are important in the sense that they demonstrate the complex and varied systems at play in the production, reception, and commodification of drama in this period, the term "textual patronage" is unhelpfully encompassing—in fact, it is used to refer to the prefatory materials themselves, and the process through which the various writers of such material appealed to patrons and readers for protection and support.

By formulating paratexts as containers of "authorial soliloquies" which push "private thoughts" onto a public stage (16), Bergeron limits and even contradicts his argument that "[t]extual patronage . . . includes printers and publishers who intrude into dramatic texts and embrace the genre of paratexts" (23). Presumably, he means to imply that writers of prefatory materials such as Heminges and Condell—who are credited with giving "new vitality to textual patronage" (154)—sustain a version of "the 'author's' voice" in order to enable "textual patronage" for the author's work (16). Certainly, that is what his juxtaposition of the first Folio's perpetuation of "Shakespeare's remains" with Jonson's 1616 Folio's promulgation of a self-constructed authorial voice into the public domain suggests (154). Nevertheless, it is quite clear here that the notion of dramatic paratexts as "authorial soliloquies" is an inadequate way of describing the politically layered processes involved in courting a diverse body of potential readers to bolster the perceived value of a given text (16). Unfortunately, that contradiction tends to detract from the book's innovative examination of the "self-justification and self-advertising" implicit in printers' paratexts (25). And, in a similar way, the book's demonstration of an important diversification in the sources of support and in the processes involved in seeking support that writers might mobilize, and its intelligent assertion that "[a]ddresses to readers and dedicatory epistles signal an active component of the economic marketplace" (46) is destabilized by the insistence that "in the long run [paratexts have] little to do with money but much to do with status and protection" (15).

In summary, this book brings the paratexts of Renaissance printed drama to bear on interrelated questions pertaining to the decline of aristocratic patronage as an influence on literary production and to the emergence of the professional author in the marketplace of print. Although it struggles at times to adequately define the idea of "textual patronage" and to explicate its relation to the conflicting economic systems which it appears to conflate, it remains a rich and valuable study. Indeed, Bergeron's book ambitiously forges new ground in the field of Renaissance print culture by scrutinizing prefatory

266 REVIEWS

materials in the kind of substantial and necessary way that no other study has attempted before. In that sense, it lays the foundations for future investigation, illuminating the undeniable complexities of the playwright's transition from stage to text, and from a market of patronage to a marketplace of print.

Notes

1. Douglas A. Brooks, *From Playhouse to Printing House: Drama and Authorship in Early Modern England* (Cambridge: Cambridge University Press, 2000); Joseph Loewenstein, *Ben Jonson and Possessive Authorship* (Cambridge: Cambridge University Press, 2002).

2. Richard Helgerson, *Spenser, Jonson, Milton and the Literary System* (Berkeley: University of California Press, 1983).

3. "A New Way to Pay Old Debts: Pretexts to the 1616 Folio," *Ben Jonson's 1616 Folio,* ed. Jennifer Brady and W. H. Herendeen (Newark: University of Delaware Press, 1991), 38–63; cited from 41.

Love and Conflict in Medieval Drama: The Plays and Their Legacy, by Lynette R. Muir. Cambridge: Cambridge University Press, 2007. Pp. xv + 294. Cloth $96.00.

Reviewer: CHET SCOVILLE

Like Lynette Muir's *Biblical Drama of Medieval Europe* (Cambridge, 1995), to which this book is a "companion volume" (1), *Love and Conflict in Medieval Drama* is a large-scale survey of hundreds of dramatic texts from Europe. For the most part, this book eschews biblical plays, polemical plays, and morality plays—that is, those plays that are often the main focus of early drama studies— leaving "a very substantial body of serious medieval plays on love and war" (1). Following Muir, the reader becomes aware of both the vast amount of material that is left to study off of the beaten path, and of Muir's own vast learning in that material.

Muir divides these hundreds of plays into subject categories, including saint plays, conversion plays, sacrament plays, plays about Troy, and about falsely accused queens. In each of the book's twenty-four chapters, she provides a summation of the characteristics of each subject and a comparison of the way in which the plays treat that subject. It is difficult to imagine a more comprehensive subject treatment of this material in book form than that which Muir provides.

However, this study does have some problems, the most significant of which derives from the vastness of the material itself. Muir, as noted, covers hundreds of plays from the twelfth through sixteenth centuries, from France, England, Italy, Germany, and elsewhere. Given that enormous scope, Muir rarely is afforded the space to construct sustained arguments or analyses; often, the coverage of the plays consists of little more than plot summary. Furthermore, Muir's categorizing of plays by subject matter leads to some curious moments. For example, chapter 11, "Domestic Dramas," is only a page and a half long; in that brief chapter, Muir deals with no fewer than nine plays, saying little more about any of them than the main plot points. There is little room for consideration of each play's local context or performance history, or for sustained analysis of the developments of each of the subjects Muir studies. Indeed, there is often little indication of *why* the plays ought to be categorized by subject in this manner.

Elsewhere, in chapter 20, "Christianity Goes West," Muir deals with the dramatizations of the crucial period in which Christianity spread from Rome into Western Europe; she begins with *Le Miracle de Clovis.* Yet, again, her analysis of this play consists almost entirely of plot summary: "Much diplomatic activity between Clovis and Gondebaut succeeds eventually in regaining the treasure which he had stolen from Clotilde's parents. Clotilde has another son and has him christened also. Clovis is angry that the child seems to be a weakling and again blames the baptism" (165). Missing from the analysis is the question of why the play depicts such a conflict, and what point it is making about the Christianization of the land of its origin.

This is not to say that *Love and Conflict* is not deeply learned, nor that it is without value; as an introduction to a huge mass of material, it is certainly impressive, and undoubtedly will be of use both for scholars and for students; its index, notes, and bibliography will allow readers to navigate to specific plays quickly, and gain familiarity with those plays' high points easily. Yet, one cannot help but wonder whether this sort of undertaking might, today, be more usefully made into a searchable electronic index of plays. A relatively short book such as this seems a highly constricted format for such a wealth of information, especially when other options are available.

Sacred Players: The Politics of Response in the Middle English Religious Drama, by Heather Hill-Vásquez. Washington, D.C.: Catholic University of America Press, 2007. Pp. vii + 229. Cloth $59.95.

Reviewer: ANDREA R. HARBIN

Heather Hill-Vásquez in *Sacred Players* examines medieval drama in its most vulnerable period, early Protestant England, suggesting we should see it as "an important second life for the religious drama in England" rather than as a time of decline (3). In focusing on the period of decline, and as she argues, change, Hill-Vásquez raises questions about the power and use of the

268   REVIEWS

drama that are a welcome contribution to the field. She argues persuasively that these late plays survived in part because they could be effectively reworked to reflect Protestant rather than Catholic concerns, and indeed that they could be used as condemnation of the earlier religion. Like David Mills (1998) and Paul Whitfield White (1993), she examines how these plays might be recycled to adapt to changing societal needs. She builds on this scholarship by theorizing that the reformation of the Catholic drama relied not only on an emendation of the text but also on a shifting audience response. These plays thus "taught" the audience how good Christians should read the play and demanded they take an active role in constructing the play's meaning.

The work has been subdivided into three sections, all of which draw on Jauss's *Rezeptionsästhetik* as their theoretical basis: "Part I: Reforming Response: Protestant Adaptations," "Part II: Sanctifying Response: The Church and the 'Real Presence,'" and "Part III: Gendering Response: Christ's Body and God's Word." In these later chapters she also draws on New Historicist and gender theories to a lesser extent, though these theoretical premises are not always clearly delineated.

The political argument in part 1 is the most complete and persuasive of her theories. In chapter 1, Hill-Vásquez examines the Chester Whitsunday play and in it sees a change in the audience role from the Catholic participatory experience in Christian history to the more intellectual Protestant view of biblical history. Where the play draws the audience into the action, she sees remnants of the pre-Reformation play. In contrast, the *Expositor,* a character she argues is likely a late addition, places the action in the past and explains the "true meaning" of the past to the audience, at times "correcting" the more Catholic elements of the play. This perhaps sets up a New Historicist argument as well that Hill-Vásquez does not yet fully explore.

In chapter 2, *"The Conversion of St. Paul,"* Hill-Vásquez argues that the subject matter of this play made it more easily adaptable to Protestant theology and thus saved it where other saints' plays were suppressed. She states that, like the *Expositor* in the Chester play, the Poeta in *The Conversion of St. Paul* consistently reminds the audience of the importance of Scripture, privileging it over the more participatory nature of the play itself. Hill-Vásquez's argument here is intriguing, yet the play itself does seem to embrace much of the view of Catholicism as well. The audience is clearly drawn into the play in a way that blurs the boundaries of past and present, making them part of Christian history and contemporaneous witnesses to Paul's conversion. The exhortations of the Poeta to the learned men that the procession continue "under the correccyon of them that letteryd be" (line 355) would be more persuasive as a Protestant interpolation if it did not follow the more general "under *your* correccyon" (line 8; my emphasis).

In part 2, Hill-Vásquez examines how even in the medieval Catholic drama plays could be used to mold audience response into its "proper" form, cor-

REVIEWS

269

recting and criticizing the behavior of established authority. This analysis thus furthers her argument about the power of drama to shape belief, yet it does not substantively contribute to her larger argument about Protestant reform. Her third chapter explores the question of who should have access to the sacred, examining *The Tretise of Miraclis Pleyinge* and the Croxton *Play of the Sacrament*. She argues that while the *Tretise* cautions against religious drama because it inappropriately merges the sacred and the mundane, the Croxton play demonstrates both the danger in inappropriate handling of the divine and the audience's ability to correct that misuse through proper behavior.

Hill-Vásquez turns to a New Historicist argument in chapter 4, asserting that the York Corpus Christi plays emphasize the connection between human and divine labor; at the same time they question the sanctity of the mercantile class, condemning work that is not creative. She argues that this may be a response to the control that the ruling elite had over the Corpus Christi plays, and their use of the plays, and the fines levied in their benefit, to control the crafts. This argument assumes that the support of the plays was primarily involuntary, and supposes an essentially oppositional relationship between the merchant and craft trades.

In the third part, Hill-Vásquez returns to the question of Protestant versus Catholic response in drama, examining gender roles in medieval and Protestant examples. Her fifth chapter investigates the role of gender in the Digby *Candlemass Day and the Killing of the Children*. She asserts that gender roles become fluid in these plays and this echoes the fluidity of temporal and sacred bounds that we see elsewhere in medieval drama. Her last chapter once again returns to the question of post-Reformation medieval drama. Where the fluid gender roles of the "Catholic" play encouraged the crossing of gender boundaries in order to attain a complete religious experience, in Lewis Wager's Protestant play *The Life and Repentance of Mary Magdalene,* the feminine becomes a sign of the "old" religion and thus a point of "contention, critique, and religious condemnation" (169). Her return to the question of Catholic versus Protestant response in chapter 6 is a welcome reminder of the overall argument about the revision of medieval drama, a thread that gets lost a bit in her exploration of Catholic drama in part 2.

The questions raised by Hill-Vásquez in *Sacred Players* about the role of late medieval drama in a new Protestant society are good ones, and she supports her analysis well with careful close reading of the texts. While the focus moves away at times from what I see as the central argument of the text—the transformation of Catholic to Protestant drama—and per force relies at times on assumptions about audience response, it is, nevertheless, both well researched and clearly written. More important, it asks us to consider late medieval drama as both reflective of societal change and as a means of effecting that change.

270

REVIEWS

The Third Citizen: Shakespeare's Theater and the Early Modern House of Commons, by Oliver Arnold. Baltimore: Johns Hopkins University Press, 2007. Pp. xii + 308 pp. Cloth $55.00.

Reviewer: CHRIS FITTER

Like obsessive paparazzi squinting down narrow lenses for sightings of the blue-blooded and super-rich, the New Historicists have long been fixated on early modern court and monarchy to the exclusion of lesser actors, such as the Houses of Parliament. Stephen Greenblatt and his followers, Oliver Arnold rightly chides in *The Third Citizen,* have "discovered the crackle of art and psychic complexity in Elizabeth's speeches and James' many writings, but [the] ocean of parliamentary discourse remains unexplored" (26). The House of Commons, having gained a permanent meeting place in 1549 in St. Stephen's Chapel, was in Elizabeth's reign increasingly sought by the public as an authority for redress (65); and partly in consequence it was battling—*pace* the denials of the revisionists—for greater power relative to the House of Lords and the crown. Its weapon of choice was the rhetoric of truly national representativeness. "[Her] Majesty and the Nobles being every one a great person, represented but themselves," argued Edward Coke: "but [the] Commons though they were but inferior men, yet every one of them represented a thousand of men." Disconcertingly, Arnold gives both 1593 and 1601 as the date of these words from Coke (15 and 85), but he adduces several similar quotations from the Elizabethan and early Jacobean periods. In William Shakespeare's lifetime, ten parliamentary elections took place, in a number of which both he and his father were eligible to vote; and the excitements of an election, however rigged by local power brokers, supplied the "astoundingly anomalous spectacle . . . of the high submitting themselves to the low (landlords to tenants, dukes to the cobblers who made their shoes, mayors to tradesmen)" (24). Mustering large crowds like fairs or riots, flowing with ale laid on by the candidates, and climaxing in an uproar of voices clamoring assent or repudiation, such memorable occasions, Arnold suggests, smacked both of theater and carnival.

One trouble, however, with the claim that, in the words of one Elizabethan M.P., "I speake for all England, yea, and for the noble English nation" (88), was that the Commons kept its deliberations aggressively secret, and punished any member of the public who managed to infiltrate the chamber, even using its gatehouse as a jail (67). "The Elizabethan and Jacobean Commons never authorized a formal or even informal canvassing of public opinion," seeking actually "to inhibit the development of an informed, effective political public" (62). Further contradicting the ideology of universal representation were the narrowly restrictive demographic of the Commons (just 450 or so members, almost exclusively from the propertied classes), and the consequently self-interested nature of its legislation. Arnold quotes valuably from skeptical contemporaries, such as the reformer Henry Brinklow who complained in 1542 that it was unlikely the Commons would aid the poor, since in elections, the people have none to vote for "but such as be rych" (35). M.P. Arthur Hall lamented in a publication of 1576 that many members were "hirelings," "corrupted with brybes of the great ones" (111). Were the jubilant carnivals of popular election, then, mere ideological ruse? These, the extraordinarily interesting, neglected, and important historical coordinates within which Arnold examines Shakespeare's dramaturgic analysis of popular political representation, promise a pioneering study, perhaps of landmark magnitude.

Such possibilities unfortunately leave one the more disappointed with *The Third Citizen,* for its readings confer stylistic sophistication upon the polemical effacement of nuance and complexity. Arnold's foundational contention is that the institution of popularly elected representative assembly was, and remains today, a catastrophe for ordinary people, duping them into consent through the illusion of freedom while alienating them from their own agency. "Political representation per se disempowers the people" he insists repeatedly, since representatives always usurp the popular voice and displace the masses (191). Enfranchisement merely mystifies power: "the voice of the people is always, in the culture of representational politics, a fiction, a fabrication" (156). In a book riddled with half-truths, this claim typically absolutizes what is historically contingent; but its "representation-as-containment" thesis is clearly a variant on the seminal Foucauldian/Greenblattian model of political containment operating through the appearance of subversion. The poverty of its historicism is clearest in Arnold's contradiction of facts resisting his reductivism. He conveniently ignores the record of limited paternalist legislation (there was some); and, tilting at Annabel Patterson's *Shakespeare and the Popular Voice* (1989), Arnold lays down that "The people of England were not 'in desperate need of representation': they had it already in the House of Commons . . . a wider franchise [only] swells the legions of the deluded" (11–12, 189). Had Arnold read, for example, Tim Harris's *The Politics of the Excluded* (2001), he would have learned that England had been for centuries an "unacknowledged republic" of parochial self-governance, and that late Tudor England was in fact riven by desperate electoral struggles in town and village as local oligarchies sought to disenfranchise the wider community—whose poorer members then became subject to repressive policing and intimidation, and found their traditional revels and pastimes criminalized as disorder. Arnold's gloomy predestinarian ontology misses the fact that the franchise was thus a consequential, hot-button issue throughout Shakespeare's life, if more so at local than at parliamentary level.

Though he damns all parliamentary process as treacherous placebo, Arnold nowhere suggests an alternative (Anarcho-Syndicalism? Menshevism?), nor can his simplification account for the benefits that have historically accrued

272   REVIEWS

within (pressured and infiltrated) bourgeois parliamentary rule since Shakespeare's time: freedom of speech, assembly, and worship, abolition of slavery, female enfranchisement, and the welfare state. Arnold's literary criticism is predictably Procrustean: "Shakespeare *invariably* represents the relation between representative and represented as hierarchical and antagonistic" (13). Thus the tribunes in *Julius Caesar* and *Coriolanus* are purely selfish and bamboozling and countermand the popular will. (But if Marius and Flavius seek only their personal interests, why do they so dangerously oppose Caesar at the zenith of his popularity? And are not the tribunes in both plays correct in their identification of authoritarian threat? And does not the fickleness of the Roman plebeians require countermanding?) Election of tribunes in *Coriolanus* is dismissed as "empty ritual" (192), yet Arnold later admits "The plebeians, to be sure, get some corn 'gratis', and help to banish Coriolanus from Rome" (199). Salisbury, representing the people's views in *2 Henry VI,* is labeled "self-serving and contemptuous of the people he represents"; but as Arnold can find no evidence here, he indicts Warwick instead, implying we should lump the two together (93–94). Titus Andronicus "seeks power even as he refuses the 'palliament of white and spotless hue,'" scheming for influence as a kingmaker (112): thus "political representatives and emperors . . . are doubles rather than opposites" (118). (But if Titus sought personal power, why did he turn down the emperorship offered him?) "Brutus' ventriloquizing of Rome is an act of bad faith" (155), commencing "a populist justification for the assassination of Caesar at the same instant he fears the people have willingly acclaimed Caesar their king" (148).

Observing, however, that the Elizabethan theater functioned in its applause or booing as a kind of democracy, Arnold identifies two positive political moments in Shakespeare, both theatrical, when a leader is entirely "wholly the people's creature" (151), commanded by their unmediated voice, just as an actor is dependent on his audience. (The latter, of course, is another half-truth.) The first is Jack Cade's exemplary "politics of total presence," wherein Cade "effaces any mediation between himself and the people." Cade "felicitously represents the desires of his followers . . . is not a ventriloquist" (96–98). The second is Julius Caesar, who in his role of "Caesar" is "the sovereign people's subject" (160), in "utter subjection to the audience" (178). This view of a meekly submissive Caesar (he "submits himself directly to the people's judgement" [177]) strangely overlooks the autocrat who infamously marched his legions across the Rubicon to influence political will in Rome, and is tempted to the Capitol by hint of a crown from the Senate, even though the people have already booed that prospect. The paean to Cade ("he never hesitates to put his fate in their hands" [98]) overlooks his slashing his way through their ranks with his sword once they switch allegiance at 4.8.60–65. Nothing clear is concluded from all this. "Elizabethan and Jacobean elections may have made a radical rather than a reformer out

REVIEWS   273

of Shakespeare," suggests Arnold (189). But what political form would an
Elizabethan radical have endorsed? Armed popular insurgence was not an
end in itself, as Arnold seems sometimes to suggest ("Rome's plebeians
should never have traded in their rebellion for representation in the first
place" [192]). On the other hand, Arnold tergiversates in an endnote, "To
claim that Shakespeare figures theatrical relations of power as democratic is
not to claim that Shakespeare endorses democracy" (254). The subtle prose
of *The Third Citizen* masks an evasive engagement both of literature and politics.

Treason by Words: Literature, Law, and Rebellion in Shakespeare's England,
by Rebecca Lemon. Ithaca: Cornell University Press, 2006. Pp. 256. Cloth
$45.00.

Reviewer: **DENNIS KEZAR**

To mangle Stein on Oakland, there is not always much there here. Rebecca
Lemon tantalizes us with what at certain points sounds like a compelling thesis for students and colleagues working with Renaissance English literature
(historians, political scientists, and legal scholars are not encouraged by this
reviewer to go any further). In its most invigorating formulation (for those of
us invested in the importance of words), Lemon's advertised thesis seeks to
remand the study of early modern treason law to language alone. What matters here is words (broadly and finally amorphously defined), and what matters much less is deeds, the "tyranny of things" promoted by scholars such
as Chicago's Bill Brown, cultural artifacts, and so forth. There is absolutely
no reason I can imagine that scholars of Renaissance literature should
not—as I initially did not—find themselves immediately attracted to and
sympathetic with such a project, as such a project is very much what our
professional lives depend upon.

The problem—or, to be more fair, my problem—is how this project of linguistic remanding devolves quickly into plot summary and diacritical recur-
sivity (as opposed to diacritical intervention). I cannot imagine a legal
historian worth her or his salt not aware of the important (and well re-docu-
mented in this monograph) transition from Edward III's 1352 statute defining
treason as, to use Lemon's language, focused "mainly on action" (5). Of
course this statute itself notoriously deploys the problematic language—also
well rehearsed in Lemon's whiggish history of what finally (in the afterword,
which begins with an epigraph from late Justice Rehnquist) becomes a thinly
veiled allegory of presidential usurpation of republican rights: "When a man
doth compass or imagine the death of our lord the king, of our lady his
Queen . . ." (5). As Lemon dutifully notes, subsequent monarchs (Henry,
Elizabeth, James) interpretively burden the word "imagine" with a wealth of

274   REVIEWS

allegedly "strict constructionist" legal freight. But nowhere in this book appears a theoretical dialogue with the important legal-historical scholarship on the debates over *mens rea* in early modern common law; nor in this book could I find any evidence on the continuing and neglected relevance of speech-act theory to literary scholars working on the nexus of law and ethics in the Renaissance. What is delivered instead sounds a bit tautological. Lemon wants to talk about "the proliferation of textual materials" and "textual explosions" because, well, she wants to talk about words and texts (see pages 3, 11, 13). Fair enough, but other problems become apparent when she attempts to do so.

Theoretical impoverishment (not that there's anything wrong with that) can only be justified by readings of literary texts that justify themselves. Structurally and thematically (and effectively) this book revolves around the Essex Plot and the Gunpowder Plot. Textually (and mostly sensibly) this book concerns itself with Hayward's *Henry IV,* Shakespeare's *Richard II* and *Macbeth,* Donne's *Pseudo-Martyr,* and Jonson's *Catiline.* It is of course unfair to complain about textual selection, but one wishes *Measure for Measure,* with its thematizing of *mens rea v. actus reus* ("thoughts are no subjects") had made an appearance. More puzzling is the inattention in Lemon's reading of *Richard II* to the Exton episodes (genealogically related, of course, to Marlowe's treatment of treasonous epistolic communication/interpretation in *Edward II,* also ignored). One frequently gets the sense that Lemon's thesis has gotten lost in the local readings (again, not necessarily a bad thing). But from the local readings we learn that Hayward was more loyal than his punishment would imply; that York is a figure of the conflicted recusant writer uncomfortably trying to get along with a shifting political/religious plot; that Malcolm—a Jacobean version of York—is similarly torn between duty and "monarchomachs"; that Donne's conflicted position as a fairly recent and dubious convert made him—well, circumspect with regard to absolutism and rebellion; and that Jonson's (similarly complicated political and religious position) contorted representations also suggest the difficulty of negotiating the *via media.*

These local readings suggest to me an abbreviation of *Hamlet*'s "There needs no ghost, my lord, come from the grave / To tell us this." In the interest of space, let's call it TNNG.

Perhaps my problem, as a reviewer, is that the rubric of the book raises expectations to an impossible level. I wanted and tried to like the book more. I have no doubt that an important book—aimed at literary scholars—could be written on the topics that Lemon raises. In fact many such books have been written and show up like perennials in Lemon's bibliography and notes (in no particular order: Cyndia Clegg, David Norbrook, Katharine Maus, Susanne Wofford, Annabel Patterson, Constance Jordan, Fran Dolan, Heather Dubrow, and Peter Lake [there is not enough of Debora Shuger]). The prob-

REVIEWS 275

lem for Lemon's book on law, though, is that these important scholars are invoked as either authorities or as distinctions without differences that the author can or will define.

As yet another literary-critical book with "Law" in its title, Lemon's project finally defines itself as topic-driven, not thesis-driven. Thesiphobia prevents the author from attempting any kind of differentiation between—and definition of—the other rubrics in her title that raise important questions: Is an early modern playtext, properly speaking, "literature"? Since the book begins with an instance of letter reading, what is the literary status of a letter read onstage? Is "rebellion"—at least before Milton's "dragon's teeth" appear ominously in *Aereopagitica,* ever understood as an explicitly and discretely "literary" phenomenon in the English Renaissance?

This last question may be the most important that this book provokes. It seems highly unlikely—given the evidence Lemon marshals—that early modern jurists, citizens, and writers working under the law, would have recognized a category such as "discretely literary." These thinkers, after all, inhabited a period in which the boundaries between word and deed had been profoundly blurred by law, by religious controversy, by stage, by state. TNNG. An important project begun but left unfinished by *Treason By Words* involves a question that will require sophisticated theoretical and interpretive work: To what extent could the early modern subject consider *words alone* (in the absence of interpretation, *mens rea,* mobs, audiences, and so forth) potentially treasonous or harmful? This question of course runs the risk of thought experiments such as Steven Knapp's authorless poem discovered on a beach. But if this book has established any kind of beachhead, it is only here.

The Invention of Suspicion: Law and Mimesis in Shakespeare and Renaissance Drama, by Lorna Hutson. Oxford: Oxford University Press, 2007. Pp. x + 382. Hardback $99.00.

Reviewer: **DEBORA K. SHUGER**

The Invention of Suspicion is a brilliantly suggestive study of the law's relation to Elizabethan drama. The book focuses on the impact of three intertwined factors: classical forensic rhetoric, Roman New Comedy, and the common law. From the rhetorics of Cicero and Quintilian, Tudor schoolboys learned how to evaluate evidence, construct verisimilar narratives, create suspicions—and how to analyze the comedies of Plautus and Terence, also standard sixteenth-century school texts. As the Roman rhetoricians used New Comedy to exemplify forensic strategies, so Renaissance editions of Plautus and Terence invoke forensic rhetoric to explicate the supposes and suspicions by which New Comedy's wily slaves and young lovers triumph over disap-

276 REVIEWS

proving daddies. The pervasively forensic character of New Comedy stands behind the Elizabethan association of dramatic mimesis with judicial rhetoric.

Moreover, as Hutson shows, the Elizabethan dramatists who first adapted New Comedy to the English stage had close ties to the Inns of Court and to parliamentary circles working on legal reform. Their refigurations of Roman comedy bear the imprint both of the newly sophisticated evidential concepts reshaping the common law and of a "civic" perspective on law as the visible form of local government. For Hutson, these legal developments are pivotal, since it is they that give cultural and political meaning to the drama's borrowings from antiquity. Against the Foucauldian view of law as the instrument of the early modern state, *The Invention of Suspicion* argues for the strongly participatory character of English criminal justice, with its volunteer officers of the peace and jury trials. Marian statutes required JPs, many of whom knew Roman forensic rhetoric from their school days, to take preliminary statements, to make an initial assessment of the evidence, and to write up a summary for the information of the court. The JPs' new authority supplemented rather than supplanted the detective work of the community, where the victim, aided by neighbors and amateur constables, remained largely responsible both for identifying suspects and for conducting the prosecution. The roles of both JPs and jurors "increasingly involved the exercise of discretion, judgment, and a sense of how to weigh evidence," enhancing "the investigative procedures of the common law" with a "new cultural centrality and moral exemplarity" (5). Early Elizabethan writers thus laud *pro-et-contra* forensic argument as "best for boulting out of the truth" and express their confidence in the capacity of ordinary people to discern the "credit of the Testimonie" and find "the trueth [that] lieth hid in evidence" (76–77, 147).

Hutson's account of how these interrelated aspects of legal culture and humanist education spilled over into Elizabethan drama is complicated, involving what seem three quite different strands: one formalist, another political, and the third (for want of a better term), Shakespearean.

She thus describes how late Elizabethan formal developments in plotting and characterization drew on techniques of forensic rhetoric. From its lessons in the weaving of circumstantial narratives peopled by figures "immersed in complicated relations extending back into the recent and the remoter past" (128), narratives that let us see how occasions inform against suspect and how events serve as evidence of unacknowledged motives, guilty secrets, and that within that passes show, Elizabethan playwrights learned to produce "the illusion that behind speech headings and speeches are the consciousnesses of 'characters'" (7). Throughout the drama of this period one finds characters engaged in forensic "supposing" about the true aims and feelings of their fellow *personae*. Such "conjectures of suspicion" about others, however, bear inadvertent witness to their speakers' own "anxieties, desires, and the pretentious fantasies that Jonson called 'humors'" (289), thereby inviting the audience "to infer, in quasi-forensic manner, motives for . . . [the speakers'] false surmises, and so build up a sense of their histories and inner lives" (314). It is from Helena's constant assumption that she is being mocked by the men who claim to love her that we "infer a psychic history of increasing insecurity about her beauty" (289). Forensic rhetoric, that is to say, transformed dramaturgy by producing the sense that characters have inner lives and histories.

This sort of historicized formalism seems compelling and fresh. By contrast, Hutson's treatment of the political import of Elizabethan drama's legal heritage at moments seems to be heading down well-trodden ways. In demanding to know the cause of Humphrey's death, the commons in *2 Henry VI* does act as "a kind of jury" (245), but Hutson's account of the scene as depicting a "civic ideal of Justice" where the "participatory justice" of the common law blossoms into "popular political agency" (251, 254) overlooks the commons' threatened pre-trial lynching of Suffolk (3.2.252ff). The book is openly invested in this populist-participatory ideal. Yet, if this investment produces a sanitized picture of *2 Henry VI,* elsewhere it yields more suggestive and powerful readings. In particular, the attempt to find in the drama some counterpart to the common law's validation of popular participatory justice informs Hutson's striking re-examination of revenge tragedy. Rejecting the conventional opposition between revenge and justice, which sees the former as a private person's misappropriation of the state's penal violence, on the grounds that the Tudor courts, by leaving criminal prosecution largely in the hands of victims and kin, melded public justice and private revenge, Hutson instead approaches the politics of revenge tragedy by a path that begins in Purgatory—or rather, with the loss of Purgatory, with the loss, that is, of the place that "was supposed to correct the inequalities and injustices" of this world by enabling discriminations more complex and more responsive to complexities, ambiguities, uncertainties of human experience than the binary of eternal torment or eternal bliss (267–68). Its loss confronted Protestant England with two nightmares of failed justice, and it is with these that revenge tragedy wrestles. If an evildoer does *not* repent, God's justice will settle scores in hell. But what if Claudius had truly repented? Prior to the Reformation, priestly absolution would have freed him from guilt, but not from the debt to divine justice, which he would pay willy-nilly in Purgatory. But if there is no Purgatory, then payment can only be exacted in this life. Revenge tragedy, Hutson argues, plots this secularization of purgatorial satisfaction as providential vengeance in this world, where "the gradual agency of forensic investigation, work[s] to satisfy the community—God's people— that justice had been done" (275). But what of the *avenger*—who does not repent and whose pursuit of justice plunges him into a quicksand of moral ambiguity? Purgatory could deal with such complexities, but for Kyd's Hier-

278   REVIEWS

onymo there is only heaven or hell. *The Spanish Tragedy,* Hutson suggests, emphasizes the avenger's careful forensic detective work, because Hieronymo's judicial deliberateness "works, though precariously and uncertainly, to decontaminate the revenger from the guilt inherent in his desire for justice" (269). *The Spanish Tragedy* and its successors validate the competence of ordinary persons to evaluate evidence, to pass judgment in cases of life and death, and, more controversially, under exceptional circumstances to do so on their own authority. The plays' implicit "link between judicial and political participation" thus has a "significant *political* charge" (103–5).

Yet one of the most admirable features of Hutson's book is that, despite its open commitment to populist-participatory ideals, it acknowledges the exceptions, including the huge exception named Shakespeare. Hutson thus points out that the early Elizabethan adaptations of New Comedy rework their models' carnivalesque intrigue plots into dramas of intrigue punished by a heroic magistrate-detective. Although some of these adaptations celebrate the power of forensic reasoning to find "the trueth [that] lieth hid in evidence," others register "the slippery, *pro-et-contra* deceptiveness" of such arguments, their fearful capacity to "dazzle and deceive" (173). However, given all the cultural baggage that Shakespeare's politics still carries, the book's willingness to allow for the complexity of his position vis-à-vis its thesis is as remarkable as its account of his plays is compelling. Whereas earlier Elizabethan plays (including *Titus* and *2 Henry VI*) borrow the forensic strategies of New Comedy to craft a politically engaged civic humanist drama, Shakespeare's later histories use the same "forensic strategies" to create "an illusion of inwardness" (218–19). Moreover, in a series of plays written around 1600, "the mimetic power of these very forensic techniques" comes to be associated "with the forces of evil." Polonius is Shakespeare's magistrate-detective, Iago his master of circumstantial *narratio* (308). *Much Ado* dramatizes "the ease with which an invention of sexual suspicion . . . accumulates[s] its own irrefutability." The play refuses to allow "examination of *evidence*" to provide "a solution to Hero's plight," but instead foregrounds Benedick's "act of faith" in Beatrice and therefore in her "belief in her cousin's innocence"—an act of faith that, like "compurgation in medieval folklaw," is not a forensic strategy (344–45).

Hutson's aside about compurgation being "medieval folklaw," however, seems odd. The church courts were using compurgation to rebut sexual calumnies into the 1640s. While *Invention of Suspicion* is a splendid book—perhaps the single best recent study of the imbrications of law and literature in Tudor England—like most works in this field, it doesn't know enough about the legal world outside the chambers of postmedieval common law. Its discussion of equity virtually ignores Chancery; instead Hutson inexplicably argues for a "translation of the Church's penitential jurisdiction over conscience into a common law jurisdiction over the evidential [*equitable?*] reconstruction of intention" (22, 50, 55–56). The church's penitential forum

REVIEWS 279

(i.e., confession, not the church courts) concerns the consciences of individual sinners; the common law "jurisdiction" has to do with interpreting statutes in light of the lawmakers' presumed intent (as, for example, my conjectural emendation of "evidential" to "equitable"). Chancery's jurisdiction over the consciences of individual malefactors parallels the church's penitential forum, but the common law principle of equitable interpretation is a horse of a different color (and doesn't apply to penal statutes). Nor is St German's claim that "English law tells us which taking is just and which unjust," and therefore whether or not restitution is due, an "extraordinary" usurpation of priestly authority (50–51) but a standard principle of canon law (*Decretum Gratiani,* prima pars, d. 8, c. 1). Nor did the Reformation sever the Eucharist from the obligations of restitution and reconciliation (20–21), as the preface to the Communion liturgy in all three Tudor Books of Common Prayer makes clear. Nor were medieval criminal trials a "formalistic procedure which," unless the accused pled benefit of the clergy, "would inevitably lead to hanging" (34), given that the acquittal rate, even for homicide, could run as high as 80 percent.[1] Nor, as Hutson herself at points acknowledges (74), did jurors only begin to evaluate evidence in the sixteenth century (6, 45, 63, 90; *see* Fortescue, *De laudibus legum Angliae*).

One can find more such errata, yet I'm not sure that they vitiate the book's argument in any essential way, although they do soften Hutson's contrast between medieval and Tudor contexts. In truth, such softening is probably justified, since, although medieval drama may not resemble New Comedy, Chaucer's "Miller's Tale" does; and although a character in an Elizabethan play who dreamt a loved one were really a criminal might well question such evidence (41–42), Spenser's Red Crosse, like the fifteenth-century Mankind, does not. More troublingly, Hutson's over-sharp contrast between medieval confessional theater and Elizabethan forensic dramaturgy requires her to ignore the latter's use of soliloquy. Our knowledge of Hal's and Hamlet's inward truth is partly inferential, but also partly, if not largely, derived from their confessions.

Notes

1. Thomas Andrew Green, *Verdict According to Conscience: Perspectives on the English Criminal Trial Jury* (Chicago: University of Chicago Press, 1985), 32n.

Revenge Tragedy and the Drama of Commemoration in Reforming England, by Timothy Rist. Aldershot, U.K. and Burlington, VT: Ashgate Publishing, 2008. Pp. 165. Hardback $89.95.

Reviewer: THOMAS P. ANDERSON

Timothy Rist's study of Jacobean revenge tragedy moves in two directions. First, the book examines the myriad forms of funerary commemoration that

280   REVIEWS

populate revenge tragedies by important early modern dramatists such as
Shakespeare, Kyd, Middleton, Webster, and Marston. In Rist's analysis, the
sheer plentitude of forms of commemoration in putatively reformed plays is
evidence that the plays enact a Catholic longing. The book's second objective
is to "systematically" (2) revise the relatively recent critical trend that argues
revenge tragedy, indeed the early modern stage in general, is a reformed
genre that both reflects and actively encourages Catholicism's waning influence in early modern London. Because of the book's strident insistence on
the second objective, it risks rendering moot its most insightful observations
about the persistence of unreformed funerary ritual and scenes of mourning
in revenge tragedy.

With its emphasis on the style of the enacted devotions to the dead, Rist's
book is part of Ashgate's *Studies in Performance and Early Modern Drama*
series that, according to the series editor, focuses on performance "in defi-
ance of theatrical ephemerality." In establishing a performative dimension to
Renaissance funerary commemoration, Rist locates an "aesthetics of mourning" unique to Renaissance revenge drama which encourages acts of judgment by theatergoers (15). And, according to Rist, as the early modern
spectator sat in judgment on scenes of mourning in the aftermath of violent
events on stage, theological considerations determined the gap between the
"performative ideal" and the degree to which the acts of mourning were actually reformed (22). Rist establishes a conceptual frame in a wide-ranging introduction that touches on many important points in current scholarship on
the historical, cultural, and political impact of the Reformation in Elizabethan
and Jacobean England. Drawing on Frances Yates's influential study of the
art of memory, Rist's central assumption is that death in the period was "remembrance's 'animating impulse'" and that "England's Reformed challenge
to Christian 'memoria' was an earthquake" (4, 5).

Arguing that traditional aides-mémoires for the dead—churches and mon-
asteries, including the Blackfriars and the Whitefriars—were increasingly put
to theatrical use, Rist's study contemplates the effect of this transformation
on purpose-built playhouses. Chapter 2 of Rist's book looks at the playhouse
at St. Paul's and its production of *Antonio's Revenge* as a model for this blend
of theater and religio-politics. This chapter proves to be the book's most interesting section, providing an analysis of how physical space, theatrical performance, and ritual commemoration work together to undermine the sense
of reform that putatively characterizes revenge drama. For Rist, St. Paul's
embodies "shrouded remembrance," a "contested monument containing
subsidiary, contested monuments" that simultaneously bears on the theatricality of the age and the complicated, contradictory processes of remem-
brances of the dead (77, 76). Performed in a monumental space with
conflicted significance, Marston's play, Rist concludes, presents a "divided
view of remembrance" that highlights "a development in the emphasis of

REVIEWS   281

revenge tragedy and an insight into a divided, Protestant mentality, even as the presentation of mourning in a *monument* reveals theatre and church entwined" (95).

The other two chapters in *Revenge Tragedy and the Drama of Commemoration in Reforming England* offer readings of revenge drama that privilege Catholic interpretations of scenes of mourning and commemoration, arguing that overt and covert Catholic affect is the plays' sincere expression of religio-political sensibility. As an accumulation of Catholic readings of plays such as *Titus Andronicus, The Revenger's Tragedy, The Spanish Tragedy, Hamlet, The White Devil,* and *The Duchess of Malfi,* Rist's book counters the prevailing trend that views the Renaissance public stage as one characterized by its reformed and reforming sensibilities. However, the book's hostile stance against what the author describes as a Broudian school of criticism, named after Ronald Broude's influential argument about the reformed nature of revenge tragedy over thirty-five years ago, at best distracts from many of Rist's interesting revisionist readings—and at worst turns disinterested argument into biased polemic. If it is the case that Broude's classic theory of early modern revenge drama is indeed "simplistic" (1), as Rist maintains in the introduction, then what is to be gained by establishing a Broudian reading as the impetus for each chapter's insistence on unreformed interpretations of acts of mourning and commemoration?

As an example of the unnecessary polemical tone of the attack on Broude and those influenced by his work, Rist begins the book's first chapter by addressing Broude's Protestant interpretation of *The Spanish Tragedy,* as well as Eugene Hill's more recent analysis of the play based on Broude's 1971 argument. Rist begins the chapter "without apology" with a consideration of the flaws Broude's and Hill's less persuasive, local readings of the play and promises to offer an unreformed reading that more holistically addresses Kyd's revenge tragedy—and the entire genre more generally—by focusing on commemoration and mourning (27).

The polemical tone, highlighted by a gratuitous exclamation point following a challenge to Broude's approach (29), and the premise that critical conversations might require apologies prove distracting to the Catholic readings that follow. Describing another critic who sees anti-Catholic imagery in Kyd's play as "too far under the influence" of a Broudian approach, Rist runs the risk of lumping competing critical voices into one facile category that diminishes their substance and nuance (36). Indeed, Rist's insistence that revenge drama expresses unreformed desires that overshadow reformed sensibility seems itself a limiting hermeneutic that ignores the productive religio-political ambiguity that more recent critics have identified in revenge tragedy.

In recent years, historians such as Eamon Duffy and David Cressy have written persuasively about the residual impact of the lingering traces of Cath-

282 REVIEWS

olic ritual in Protestant England not to claim an identifiable unreformed truth in English identity. Instead, their recent work suggests, that dominant cultural formations such as Catholicism persisted in residual cultural articulations even as emergent social formations such as Protestantism attempted to supersede it.

Revenge Tragedy and the Drama of Commemoration in Reforming England succeeds as a polemical attempt to counter critical tendencies that read reformed sensibilities in revenge tragedy at the expense of a pronounced residual Catholic legacy most evident in acts of commemoration and mourning. Rist's book, however, falls short of advancing the critical conversation that in recent scholarship has begun to reconsider dichotomous interpretations of the religio-political status of early modern revenge drama.

Locating Privacy in Tudor London, by Lena Orlin. Oxford: Oxford University Press, 2008. Pp. 392. Hardback $99.00.

Reviewer: AMY SMITH

Lena Cowen Orlin's *Locating Privacy in Tudor London* gracefully and convincingly challenges what have become commonplace assumptions about privacy in the early modern period. Taking on scholars such as Ariès, Girouard, and Hoskins, this book questions "the notions that personal privacy is something desirable and something progressive" (9). Privacy, in Orlin's narrative, is neither widely sought after for the purpose of solitary contemplation nor the impetus behind the changes in space evidenced by the Great Rebuilding and the proliferation of closets. Rather, privacy is seen as more connected to confidential conversation than solitariness, as less available in domestic space than corporate, and as a sometime threat to public discipline rather than a universally valued state. In (re)locating privacy, Orlin compels us to rethink other conceptual frameworks—subjectivity, inwardness, and our (often resisted but still powerful) Burckhardtian vision of the Renaissance as the rise of the individual.

Orlin's methodology avoids both old historicism's often unexamined reliance on elite sources and New Historicism's sometimes too fleeting attention to the material world of the middling classes. The book has two narrative threads—one is an architectural history and the other is an in-depth case study of an ambitious alderman and member of the London Draper's Guild, Francis Barnham, and his wife Alice. Indeed, Orlin's chapters connect with and enrich one another as each historiographical chapter (chapter 2's history of household space, for example) is paired with a detailed analysis of the Barnham's experience (chapter 3's attention to the uses of Alice Barnham's parlor). Thus chapter 2 re-examines the assumption that the particularization of spaces in private homes was engendered by a desire for privacy and self-

REVIEWS 283

expression, suggesting instead that the atomization of space may actually have resulted in less privacy (guests were now invited into more domestic spaces than in the days of the medieval great hall) and been largely a result of the desire to display one's possessions. Chapter 3 further enriches this argument by arguing that the rebuilding of homes such as Francis Barnham's was the result of the need for a space that could meet various civic and business needs; the parlor, far from the private female domain of Alice Barnham, was the site of countless public feasts and functions. Here, and throughout the book, the inclusion of Alice Barnham's story helps Orlin unsettle the gendered assumptions often made about privacy.

What is perhaps most impressive about *Locating Privacy* is the breadth of evidence to be found in its pages. To suggest the importance placed on obtaining knowledge about other people in early modern England, for example, Orlin examines everything from the peepholes found in building remains to Francis Barnham's business records. Doing so allows her to see surveillance as a practice with varied benefits. For ordinary citizens in a London increasingly seen as anonymous, "privacy seemed a menace to public well-being," and threatened their sense of "social responsibility" (192). For businessmen like Francis Barnham, "privacy had less commodity value than did vigilance and the knowledge it produced" (193). Because where we look for answers to our questions inevitably affects the answers we find, Orlin's willingness to look in so many places (paintings, church court records, architectural plans, wills, etc.) enriches and complicates her answers regarding the prevalence and value of privacy in early modern England. She is also careful to suggest the limits of her evidence, suggesting that while the omission of information in an archive may give the appearance of privacy, it may simply be a function of accident or the incomplete nature of any one archive; thus she cautions us not "to presume that things not knowable now were things not known then" (264). Again Alice Barnham provides an insight into the gender bias of such silences—she was a silkwoman, but because they never formed a guild, they left behind no institutional records; "thus a career that was not at all secret in its own time is barely recoverable in ours" (294). In contrast (not surprisingly), the available evidence and incipient analysis of the Ridolfi plot and the rebellion of Northern Lords is almost overwhelmingly detailed.

Scholars of early modern drama may be especially interested in the connections between physical space and privacy that Orlin explores. She argues that early moderns were especially interested in the ability to have a private conversation and that the very act of doing was usually perceived as incriminatory. Indeed, "Elizabethans were keenly observant of those behaviors which demonstrated an *intent* to be secretive, because it was almost always a dangerous desire" (247). While Orlin says little about literature, we might use these ideas to enrich our thinking about asides, architectural settings, character groupings, and the nature of soliloquies. Her arguments about the

284 REVIEWS

relationship between particular rooms and privacy turn many previous narratives about space on their heads, suggesting the need to rethink the connections between enclosure and openness and privacy. It is the gallery, the most open, spacious, and "most distinctive architectural innovation" of the early modern period, rather than the personal chambers or closet, that is most amenable to privacy in the form of private conversations (227). Orlin argues that while closets "are convenient conceptual containers for the subjectivities, genderings, and sexualities in which we persistently interest ourselves," the Tudor closet actually began as storage for material possessions and was "less about keeping people preclusively out than about keeping goods safely in" (297, 304). Thus locating privacy is an elusive task; Orlin finds it contested, the object of suspicion, and often inhibited by the very architecture of early modern England. She does however conclude that, "despite all the impediments that have been the subject of this book, privacy sometimes happened" (326).

While Orlin's methodology keeps her deftly attuned to gender, class, and religion throughout her analysis, from the start she claims economics as her "dominant discourse" (11). This is especially fitting in a book with such a detailed analysis of an early modern businessman and his wife, yet I hope that her reading of the economic motivations for and against privacy isn't used to create the type of overdetermined readings she sees as a danger for those who use everything from feminism (Is every Renaissance painting of a woman pointing to the absence of a man?) to Foucault (Are the disciplinary effects of architectural formations always already in place?) in limiting ways. Her nuanced readings discourage such simplifications because Orlin sees the resistance to privacy as contested as well as evidenced by a variety institutions and ideologies. For example, she complicates the notion that the Reformation's emphasis on a direct connection with God necessarily resulted in more privacy, reminding us that church courts replaced private confessions, and public punishments replaced private penance. Here and throughout this detailed analysis, we see an author who empties prior assumptions and follows the trails of multiple sources to present us with a more contested and complex view of privacy than her predecessors were able to—one which will surely enrich our reading of early modern literary texts as well.

Shakespeare's Modern Collaborators, by Lukas Erne. In *Shakespeare NOW!* Series, edited by Simon Palfrey and Ewan Fernie. New York and London: Continuum, 2008. Pp. 129. Hardcover $90.00, Paperback $19.95.

Reviewer: ROBERT E. STILLMAN

If every audience is a fiction, Simon Palfrey and Ewan Fernie can be credited with imagining a sympathetic fiction for *Shakespeare NOW!,* a new se-

REVIEWS   285

ries seeking to bridge the gap between the specialized conversations of scholars and the discourse of "regular playgoers, readers, or indeed actors" (ix). Palfrey and Fernie imagine a readership of nonspecialists who both enjoy Shakespearean drama and can be engaged by "powerful, cutting-edge scholarship" articulated in "shareable" language (ix–x). That audience is a sympathetic fiction because it points to a public domain inside which ideas from the academy can circulate energetically, and even more so because it suggests an academy responsible for explaining itself to a public beyond. What a pleasure to conceive of scholars called upon to justify "why [they] are bothered with these things [these Shakespearean plays] in the first place. Why [they] read? Why [they] go to plays? Why . . . they [are] important?" As its scope, then, *Shakespeare NOW!* promises compact, clearly written, lightly documented volumes by top-notch academics communicating scholarly labors as (what the editors assert they are) "intellectual adventure stories" (x). All this verbiage about fiction has a point, but first it would do well to consider one distinguished contribution to this series in relation to that promise.

Lukas Erne's *Shakespeare's Modern Collaborators* offers a defensive maneuver as prelude to a ground-clearing operation: against the ordinary person's vision of the editor as harmless drudge and the rival academic view of the editor as harmful obfuscator (*pace* Michael Warren or Leah Marcus), this short, dispassionate, lucidly argued volume seeks to illuminate the value of a fully mediated, "fully edited" version of the plays (7). It is worth noting the book's dispassion because while its title nods in the direction of sometimes self-indulgent celebrations of the editor as poetic compatriot (i.e., collaborator), Erne's argument is conspicuous for its moderation. Editors give us a more accessible and (important for Erne, author of *Shakespeare as Literary Dramatist*) a more readable Shakespeare: instead of wearing the poet's pants, Erne's editors spend their time mending textual breeches. And as Erne's first two chapters engagingly recount ("Establishing the Text" and "Framing the Text"), there is much mending to do. Addressing nonspecialists, these chapters describe the editor's job of updating spelling and punctuation, making emendations, and introducing lineation, and act and scene divisions. Even comparatively unexciting discussions about variant names of Shakespeare's characters yield reader-friendly facts about individual figures like Lady Macbeth— universally known as such, but never named "Lady Macbeth." Erne also explains the value of annotations, collations, footnotes, and introductions, and attends to complicated questions of canon selection and play titling. With every new point, a new illustration appears verifying the editor's virtue as mediator of things Shakespearean.

In two more chapters, Erne records contemporary debates about editing stage action—as he details the rise of performance criticism—and current discussions about how to edit (indeed, how to identify) the "real" *King Lear.*

286   REVIEWS

These are the most revealing chapters in the volume, partly because of the complexity of the issues raised—Is the play heavily edited with stage directions an aid to appreciation or an editorial intrusion? Is the reader of *Lear* better served by a single conflated text or by two different *Lears?* Partly, too, these are the most revealing chapters because they highlight the virtues and the vices of the *Shakespeare NOW!* series format. Concise discussion has its appeal, but Erne clearly does not have the necessary space to explain both the complexity of debates about performance-based editing or to illustrate fully his preferred alternative to the performance paradigm in contemporary practice: a new-style "literary" edition enabling readers to visualize both "the staged theatrical representation" and "the represented dramatic fiction"—both Hamlet leaping "under the Stage" and Hamlet leaping "into the Grave" (84–85). Constrained by limits of space, Erne has even less room to clarify why debates about the status of the text as performance script or literary artifact have such currency or to contextualize those debates in relation to the shifting paradigms of scholarly discourse from Foucault (and death-of-the-author deconstruction) to Kastan (and after-theory materialism). If *Shakespeare NOW!* hopes to create a public discourse that really engages ideas, it needs to provide sufficient space for ideas to be engaged.

More than constraints upon space are at issue. There are also assumptions about that imagined audience of readers that bear questioning, especially as they concern scholarly efforts to address a broader public. After a concise, critical review of editions of *Lear* from the early modern to the postmodern, Erne notes that in the last twenty-five years "scholarly editors [by virtue of contrasting textual mediations] have produced more than ten radically different *Lears* and a similar number of *Hamlets*" (101). That point is preliminary to his claim that "the real *Lear* no longer exists but has given way to the editor's *Lear*"—to various editions (that is) as "performances" in print, none of which can ever seek to be definitive (101–2). His ontological argument is as familiar to academics as a footnote. However, to the volume's wider readership, hoping (say) to scarf a cheap online edition from Amazon, the academically familiar is likely to seem strangely disorienting, informed now (as they are) to purchase not one, but two (even ten) *Lears* with the knowledge that the "real one" doesn't exist. Erne's ontology may be right, but some explanation seems needed about why substituting the "editor's *Lear*" for what ordinary readers would assume is Shakespeare's *Lear* is either valuable or useful—valuable or useful to anyone, that is, besides the professionals, commercial and scholarly, who profit from it. Instead, that substitution is presented as a fact of professional life, a construction determined by shifting forces of cultural change and editorial logic. (The "manifold operations" of editing "are often of considerable complexity and continue to be subject to change" [103].) Earlier efforts on Erne's part to argue for the meaning and value of editorial practices give way to arguments from necessity. Could Erne

REVIEWS 287

have introduced such arguments? Perhaps so. The fact that he does not speaks to the difficulty of academics—to our collective difficulties—in communicating beyond the walls of the academy (101–2).

We are not accustomed to clarifying the value of what we do to a larger public, to entertaining real, complex discussions about why what we do matters. We are not so accustomed because even in a series like *Shakespeare NOW!*, edited by academics producing books written by academics for review in a forum read by still more academics, we are still obsessively talking among ourselves and to ourselves—whatever the stated intentions of series editors. The nonspecialist audience of Palfrey and Fernie's introduction is revealed in the conclusion to Erne's volume to be a fiction indeed. "I have written this short book," the conclusion reads, "in the conviction . . . that students have much to gain from their own hands-on editorial experience, an exercise to which this book might serve as prolegomena" (105). Erne's fine book is an excellent prolegomena for academics who would like to teach the complexities of editing (and therefore reading) Shakespeare—and an excellent book for graduate students pursuing that study themselves. It is also, however, a reminder about the limits of academic discourse—even high-quality academic discourse—in communicating across that real gap between scholars and non-specialist readers and audiences of Shakespeare. A truly public discourse is a fiction that contemporary Shakespearean scholars have yet to make real.

Index

Aaron, Melissa D., 251–53
Addison, John, 98, 99
Alleyn, Edward, 86
Altick, Richard, 111
Anderson, Thomas P., 279–82
Appian, 51
Arnold, Oliver, 270–73
Augustine of Hippo, 136

Ballad tradition, 23, 24, 27–41
Barker, Francis, 61
Barroll, J. Leeds, 92
Baskerville, Susan, 144
Bastwick, John, 183
Bawcutt, N. W., 179–200
Beaumont, Francis, 192, 192
Beith-Halahmi, Esther Y., 27
Bell Savage Inn, 144
Bentley, G. E., 82, 88–89, 195
Bergeron, David, 263–67
Berry, Herbert, 144
Biberman, Matthew, 261–63
Birth of Merlin, 207–9, 216
Blackfriars playhouse (first and second), 102, 186
Bliss, Lee. 65, 67
Bloom, Gina, 234–37
Bly, Mary, 242–47
Boar's Head Inn, 144
Boy actors, 242–47
Bradshaw, Richard, 87–89, 122–23
Brandon, Samuel, 24, 42, 46, 47
Britland, Karen, 237–39
Brome, Richard, 191, 194, 211
Bruce, Yvonne, 24, 25, 42–59
Bruegel, Pieter, 131
Bull Inn, 144, 156, 157
Burbage (James and Richard), 86, 154
Burghley House, 91
Butler, Martin, 180–83, 186–188, 192, 195
Butler, Samuel, 19

Cane, Andrew, 184, 192
Carey, Henry, 164
Cary, Elizabeth, 24, 25, 46
Castle of Perseverance, 136, 139
Catholicism, 183, 192, 239, 267–69
Cavendish household, 109–11, 119
Cato the younger, 45
Cecil, William, 107
Chambers, E. K., 81–82, 85, 87
Chapman, George, 24, 60–77
Chappell, William, 27
Charles I, 180, 181, 183, 188, 191, 192
Chaucer, Geoffrey, 222–25
Christian Stoicism. *See* Stoicism
Cicero, 43, 44
Cholmley, Richard, 98, 103, 105, 111
Cleveland, John, 191
Clifford, Anne, 46
Clifford household, 85, 91, 97, 99, 107–10, 119
Closet drama, 24, 42–59
Cokayne, Aston, 195
Coke, Edward, 93
Collier, J. P., 82
Constancy (concepts of), 42, 43
Conversion of St. Paul (Digby), 132
Cosmetics, 231–34
Costume, 248–51
Court drama, 237–39
Cowley, Abraham, 182
Craythorne, Margaret, 144
Criminality, 128–43
Cross Keys Inn, 144–178
Crupi, Charles, 34, 39–40

Daniel Samuel, 42, 46–53
Danter, John, 30
Davenant, William, 182, 192
Davidson, Clifford, 128–43
Davis, Norman, 128
De Ormesby, William, 128

INDEX

Dekker, Thomas, 21–23, 95, 179, 211
Deloney, Thomas, 37
Dessen, Alan C., 100
D'Ewes, Simonds, 185
Dio Cassius, 51
Disley (actor), 89, 90, 125–26
Dollimore, Jonathan, 180
Donne, John, 71
Drake, Francis, 93
Dudley, Robert, 87, 88
Du Vair, Guillaume, 42–44
Dyke, Daniel, 190

Earl of Derby's Men, 83, 91, 99, 120–22
Earl of Leicester's Men, 94
Earl of Pembroke's Men, 90, 94
Earl of Shrewsbury's Men, 89
Earl of Worcester's Men, 85
Editing, 284–87
El Sabio, Alfonso, 138
Elizabeth I, 47, 51, 95
Ephraim, Michelle, 261–63
Epictetus, 44
Erne, Lukas, 282–87
Everyman, 234, 139

Field, Nathan, 22, 23
Firth, Charles, 189
Fitter, Chris, 270–73
Fleay, F. G., 82
Fletcher, John, 192, 194, 195, 221–25
Ford, John, 211
Fortune Playhouse, 194
Fouquet, Roger, 110
Frith, Mary, 19, 21–23

Galloway, David, 103
Garnier, Robert, 47
Gasper, Julia, 179
George, David, 85
Gesta Romanorum, 130, 131, 134, 135, 138
Gibson, James M., 92
Girard, René, 62
Gossett, Suzanne, 237–39
Greene, Robert, 204, 206, 207, 215, 216
Greville, Fulke, 42, 46, 47, 49–52
Gurr, Andrew, 21, 82, 107
Gwynne, Nell, 19

Hall, Joseph, 43–45
Harbin, Andrea R., 267–69

Harrison, Joan, 144
Heal, Felicity, 96
Heinemann, Margot, 179, 180
Helgerson, Richard, 27, 29, 30, 37, 38
Henslowe, Philip, 86
Herbert, Mary (Sidney), 47
Heylyn, Peter, 193
Heywood, Thomas, 23, 24, 27–41, 211
Hieatt, Constance, 132
Hill-Vásquez, Heather, 267–69
History play, 27–41
Hodgson, Elizabeth, 60–77
Hoghton, Alexander, 85
Holbrook, Peter, 27
Holden, W. P., 179
Hotson, Leslie, 95, 189
Hutson, Lorna, 275–79

Ingram, Arthur, 98

James VI and I, 45, 95, 179
Jerman, James, 135
Jews (in performance), 261–63
Jewell, Simon, 94
Jones, Marion, 135, 136
Jonson, Ben, 19, 20, 23, 60, 95, 191, 192
Juvenal, 20

Karim-Cooper, Farah, 231–34
Kathman, David, 144–78
Kastan, David S., 180–81, 186, 187
Kemp, Will, 104
Kezar, Dennis, 273–75
King's Men, 84
Knutson, Roslyn L., 253–57
Korda, Natasha, 19, 20, 23
Kyd, Thomas, 44

Lady Elizabeth's Men, 93
Lamb, Mary Ellen, 42, 54
Laud, William, 193
Law, 273–75, 275–79
Layston, Alice, 144–78
Lemon, Rebecca, 273–75
Levin, Richard, 210–30
Lipsius, Justus, 43–45, 52
London playing companies, 82, 84, 90
Lord Admiral's Men, 89, 90
Lord Chamberlain's Men, 90, 145
Lord Dacre's Men, 85
Lord Dudley's Men, 87–89, 123–25
Lord Eure's Men, 95

290 INDEX

Lord Hawarth's Men, 85
Lord Mountjoy's Men, 94
Lord Strange's Men, 145
Love, Genevieve, 234–37
Lowin, John, 195

MacLean, Sally Beth, 103
Magic, 201–30
Markham, Gervase, 108
Marprelate controversy, 190
Marvell, Andrew, 60
Masque, 248–51
Mary Magdalene (Digby), 129
Maus, Katherine, E., 61, 64
Mayne, Jasper, 182, 194
McMillin, Scott, 94, 103
Middleton, Thomas, 21–23, 95, 179
Montaigne, Michel de, 45
Montsarrat, Gilles, 45
Moore, John, 185
Moretti, Franco, 180
Mucedorus, 194
Munro, Lucy, 242–47
Murray, John T., 82, 84–85, 88, 90
Myers, A. M., 179

N-Town collection, 129, 132
Nationalism, 206

Orlin, Lena C., 35, 282–84
Otto, Martin, 98
Ovid, 65

Palmer, Barbara D., 81–127
Parker, Henry, 190
Parliament, 184, 185, 187, 188, 270–73
Parrott, Thomas M., 71
Patronage, 263–67
Peacham, Henry, 21
Pearson, Peter J. G., 110
Pembroke circle, 42, 47, 86
Percy household, 107
Performance, 81–127, 248–53, 261–63, 270–73
Petronius, 61–62, 65
Phaedrus, 61
Phoenix Playhouse, 186
Play of the Sacrament, 138
Playgoers, 20–22
Plutarch, 51
Porter, Gerald, 27, 28
Potter, Lois, 187, 192

Powell, Gabriel, 45
Prince Charles's Men, 86
Prince's Men, 86
Prince Palatine's Men, 86
Princess Elizabeth's Men, 84
Privacy, 282–84
Protestantism, 44, 46, 47, 183, 267–69
Presbyterian preachers, 191–92
Preussner, Arnold W., 69
Provincial playing (*see* Touring)
Prynne, William, 181
Puritanism, 87, 179–200

Queen's Men, 86, 90, 91, 94, 103
Queen's Revels, 86, 242–47

Raber, Karen, 239–42
Ravelhofer, Barbara, 248–51
Raylor, Timothy, 248–51
Reade, Timothy, 184
Rebellion, 273–75
Red Bull Inn/Playhouse, 144, 186, 192, 194
Religious drama, 128–43, 267–69
Revels, Master of, 82, 100, 184
Rist, Timothy, 279–82
Rollins, Hyder, 189
Rowe, John, 194
Rowley, William, 211

St. Christopher play, 103–5
Salisbury Court Playhouse, 189
Salvation, 128–44
Scherb, Victor I., 128–29
Scot, Alison V., 263–67
Seneca, 42
Shakespeare, William: 86, 192, 201, 209, 251–53: Plays: *Hamlet,* 60, 61, 65; *2 Henry VI,* 210, 212, 213, 218; *Henry V,* 28–30; *King Lear,* 103–5 *The Merchant of Venice,* 214; *Pericles,* 103–5, 218; *Romeo and Juliet,* 219–21; *The Taming of the Shrew,* 101; *The Tempest,* 211–21; *Troilus and Cressida,* 210; *Twelfth Night,* 65, 68; *The Two Noble Kinsmen,* 221–25; *The Winter's Tale,* 218
Shirley, Anthony, 104
Shirley, James, 192
Shuger, Ebora K., 275–79
Sidney, Philip, 44

INDEX

Smith, Amy, 282–84
Smith, Irwin, 102
Southern, Richard, 100–102
Spearing, Elizabeth, 22
Spectacle, 84
Spencer, Gabriel, 89
Staging, 231–37, 239–42, 248–51
Stanley, Thomas, 194
Staunton, Edmond, 187
Stern, Tiffany, 251–53
Stevenson, Laura C., 34
Stillman, Robert E., 284–88
Stoicism, 24, 42–59
Straznicky, Marta, 53

Taylor, Jeremy, 63
Taylor, John, 63
Taylor, Joseph, 195
Teague, Frances, 231–34
Thompson, E. N. S., 179
Thomson, Leslie, 100
Tiner, Elza C., 253–57
Todd, Janet, 22
Tomlinson, Sophie, 239–42
Touring, 81–127, 183
Tragedy, 180, 279–82

Tragicomedy, 60
Treason, 273–75
Tricomi, A,bert, 65

Unton, Henry, 101

Vives, Juan Luis, 63–64, 66

Wager, W., 136
Waller, William, 193
Walsingham (shrine), 129
Walsingham, Francis, 163
Weir, Anthony, 135
Westerfield family, 146, 158–59, 160–62
Wharton, Philip, 98
Wharton, Thomas, 106
Widows/Widowhood, 60–77
Willoughby, Francis, 98, 100
Wilson, R. M., 135
Wiseman, Susan, 186
Witherspoon, A. R., 42
Women, 19–77, 144–77, 237, 239–42, 261–63
Woolf, D. R., 27
Wotton, Henry, 96
Wynne-Davies, Marion, 19–26